30 POWERFUL LAWS
OF PERSONAL AND PROFESSIONAL SUCCESS

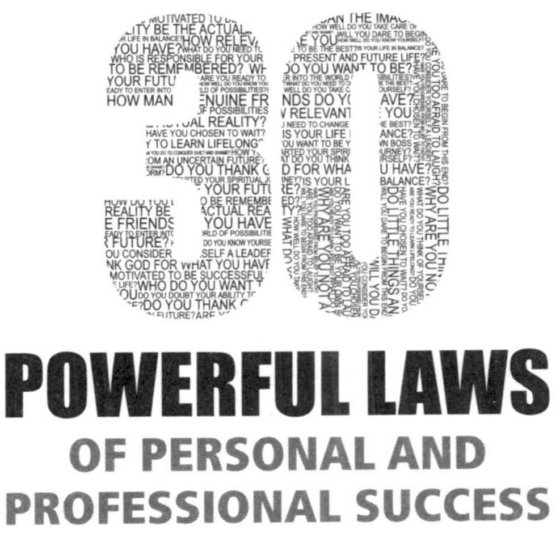

POWERFUL LAWS

OF PERSONAL AND PROFESSIONAL SUCCESS

ANUPAM KURLWAL

New Delhi | Mumbai | Chennai | Kolkata | Bengaluru | Hyderabad | Kochi | Guwahati

Publisher's note

Every possible effort has been made to ensure that the information contained in this book is accurate at the time of going to press, and the publisher and author cannot accept responsibility for any errors or omissions, however caused. No responsibility for loss or damage occasioned to any person acting, or refraining from action, as a result of the material in this publication can be accepted by the editor, the publisher or the author.

Every effort has been made to trace the owners of copyright material used in this book. The author and the publisher will be grateful for any omission brought to their notice for acknowledgement in the future editions of the book.

First Published 2014
Reprinted 2015

Viva Books Private Limited

- 4737/23, Ansari Road, Daryaganj, New Delhi 110 002
  Tel. 011-42242200, 23258325, 23283121, Email: vivadelhi@vivagroupindia.net
- 76, Service Industries, Shirvane, Sector 1, Nerul, Navi Mumbai 400 706
  Tel. 022-27721273, 27721274, Email: vivamumbai@vivagroupindia.net
- Megh Tower, Old No. 307, New No. 165, Poonamallee High Road, Maduravoyal, Chennai 600 095
  Tel. 044-23780991, 23780992, 23780994, Email: vivachennai@vivagroupindia.net
- B-103, Jindal Towers, 21/1A/3 Darga Road, Kolkata 700 017
  Tel. 033-22816713, Email: vivakolkata@vivagroupindia.net
- 7, Sovereign Park Aptts., 56-58, K. R. Road, Basavanagudi, Bengaluru 560 004
  Tel. 080-26607409, Email: vivabangalore@vivagroupindia.net
- 101-102, Moghal Marc Apartments, 3-4-637 to 641, Narayanguda, Hyderabad 500 029
  Tel. 040-27564481, Email: vivahyderabad@vivagroupindia.net
- First Floor, Beevi Towers, SRM Road, Kaloor, Kochi 682 018
  Tel. 0484-2403055, 2403056, Email: vivakochi@vivagroupindia.net
- 232, GNB Road, Beside UCO Bank, Silpukhuri, Guwahati 781 003
  Tel. 0361-2666386, Email: vivaguwahati@vivagroupindia.net

www.vivagroupindia.com

ISBN: 978-81-309-2761-9

Published by Vinod Vasishtha for Viva Books Private Limited, 4737/23, Ansari Road, Daryaganj, New Delhi 110 002.

Printed and bound by Raj Press, R-3, Inderpuri, New Delhi 110 012.

SUB-0026

Contents

This Bible of Believers is a tribute

To Those Who Believe They Can

Dare to dream 'the best life' and

Take 'inspired action' to create it.

I respect and salute you!

An Appeal To The Parents

I urge the parents that it's only you who can shape the future of your country and of the world. You have got a wonderful opportunity to guide the coming generation. Remember: Though every seed has a potential to become a fruitful tree, yet not every seed gets an opportunity to become a blossoming tree until it gets positive circumstances. Children are our biggest assets. You can do wonders if you just concentrate on your child leaving all worries about the society and the world. How? You have to be vigilant and concerned about the company of your child, development of his health, his approach towards problems and growth of his life skills. You should be extra careful about the company of your child because a child learns more through imitation. I urge all the parents: Please spend one hour quality time daily with your children. Tell them about this book. Teach them laws of success. I will feel amply rewarded if all the children get golden guidance from their parents who have understood and got the wisdom contained in the 30 powerful laws of this Bible of Believers.

Author

Acknowledgements

Alfred North Whitehead, the originator of process philosophy once said, "No one who achieves success, does so without acknowledging the help of others. The wise and confident acknowledge this help with gratitude." The present book is no exception to the law that "Nothing big can be achieved alone." I have received help and support from numerous people, administrators, books, institutions, libraries, websites, blog writers and teachers. I extend my deepest heartfelt gratitude and thanks:

- to Prof. (Dr.) Naresh Sharma, my mentor, who taught me the art of writing on legal subjects and from there I grew my writing skills.
- to Prof. (Dr.) M.P. Singh, Chancellor of Central University of Haryana, Mahendergarh and Chairperson of Delhi Judicial Academy for his valuable suggestions on various concepts of leadership.
- to Mr. Vinay Singhal, Managing Director, SJV Consultants Pvt. Ltd, who shared practical things in business life with me that really helped me a great deal.
- to Prof. (Dr.) Gurpal Singh, who has always been my ideal in dedication and discipline; whatever commitment I have towards my work, I have learnt from him.
- to Prof. (Dr.) K.P.S. Mahalwar, for teaching me the integrity, care and honesty. You have always encouraged me to write, speak and contribute in diverse fields.
- to Prof. (Dr.) Preet Singh, for imbibing in me, the attitude of working even in adverse circumstances, and to place my work at priority.

- to Prof. (Dr.) Raj Kumar, for teaching me the art to win friends and influence people. You have been a major impact in the change of my thinking patterns.
- to Prof. (Dr.) Satish Arya, who has always been with me through thick and thin and never let me feel down even in the most turbulent times of my life.
- to Prof. (Dr.) Poonam Datta, for those extensive conversations specially on literature that in fact steered the progress of this work in the right direction.
- to Dr. Vinay Naryan Paranjape, the son of legendary Prof. (Dr.) N.V. Paranjape, for keeping me enthusiastic while I was on crossroads in reaching at conclusions on concepts.
- to Dr. Tarun Arora, for inspiring me to learn valuing relationships, I know now, just because of you, how to greet, respect and hold people.
- to Dr. S.K. Nara, for the discussions in the car, during the drive to the workplace, that have also laid the foundation of this philosophy.
- to Dr. Vijay Rathee, for those lengthy discussions on business and finance, that proved to be the foundation of my chapters on business, finance and leadership.
- to Mr. Sandeep Aggarwal, for infusing in me a sincere desire to excel and make a difference in the lives of people in the circle of my influence by the way we do our work.
- to Dr. Praveen Gupta, words can never convey how much I appreciate your care and support. You are an awesome friend.
- to Dr. Swasti Sharma, for showing medical concern for the health of my family. I love and appreciate your support and encouragement.
- to Dr. Anil Dahiya, for promoting me in the field of occult sciences. Thank you for your confidence in my abilities to heal people.
- to Rajnarain Panghal, my best well-wisher, for persuading me to achieve excellence and making me conscious of the fact that people expect wonders from me.

- to Mr. M.M. Alam, my distinguished friend, for placing the reliance in my capability to teach and for giving me the opportunities to enhance my potential as a teacher.
- to Mr. Narender Kumar Rajliwal, public relation executive, PGI Chandigarh, for those frequent telephonic conversations on various topics of this book. Your practical instances helped a lot to understand life in its actual reality. Thanks a lot.
- to the dead poet, for contributing the theme poem that summarizes the key principles contained in the 30 laws of this book. This poem is really heart touching and inspirational. It is an honour to have you in my resourceful psyche group.
- to my parents, Sh. Daryao Singh Kurlwal and Mrs. Bimla Devi, for giving birth to me at first place and for providing me with the values and work habits that have allowed me to create the level of success that I have.
- to Rishi and Ashish, for being such good brothers. I couldn't be where I am without you. Thank you for being the models of brotherhood.
- to Honey Tigala, my lovely wife, for understanding the long sittings before my computer, being with me in the nights that turned into mornings, feeding me like a child with your hands when work was my main concern, your hilarity in between the work to keep me fresh and relaxed. Thanks for being so supportive, caring and loving.
- to my angel daughter Megan and my little prince son Parth, who were so lenient with my obsession with work. Thank you for the sacrificed weekends and cancelled vacations that were needed to complete this work.
- to Sir Nitin Vats, my incredible gentleman. The way in which you do the things and the results you produce are awesome.
- to Nitin Chauhan, my personal fitness coach and chief trainer at Hercules Gym, Gurgaon for those long training sessions and expert advices to keep my physique fit and healthy.

- to my taught students of National Institute of Law of Kurukshetra University, C.R. Law College Hisar, Bhai Gurdas Law College Sangrur and University Institute of Law & Management Studies Gurgaon for being with me in whatever mission or project I have taken. I appreciate your valuable faith in my pursuits.
- to the daily visitors of my website, facebook page, twitter and other social media sites who trust my commitment to serve people and give me the courage to continue and expand what I believe is right.
- to well-known authors of numerous great books, prominent column writers in newspapers, outstanding writers of many blogs, owners of various websites and the eminent generators of working ideas, principles and strategies. I am grateful for the inspiration and wisdom of many thinkers, whose writings, I have consulted for writing the present book. Your ideas, insights and spirit are woven throughout. I have duly acknowledged each and every word in my book and if there is any failure on my part, I will give due credit in the next edition. It is your tireless efforts, your attention to details and your commitment to excellence, which have found manifestation in my success philosophy.
- to Viva Books, for believing in my laws, strategies, ideas and more importantly in my success philosophy. I feel privileged on being a part of such a visionary brand of book publishing.

Jack Kerouac said, "All human beings are also dream beings. Dreaming ties all mankind together." Therefore, I dedicate this Bible of Believers to all those who believe they can dare to dream "the best life" and take "inspired action" to create it. I respect and salute you.

A Personal Note From The Author

Dear Success Seeker,

Welcome to the world wherein
Impossibilities are rare and
New possibilities become probabilities
Every moment in Personal & Professional Life
And, believe me, it happens in this world.

Once upon a time Virgil said, "They can conquer who believe they can." This book is for those who believe they can race against the time and be successful in living the life of their dreams. This Bible of Believers is for those who listen to themselves and not to the world. My friend! This book is for you. The fact that you are reading this book indicates that you want to live a richer, better and more rewarding life than you have now. I do firmly believe that we are all important. Yes! You too, my friend, who have just started the success journey by choosing to read this book.

Success is what everyone dreams of. Why do we want to succeed? There are many reasons for wanting success, for example life plans, past failures, desire to win and problems of present life etc. Success provides a stimulus to act. We want to compensate for the past failures. We want to do away with the feeling of lacking. We look at success as a solution to end our problems in present life. The word *success* is very powerful and inspiring for each of us.

Success has a personal colour. When a student secures 100 out of 100 in mathematics; a housewife cooks a dish well; a doctor operates a major operation, each of them consider himself/herself successful. A businessman says, "Success means being extremely wealthy." A young boy says, "It means being able to enjoy the life you have now." A family woman will say, "It means having the love and support of your family and friends." A religious person may say, "I believe that success is being able to wake up each morning, look in the mirror and be satisfied with your life." Every individual has his or her own definition of success.

I looked up the word success online, and I retrieved the definition, "the attainment of wealth, position, honours, or the like" (dictionary.reference.com, 2013). In my view, success is, "A journey in which one realizes his/her short-term, mid-term and long-term goals in a way that it brings feelings of achievement, happiness and relevance."

No matter what your definition of success may be, you can find yourself one step closer to achieving that goal only if you have the right personal philosophy. It also means that I am asking you to believe in me and my laws of success. This is the first step you have to take i.e. to hold my offered hand and then I promise you once again that I will train your mind step by step in those top secrets or fundamental laws of success, employing which you will certainly have a balanced life and what you have always wanted like excellent health, higher income, good wealth, cordial relations, celebrity status, powerful leadership, greater satisfaction, enjoyment in life and better spiritual life, etc.

Any training program, and that's precisely what this book is, must do three things. It must offer content, the what-to do. Second, it must supply a procedure, the how–to–do–it. And third, it must meet the acid test; that is, get the domino effect. This training program is a result of my life experiences researched over ten years through "examine and experiment technique" that has helped me evolve these timeless laws of success, compiled in the form of this book.

I've been studying, applying and teaching the secrets of success for one decade and this book is your chance to learn from my experience and knowledge to create the life that you want and deserve. Believe me! I have shared my top strategies that I use personally for getting my things done. I have steered the most extraordinary successes in reputed professions, business, relationships, and beyond out of these laws. But here the situation is different, you are training yourself, and there is nobody to supervise you on a personal level. This is a tele-training. You will define your own version of success because life is a *do it by yourself* project. Obviously, I believe your mind can be programmed for super-success and I also believe that you'll be richer in many ways if you utilize this philosophy for which I spent over 2,000 hours of refining and committing to paper.

You will find yourself in the middle of many situations wherein you get surprised – Why success is not occurring fast? When am I going to get my dream job? When am I going to be of my ideal weight? You must not get discouraged but should go on with your passion. You have to know and believe that success takes time, determination, and a lot of hang around. I am quite sure that if you apply all of the laws and techniques revealed in this book you will realize your goals, or rather you will realize your dreams. However, it won't occur at once. You will grow like a baby matures.

You must also accept that you have done, maximum times if not always, the best that you could with the skill and knowledge you had at the time. Now you are going to learn, unlearn and relearn many things. The knowledge that you'll get from this book will liberate you from the chains of ignorance and you will start looking at the same world from a totally positive perspective and more importantly you will have the right kind of thinking approach that will prove to be, I see, the change, you are looking for quite a long time, and that to me is my role as an author, teacher and an awakener whose mission is to help transform people's lives by finding the small changes that make the big difference. "I am not a teacher," said Robert Frost, "but an awakener."

On a final personal note, I have enjoyed writing this success philosophy, and I along with many others who believe in my success philosophy, sincerely work every day to implement and live by the laws of this book, in personal and professional life also. I hope that this philosophy will bring a lasting happy change in your life and the organization you work for. With the blessings of the Almighty, I feel great pleasure in placing this book before the worthy readers.

To your best success and achievement, Good luck!

Anupam Kurlwal

What Kind Of Book Is This? And How Is This Book Different From Any Other Book You Have Read On The Subject?

The market is flooded with what we call self-help books, and to you, it may look like that this book might not be different from others. There must have been the same old question in your mind when you picked up this book. Is this book an exceptional stuff or a normal self-help paperback? It is not "the same old thing." *This magnum opus* self-help tome indeed is not a common paperback because it provides a road map for changing your thought patterns. It helps to create an empowering life philosophy, a way that will perpetuate success. However, the genre of the present book is also self-help and yes, it is a non-fiction book, because success is a serious issue and it has to be dealt with in a serious way.

Let me promise you at the outset that this Bible of Believers is going to change your life, more importantly your thinking pattern, as I strongly believe, "What you have outside is a manifestation of what you have inside." This book is a philosophy but there is a gentle theory involved. The ideas, procedures and techniques come from a lifetime of living. Nevertheless, we need regular reminders. In that line, this book is a reminder.

Combining rock–solid research with common sense and realistic experience, this user-friendly guide reminds you that there is always more to learn and it also fills a nagging gap you have had for some time. This book is a step-by-step remarkable resource that allows you to multiply your success, chart your progress, and achieve any desire. There is a lot of experience condensed into this book. The strength of this book is that I have made an effort to bridge the different aspects of life in a simple presentation of success principles, with no complex theories. That is a significant accomplishment in itself and puts this book in the rare breed of books. Definitely, the book's greatest strength, however, is to make this information attainable to the average person. I have also defined oft-foggy concepts like leadership, values, vision, mission and other things in a simple and understandable language. Although, the author is in the habit of using universal language but the same is done with proper back up of various authorities. Anyone with a strong interest in helping oneself or others will be well rewarded by reading this book. Buy three copies, one for you and two others for those you love, and circulate them now. Those who will read it will thank you. This is a self-help treasure.

I have written a much needed book especially for this day and age. The dedication says a lot, success and happiness come **To Those Who Believe They Can** step out of mediocrity and endeavour to create the life of their dreams. This book makes a big promise with its title, *30 Powerful Laws of Personal and Professional Success* and I have made every effort to fill this guide with lots of long-overdue practical tips, real world examples and well-researched "how to" actionable suggestions. Following these, will at the very least, help you to focus on the right things. I have been most careful to see that no impractical information, suggestions or instructions are incorporated, because of my heartfelt passion to be helpful.

Every lesson begins with the objective of it, an overview of what's to come, followed by thought of the day, to set the tone of the day. Each lesson ends with a suggested strategy, assignment for the day, visualization for the day and self suggestion for the day to review the lesson's content and drill it in deeper for better understanding and implementation. Each chapter features a number of'end-of-chapter' exercises to help you move in the right direction. I firmly believe that success leaves clues, so every topic and idea is well referenced from the authoritative writings and established experts in that field. Each lesson, one by one, builds upon the next to create consciousness success about. When reading this book, you will feel like you and I are in a conversation (rather than in a lecture) discussing you and your future and this feature makes this book special. You'll praise the book for its quotes also. While opening chapters and adding the occasional quote is a practise usually used, I found a variety of really motivating, totally appropriate and quotable quotes to keep you on your toes. I have focused, throughout the book, on unleashing the great potential you have within yourself because I believe each of us is born to be a genius. During this life-changing change, I won't just give you information. I'll also help you to change permanently. Yes, I promise that our ride together will be full of inspiration.

Some of the ideas I preach for are not mine. I borrowed them from highly successful businessmen. I took them from good wives, good husbands and good students. I swiped them from many best books of success philosophy. Change is the law of nature but there are certain rules that never change. And I have put them in this book. Therefore, in one way, it is a synthetic approach because the present book compiles all the ageless proven techniques of success at one place. This book is a humble effort towards that direction. All things change. Many things have changed. We have changed with them too. Therefore, many of the techniques and strategies are the outcome of long processes of thinking and verifying their truth in practical life. In other words, it is a product of creative imagination and application.

This Bible of Believers directly focuses on the leaders themselves, because whoever you are and whatever you do, you have to lead in your life inside out. The laws of this book, by the same token, will help business leaders, executive coaches and human resource executives because they get to know what each needs to do to really shine in leadership and life. This book is full of street-tested success principles and techniques you can immediately put into practice in your life.

You may also notice that you're already familiar with some of the concepts mentioned in the book. That's great! But ask yourself, "Am I presently working on them?" If not, make a commitment to put them into action—Now! You will not know whether they will work unless you give them a try. And here's my pat—no one else can do this for you. Only you can do it.

How And Why This Book Was Written

A normal person gets inspired by great leaders, and certainly, I am not an exception. I had been searching for years to discover a working instruction book on a balanced, successful and relevant life. Since no such book existed, I have endeavoured to write one. And, here it is.

The book you are now holding in your hands is the result of nearly ten years of my research. It's a product of a decade's experience of speaking, writing, counselling, teaching and coaching thousands of students and people. It all began in 2004, when after my class, several students approached me to say how much they appreciated the motivational examples I used in the classroom teaching. They told me that listening to my motivational philosophy always helped them to make constructive and positive changes in their lives, and they suggested that I should write a book on success philosophy. I promised I would think about it. This was the first motivation. I took an inspired action. I purchased some books on success philosophy and read them and then I started to take notes on my computer. I was quite eager, at that time, to know the secrets of success. Although, I had learnt many lessons on psychology of winning, when I saw my spiritual master in action, still, I wanted to identify what it takes to become a great leader, the type who is a magnet for the followers and make things happen.

The second motivation came on my 29th birthday, after my meditation, on 16th March, 2007, in the morning; I discussed the development of the book with Honey, my wife. She said, "You have always inspired others."

She added further. "This is a noble cause. You must continue to work on it." I was living, at this time, by doing, what everybody does, what was most convenient for me rather than doing what was in my best interest. I purchased many self-help books; over a hundred I guess, and went through them. I used to knock out a complete book in one sitting. Will Durant said, "Education is a progressive discovery of our own ignorance." I also gradually realized that I was in need of a training book myself. Therefore, this book wasn't written in the normal sense of the word. It grew as a baby grows.

I was in a confident state of mind in September, 2011, when I got my law book "An Introduction to Alternative Dispute Resolution System" published by Central Law Publication, Allahabad. I gained a good momentum at that time. While preparing for the book, at that time, I read everything that I could find on the subject of lessons. I searched many libraries for some old classic books and bought new books online. I studied many newspaper columns, magazine articles, books on psychology, biographies and autobiographies of successful persons. I spent many nights on my computer searching online also. The idea was to accumulate the principles essential to accomplish success and I was so determined to spare no time, no expense, and no source to discover every practical idea that anyone had ever used to get super-success.

Sir Nitin Vats, my greatest enthusiast, also liked the proposal and provided the much needed motivation at my 5th marriage anniversary party on 7th February, 2012 when he said, "Sir, I hope your book will be a fountain of inspiration and a much needed direction in itself. Everybody wants to succeed but lacks the direction and motivation." I had a list of many laws, at that time, compiled from many resources. I saw their practical application in the lives of successful people ranging from top businessmen to good housewives. To my surprise, the list developed out of great self-help books and other sources didn't cover all the aspects of life and then the whole direction of my book writing changed. I shifted to creative imagination instead of synthetic approach. Care Rogers said, "The only person who is educated, is the one who has learned how to learn and change." I thought about one law throughout the week and sometimes I worked on a law even for a month. I looked at mine and others' past successes; discussed the same law with many successful people and identified the success patterns and then from those patterns, secrets were drawn and put in the form of a lesson. Consequently, this Bible of Believers grew and developed out of the laboratory of life.

It's my honest feeling that I was connected to infinite intelligence during the writing of this book especially in the last period. Whatever principle, I worked upon at that time; the supporting stuff came to my aid, whether in the form of people who were living that law or an event that was a superb example of that law. I found the theoretical reflections in the self-help books also; I left, considering incomplete. Frank Lloyd Wright said, "In order to achieve anything worth having, you have to go wholeheartedly." I was so passionate about getting this book completed that I left exercising and skipped food many a time due to excessive mental involvement. My wife, most of the times, made me eat like a child, with her hands, while I was busy in my writing, and believe me, I avoided sleep even sometimes for the rude logic that I didn't want to lose the momentum. It was an autonomous period; I should call it, because everything went on its own.

However, I managed my schedule later because my health started to deteriorate. This incident taught me another law, which I have put in the form of a lesson: HOW WELL DO YOU TAKE CARE OF YOURSELF? We take our lives and health for granted and this thinking is responsible for severe health breakdowns. I urge that we should look out for a balanced life and learn time management to make each day a separate life in itself. We should devote our time as per the needs, on family, finances, career, friends, social life, health and spirituality in our life.

Everybody counts our success by the quality of things we have rather than by the quality of person we have become. People are chasing goals that will never make them blissful. They are always on the run for positions, cars, big homes and big bank balances. They are chasing their tails whereas significance requires success as a stepping stone. Success comes when you add values to yourself and significance requires that you add values to others. This is the ultimate concern of this book, to make you achieve the highest level of excellence – 'Relevance', to be exact, being able to matter. You'll be remembered for your contribution and not for your personal success. I strongly accept this fact as true: "Relevance and not the excellence is the highest manifestation of human life." He who shares does not lessen, but greatens his life.

You feel less stress and enjoy every moment when you are in balance. I have put emphasis on relevance in this book making you a successful and a balanced person who has great health, wonderful relationships, financial independence, wealth and freedom. This is real greatness. At the end of life, if you are not a good husband in the eyes of your wife, a good father in the eyes of your children, a good citizen in the eyes of society and a good friend in the eyes of your friends what is the purpose of your life?

This book is *a call for action* because through its suggested strategies, assignments, visualizations and self suggestions, it'll ask you to put laws into practice. This book is going to change your thinking pattern. The laws in this book are universal. They are applicable in any condition, company or country. As Plato said, "Truths are eternal." It's an Inside–Out approach to personal and interpersonal effectiveness. I am sure that your life will be full of love, joy and spiritual bliss once you'll start living by my laws.

Peace and Blessings,
Anupam Kurlwal

How To Get The Most Out Of This Book

This Bible of Believers is specially designed for *you*, the reader, who has a burning desire to learn the ways to maximize personal and professional achievements. You can read this book at one go and then put this book in your bookshelf, but, believe me, this book should never be treated as a material, as it is structured to be a companion in your change process. In order to get the most out of this book, there is a systematic approach. This book will turn in to our book by this approach.

1. As you read, stop at any suggestion or an idea to ask yourself how you can apply the same in real life.
2. Write marginal notes to yourself.
3. Use blue ink pen at the first glance, red ink pen at the second reading and green ink pen at the third and final master study.
4. As you read, underline the words, sentences and paragraphs that seem vital, or especially applicable to you. Draw a line besides a suggestion and mark the suggestion with four or five stars. Marking and underscoring will make this book more interesting and far easier to refer to the points quickly.
5. Discuss the concepts in each chapter with your spouse or partner, or with a close friend and ask them to catch you violating the success laws, and you must give them rewards for this activity. Please take criticism in a lighter mood.

6. You should try to do the suggested strategy, assignment, visualization and self suggestion on the same day to make it more effective. Someone said, "Do something today that your future self will thank you for." These techniques and methods have been developed on the premises, "What you do today can really improve all your tomorrows."
7. Sit quietly for several minutes each morning after rising, and each evening before retiring, and relive the law mentally. Allow spiritual guidance and divine communication to come to you during this period.
8. The recommended approach is to read each chapter thrice (and you should) and then do the suggested things, complete the given assignments before going on to the next one so that each lesson becomes your primary nature. Studying the contents of this book three times is necessary for induction program and reviewing it once a month is a must for refinement so that you inculcate the fundamental changes in your personal philosophy. Each additional month you follow the thirty laws, you'll experience them on a different level. The fastest way of learning is little by little and day by day. Every day is a test and a separate life in itself.
9. Use this success system as your workbook. Treat this book as a blessed companion, a lifelong friend by applying its ageless principles in solving your daily problems because learning is a process and we learn by doing.
10. Spread the message contained in the book as a "Professor of Happiness" by helping the needy people in turbulent times.
11. Observe your progress each week, each month and each year because you are attempting a new way of life. Don't hesitate. Change is most effective when it is slow but sure.

This approach is suggested to acquire a complete mastery on the principles and their reflections in practical life. The more intimately and minutely you'll study this resource, the more you'll see and the more incredible wisdom you'll get. By browsing the initial paragraphs for the 30 laws in the table of contents, you can identify the pertinent law.

Note: Throughout the book I have used masculine gender, only for the purpose of ease in writing. The laws apply to both the genders.

1

Who Is Responsible For Your Past, Present And Future Life?

OBJECTIVES

- To learn the "Law of Chosen Response",
- To understand that your present is the product of past choices and
- To take full responsibility of your actions in future.

GOLDEN GUIDANCE

> *"The price of greatness is responsibility."*
>
> Winston Churchill (1874–1965)

NEED TO CHANGE

> *"Nothing changes if nothing changes, and if you keep doing what you've always done, you'll keep getting what you've always got, and will keep feeling what you always felt."*
>
> An old wise saying

You deserve a special pat on your shoulder because you have made a fresh start today. It's a good beginning. Beginning is always tough but a journey of a thousand miles begins with a single step. You have taken the first step by choosing this book. Change will not come if you hang around for some other person or some other time. Warren Buffett once rightly asserted:

"You know ... you keep doing the same things and you keep getting the same result over and over again." I mean, you should treat your life as an occasion, and then you must rise to it. You are the change that you look for. If you have the guts to start, you also have the guts to succeed. This moment looks on you. You are the one you've been waiting for. This era belongs to you. This is your time. You must also understand this, that it is not the beginning of a new chapter in your life; this is the beginning of a completely new book (a new life). The moment you began reading this book the old book got automatically closed. This latest book is only just opened and has just begun. Look! My Dear, you're on its first chapter! Is it not a gorgeous one!

Let me suggest you to ask yourself a question. Do you consider yourself successful? Stop for five minutes and think. Don't move forward. Think for five minutes and write your thinking pattern on a plain paper. Be honest and complete this exercise.

When you were finding your answer to this question you must have reflected on your past life and considered your present position. Probably, most of the people will come up with a negative reply. What next? Now, you must have some questions in your mind. For example, Why haven't you accomplished your aim by now? Why aren't you wealthy already? When are you going to realize your dreams? What do you need to change to get what you want? What is the secret of success? Why is it that often, you find yourself in a hopeless situation, powerless to make urgently needed changes in your life? My sincere apologies! I need to be honest. I can't tell you the answer in one sentence because change is a many-sided process that involves many factors.

You'll get your answers to these questions as you'll read the chapters of this book all the way through. That's my promise! But, one thing is certain that you need to change. If you change nothing, nothing will change. But taking on too much, too fast usually doesn't last. Therefore, we must start slowly if we are to change at all. Once a law becomes your first nature, take on the next law.

YOUR GREATEST LIBERTY

> *"Every human being has four endowments – self-awareness, conscience, independent will and creative imagination. These give us the ultimate human freedom ... The power to choose ... to respond ... to change."*
>
> Stephen R. Covey (1932–2012)

There are thousands of small things you can change. How will you respond to this powerful statement, if I declare: "The power to change lies in the power to choose your response"? Actually, this statement is the rider.

You must make a choice to take a chance for changing your life. You must choose to make a change. In fact, you already have, at your disposal, all the resources you need to effect a change; all the energy, time, health, faith, motivation and money; the only thing is that you need to reconnect with these resources. This present book contains numerous resources in powerful lessons; to those you must (re)connect, in order to produce a "Changing Change" in your life.

I would like to put forward a thesis: "You are the product of your brain." You can't become what you want to be; you can't be extremely happy; you can't believe yourself as successful and you can't intermingle effectively with others unless your brain functions in success patterns.

Albert Camus has very rightly quoted: "The truth is that everyone is bored, and devotes himself to cultivating habits." The phrase or cliché 'I am feeling bored' is a worthless thing to say. You live in a great, gargantuan and giant world. You are breathing. Is it not amazing? Therefore, don't say such a thing again. Then, what compels us to feel bored. It's the brain pattern. It is a fact that failure brain patterns make people a failure. The book in your hands discusses the success brain patterns employed by all time greats like Alexander, Joseph II, Lao Tzu, Mao Zedong, Mahatma Gandhi, Martin Luther King, Napoleon Bonaparte, Bismarck, Franklin Delano Roosevelt, Eleanor Roosevelt, Winston Churchill, Adolf Hitler,

Henry Ford, Benjamin Disraeli, Muhammad Ali Jinnah, Abraham Lincoln, Edison and Lenin etc. Your brain patterns are responsible for your marriage, parenthood, professional status, personal beliefs and religious faith, along with your experiences of the two great masters under which nature has placed all human beings – pleasure and pain. The good news is that you can change feeling about circumstances and the circumstances eventually by changing your brain patterns with the help of exercising your greatest freedom – the freedom to respond.

SOMEBODY WOULD DO IT

> *"Power flows to the man who knows how. Responsibilities gravitate to the person who can shoulder them."*
>
> Elbert Hubbard (1856–1915)

Most of us read the noticeboards; we immediately suppose all the notices are addressed to others. However, Big Dreamers take full responsibility of their past, present and future actions. In my view, the buck stops at the top of the pile. Long time ago, I read a short story about responsibility, which I often tell to my final year students. Whether or not you've heard it before, it's worth a laugh and a moment's thought. A classical tale and one of my favourites: This is a little story about four people named Everybody, Somebody, Anybody, and Nobody. There was an important job to be done and Everybody was sure that Somebody would do it. Anybody could have done it, but Nobody did it. Somebody got angry about that because it was Everybody's job. Everybody thought that Anybody could do it, but Nobody realized that Everybody wouldn't do it. It ended up that Everybody blamed Somebody when Nobody did what Anybody could have done.

Moral of the story:

1. Either do the work yourself or make sure you delegate the work to somebody, otherwise nobody will do it.

2. You must always know WHO is doing the job and HE/SHE must be identified.
3. Improvement begins with you.
4. Most people are afraid of responsibility.
5. Responsibility is what one expects from others.

STIMULUS AND RESPONSE

> *"A life of reaction is a life of slavery, intellectually and spiritually. One must fight for a life of action, not reaction."*
>
> Rita Mae Brown, an American writer

All the common men look in the direction of the government, the top management and super-leaders. But why do people expect from the government, the top management and super-leaders? The answer is: To whom, plenty is given, plenty is expected. Who can forget the famous dialogue of the Spiderman Movie: "With great power comes great responsibility." This plenty that is required, is the ability to perceive, believe and proceed. Winston Churchill (1874–1965) is widely regarded as one of the greatest wartime leaders of the 20th century. He was the Prime Minister of the United Kingdom from 1940 to 1945 and again from 1951 to 1955. He is also the only British Prime Minister in history to have received the Nobel Prize in Literature, and was also the first person to be made an Honourary Citizen of the United States. He excelled in his whole life because he was ever ready to accept the responsibility. You must be able to predict upcoming effects of your decisions, choices, attitudes and behaviours. Believe me. This quality to judge the future effects can give you the ability to "Set and Act" priorities in your personal and professional life. You have to pay the price for being great, and the price is to accept the responsibility. Each great power comes with equal great responsibility. It is the responsibility of choosing the right response. Choosing the right response is often a hard thing, and I can tell you from my own experience that, often a hard thing is a right thing.

Allow me to ask another question. Do you know the difference between Stimulus and Response? O.k., why don't you react before your teachers or bosses with same intensity as you do before your friends? Just stop for five minutes and think over it. Be honest and complete this exercise. I think you have reached at the right answer. A stimulus stimulates you and a response is how you respond. If you are stimulated by cold water your response may be to shiver. If you place your hand on a hot pot the heat will stimulate your skin (ouch!) and your response will be to withdraw your hand often even without thinking. Can you guess the advice? Pain is inevitable but suffering is optional. Your happiness is your choice. Why is it so hard to make lasting changes in our companies, in our communities, and in our own lives? The primary obstacle is a conflict that's built into our brains. I know it can be hard to get started and find your own way. I've been in the very same place before.

I have noticed, during the writing of this first chapter, that our minds have two conflicting systems. One is the sensible mind and the other is the exciting mind. The sensible mind is conscious and hence slow in its functioning because it tries to be logical. The exciting mind is unconscious and hence its functioning is quick because it is emotional. Many observances of this thesis can be found in our daily life. You must have observed that the sensible mind wants a great physical shape; the exciting mind wants to try new tasty foods.

Why I am stressing upon distinction between stimulus and response is due to the fact that in Life-Changing Events you have to respond with your best self. In an interview, that can change your life, an interview board member comments on your dressing sense, instead of responding with a smile and accepting your mistake, your whole personality comes at threat. When you spoke for the first time on a stage, your so called good friend commented on you with surprise, "Would you speak?" and the whole stage drama happened. And, now you don't want to give a try to all those things in which you have been a failure. Nevertheless, My Dear! I tell you the law of success: "Your success is determined by your action and not by your reaction. Reaction is the worst form of slavery. Action is the choice. Your life is built 10% by what occurs with you and 90% by how you act in response to the occurrences."

SELF-AWARENESS

> *"We are each responsible for our own life – no other person is or even can be."*
>
> Oprah Winfrey, best known for her
> Oprah Winfrey Show

Animals react to stimulus automatically. Only a man has the power to choose his response. Your unique natural gifts lift you above the animal world. The Fountain of Freedom: "The space between stimulus and response generates your greatest power—the liberty to choose." The source of action is not the thought but the sense of responsibility. Your character is established when you take responsibility. All the self-respect will come from accepting responsibility. Tons of blame can't change you but an ounce of taking responsibility can change you completely. There is only one person who is accountable for the class of the life you are living. That person is you. You are the captain of your ship i.e. life.

There is a common sense observation. Stephen R. Covey says that you can break the word "Responsibility" as response + ability and then you can have the true meaning of this word—ability to choose your response. We are responsible for our life. The Power of Choice is not just positive thinking, but it involves what I call "Positive Doing". It requires you to use your ears to see and your eyes to hear – A Complete Observation. It requires sense intelligence – to be able to make the fine distinctions through the use of all senses. Positive people choose their response to the external stimuli. They are aware of their true self and know what self-awareness means.

DECISION AND CHOICE

> *"One's philosophy is not best expressed in words; it is expressed in the choices one makes... and the choices we make are ultimately our responsibility."*
>
> Eleanor Roosevelt (1884–1962)

When we choose, we taste for curiosity, it's like picking an item from a menu, selecting from many options, taking the responsibility of an end result, whether good or bad. In decision, we conclude, there is no personal responsibility as you use the evidences before you to judge, and if there is any problem, you always have those evidences as your shields or excuses. You decide in your offices. You choose your friends, foods and dresses. Decisions and choices build your character and form your life path.

Your decision comes from your head and is more often based upon prejudices but your choice is a manifestation of your heart, the creative solution. A choice means choosing a response and solving the problem by collective effort for example, with a total involvement of the same problematic individual. The technique is to use the individual as a solution instead of treating him as a problem. Successful or creative people are a part of the solution and in reality a solution themselves whereas negative people are a part of the problem and in fact, a problem themselves.

GOOD-SELF AND EVIL-SELF

> *"You always have an option to choose between your evil-self which makes you negative in your approach and your good-self which always ask you to be positive in all the circumstances."*
>
> Bhagavan Nayagar (1951–2001)

Prosperity comes from your good-self and the poverty reflects through your evil-self. Your personality is divided into two selves; one is your good-self i.e. Soul and the second is your evil-self i.e. Ego. I call the evil-self an agent of satan or negative power. All the negative feelings of fear, poverty, ill health, hatred, bad relationships and materialism are reflections of this evil-self. Our bad self wants us to stay away from God, that's why negative people are neither self-believers nor believers in God and, they try to take short-cuts and commit crimes. Another good way to deal with this self-criticism i.e. evil-self is to give yourself the approval and support that you deserve. When you do something well, it is imperative to reward yourself, count and build up on that victory. Over time, this method will push out the self-critical scripting from your mind and make you more positive in your outlook.

No external or internal stimuli of any nature can hurt you except when you submit. It's not what happens to you, but your response to what happens to you that hurts or uplifts you. No one can hurt you without your consent. No one can be comfortable without his own approval. I have found that most people find it far easier to dismiss other people's negativity towards them, but find it much harder to deal with their own evil-self. The concept of evil-self and good-self can be useful in any circumstance.

RESPONSIBILITY AND BLAMING

"The thorns which I have reap'd are of the tree
I planted; they have torn me, and I bleed.
I should have known what fruit would spring from such a seed."

Lord Byron, *Child Harold's Pilgrimage*

High achievers choose to act in a positive manner and create suitable circumstances instead of blaming the unsuitable circumstances. All the astrologers will blame the stars for an unhappy incident. Priests will blame the gods. A manager will blame the staff. Staff members will blame the manager. But my point is that when you shift the blame you lose an occasion to change yourself. Positive or proactive people take responsibility for their choices and the consequences that follow. Yes, you are the outcome of your decisions. Remember the times when you made a decision of "not to act but to be acted upon". Positive people do not blame circumstances, conditions, or conditioning for their behaviour. Their behaviour is a product of their own conscious choice, based on values like imagination, conscience, independent will and more importantly self-awareness, rather than a product of their conditions, based on feeling.

Nature has made humans to act and not to be acted upon. The best example of leadership is leadership by example. It is depressing to see so many leaders, when failures occur, point fingers at others instead of taking responsibility. They don't realize that when anyone points his index finger towards the other, four fingers of his own hand are pointing towards himself. I believe that no one has got a right to point a finger unless he has lent his hand to the pointed person earlier. I have read, seen and met many great leaders and my one time conclusion about great leaders is: "A true leader accepts the failures and enjoys the successes." They are extremely positive people and they use positive language, "I am responsible for my action." Negative people use blaming language, "Excuses like Traffic Jam." So, *here is the golden tip*: "You should firmly believe that responsibility is an opportunity for you to go beyond yourself. You should consider it as a platform to build upon, and not as a burden to have grievance against. Responsibility is often considered against the notion of liberty but actually it is a driving force for self-transcendence. The Numero Uno Law to become a winner is to accept the responsibility for your actions." Your evil-self that uses blaming language can make you live in mediocrity, as it discourages you to make choices and makes you decide to wait. It is high time to do something about your evil-self because it shifts responsibility and if you keep shifting it then you will fail to understand the real meaning of your existence.

YOUR DECISION LEADS TO REWARDS AND CONSEQUENCES

> *"The world is full of BAITERs, who believe that the means are justified by the end, and live selfish life. These people are backstabbers, abusers, imposters, takers, exploiters and reckless."*
>
> Philip C. Mcgraw, *Life Code*

The biggest day of your life is when you take complete responsibility for everything you think, say, feel, and do. Abraham Lincoln, the 16th American President, gives a million dollar advice: "You cannot escape the responsibility of tomorrow by evading it today." For example, you reach late in your office and your boss gets angry at you. Ninety-Nine out of hundred people will decide to employ the age-old excuse of "Traffic Jam" and one out of hundred dares to choose: "I am late because I got up late and I promise you, I will never ever be late again." Colette Carlson calls negative thoughts as "LIES – Limiting Ideas Eliminate Success." She also describes inner critic as a "LIAR – Lets Inspire Another Response." Excuses like traffic jams are LIES whereas accepting the responsibility is an outcome of LIAR.

You can find the observance of law of chosen response in the life of many great leaders. Winston Churchill was a British politician who is widely regarded as one of the greatest wartime leaders of the 20th century. Fifty years ago at Harvard, Winston Churchill delivered his great clarion call for Anglo–American brotherhood. He said the golden words: "The price of greatness is responsibility." Harry S. Truman, the 33rd President of the United States, never shirked his duties and always accepted full responsibility for his decisions. Anna Eleanor Roosevelt was the longest-serving First Lady of the United States, holding the post from 1933 to 1945 during her husband Franklin D. Roosevelt's four terms in office. President Harry S. Truman later nicknamed her the "First Lady of the World" in tribute to her human rights achievements. She modelled civic and national responsibility as a social activist. On October 2, 1996, then aged 25, Lance Armstrong was diagnosed with testicular cancer, but he overcame stage three (advanced) cancer. He emerged as a superhero. Several people blamed him for using doping. Armstrong admitted his seven Tour de France titles were fueled by an array of drugs, reversing years of denials in an interview with Oprah Winfrey.

Positive people keep their promises and only negative people may say it for a change of excuse. You will never ever be late in future because you believe in yourself. When you say something, you mean it. You should treat your negative thoughts or limiting beliefs as reflections of your evil-self and you should never let them dominate your existence. As an alternative you should commit a law to your memory that in every endeavour—communication (whether external or internal) is the key. I recommend you to use your language to paint, and then each interaction becomes splendid. Someone said in this context, "Don't raise your voice rather improve your argument."

You can choose a better response in place of a limiting thought that will empower you. I call our inner critic as a liar. This reminds me of a beautiful and wise question: "A year from now what will I wish I had done today?" This question can be your guiding star. It is intended to guide your efforts and can be used for the times to come. An indicator of wisdom and maturity is when you honestly know that your decisions lead to rewards and consequences. You are responsible for your life, and your ultimate success depends on the choices you make. The role of parents is crucial as they can raise the child with a sense of responsibility. You can teach your child to return library books on time, complete school assignments on time, keep a promise, call parents if he is late, take good care of personal possessions and apologize if he is wrong.

GOOD THOUGHTS—REFLECTIONS OF SOUL

"It is character that gets out of bed, commitment that moves us into action and discipline that enables us to follow through."

Zig Ziglar (1926–2012)

The *Bhagwad Gita* (Holy Book of Hindus) claims: "Soul is pure and can never be impure." So, the reflections of your good-self are always pure and positive. Therefore, it is just a matter of believing in yourself and activating your good-self and switching off the evil one. You need to start right from here and right now. The age of 65 till death is an age of retrospection where we retire and slow down. I met many old age people during the writing of this book. I found that during senior citizenship, we develop honour as a virtue if we have lived a successful life, and, if we have been unproductive, we tend to develop despair or depression. It all starts from childhood and gets strengthened during the coming years. I advise the depressed men: "Don't let your past use up too much of your present." After all, it's never too late to make a fresh start.

SPEAKING TRANSMITTERS

"Fire and swords are slow engines of destruction, compared to the tongue of a Gossip."

Richard Steele (1672–1729)

Most people are serious for the way others perceive them. They often wonder what others say about them when they're not around. So, in response to this we try to satisfy our ego or evil-self by what we describe tittle-tattle. Gossipmongers, or "Speaking Transmitters" as I call them, are those who actively seek out and spread rumours by spicy-stories. It is a fact that people never trust gossipmongers. Just stop for a moment and visualize the times when you were part of this chit-chat process. Dr. M.S. Verma, a Supreme Court Lawyer, opines: "Take it for granted that any loose talk will reach to the concerned person. In fact, many people use it as a weapon i.e. they say whatever they want to reach to the targeted person. It kills the relationship." Let me ask you a question. Have you ever tried going to office one day without talking about another person? I urge you to give it an honest try. Go for one week next time.

A gossip in any form and at any place is talking about someone else. Although it is a human nature, a gossip is often destructive for the inner world. A gossipmonger is not a highly capable individual at his/her core personality. Gossips can ruin long friendships, isolate groups and break families. Gossips lower your self-esteem as it involves the passing of rumours from person to person and ultimately make the person self conscious. Small people talk about others. Average people talk about things. Great people talk about ideas. Decide your category!

EGO FOLLOWS POSITION AND POWER

> *"Never let your ego get so close to your position that when your position goes, your ego goes with it."*
>
> Colin Powell, an American statesman

Ego is the biggest hurdle in accepting responsibility. Sigmund Freud has divided human personality into three elements known as the id, the ego and the superego. These three work together to create complex human behaviours. The id is present right from birth and plays a major role in early childhood needs because it is based on natural instincts and reflected through emotions, for example a baby cries when he is hungry. The ego develops from the id and ensures that the impulses of the id can be expressed in a manner acceptable to the society. The superego is the set of values a person has, that he derives from his surroundings and develops with experience. Superego begins to emerge from the age of five. In fact, I call super ego the good-self. The point I want to make is: Immature and underdeveloped people have a strong id, self-centred people have a strong ego and high achievers have strong good-selves. An egoistic person wants to be in the chair but doesn't want to come in the front to share the burdens. I consider ego as the negative side of human being. Friedrich Nietzsche once said: "Whenever I climb I am followed by a dog called Ego."

I tell you a famous story on ego. Over a river there was a very narrow bridge. One day a white male goat was crossing this bridge. Just at the middle of the bridge he met another black male goat. There was no room for them to pass. "Go back," said the black male goat to the white, "there is no room for both of us." "Why should I go back?" said the white male goat. "Why shouldn't you go back?" "You must go back," said the black male goat, "because I am stronger than you." "You are not stronger than me," said the white male goat. "We will see about that," said the black male goat, and he put down his horns to fight. "Stop!", said the white male goat. "If we fight, we will both fall into the river and be drowned. Instead I have a plan – I shall lie down, and you can walk over me." After that, the wise one laid down on the bridge, and the egoistic one proudly walked over him. So they passed each other, and went on their ways. Although the black male was still thinking that he made the other one lay down. The white one was appreciating his calmness that he didn't get angry otherwise both would have fallen down from the bridge and died.

Moral of the story:

1. We should use wisdom instead of ego in a problematic situation.
2. An inconsiderate person believes that everything revolves around him.
3. A self-seeking person wants to dominate others and treats others as fools.
4. Ego takes away the ability to think in the right direction.
5. A self-centred person wants attention at all places and at all times.
6. An egoistic person will consider the wise as weaker if the wise man shows modesty.
7. Ego is very powerful especially in feeble minded persons.

MONKEYS WITH A MESSAGE

> *"People are often unreasonable and self-centred. Forgive them anyway.*
>
> *If you are kind, people may accuse you of ulterior motives. Be kind anyway.*
>
> *If you are honest, people may cheat you. Be honest anyway.*
>
> *If you find happiness, people may be jealous. Be happy anyway.*
>
> *The good you do today may be forgotten tomorrow. Do good anyway.*
>
> *Give the world the best you have and it may never be enough. Give your best anyway.*
>
> *For you see, in the end, it is between you and God. It was never between you and them anyway."*
>
> Mother Teresa (1910–1997)

Activating the good-self is very tough and not as easy as it looks; you will have to be watchful to whatever you say, hear, see and do as symbolized by "Gandhi's Three Monkeys".

The monkey with its two hands shutting the mouth says, "Always say positive words" (Never say negative words). It also means that you should be respectful to yourself as well as to others by making a choice of speaking only the positive words as you have said goodbye to the "world of impossibilities" once you have started reading this book. I strongly advise you to stay away from any kind of backbiting, as I have seen that it pollutes even the strongest relationships.

The second monkey with its two hands on both the ears says, "Always hear positive words" (Never hear negative words). It also means that your ears are closed for any type of negative thoughts and feelings for others and for yourself and you are open only for positive affirmations since you listen to your good-self only. By believing in this, you will naturally avoid listening to any backbiting.

The third monkey with its hands closing both the eyes says, "Always see positive things" (Never see bad things). It also means that you are conscious while viewing and you see only the positive side of things and avoid the negative view. This thought will open a new world of possibilities for you and after some time, it will become a part of your being to possibilities instead of impossibilities. Its another implication is that by activating your good-self you will only do good to others and avoid any kind of harm to yourself and to others as well. It also means that you will not indulge yourself in negative things even mentally.

And, there is a fourth monkey, Dr. Anupam's Monkey with its hands crossed and locked that says "Always do positive deeds" (Never do bad things). Breathe in the fantastic future and breathe out the pathetic past. It means that you must not involve yourself in negative actions, as an alternative you'd always look out for positive responses and goal oriented actions. It also implies that you should stay away from "Bad Habits" like adultery, gambling, drinking, drugs and smoking etc. The message is crystal clear: "Always say positive words. Always hear positive words. Always see positive things. Always do positive deeds."

If you are in the habit of smoking, and just in the name of excuses, you continue smoking, you can never quit smoking. Similarly, if you are not satisfied with your current life then you have to change your current behaviour in your inner and outer world, and that to me, is the only way to experience changes in the outer world.

SUGGESTED STRATEGY

> *"Attack the evil that is within yourself, rather than attacking the evil that is in others."*
>
> Confucius (551–479 BC)

I consider, for proper implementation of this Self Theory, you will require another auxiliary principle of "Reflect before you Act."

I also call it "Forever Respond & Never React Policy." My spiritual master used to compare me with a lion. Whenever he saw me sad, he used to say: "A mice plays with the moustaches of a lion but the lion does not get angry by this play. It simply hits the mice with its paw and makes the mice run." The thing is that in all the events ego or evil-self jumps first to react but you should pause for a moment and respond from good-self. I suggest you to take a moment of silence—"pause before you respond" and then let your good-self slowly dominate your whole personality, let the good words flow from your mouth and let the positive vibrations spread in the environment and connect with the infinite energy. Therefore, make a pledge to respond with your good-self forever and activate your good-self right now. Always keep in mind what great M.K. Gandhi (1869–1948) said: "They cannot take away our self-respect if we do not give it to them."

Ask and you will be answered. The answer will come through your friends and more importantly from your good-self and it means God is answering your question. Like you put a break to your car in speed and go slow and then you cross the dangerous way quietly and cautiously, in the same way, put your whole existence on a complete stop in a heated situation and then emerge with your best self and never let your ego dominate you. You only have to control over four things in your life—the thoughts you think, the talks you hear, the images you visualize, and the actions you take (your behaviour). How you use these four things determines everything you experience.

My submission is: "Go for a complete smiling silence and never speak unless it is mandatory to speak. Break this bliss for laughing and spreading your good-self for a KISS—Keep It Short and Simple." Laughter is transmittable. It is the rhythm and music of life. Accordingly, you must get out of the "Smiling Bliss" only to play the music of life and spreading your fragrance of love. Wayne Dyer, American self-help author, rightfully speaks: "Be miserable. Or motivate yourself. Whatever has to be done, it's always your choice."

ASSIGNMENT

1. Try to be positive in your overall outlook and live a "larger than life" image.
2. Try to be a role model – Do not blame rather accept mistakes, learn and correct them. Lead yourself first i.e. inside out before leading anyone. You pick a coin seeing one side, however, later on it turns out to be a counterfeit-coin, then you must accept that, it was you who picked it up.
3. Try to see people as solutions – Never look at people as problems. It's not what they're not doing or should be doing that's the issue. The issue is your own chosen response to the situation and what you should be doing. If you start to think of any person as a problem, stop yourself. That thought is the problem. Either work on a bitter relation or leave it.
4. Try to analyze the results – Results don't lie. Ask in yes or no. Either you are achieving or not achieving your targets. Do not be afraid to ask others about your current going. Truth is truth.
5. Try to maintain a journal – Keep a journal of daily life, in which you should write daily changes and philosophies. This idea is the outcome of an old saying "the faintest ink is better than the best memory." Please Mark: I am asking you to maintain a journal not a diary.
6. Listen to the audio program *The Art of Exceptional Living* by Jim Rohn. You can also search www.booksshouldbefree.com for more works.

VISUALIZATION

At the end of day, visualize as to what you saw, said, heard, thought and acted in the whole day. Make observations and then re-visualize the problematic incidents with positive changes. Visualize that all the four monkeys are living in you and guiding you to do the right things only.

Remember: When a mice plays with the moustache of a lion, it does not get irritated, it does not roar, it simply smiles and just gives a gentle stroke with its paw to make the mice run.

SELF SUGGESTION

I accept 100% responsibility for everything I think, say, feel and do.

Bear in mind: Super achievers always keep their commitments.

[*Promise & Put Your Signature Here With Date*]

2

How Well Do You Know Yourself?

OBJECTIVES

- To learn the "Law of Living the Values",
- To understand your true or real self, and
- To create your value and ethics statement.

GOLDEN GUIDANCE

"Know your enemy and know yourself and you can fight a hundred battles without disaster and your victory will not stand in a doubt."

Sun Tzu (C. 544 BCE–C. 496 BCE)

HOW DO YOU GET TO KNOW YOURSELF BETTER?

"The first thing you have to know is yourself. A man who knows himself can step outside himself and watch his own reactions like an observer."

Adam Smith, *The Money Game*

Do you think that getting to know yourself is important? The maxim, or aphorism, "Know thyself" has a variety of meanings attributed to it in literature. But here I suggest you to ask yourself: How did you get close to your friends? Stop for a moment and recollect your friendship times. Yes, your guess is very much right—you got close to your friends by spending time with them. There are many personality tests (Know Thyself) available online that tell you how to get in touch with your true self, spare some time in this exercise and you will certainly fall in love with yourself.

Let me ask you a few questions once again. Take a notebook and write questions one by one and write your answers honestly at least in one page – one answer in one page. Ask yourself. Have you spent enough time to know yourself? Are you living a double life? How can you love yourself unless you work on knowing yourself? How will you lead the whole world if you cannot lead yourself? If you feel that your life is full of events because you wander here and there all day, then let me tell you my dear friend, you don't even know that whatever you are doing is your true self or wishes of others. Thus, it's high time to know yourself and more importantly to love yourself. The point is that you see clearly but with the eyes of love. So, *here is the golden tip*: "In the exercise of knowing yourself you will find that you don't have everything but you must learn to love everything you have. You must make an honest effort to love who you are inside and out."

KNOW WHO YOU ARE

> *"He who knows others is wise and he who knows himself is enlightened."*
>
> Lao Tzu (6th Century BCE)

Many times in our life we become sad, unenthusiastic and weak by the outcomes of choices we make and the circumstances that happen with us. We think as though we are of no value. Aristotle (384 BC–322 BC) who was a Greek philosopher, a polymath, a student of Plato and a teacher of Alexander the Great once said: "Knowing yourself is the beginning of all wisdom." Understand the law of self-respect: Despite what has occurred or what will occur, you will never lose your value.

There is a short story about human value. Tom said to his father, "I am feeling depressed. I have failed in my high school examination three times. I am worthless." Tom's father Robert was an intelligent man. He decided to teach his son the value of human life. Robert picked up a gold coin and held it high in his hand. He asked Tom, "Would you like to have this gold coin?" Tom raised his hand. He said, "Surely, give it to me please." Robert said, "I am going to present this gold coin to you but first, allow me to do this." He proceeded to scratch the gold coin with a knife. He then asked, "Do you still want it?" Still Tom raised his hand in the air. Then, Robert asked, "What if I do this?" and he dropped it on the floor, and ground it with his shoe. He picked up the coin, now scratched and dirty, and said, "Now, Do you still want it?" Still Tom raised his hand into the air. Robert said to Tom, "My Son, you have learned a very valuable lesson. Regardless of what I did to the gold coin, you still wanted it because it did not decrease in value. It was still a gold coin. You are also worthwhile in this world."

Moral of the story:

1. Dirty or clean, you are always precious to those who love you.
2. The worth of your life comes by who you are.
3. Don't ever forget: You are fabulous.
4. Values that you cherish are really free of worldly interruption.
5. Life takes a test of trust.

FOUR THINGS YOU MUST DO

> *"There can be right action only when there is right thinking and there is no right thinking when there is no self-knowledge. Without knowing yourself, there is no peace."*
>
> Jiddu Krishnamurti (1895–1986)

In an attempt to change unnecessary habits and actions, it is imperative to take the time to get to know yourself. Most of us nod our heads in any motivational seminar and claim, "I have the same belief", and then we go outside and do just the same things, as we have been doing for the past few years. We have to become conscious of the menace of unknown-self. Only "IM—Innermost Makeover" will bring right balance. It guides the right external action. Caution: Innermost makeover is not loneliness. It is not abandonment of external action. There are a few things you must do in order to exist here with a meaningful life. They are as follow:

1. Accept what you are (self-awareness)
2. Spend time in knowing your true self (life mission)
3. Improve yourself consistently (vision)
4. Learn what you want in life (goal setting)

You must have understood by now that it is during the turbulent times, you are far remote to yourself and you experience yourself deeply. You see and sense who you truly are. Use "I can be" approach instead of "I do not have." Believe in, "I can be more creative" instead of "I do not have money." The most constructive way by which you can influence your situation is to work on yourself, on your being. By making and keeping promises to ourselves and others, inch by inch, your "Reputation and Reliability" become bigger than your moods.

HONESTY IS THE NUMBER ONE VIRTUE

> *"Here are the values that I stand for: honesty, equality, kindness, compassion, treating people the way you want to be treated and helping those in need. To me, those are traditional values."*
>
> Ellen DeGeneres, the famous host of
> *The Ellen DeGeneres Show*

Every successful leader looks for three qualities in people. Honesty is number one, respect the second one, and absolutely the third is loyalty. There is an old and well-known story on honesty. Once upon a time, a woodcutter was cutting wood in the forest near a river. Suddenly, his axe fell into the river and he became unhappy as he would not be able to cut wood and earn money for that day. The Goddess of river appeared before the woodcutter and asked him, "Why are you sad?" He replied, "I have lost my axe in the river." The Goddess went away and appeared again with a golden axe and asked him, "Is this your axe?" He refused to the golden axe. Then, she came with a silver axe and asked him, "Is this your axe?" He answered in negative. Afterwards, she appeared before the woodcutter with an iron axe and asked the same question. The woodcutter replied in an affirmative way and accepted that it was his axe. The Goddess was happy with his honesty and gifted him all the three axes—golden, silver and iron for his honesty.

Moral of the story:

1. Honesty is the best policy.
2. Honesty is absolutely essential for success in life.
3. Any difficulty will move in the face of honesty.
4. An honest man is generally humble.
5. Honesty is the first virtue of a man who has wisdom.

WHAT ARE VALUES?

"The most incredible architecture
Is the architecture of Self,
Which is ever changing, evolving, revolving
And has unlimited beauty and light inside
Which radiates outwards for everyone to see and feel.
With every in breathe you are adding to your life, and
Every out breathe you are releasing what is not contributing to your life.
Every breathe is a re-birth."

Allan Rufus, *The Master's Sacred Knowledge*

Values are concepts, principles, or standards that drive one's decisions and actions. Examples of values are honesty, persistence, dependability, self-sufficiency, and faith. I see values as "One's judgement of what is important in life; an ideal accepted by some individual or group." You'll gain the value of respect by accepting differences and holding others in high regard. You'll gain the value of responsibility by being responsible for your own actions and behaviours. You'll gain the value of care by feeling for others and helping the deprived. You'll gain the value of self-discipline by controlling your emotions well and abstaining from words and actions that hurt yourself and others. You'll gain the value of inter-dependence/co-operation by working in a team to achieve common goals. You'll gain the value of excellence by having the approach of 'do the best and be the best' in all your pursuits. The infinite intelligence will provide you all the opportunities to put values into action. The onus is on you to act upon.

VALUES v. GOALS

> "Seven Deadly Sins
> Wealth without work
> Pleasure without conscience
> Science without humanity
> Knowledge without character
> Politics without principle
> Commerce without morality
> Worship without sacrifice."
>
> Mahatma Gandhi (1869–1948)

One of the main difference between values and goals is that values are impersonal; universally applicable whereas goals are of personal nature. Values are considered important for humanity and goals are objectives which you must strive hard to excel in your life. A good human being keeps his value intact in realizing his dreams. When we look at the lives of well-known people, we often see how personal values guided them, propelling them to the peak of their fields.

IT'S ALL ABOUT LIVING THE VALUES

> *"Everybody who flashed the signs of loyalty he took to be loyal. Everybody who flashed the signs of intelligence he took to be intelligent. And so he had failed to see into his daughter, failed to see into his wife, failed to see into his one and only mistress—probably had never even begun to see into himself."*
>
> Philip Roth, *American Pastoral*

Women have to assume a more powerful role in present times than ever. I would like to share an incident from my personal life. My wife Honey Tigala, when she got married to me in 2007, was working in an excellent company at a good post. In India, things change a lot after marriage especially for a woman because marriage is a complete uprooting from her parental family and re-plantation in her in-laws family. It was time to organize and plan things for both of us. We had planned each and everything except one issue. The condition of my father was critical at that time and he needed total care and protection due to his paralysis and recent heart attack. Both of us were working. One of us had to leave the job. I was hesitant to have a talk with her on the issue of leaving the job. How could an educated man like me even ask his wife to leave the job? Things could go in a wrong direction if the decision was not taken in a couple of days. The general perception in Indian society is that a man is the bread earner and the woman takes care of household affairs. My wife is a lady of independent thoughts and hails from the national capital, Delhi whereas my city, Bhiwani is comparatively less developed both in terms of materialism and society. Thanks to my fortune! She has a unique quality of noticing things even without a single word being said. One day she asked me, "Is something wrong? Are you all right? I told her the whole dilemma. I also told her, "I can leave the job but your impression will not be good in our society. My parents are educated enough to understand the situation. Jobs are hard to get these days. The problem is the society.

The reputation of my family, me and you are equally at stake." She said, "I understand that serving the parents is considered as a duty of a son and son's wife. Rest assured. I will do the needful." Three days after, we were in a restaurant, on our favourite table. It was exactly 8.30 p.m. I ordered the dinner. Before the bearer came, she gave me an envelope. I found a letter in it mentioning the acceptance of her resignation from the job. She had left her job. Her sacrifice becomes more important because of the fact that she was earning more than me at that time. She was also more settled and secured. The problem arose thereafter. A working lady can't sit idle at home. It was my turn this time. I told her, "It's all about living the values. Interdependence is bigger than Independence. My mother was the root of our family tree and now you have assumed her position. Your new role as a housewife will be more challenging and demanding." I convinced her about the well-being of family members and the legacy. She was pumped up to take the new assignment. She served well and did all the things she could for the next three years. She shows the same level of dedication and commitment now towards me and our children. It's a mission for her more than anything else. Her vision: A Healthy and Successful Acharya Family. She sends everybody to his/her destination. All the wishes and choices of family members in respect of daily food are to be taken care of by her on daily basis. She manages everything from education of children to health of family members.

Moral of story:

1. Managing the home is tougher than working in a company.
2. Home management calls for true leadership traits on daily basis.
3. There is more discipline in a housewife as compared to a CEO of a company.
4. You live your values – whether negative or positive.
5. A higher value demands bigger sacrifice.
6. Values are always your saviour.

DO YOU LIVE YOUR VALUES?

> *"When Thoreau considered 'where I live and what I live for,' he tied together location and values. Where we live doesn't just change how we live; it informs who we become. Most recently, technology promises us lives on the screen. What values, Thoreau would ask, follow from this new location? Immersed in simulation, where do we live, and what do we live for?"*
>
> Sherry Turkle, *Alone Together*

What are the life values that you hold close to your heart? The answer to this question decides your future. There are many reasons why people don't have a proper value system. The first thing is "Time Factor" that people don't have much time left to fulfill their desires and life mission. Secondly, the "Distraction Factor" distractions are too many to live one's values meaningfully. "The Law of Living the Non-Negotiable Values" ask you to make your life resonate with your values. So, whatever time you are left with, you must invest your time in living the life after death and getting closer to your destination. Values are important as your actions are manifestations of your values and your behaviour is outcome of your ethical system.

MAKE YOUR "VALUES OF LIFE" LIST

> *"I think a power to do something is of value. Whether the result is a good thing or a bad thing depends on how it is used, but the power is a value."*
>
> Richard P. Feynman, *The Meaning of It All: Thoughts of a Citizen-Scientist*

The question to ask yourself is this: What is "Value of Essence" that establishes presence of your life? You can look many of your dimensions in creativity. I often advise to make use of the creative process like singing, writing, art and dance to know yourself better. You should create a list of your life-values. Firstly – choose as many values randomly as you like, secondly – reduce them to 15 values like commitment, loyalty, dedication, love, etc. and define how you apply them to yourself. For example: I am committed to my wife and children. And now brainstorm and prioritize your list putting first things at first place and secondary at second place and rearrange these values up to 15 places. You can see the list of values for choosing your "Values of Life". Suppose a person chooses following values first through random selection:

1. Health 2. Wealth 3. Love 4. Peace 5. Success 6. Fun 7. Happiness 8. Learning 9. Courage 10. Leadership 11. Excellence 12. Family 13. Originality 14. Mastery 15. Security

You can see the difference of approach in one's life through Prioritized List, if somebody put success at first place that means he will devote less time in his family and if a person puts health at his first priority that means he will read more health oriented books and watch similar videos. You must also change your list from time to time to maintain a challenge in your life. For example, when I placed my health as my first priority, I devoted more time in regular exercise and supervision of my personal hygiene and food habits and when I choose a writing project, the centre of gravity of all my actions becomes my book. This value driven approach keeps you on your toe and let you exploit your resources to the maximum.

LIST OF "VALUES OF LIFE"

"The whole problem with people is they know what matters but they don't choose it."

Sue Monk Kidd, *The Secret Life of Bees*

Placed below is a list of 439 values (or LOV–439) culled from years of scrutinizing individual achievements and organizational successes, however it is not exhaustive, so feel free to add your own values.

Words of values beginning with A

1. Ability; 2. Abundance; 3. Acceptance; 4. Accessibility; 5. Accomplishment; 6. Accountability; 7. Accuracy; 8. Achievement; 9. Acknowledgement; 10. Activeness; 11. Adaptability; 12. Adoration; 13. Adroitness; 14. Advancement; 15. Adventure; 16. Affection; 17. Affluence; 18. Aggressiveness; 19. Agility; 20. Alertness; 21. Aliveness; 22. Altruism; 23. Amazement; 24. Ambition; 25. Amusement; 26. Anticipation; 27. Appreciation; 28. Approachability; 29. Approval; 30. Artfulness; 31. Articulacy; 32. Artistry; 33. Assertiveness; 34. Assurance; 35. Attentiveness; 36. Attractiveness; 37. Audacity; 38. Authenticity; 39. Availability; 40. Awareness; 41. Awe

Words of values beginning with B

42. Balance; 43. Beauty; 44. Being-ness; 45. Being the best; 46. Belongingness; 47. Benevolence; 48. Blissfulness; 49. Boldness; 50. Bravery; 51. Brilliance; 52. Briskness; 53. Buoyancy

Words of values beginning with C

54. Calmness; 55. Camaraderie; 56. Candour; 57. Capability; 58. Care; 59. Carefulness; 60. Celebrity; 61. Certainty; 62. Challenge; 63. Change; 64. Charity; 65. Charm; 66. Chastity; 67. Cheerfulness; 68. Clarity; 69. Cleanliness; 70. Clear-mindedness; 71. Cleverness; 72. Closeness; 73. Comfort; 74. Commitment; 75. Community; 76. Compassion; 77. Competence; 78. Competition; 79. Completion; 80. Composure; 81. Concentration; 82. Confidence; 83. Conformity; 84. Congruency; 85. Connection; 86. Consciousness; 87. Conservation; 88. Consistency; 89. Contentment; 90. Continuity; 91. Contribution; 92. Control; 93. Conviction; 94. Conviviality; 95. Coolness; 96. Cooperation; 97. Cordiality; 98. Correctness; 99. Country; 100. Courage; 101. Courtesy; 102. Craftiness; 103. Creativity; 104. Credibility; 105. Cunning; 106. Curiosity

Words of values beginning with D

107. Daring; 108. Decisiveness; 109. Dedication; 110. Decorum; 111. Deference; 112. Delight; 113. Dependability; 114. Depth; 115. Desire; 116. Determination; 117. Devotion; 118. Devoutness; 119. Dexterity; 120. Dignity; 121. Diligence; 122. Direction; 123. Directness; 124. Discipline; 125. Discovery; 126. Distinction; 127. Discretion; 128. Diversity; 129. Dominance; 130. Dreaming; 131. Drive; 132. Duty; 133. Dynamism

Words of values beginning with E

134. Eagerness; 135. Ease; 136. Economy; 137. Ecstasy; 138. Education; 139. Effectiveness; 140. Efficiency; 141. Elation; 142. Elegance; 143. Empathy; 144. Encouragement; 145. Endurance; 146. Energy; 147. Enjoyment; 148. Entertainment; 149. Enthusiasm; 150. Environmentalism; 151. Ethics; 152. Euphoria; 153. Evolution; 154. Excellence; 155. Excitement; 156. Exhilaration; 157. Expectancy; 158. Expediency; 159. Experience; 160. Expertise; 161. Exploration; 162. Expressiveness; 163. Extravagance; 164. Extroversion; 165. Exuberance

Words of values beginning with F

166. Facilitating; 167. Fairness; 168. Faith; 169. Fame; 170. Family; 171. Fascination; 172. Fashion; 173. Fearlessness; 174. Ferocity; 175. Fidelity; 176. Fierceness; 177. Financial independence; 178. Firmness; 179. Fitness; 180. Flexibility; 181. Flow; 182. Fluency; 183. Focus; 184. Fortitude; 185. Frankness; 186. Freedom; 187. Free Spirit; 188. Friendliness; 189. Friendship; 190. Frugality; 191. Fulfillment; 192. Fun

Words of values beginning with G

193. Gallantry; 194. Generosity; 195. Gentility; 196. Giving; 197. Grace; 198. Gratitude; 199. Gregariousness; 200. Growth; 201. Guidance

Words of values beginning with H

202. Happiness; 203. Harmony; 204. Health; 205. Heart; 206. Helpfulness; 207. Heroism; 208. Holiness; 209. Honesty; 210. Honour; 211. Hopefulness; 212. Hospitality; 213. Humility; 214. Humour; 215. Hygiene

Words of values beginning with I

216. Imagination; 217. Impact; 218. Impartiality; 219. Independence; 220. Individuality; 221. Industry; 222. Influence; 223. Ingenuity; 224. Innovation; 225. Inquisitiveness; 226. Insightfulness; 227. Inspiration; 228. Integrity; 229. Intellect; 230. Intelligence; 231. Intensity; 232. Interdependence; 233. Intimacy; 234. Intrepidness; 235. Introspection; 236. Introversion; 237. Intuition; 238. Intuitiveness; 239. Inventiveness; 240. Investing; 241. Involvement

Words of values beginning with J

242. Joy; 243. Judiciousness; 244. Justice

Words of values beginning with K

245. Keenness; 246. Kindness; 247. Knowledge

Words of values beginning with L

248. Lavishness; 249. Leadership; 250. Learning; 251. Liberation; 252. Liberty; 253. Lightness; 254. Liveliness; 255. Logic; 256. Longevity; 257. Love; 258. Loyalty

Words of values beginning with M

259. Majesty; 260. Making a difference; 261. Marriage; 262. Mastery; 263. Maturity; 264. Meaning; 265. Meekness; 266. Mellowness; 267. Meticulousness; 268. Mindfulness; 269. Modesty; 270. Motivation; 271. Mysteriousness

Words of values beginning with N

272. Nature; 273. Neatness; 274. Nerve; 275. Nonconformity; 276. Nurturing

Words of values beginning with O

277. Obedience; 278. Open-mindedness; 279. Openness; 280. Optimism; 281. Order; 282. Organization; 283. Originality; 284. Outdoors; 285. Outlandishness; 286. Outrageousness

Words of values beginning with P

287. Partnership; 288. Patience; 289. Passion; 290. Peace; 291. Perceptiveness; 292. Perfection; 293. Perkiness; 294. Perseverance; 295. Persistence; 296. Persuasiveness; 297. Philanthropy; 298. Piety; 299. Playfulness; 300. Pleasantness; 301. Pleasure; 302. Poise; 303. Polish; 304. Popularity; 305. Potency; 306. Power; 307. Practicality; 308. Pragmatism; 309. Precision; 310. Preparedness; 311. Presence; 312. Pride; 313. Privacy; 314. Proactivity; 315. Professionalism; 316. Prosperity; 317. Prudence; 318. Punctuality; 319. Purity

Words of values beginning with R

320. Rationality; 321. Realism; 322. Reason; 323. Reasonableness; 324. Recognition; 325. Recreation; 326. Refinement; 327. Reflection; 328. Relaxation; 329. Reliability; 330. Relief; 331. Religiousness; 332. Reputation; 333. Resilience; 334. Resolution; 335. Resolve; 336. Resourcefulness; 337. Respect; 338. Responsibility; 339. Rest; 340. Restraint; 341. Reverence; 342. Richness; 343. Rigour; 344. Risk-taking

Words of values beginning with S

345. Sacredness; 346. Sacrifice; 347. Sagacity; 348. Saintliness; 349. Sanguinity; 350. Satisfaction; 351. Science; 352. Security; 353. Self-control; 354. Selflessness; 355. Self-reliance; 356. Self-respect; 357. Sensitivity; 358. Sensuality; 359. Serenity; 360. Service; 361. Sexiness; 362. Sexuality; 363. Sharing; 364. Shrewdness; 365. Significance; 366. Silence; 367. Silliness; 368. Simplicity; 369. Sincerity; 370. Skilfulness; 371. Solidarity; 372. Solitude; 373. Sophistication; 374. Soundness; 375. Speed;

376. Spirit; 377. Spirituality; 378. Spontaneity; 379. Spunk; 380. Stability; 381. Status; 382. Stealth; 383. Stillness; 384. Strength; 385. Structure; 386. Success; 387. Support; 388. Supremacy; 389. Surprise; 390. Sympathy; 391. Synergy

Words of values beginning with T

392. Tactfulness; 393. Teaching; 394. Teamwork; 395. Temperance; 396. Thankfulness; 397. Thoroughness; 398. Thoughtfulness; 399. Thrift; 400. Tidiness; 401. Timeliness; 402. Traditionalism; 403. Tranquility; 404. Transcendence; 405. Trust; 406. Trustworthiness; 407. Truth

Words of values beginning with U

408. Understanding; 409. Unflappability; 410. Uniqueness; 411. Unity; 412. Usefulness; 413. Utility

Words of values beginning with V

414. Valour; 415. Variety; 416. Victory; 417. Vigour; 418. Virtue; 419. Vision; 420. Vitality; 421. Vivacity; 422. Volunteering

Words of values beginning with W

423. Warmheartedness; 424. Warmth; 425. Watchfulness; 426. Wealth; 427. Well-being; 428. Wholesomeness; 429. Wilfulness; 430. Willingness; 431. Winning; 432. Wisdom; 433. Wittiness; 434. Wonder; 435. Worthiness

Words of values beginning with Y

436. Youthfulness

Words of values beginning with Z

437. Zeal; 438. Zest; 439. Zing

IT'S A GREAT EXPERIENCE

> *"The first principle of value that we need to rediscover is this: that all reality hinges on moral foundations. In other words, that this is a moral universe, and that there are moral laws of the universe just as abiding as the physical laws."*
>
> Martin Luther King Jr., *A Knock at Midnight*

Generally, you get your values from your family, education, environment and social conditioning. Whether we are consciously aware of them or not, every individual has a core set of personal values. Mahatma Gandhi had resilience. Abraham Lincoln had determination, persistence and courage. Nelson Mandela is famous for his strength, perseverance and willpower. Boldness and enthusiasm made Julius Caesar great. George Washington represents the will and character of American leadership. Winston Churchill is known for his fearlessness. Hitler was a captivating leader. His self-belief persuaded people to believe in him. Alexander the great was known for his leadership qualities. King David is well-known for his heart and mind of faith as he faced the giant Goliath with just five stones. Franklin Roosevelt faced some of the harshest circumstances in U.S. history – the depression and World War II. USA recovered because of his unfailing optimism and activism. Jesus Christ's life still continues to liberate the souls of men and women. These all time greats knew themselves inside-out. Every one of these greats has one value for which their life stands. It is a great experience to truly sit down and decide your own values. It's a bliss, when you become clear about who you want to be and what you are going to do in your life. I advise you to look in five or six of your past successes and figure out what values you think contributed to each success and then you can also add values to your list by visualizing yourself in each situation.

VALUES v. ETHICS

"In law, a man is guilty when he violates the rights of others. In ethics, he is guilty if he only thinks of doing so."

Immanuel Kant (1724–1804)

What is the difference between values and ethics? Values are "Rules of Decision" – the foundation of what you believe; a system that determines and answers what is right or wrong. While, ethics is a set of moral values that decide your doing of what you believe right or wrong. Morals underline your ethical approach. Ethics is a philosophical study of moral values. For example in US, the values of liberty and freedom hold great significance and the behaviour and actions of people in the society are guided by these values. Morals are – "Is Norm" what we do i.e. character that's why we tend to judge others by morals instead of values. Values are how we think i.e. personality and Ethics is "Should Norm" – how we respond and behave in certain situations based on group or profession expectations to which a person belongs. Advocacy ethics demand to defend a criminal while personal moral conduct does not approve crimes.

In conclusion, it can be said that values determine how you will face the world and relate with people as an individual, group, culture and society. Morals give you a right or wrong thing to which values assign a duty to perform or not and you act keeping ethics as standard expectation. Let me give you some examples –

An ethical person knows "One should not cheat on spouse." (Ethics)

Moralistic person knows he/she will never cheat his/her spouse in life. (Moralistic Conduct)

The value you believe in: Loyalty (Guiding Light)

CULTURE v. BEHAVIOUR

> *"The world is my church. My actions are my prayer. My behaviour is my creed."*
>
> Steve Maraboli, *Unapologetically You*

Even if you don't understand the difference, one thing is obvious, your values, morals and ethics effect and affect your line of thought, decision, action and more importantly your behaviour. At least, you know you are taught to behave ethically. Good leaders develop organizational ethics (a system to respond to external or internal stimulus) which is interdependent with organizational culture. We should try to cultivate a culture where ethics become a way of life and the question "What is right?" should never arise in the mind, because we will do right only when we have a right culture. In good teams, players behave and get selected on the basis of performance i.e. character ethics and not on name image i.e. personality ethics.

VALUE STATEMENT

> *"There is only one corner of the universe you can be certain of improving, and that's your own self."*
>
> Aldous Huxley (1894–1963)

A value statement is an expression of a company's or individual's core beliefs. A personal value statement is written by an individual to express their personal values and beliefs. Companies write the statement to identify and connect with the employees and consumer. The value statement, along with a mission and vision statement, will form the corporate culture and climate. Just as individuals subscribe to values, so do organizations and institutions, Microsoft's value statement is as follows: "As a company, and as individuals, we value integrity, honesty, openness, personal excellence, constructive self-criticism, continual self-improvement and mutual respect.

We are committed to our customers and partners and have a passion for technology. We take on big challenges, and pride ourselves on seeing them through. We hold ourselves accountable to our customers, shareholders, partners, and employees by honouring our commitments, providing results, and striving for the highest quality."

WRITING VALUE STATEMENTS

> *"No one is free who has not obtained the empire of himself. No man is free who cannot command himself."*
>
> Pythagoras (570–495 BC)

Keep revising your Personal Value Statement {or PVS (1) in short} till you feel it reflects your core values. The process to form Value Statement is a fun to exercise:

1. Choose top three values from the list of your "Values of Life". Then define each value in a sentence. For example, you may write, "I value commitment because it allows me to be regular, and keep others' trust (in me) alive."
2. Now list three qualities that you know you already have like dedication, creativity and expression. Then define each value in a sentence.
3. What are the three things in your life that really mean a lot to you like my family, my friends and my work? Then define importance of each one in a sentence.
4. Now list three weaknesses in your personality that can stop you in materializing your vision like anger, anxiety and carelessness. Then define importance of each one in a sentence.
5. Combine all to have your PVS (1). The Resulted Value Statement is:

I am determined to exemplify the values of *caring, commitment,* and *courage* on a daily basis in my life. By imbibing these cherished values I will get closer to my mission and vision and have a sense of purpose to live, love and laugh to inspire others. I know that I have mastered the qualities of *creativity, dedication,* and *expression* and I look to convey these traits in every opportunity. I understand that I am blocked by my *anger, carelessness,* and *anxiety* and I am working to resolve these problems. There are three things *my family, my friends,* and *my work* which are indispensable for me. I revise my PVS (1) to commit myself to live in alignment with my vision and values.

ETHICS STATEMENT

> *"Ethics is not about platitudes, let alone tautologies, logic or mathematics, but about difficult choices – dilemmas."*
>
> Martin Cohen, *101 Ethical Dilemmas*

A personal ethics statement includes ideals that are important to a person, such as honesty or integrity. A personal ethical statement should be written and used as a guide for your dealings with everyone you come in contact with. An ethical statement should give you a sense of what is right when dealing with others. You will also notice that your actions take you beyond the confines of your ethical statement. If they do, then you may want to redraft your PES – Personal Ethics Statement.

WRITING ETHICS STATEMENT

> *"A man without ethics is a wild beast loosed upon this world."*
>
> Albert Camus (1913–1960)

Keep in mind: "Treat others the way as you want yourself to be treated." Identify your roles in different capacities. For example, your roles as a son, brother, husband and manager etc. For illustration: "I will remain a dedicated husband to my wife." "I will try to be a good father." The best method is imagining yourself before all the persons you have to deal with and then write your expected behaviour and then see the values in your conduct. For instance: If you assume yourself before your boss, and then ask yourself what ethics/duties are required to deal with him. It may be respect for the chair. I always say "I am with the chair not with the chairman." I support the value not the person. Write your ethical values from your expected behaviour in all situations and with all relations plus derive values from professional requirements also and then concretize four or five core ethical values and lastly define each value in single sentence and ultimately combine them to form a paragraph of 4 to 6 lines. Keep revising it until it resonates with your ethical standards in your personal, private, social and public zones. This can be mentioned in your resume but avoid plagiarism.

My PES – Personal Ethical Statement says: "I am a dedicated teacher who loves to teach, write and read as a habit. All my thoughts and actions are help oriented. I am determined to help others in getting their aspired success at any cost and at any time (except my values and schedule system); I listen more than my patience and help them more than their expectations."

SUGGESTED STRATEGY

> *"Unexamined life is not worth living."*
>
> Socrates (469 BC–399 BC)

There are many good habits but here I am asking you to imbibe there *three good habits* in yourself and believe me you will never be same again. Let us have a look at these:

1. The fault you see in other people may be a default in yourself. It is your "Self" that you see in others. Toni Collette rightly speaks: The better you know yourself, the better will be your relationship with the rest of world. Therefore, try to see only good things and ignoring the unhappy ones. If you look fine things in others, this habit will make you a fine human being.

2. Do you analyze before you finalize? Ask yourself before doing anything. Is it important for me? Do only those things which are crucial for your life values and delegate other things. You can focus on one value per week, giving your entire concentration to apply it in your life and then observe the results. You must act courageously if you have chosen courage as your value. Action is the key. Let me tell you a quote of Jeremy London: "I don't think anybody should get married before they're 30. You're too young to really know yourself." Well, this statement may look odd to you. But it emphasizes the need to ask yourself before doing anything, be it thinking, saying, eating and anything for that matter, and I mean anything, otherwise you will eventually do nothing.
3. In your life journal write how you spend your time, how you think, what you eat and other missions and visions. Nelson Mandela rightfully says: "A good head and good heart are always a formidable combination. But when you add to that a literate tongue or pen, then you have something very special."

ASSIGNMENT

1. Develop a PVS (1) for your beliefs.
2. Develop a PES for your behaviour.
3. Try to live, love and laugh to inspire others through your daily activities and roles based on your PVS (1) and PES.
4. Listen to the Audio program *Get The Edge* by Anthony Robbins.

VISUALIZATION

When you get up, just sit for few minutes and visualize yourself living your value driven daily life based on PVS (1) and doing all day activities on the basis of PES – Personal Ethics Statement. Remember: Despite all your mistakes and misfortunes you are still a gold coin. The ability to submit an impulse to a value is the character of a superhero.

SELF SUGGESTION

I strive to achieve ethics and values in my life. I am a positive role model to others.

Bear in mind: Super achievers always keep their commitments.

[*Promise & Put Your Signature Here With Date*]

3

How Would You Like To Be Remembered?

OBJECTIVES

- To learn the "Law of Living the Life after Death",
- To identify with the true purpose of your life, and
- To create your personal mission statement.

GOLDEN GUIDANCE

> *"Great minds have purposes. Others have dreams."*
>
> Washington Irving (1783–1859)

LIVE MEANINGFULLY

> *"A man with money is no match against a man on a mission."*
>
> Doyle Brunson, poker's most famous champion

What is your legacy? How would you like to be remembered? Will you be spoken well of? Are you working for a cause or applause? Will you be remembered with love and respect? Will you be missed with respect? These questions come to a mind of only few image conscious people, as most of people think in terms of their present needs only. Have you ever dared to ask these questions to yourself? Richard Bach, an American writer, who is widely known as the author of the hugely popular 1970s best-sellers

Jonathan Livingston Seagull and *Illusions: The Adventures of a Reluctant Messiah,* prescribes a test: "Here is the test to find whether your mission on earth is finished. If you're alive it isn't." You must decide your goals and more importantly your life mission in order to live with a purpose. You need to develop three elements so as to have a life-mission:

1. Element of Faith: You have to be basically being mindful of God.
2. Element of Sharing: You should do generous things.
3. Element of Passion: You should find what is exceptional to you – your God-Gift.

The top secret formula is: Blend what you love to do (3) and what you give (2) with God's purpose (1). How will you find God's purpose? The answer is: When you find your profound happiness in fulfilling the people genuine needs. Understand: People will remember you for your contribution to the mankind and not for your personal riches and success.

THE STORY OF A SAVIOUR

> *"The way of Jesus cannot be imposed or mapped – it requires an active participation in following Jesus as he leads us through sometimes strange and unfamiliar territory, in circumstances that become clear only in the hesitations and questionings, in the pauses and reflections where we engage in prayerful conversation with one another and with him."*
>
> Eugene H. Peterson, *The Jesus Way: A Conversation on the Ways That Jesus Is the Way*

In the beginning, when nothing existed, the word (Jesus) was with God. Word was God. Jesus, the Son of God, was sent by God to earth to free us from the bondage of Satan. God chose Mary, a simple and poor woman to show His indiscrimination. The angel Gabriel visited Mary in a dream and told her that she would give birth to the Son of God. She was a virgin who was engaged to Joseph of Nazareth, a Jewish carpenter. Gabriel told her that God's power would make the conception possible. Mary consented to God's will. The angel also told Joseph that the miraculous conception was caused by the Holy Spirit. The name Jesus was given by the angel. He was born in the year 4 BC, in Bethlehem, Judea. He was raised in the small rural town of Nazareth, where His adoptive father, Joseph, taught Him to use the tools of a carpenter. Jesus was baptized at the age of 30 by John in Jordan. After baptism, He went into the Judean desert to fast and meditate for 40 days and nights. He founded Christianity. Jesus performed countless miracles. When Jesus learned that Lazarus died, He came to Bethany. Jesus shouted "Lazarus, come forth!" And Lazarus came out. Some of His other miracles include, healing the sick and several incurable diseases, casting out demons, calming a storm, walking on water and feeding 5,000 people with five loaves and two fish, etc. He talked with Elijah and Moses, when He was on a mountain with His three disciples. A bright cloud emerged around them, and a voice said, "This is my beloved Son, with whom I am well pleased; listen to Him." This event is known as Transfiguration. On a Thursday night, Jesus met with His apostles, in the city of Jerusalem, to take the Passover meal with them. It was here on a solemn occasion, that Jesus told them He must soon die. That it was God's will that He give His life for His friends. Jesus had twelve men, also known as disciples, to whom He gave the power and authority over the Devil. They treated everybody equally irrespective of his caste, creed and position. All of them carried money bags to help the poor and needy. One day He asked before the crowd: "Whom seek ye?" The crowed answered: "Jesus of Nazareth." Then, He said: "I am he." One of his apostles, Iscariot Judas, betrayed Him and sold Him into the hands of Roman authorities in return for 30 silver coins. Jesus was arrested and brought before Pilate, the Governor of Rome. Pilate wanted to release Jesus, but when the people threatened a riot, he condemned Jesus to death on a cross. He was crucified on the cross between two robbers. Jesus' body was buried in the new tomb of a rich man named Joseph of Arimathea. Three days after His death, Jesus rose from His tomb just as

He had promised His disciples. Jesus appeared to Mary, the Mother of Jesus, Salome, Joanna and to many believers. After 40 days, Jesus led His disciples to Mount Olivet, east of Jerusalem. At last He stood on a hilltop and angels watched as He began to ascend into Heaven, as He rose, He said to his apostles, "Go everywhere and tell the good news." He commanded them to teach and baptize others. Jesus had promised to His disciples that they would receive power from the Holy Spirit. In Islam, Jesus (commonly transliterated as Isa) is considered one of God's important prophets. Bahá'í scripture calls Him as a Manifestation of God. Ghulam Ahmad's treatise *Jesus in India* suggests that Jesus, starting His journey from Jerusalem and passing through Nasibus and Persia, eventually reached Afghanistan where He met the Israelites who had settled there after their escape from the bonds of Nebuchadnezzar and from here He travelled to Kashmir where some Israelite tribes had also settled. Here He lived until His death at an old age. Life of Jesus is a pattern and an example of law of living the life after death for us if we want to be successful. Whenever you find yourself in any dilemma just ask yourself: "What would Jesus do?" and then do the replied answer honestly. Mother Teresa once rightly said: "Each one of them is Jesus in disguise."

Moral of the story:

1. When God wants something to happen, He indicates it before.
2. The lives of great leaders are well planned events by God.
3. A great man knows who he is and why he is here on this planet.
4. A great leader generates leaders.
5. A great leader leads from certainty of fixed principles.
6. A great man puts himself and his own needs second.
7. God does not discriminate between rich and poor.
8. Whatever great persons say, they do.
9. Every great man has vision to lead his and others lives.
10. A leader has to sacrifice even his life for others.
11. Great men don't show favouritism.

12. Great men are generally generous.
13. A great leader (even the God) can be cheated by friends.
14. Great men do not live self-absorbed lives.
15. High Achievers don't have hidden agendas.
16. Great men never resort to lie, dishonesty and deception.
17. Great men are merciful towards the mistakes of others.
18. Great men develop power with people.
19. Great men speak the language of love.
20. Great men even love their enemies.
21. Great leaders are sent for a mission on earth.

MISSIONS v. GOALS

> *"If you have built castles in the air, your work need not be lost; that is where they should be. Now put the foundations under them."*
>
> Henry David Thoreau, *Walden*

Everyone has his own specific mission or goals in life. Mission and goal are two words that sound similar, don't they? Many people remain puzzled while using these words. Let us first understand the difference between goals and mission. Goals are too many and mission is one or few. Each goal is an effort. In game of football, the mission is to win but you have to score goals to win. Similarly, you have different goals at different times which are necessary to be accomplished in order to realize your life mission. There may be objectives, goals, strategies, executions and tactics all used to achieve the mission. You must be absolutely clear about your mission otherwise you will end up nowhere.

YOU CAN CHANGE YOUR DIRECTION OVERNIGHT

> *"Remembering that I'll be dead soon is the most important tool I've ever encountered to help me make the big choices in life. Because almost everything – all external expectations, all pride, all fear of embarrassment or failure – these things just fall away in the face of death, leaving only what is truly important."*
>
> Steve Jobs (1955–2011)

You can change your direction overnight provided you have realized your life-mission. One can find the real life illustration of "Law of Living the Life After Death" in the story of Dynamite King. This is an inspiring tale. About a hundred years ago, a man looked at the morning newspaper and to his surprise and horror, read his name in the obituary column. The newspaper had reported the death of the wrong person by mistake. His first response was shock. Am I here or there? When he regained his composure, his second thought was to find out what people had said about him. The obituary read, "Dynamite King Dies." And also "He was the merchant of death." This man was the inventor of dynamite and when he read the words "merchant of death" he asked himself a question, "Is this how I am going to be remembered?" He got in touch with his feelings and decided that this was not the way he wanted to be remembered. From that day on, he started working towards peace. His name was Alfred Nobel and he is remembered today by the great Nobel Prize. Nobel held 350 different patents, dynamite being the most famous.

Moral of the story:

1. You should take time to get in touch with your feelings and redefine your values.
2. Your purpose in life is to find your purpose.
3. Actions of one individual can inspire the movement of change.
4. You have to be generous if you want to be remembered.
5. How will you make big choices in life? Remember that you'll be dead soon.

IMPORTANCE OF PERSONAL MISSION STATEMENT: LIFE PURPOSE

"When you truly act in alignment with your life purpose – the people, resources, and opportunities you need, the whole universe conspires to make it happen by helping you."

R.W. Emerson (1803–1882)

A personal mission statement is the personal constitution and the beginning of personal leadership. Muhammad (Peace Be Upon Him) united His people with a mission of spread of Islam. How well did He execute His mission? Islam has become one of the largest and the fastest growing religions of the world today. Mao Zedong's mission was industrialized China. Nelson Mandela's mission was a society free from apartheid. Fidel Castro's mission was a developed Cuba. Tom Monaghan, the founder of Domino's Pizza, said: "If you want to be successful over a long period, you have to have some idea why you were born and what life is about. I don't know how anybody can function without thinking that through." Kathleen Turner, an American actress and singer, uttered: "I think my mission is to become the greatest human I can. I know that sounds pompous, but what else do we have?" Mahatma Gandhi said: "My mission is not merely brotherhood of Indian humanity. My mission is not merely freedom of India. But through realization of the freedom of India, I hope to realize and carry on the mission of the brotherhood of man." Bruce Lee affirmed: "The key to immortality is first living a life worth remembering." Writing what is true about ourselves isn't as easy as it seems. We believe things because we are expected to believe them. A motor mechanic sees everything as a motor. We use our left brain more, as we are installed with measurements, numbers and logic for ages and we seldom touch the right artistic side of brain. PMS – Personal Mission Statement helps you to know why you exist. It has to be short, unforgettable and inspirational. This is theme of your advertisement campaign and the offer at which other people will join hands with you. The life statement is a way of discovering that sense of purpose by coming to know ourselves better. So writing a mission statement is really an adventure in self-discovery.

WRITING YOUR MISSION STATEMENT

Part-1

Self-Exploration Procedure: the way to detect your mission

I am prescribing a self-exploration procedure to determine your life mission, following which you can truly ascertain what you're here to do, and then you will have a mission to love, live and laugh to inspire. The procedure is equally applicable to teams, organizations and families by treating these as a single unit first and then small groups (as branch heads) and thinking in terms of "We" instead of "I". Write the answers to the questions. Take a blank notebook and write your answers with a pen on a blank page:

Step 1: Ask yourself, what is that activity doing which you feel you are giving your 110% and you feel most comfortable and satisfied. The activity, which you can continue for 8 to 10 hours non-stop without getting tired as your heart is involved, doing which you thoroughly enjoy and feel good. (Element of Passion)

Answer: What is it you are most passionate about? For example, for me it is when people listen to me and I persuade and inspire them. I suggest you to choose three activities you love to do. Examples can be teaching, computer, machines, driving, cooking, etc. Victor Frankl, an Austrian neurologist and psychiatrist, founder of logotherapy said: "We detect rather than invent missions in life." You should try to find the type of employment or livelihood in which step 1 is involved. For team members, families or organizations, they can assign the type of activity mentioned in step 1 to each one by asking question in step 1.

This can be the thing; you want to make your family famous for, like my family is an inspiring family. Family or a unit of organization can opt to work on any activity doing which they enjoy.

Step 2: Ask yourself, what is that situation facing which, you feel you are not giving your 100% and you feel most uncomfortable and unsatisfied. The activity, which you do not want to continue even for a minute and you get tired soon as your heart is not involved, doing which you feel burden and sadness. (Element of Sadness)

Answer: Any activity that is unrelated to first one. You should try to cut the time wasted on activities involved in step 2. For example, I try to avoid unproductive things like watching too much TV, wandering meaninglessly and too much sleep.

Step 3: Ask yourself, what is that time or situation, at which you feel truly confident and ready to do any challenging activity. (Element of Confidence)

Answer: For example, getting successes after successes, feeling happy or getting appreciation etc. You should try to maximize the situation involved in step 3. I suggest you to ask yourself: What are my three greatest successes and what were my biggest values at that time? Teams, organizations and families can also work on this step to increase happiness in atmosphere.

Step 4: Ask yourself, what is that time or situation, at which you feel frustrated and down in the dumps. (Element of Performance)

Answer: For example, getting no results or less than expected, fight with life partner or a friend or any criticism etc. You should try to minimize the situation involved in step 3. Teams, organizations and families can also work on this step to reduce tension in atmosphere.

Step 5: Ask yourself, what is that help or activity which you make for your life partner, family/team member or friend to feel happy, the activity doing which you think you can excel in your relationships. (Element of Enjoyment)

Answer: For example, cooking with him/her or shopping or sharing of feelings or a true help. You should try to excel in your relationships by enjoying activities involved in step 5. Teams and organizations can work on this step by doing activities which makes members and employees happy e.g. to treat with respect, equal pay for equal work and bonus policy etc. A family member can genuinely help each other. Mission Statements for business groups have to be market focused means what category(ies) of customers you are addressing to and how.

Step 6: Ask yourself, what is that natural talent in me, which is truly God Gifted, anything I do without much effort and excellently. (Element of Natural Talent/God-Gift)

Answer: For example, painting, singing, teaching, motivation or any artistic activity. You should try to look out for more occasions where you can show activities to public involved in step 6. Teams, families and organizations can work on this step by treating the gifted employee or member as a celebrity star and enhance his/her skill by giving more opportunities and sponsor the participation in further events and competitions.

Step 7: Ask yourself, if you are given ten years, a billion dollars, and good supporting staff, what would you do if you knew you would not fail. (Element of Imagination)

Answer: For example, training institute, a restaurant or a hotel etc. This an answer to the often asked question: What do you want to do in future? You must do the activity involved in step 7. This is your dream of life. Start by taking small steps. Teams and organizations can work on this step by asking their staff and members what facilities they want in the workplace.

Step 8: Ask yourself, what do you want be known as? What should you do to achieve that? What places and staff should I have for this? What values and services should I see in that company etc.? What will be my best offer for my customers and employees? (Element of Ethics)

Answer: What do you want to be in future? For example a great teacher of all time whose writing and teachings inspire people to live, love and laugh to inspire. Now other options can be the greatest scientist, engineer, human, etc. This is the image; you should live for, life after death. Step 7 is a stepping step for step 8. It can be equally good for the teams and organizations to develop their brand image. The image can be one thing for which you would be willing to risk your life, passion, and job etc. and prefer image above all. Soldiers die for country, lovers die for beloveds and fathers die for sons etc.

Step 9: Ask yourself, two days before your death, what persons would you like to invite at your last treat of this earthly life, and what tribute statements would you like them to make about your life. (Element of Character)

Answer: For example, great husband, wife, son, mother, human, manager and administrator etc. You should make every effort to be the person mentioned in step 9. Teams and organizations can work on this step by asking their staff and members what kind of character they want their team or organization to be famous for. "The Best Team Co-ordination of All Times", "Good People to Bank With" and "We Care" etc. The people should have faith in you for this character.

Step 10: Ask yourself, who are the most important people in your life, and now write what is your single most important contribution in their life. (Element of Contribution)

Answer: You must answer this question first: What one thing would you like to contribute which will have a positive impact in your professional field? For example: Writing a book on principles of success science that can change the thinking pattern of youth so that my country can excel. Guidance, help, education can now be your other options. You should contribute the quality or thing mentioned in step 10 to the future generations. I believe my photographs, books and journals will be a legacy to my family's future generations.

Teams and organization can contribute something unique to future generations of members and customers. A family can find the ways to help a person outside the family. One should ask what one value I will pass on to my coming generations, this value can be a guiding star and characteristic of any family, organization, team or any person. As an individual or a member of any team or organization, you should only do those acts which further the activity mentioned in step 10. For example, inspiration is the contribution for which each of my family members or member of organizations lives, loves and laughs. It means we as a family will do only those acts which further this aim.

Step 11: Ask yourself, what are those three things which have come often in your mind, but you have postponed those ideas. (Element of Conscience)

Answer: For example, maintenance of health, starting a guidance centre or people contact program etc. Individuals, Teams, organizations and family should stop deferring and initiate the things mentioned in step 11.

Step 12: Ask yourself, who are those three persons of past or present who have influenced your life, and what is one main attribute or value you respect most in these people. Select one from your family or nears and dears, one from past or present big personalities and one from your professional life. Think in detail why do you praise big personality? (Element of Influence)

Answer: For example, 1. Mr. X – Discipline 2. Mr. Y – Dedication and 3. Mr. Z – Faith. You should make every effort to add the qualities mentioned in step 12 into your life. Teams, organizations and families can work on this step by looking other teams, organizations and families for emotional inspiration. These can be greatest values to live, love and laugh to inspire. People should expect these traits from you and you must live for these. BPV – Big Personality Value – can be the value to achieve ideal greatness, you are looking for.

Step 13: Ask yourself in all seven areas – family, finances, career, friends, social life, health and spirituality, what is the single best activity you can do in each of the zones that will have the best constructive effect on your life and help you in becoming a man of balance? (Element of Balance)

Answer: For example, exercise, meditation, study, membership of a social club and making new friends etc. Teams, organizations and families can work on this for balancing profit with social responsibility. Define your roles in each capacity, like a great father, great husband, great teacher and great human etc. This is real greatness. You should write your all activities in Journal.

Part 2

Method: Develop Your Life Sentence

> *"To realize one's destiny is a person's only obligation."*
>
> Paulo Coelho, *The Alchemist*

I suggest you to do a great exercise, which I have developed by undergoing various exercises suggested online and in various self-help books.

1. Choose your three unique God gifted values
   Combination of all the self-exploration thirteen answers + Personal Value Statement + Personal Ethics Statement will serve as base for developing your mission statement. You have to come to those three values for which your whole life stands. For example I select: Creativity, Enthusiasm and Leadership etc.

2. Choose your Action Verbs
   We are taught in school that verbs describe the action that is taking place. Every mission statement requires action, so select the verb(s) that expresses your value(s). For example:
   Creativity: I collect and disseminate inspiring stories and principles through the "Live, Love and Laugh to Inspire" Series and I also deliver inspirational keynote speeches. I believe that when I choose to write (to use my creativity) a book (to produce a new and original thing of value) I always dream to care about readers' and my expectations so I select – Creativity: Care
   Enthusiasm: Talking of my ability to complete that task taken with eagerness and dedication (Enthusiasm), I always try to inspire others that this is the way to accomplish the goal so I select – Enthusiasm: Inspire
   Leadership: I always believe that "A true leader generates leaders." To be a good leader, you have to produce good results and complete people demands all the time that too well before deadlines. You have to lead by taking initiatives, so I select – Leadership: Produce
3. Imagine a perfect, festive and wonderful planet with outcome of your actions –
   You can also select help groups (minimum three) like students, women, children, handicapped people, diseased, depressed and poor etc.
   For example – Creativity: Everyone is realizing breakthrough and dream goals. Enthusiasm: Everyone is celebrating their life by utilizing their potential talents in full manner. Leadership: Everyone is leading oneself and creating leaders. Everyone is helping others in getting success.
4. Convert the three prior subdivisions into three sentences, starting with "to apply".

For example: To apply my creativity to help everybody in accomplishment of his breakthroughs and dream goals; to apply my enthusiasm to inspire everybody to celebrate life by utilizing potential talents in full manner; and to apply my leadership qualities to produce leaders who will live, love and laugh to inspire others.

5. Put all together. Combine all three sentences.
   For example, my PMS is:"My Life Mission is to apply my creativity, enthusiasm and leadership to help everybody in accomplishment of breakthroughs and dream goals. I inspire people to celebrate their life by employing their potential talents in an envisioned manner with fun. I am passionate about producing successful and relevant leaders who live, love and laugh to inspire others."
6. Revise and rewrite it daily for a month.
   Through PMS you will have more accuracy about "What do you want to be","What you don't want" and "What do you want" in your life. You can keep on writing and revising your mission statement until you feel it echoes "Values and Vision" of the life that you will live, love and laugh to inspire.

ORGANIZATIONAL MISSION STATEMENT

"Life is a MISSION
Fulfilled through our VISION
Live life well this SEASON
You were born for a REASON..."

Israelmore Ayivor, a life coach

This method is also easy one.

1. List what your company does like selling the law books, selling the law journals and to provide educational help to poor law students.
2. Decide your core values like high-quality, reasonable rates and upliftment of underprivileged in society.

3. Then concentrate on why (passion) you do that. Derived PMS is: to sell the quality law books and journals at a reasonable price and to help the needy law students in getting success by free distribution of standard study material.
4. As an organization, you need to carry an individual survey for having your mission statement, in which you can have other examples of vision statements and your present mission statements.
5. You need to print it on the official uniform, noticeboards and other important places and documents.

LIST OF "POWERFUL ACTION VERBS"

"My mission in life is not merely to survive, but to thrive; and to do so with some passion, some compassion, some humour, and some style."

Maya Angelou, an American author and poet

These 370 Action Verbs (or AV–370) will help to portray your skills and accomplishments when writing the first draft of your personal statements. You can use these in your resume also.

Action Verbs beginning with A

1. Accelerate; 2. Accomplish; 3. Achieve; 4. Act; 5. Activate; 6. Adapt; 7. Address; 8. Adjust; 9. Administer; 10. Advance; 11. Advertise; 12. Advise; 13. Advocate; 14. Aid; 15. Allocate; 16. Analyze; 17. Answer; 18. Apply; 19. Appraise; 20. Approve; 21. Arbitrate; 22. Arrange; 23. Ascertain; 24. Assemble; 25. Assess; 26. Assign; 27. Assist; 28. Attain; 29. Augment; 30. Authorize; 31. Award

Action Verbs beginning with B

32. Balance; 33. Begin; 34. Boost; 35. Brief; 36. Budget; 37. Built

Action Verbs beginning with C

38. Calculate; 39. Capture; 40. Catalogue; 41. Centralize; 42. Chair; 43. Chart; 44. Check; 45. Clarify; 46. Classify; 47. Coach; 48. Collaborate; 49. Collect; 50. Combine; 51. Communicate; 52. Compare; 53. Compile; 54. Complete; 55. Compose; 56. Compute; 57. Conceive; 58. Conceptualize; 59. Condense; 60. Conduct; 61. Confer; 62. Conserve; 63. Consolidate; 64. Construct; 65. Consult; 66. Contact; 67. Continue; 68. Contribute; 69. Control; 70. Convert; 71. Convey; 72. Convince; 73. Coordinate; 74. Correspond; 75. Create; 76. Critique; 77. Cultivate; 78. Customize

Action Verbs beginning with D

79. Debug; 80. Decide; 81. Define; 82. Delegate; 83. Deliver; 84. Demonstrate; 85. Designate; 86. Design; 87. Detect; 88. Determine; 89. Develop; 90. Devise; 91. Diagnose; 92. Direct; 93. Discover; 94. Dispense; 95. Display; 96. Dissect; 97. Distribute; 98. Divert; 99. Document; 100. Draft

Action Verbs beginning with E

101. Earn; 102. Edit; 103. Educate; 104. Effect; 105. Eliminate; 106. Emphasize; 107. Employ; 108. Encourage; 109. Enforce; 110. Engineer; 111. Enhance; 112. Enlarge; 113. Enlist; 114. Ensure; 115. Entertain; 116. Establish; 117. Estimate; 118. Evaluate; 119. Examine; 120. Execute; 121. Expand; 122. Expedite; 123. Experiment; 124. Explain; 125. Explore; 126. Express; 127. Extend; 128. Extract

Action Verbs beginning with F

129. Fabricate; 130. Facilitate; 131. Fashion; 132. Finalize; 133. Fix; 134. Fit; 135. Focus; 136. Forecast; 137. Formed; 138. Formulate; 139. Foster; 140. Find; 141. Fulfill; 142. Furnish

Action Verbs beginning with G

143. Gain; 144. Gather; 145. Generate; 146. Govern; 147. Gross; 148. Guide

Action Verbs beginning with H

149. Handle; 150. Head; 151. Heighten; 152. Help; 153. Hire; 154. Hone; 155. Host; 156. Hypothesize

Action Verbs beginning with I

157. Identify; 158. Illustrate; 159. Imagine; 160. Implement; 161. Improve; 162. Improvise; 163. Incorporate; 164. Increase; 165. Index; 166. Influence; 167. Inform; 168. Initiate; 169. Innovate; 170. Inspect; 171. Inspire; 172. Install; 173. Institute; 174. Integrate; 175. Interact; 176. Interpret; 177. Interview; 178. Introduce; 179. Invent; 180. Inventory; 181. Investigate; 182. Involve; 183. Issue

Action Verbs beginning with J

184. Join; 185. Judge; 186. Justify

Action Verbs beginning with K

187. Keep

Action Verbs beginning with L

188. Launch; 189. Learn; 190. Lead; 191. Lift; 192. Listen; 193. Locate; 194. Log; 195. Lecture

Action Verbs beginning with M

196. Maintain; 197. Manage; 198. Manipulate; 199. Market; 200. Maximize; 201. Measure; 202. Mediate; 203. Merge; 204. Mobilize; 205. Modify; 206. Monitor; 207. Motivate

Action Verbs beginning with N

208. Navigate; 209. Negotiate; 210. Net

Action Verbs beginning with O

211. Observe; 212. Obtain; 213. Open; 214. Operate; 215. Order; 216. Orchestrate; 217. Organize; 218. Originate; 219. Outline; 220. Overcome; 221. Overhaul; 222. Oversee

Action Verbs beginning with P

223. Participate; 224. Perform; 225. Persuade; 226. Photograph; 227. Pinpoint; 228. Pilot; 229. Pioneer; 230. Place; 231. Plan; 232. Play; 233. Predict; 234. Prepare; 235. Prescribe; 236. Present; 237. Preside; 238. Prevent; 239. Print; 240. Prioritize; 241. Process; 242. Produce; 243. Programme; 244. Project; 245. Promote; 246. Proofread; 247. Propose; 248. Protect; 249. Prove; 250. Provide; 251. Publicize; 252. Purchase

Action Verbs beginning with Q

253. Qualify; 254. Question; 255. Quote

Action Verbs beginning with R

256. Raise; 257. Run; 258. Rate; 259. Reach; 260. Realize; 261. Reason; 262. Receive; 263. Recommend; 264. Reconcile; 265. Record; 266. Recruit; 267. Reduce; 268. Refer; 269. Regulate; 270. Rehabilitate; 271. Relate; 272. Remodel; 273. Render; 274. Reorganize; 275. Repair; 276. Replace; 277. Report; 278. Represent; 279. Research; 280. Reshape; 281. Resolve; 282. Respond; 283. Restore; 284. Retrieve; 285. Review; 286. Revise; 287. Revitalize; 288. Route

Action Verbs beginning with S

289. Save; 290. Schedule; 291. Screen; 292. Search; 293. Secure; 294. Select; 295. Separate; 296. Serve; 297. Shape; 298. Share; 299. Simplify; 300. Simulate; 301. Sketch; 302. Sell; 303. Solve; 304. Sort; 305. Spearhead; 306. Specialize; 307. Specify; 308. Speak; 309. Sponsor; 310. Staff; 311. Standardize; 312. Start; 313. Streamline; 314. Strengthen; 315. Structure; 316. Study; 317. Suggest; 318. Summarize; 319. Supervise; 320. Supply;

321. Support; 322. Surpass; 323. Survey; 324. Sustain; 325. Synthesize; 326. Systematize

Action Verbs beginning with T

327. Target; 328. Teach; 329. Terminate; 330. Test; 331. Tighten; 332. Total; 333. Track; 334. Trade; 335. Train; 336. Transcribe; 337. Transform; 338. Transmit; 339. Translate; 340. Travel; 341. Tutor

Action Verbs beginning with U

342. Uncover; 343. Understand; 344. Undertake; 345. Unify; 346. Unite; 347. Unveil; 348. Update; 349. Upgrade; 350. Use; 351. Utilize

Action Verbs beginning with V

352. Validate; 353. Value; 354. Verbalize; 355. Verify; 356. Vitalize; 357. Volunteer

Action Verbs beginning with W

358. Weigh; 359. Widen; 360. Win; Witness; 361. Work; 362. Write

Action Verbs beginning with X

363. Xerox

Action Verbs beginning with Y

364. Yield

Action Verbs beginning with Z

365. Zap; 366. Zip; 367. Zoom out; 368. Zero in; 369. Zoom in; 370. Zone off

SUGGESTED STRATEGY

"When you're thirsty, it's too late to think about digging a well."

A Japanese Proverb

You should begin each day with the Life-Image as the standard by which everything else must be scrutinized. Each part of your life must be examined in the background of what really matters most to you. By keeping that Life-Image in mind, you can make certain that whatever you do on any particular day is in keeping with the PMS you describe as extremely significant, and that each day contributes in a significant way to the vision you have of your life as a whole. Your last words before you die should be: "Mission Accomplished."

ASSIGNMENT

1. Develop a PMS for your life and shift yourself from an ordinary existence to an extraordinary existence – a journey to success.
2. Try to live, love and laugh to inspire others through your daily activities and roles based on your PMS.
3. Listen to the Audio program *Action Strategies for Personal Achievements* by Brain Tracy.

VISUALIZATION

When you get up, visualize yourself doing all day activities on the basis of PMS – Personal Mission Statement. Remember: Each one of us is Jesus in disguise. Just continue asking yourself: What would Jesus do in this situation?

SELF SUGGESTION

I pursue my life's mission in my activities.

Bear in mind: Super achievers always keep their commitments.

[*Promise & Put Your Signature Here With Date*]

4

What Vision Do You Hold Of Your Future?

OBJECTIVES

- To learn the "Law of Envisioned Future",
- To develop your "Vision Statement", and
- To take decisions based on Vision Statement in future.

GOLDEN GUIDANCE

"Vision is the art of seeing things invisible."

Jonathan Swift (1667–1745)

ONE INCIDENT CHANGES THE ENTIRE VISION

"A leader has the vision and conviction that a dream can be achieved. He inspires the power and energy to get it done."

Ralph Lauren, an American fashion designer

This is a story about how the Stanford University was founded? In 1876, former California Governor Leland Stanford purchased 650 acres of Rancho San Francisquito for a country home and began the development of his famous Palo Alto Stock Farm for trotting horses. He later bought adjoining properties totalling more than 8,000 acres. The little town that was beginning to emerge near the land took the name Palo Alto (tall tree) after a giant California redwood on the bank of San Francisquito Creek. The tree itself is still there and would later become the university's symbol and centrepiece of its official seal. For almost a decade, the only residents of this area were the Stanfords, their farm hands, and their horses. In 1884, tragedy struck the family when Leland and Jane's only child, Leland Stanford, Jr., died of typhoid fever while travelling in Italy at a young age of 15. After the death of their beloved child, the Stanfords thought incessantly about an appropriate memorial in his honour. Within a few hours of his son's death, Stanford said to his wife, "The children of California shall be our children." They decided to convert part of their Stock Farm into a university in their son's honour. That was the beginning of Stanford University.

Moral of the story:

1. One incident can change the vision of the entire region.
2. The best reforms are carried out when sentiments operate.
3. A great vision is carried out by helping the others.
4. Education is the best tribute one can give.
5. A visionary man can see and sense the invisible.
6. Big thinking always brings big results.

ALL GREATS HAVE A VISION

> *"We must be the epitome – the embodiment – of success. We must radiate success before it will come to us. We must first become mentally, from an attitude standpoint, the people we wish to become."*
>
> George H. Allen, an American football coach,
> inducted in Pro Football Hall of Fame in 2002.

Stanford story reveals the importance of big thinking and is an example of law of envisioned future. Big thinking always has magic – the magic to produce big results. The key lies in setting goals that fill you with excitement and anticipation of the day when that dream will become a reality. Fidel Castro is well known for his vision for Cuba that still stands. Martin Luther King and Nelson Mandela envisioned a society free from racial discrimination. Mahatma Gandhi saw an independent India in his dreams. Swami Vivekananda dreamed of bringing glory to Hinduism. Muhammad (Peace Be Upon Him) saw the spread of Islam in his dreams. Cyrus the Great (576 BC–530 BC) dreamed of establishing the Achaemenid Empire. Muhammad Ali Jinnah always felt a desire to have a separate land for Indian Muslims. Vision can propel you and inspire those around you to reach their own dreams like Dr. A.P. J. Abdul Kalam has advocated plans to develop India into a developed nation by 2020 in his book *India 2020*. The Book is dedicated to a young girl whom Kalam met and asked as "what is your dream" for which the young girl replied, "I want to live in a developed India." It is up to you. You're a brand in yourself. You must pledge your loyalty towards yourself and you must strive hard to glorify your name with honour and dignity. You must strive to excel and give your all. The "Will to Work" with honesty and 100% dedication is the key. So, *here is the golden tip*: "It's high time to plan your vision to achieve success. Your family, the whole society around you and in fact the whole world want to know only single thing – Have you realized success?"

YOUR VISION OF FUTURE

> *"If we are intelligent enough to invest our experiences of the past, and wise enough to borrow the excitement and inspiration of the future by clearly seeing that future in the mind's eye, then past experiences and future excitement become today's servants."*
>
> Jim Rohn (1930–2009)

What vision are you holding of your future? Discouragement and dissatisfaction are outcome of not having a great vision. Peter Senge defined vision as "What you want to create of yourself and the world around you." The thoughts and feelings that you have today are crucial, for they are contributing to our future. A super-leader combines vision with venture. All great leaders transform vision into reality by good execution. Adolf Hitler successfully invaded more than 10 countries with his brilliant strategy and meticulous planning. The International Federation of Red Cross and Red Crescent Societies (IFRC) is the world's largest humanitarian organization because of vision. The IFRC vision: "To inspire, encourage, facilitate and promote at all times all forms of humanitarian activities by National Societies, with a view to preventing and alleviating human suffering, and thereby contributing to the maintenance and promotion of human dignity and peace in the world."

IMPORTANCE OF HAVING A PERSONAL VISION

> *"Big thinking precedes great achievements."*
>
> Wilferd Peterson (1900–1995)

Many authorities on leadership and personal development give emphasis to how vital it is for you to craft your own personal vision for your life. Warren Bennis, Stephen R. Covey, Peter Senge, Jack Canfield and others draw attention to a commanding vision that can help you succeed. How can we set the vision? Pt. Shiv Bhagwan is one of my good friends and an important member in my resourceful psyche group. He is a reputed journalist. He opines: "You must calculate your needs and then set a vision for your life. You must stick to that vision. You should not divert or dilute your vision. At the same time, you should not get carried away by other's success and must continue to believe in yourself despite all adversities." Right vision comes from right knowledge. Right knowledge is good power but bad knowledge often becomes a handicap. Most of the people, generally, live in past, but I always mention that we should try to create future from future. This is the only way. Another friend, Vipin Singhal who is a Civil Engineer speaks: "Building a life or professional career is like building a home. You must see minute details in advance in order to have a life of your dreams." Hence, the most motivational vision you can have for yourself and others is: "*Be The Best!*" All the successful people in the world plan their future and that too well in advance, by applying 1–3–10 formula. Live your present life in order to meet the one year, three year and ten year goals. You must envision your life as a meaningful, vibrant and exciting learning experience that expands your capabilities and capitalizes on your potential to the fullest. As a mission, you have to be dedicated towards imbibing in yourself an attitude of life-long learning, power of character and service to others that are consistent with your values. You ought to realize, as your motto, your aspirations by believing in your own abilities and by being single-minded to strive for success.

Saranendu Chaki (Chaki Da) is the man in my resourceful psyche group who specializes in promotion and advertising. He is the founder of Brandbox Solutions, New Delhi.

I asked him, "Chaki Da! How will you define Organizational Culture?"

He replied, "It means how managers, subordinate staff and customers treat each other."

I asked once again, "What other things does it include?"

He answered, "It also includes formality of procedures and other systems."

"One last question. This bothers me a lot," I requested.

He said, "Okay, let it come out."

I asked, "Can a visionary leader really change the organizational behaviour?"

He replied, "A true vision can effect a change in organizational culture also because it is linked with behaviours. A great leader translates vision into reality."

I've learned in my own life and in working as a motivational teacher that if you don't make out your vision, others will suggest or control your life for you. I've seen too many people who late in their lives said, "If I were only younger . . . ." "If I could save some money . . ." "If I had good health . . . ."

However these are common alibis. I don't want you to be one of them and you don't want to be one of them either. Do you?

FIND YOUR VISION

> *"To the person who does not know where he wants to go there is no favourable wind."*
>
> Seneca (ca. 4 BC–AD 65)

I urge you to find out answers to the following questions. Be honest and complete this exercise.

1. What does your vision include?
2. Do you yearn to stay fit and healthy throughout your life?
3. Do you want to make a fundamental change in your professional area?
4. Do you dream to run your own business?
5. Do you desire to raise wonderful and well-adjusted offspring?
6. Have you rescheduled your decision to write a book this year also?
7. Did you ever think of living on a beach?
8. Do you wish to visit every part of the world with your beloved?
9. Do you crave to assist others with their spiritual growth?
10. Do you wish to live a balanced and a relevant life?

All of these ten significant questions are ingredients for crafting your personal vision and if the answers to above ten questions are in YES, when you'll do these things.

WHAT IS VISION STATEMENT?

> *"Destiny is not a matter of chance, but of choice. Not something to wish for, but to attain."*
>
> William Jennings Bryan (1860–1925)

A vision statement is your ticket for the success journey. It is basis of all your plans and strategy. It helps you to get to your destination. It is picture of your future or future of your organization. A vision statement gives you the motivation and inspiration for your daily activities. It guides your life and provides the direction indispensable to chart the course of your days and the choices you make about your career. It is the light shining in the darkness towards which you turn to find your way. It lights up your way. Vision is the large picture. The word *vision* means the scheme of an image. In a vision statement you say where it is you want to go. It is "Where you want to be."

Here is an example: "By the end of 2014, I will be the most successful agent in XYZ Company. I will earn 1 lakh rupees per month and be the head of my unit." You can develop a vision based on this model example.

You need to train and reinforce yourself or your people in values of vision statement and provide rewards and punishments to yourself and to your people for keeping or not keeping the values. You need to align your activities or your services with your values. For example, you want to put 100% effort for complete satisfaction of your customer. Vision statement can be quality statement, competitive statement and superlative like number one or the best company etc.

VISION DIRECTS

> *"Dream lofty dreams, and as you dream, so shall you become. Your Vision is the promise of what you shall one day be. Your Ideal is the prophecy of what you shall at last unveil."*
>
> James Allen (1864–1912)

Passion fuels the rocket, but vision directs the rocket to its ultimate destination. Passion relates to two questions – "What are you good at?" and "What do you love to do?" Although if you want to succeed, you must identify the necessary things at what you aren't good at now, but you'd like to be. Two people can see exactly the same thing, but perceive it differently, based on their vision. In 1976, when Jobs and Steve Wozniak co–founded Apple, Jobs' vision was to put a computer in the hands of everyday people. In 1979, Jobs saw an early and crude graphical user interface being demonstrated at the Xerox research facility in Palo Alto, California. He knew immediately that the technology would make computers appealing to "everyday people." That technology eventually became "The Macintosh", which changed everything about the way we interact with computers. Xerox scientists didn't realize its potential because their "vision" was limited to making new copiers.

MISSION STATEMENT v. VISION STATEMENT

> *"If one advances confidently in the direction of his dreams, and endeavours to live the life which he has imagined, he will meet with success unexpected in common hours."*
>
> Henry David Thoreau (1817–1862)

We live in a world which is so lively and the only constant is change. However, companies or individuals summarize their goals and objectives in Mission and Vision statements. Both these things serve different purposes for the company or for the individual but are often confused with each other. What's the difference? Think of it this way; a mission statement answers the question "Who are you?" What the company does? What is the structure? What are the plans? It expresses the present leading to future. It lists the broad goals for which the organization is formed. Its prime function is intrinsic; to define the key measure or measures of the organization's success. It informs you about your desired level of progress.

The vision statement answers the question "Where are you going?" "Why are you here?" It expresses desired future only. It lists where you see yourself some years from now. It inspires you to give your best. It gives you criteria for decision-making. It shapes your understanding of why are you working here. What do you want to do going forward? When do you want to do it? How do you want to do it? Mission statement gives you the "How" and Vision statement answers "Where". Your mission statement may change, but it should still tie back to your core values and vision. Your vision should remain intact, even if the market changes dramatically, because it speaks to what you represent, not just what you do.

THE IDEA BEHIND VISION AND MISSION IS VALUE

> *"Has your soul a special mission? Yes. Your mission is in the inmost recesses of your heart, and you have to find and fulfill it there. There can be no external way for you to fulfill your mission. The deer grows musk in his own body. He smells it and becomes enchanted, and tries to locate its source. He runs and runs, but he cannot find the source. In his endless search, he loses all his energy and finally he dies. But the source he was so desperately searching for was within himself. How could he find it elsewhere? Such is the case with you. Your special mission – which is the fulfillment of your divinity – is not outside you, but within you. Search within. Meditate within. You will discover your mission."*
>
> Sri Chinmoy, *Yoga And The Spiritual Life; The Journey Of India's Soul*

I look at a mission statement as something that describes what the company or an individual is and wants now and the vision statement describes what the company or an individual wants to be in the future. You must have vision to inspire yourself and mission to introduce yourself to others. Mission is the starting point and the marching orders to get to the envisioned final destination. The vision is something that good leaders can create passion around. True leader have this vision where they want to go and know how to communicate effectively. Managers then organize the change. Vision is more like a dream with deadline viz. vision 2020. The mission statement states what you are doing to achieve current goals. Mission tells you what you're all about and vision concerns what you want to become. However, the idea behind all these is to describe your intentions in detail. It is very important to have a set value system that guides the actions along the journey. Mission is the reason of existence and vision is the dream of excellence. Vision comes from creative imagination, often from your faith. Mission calls for your actions.

A WORD OF CAUTION

> *"You've got to think about big things while you're doing small things, so that all the small things go in the right direction."*
>
> Alvin Toffler, an American writer and futurist

During this process it is critical to ensure consistency between values, the vision statement, and the mission statement. If these three components are not consistent, it is not possible to devise a workable plan. For example, for Virgin Trains, mission is "to run a high-quality, efficient and cost-effective rail service" and vision is "to become the most safe, consistent, reliable and profitable of the train operating franchises in a climate that respects different views and people need not be afraid to be open and honest." The vision statement of VT describes everything in detail, for example values of safety, consistency and reliability, commercial target of profitability and relationship with people. The organizational culture at VT places customers and their experiences of travel as their main concern. No surprise, VT has a great reputation for quality and service.

I'd like to quote motto/slogan/tagline of Hospital Corporation of America: "It's you, it's me, it's all of us." A tagline stays with you all the time. It'll only change when you want to completely redefine your company. It represents your feeling for your product. Example of Disneyland's tagline: "The happiest place on Earth."

WHICH COMES FIRST?

> *"Don't underestimate the power of a vision. McDonald's founder, Ray Kroc, pictured his empire long before it existed, and he saw how to get there. He invented the company motto – 'Quality, service, cleanliness and value' – and kept repeating it to employees for the rest of his life."*
>
> Kenneth Labich, a veteran
> New York journalist

For a new start up business, new program or plan to restructure your existing services, I recommend that the vision statement should be prepared first as it'll direct the mission statement and other strategies. For an established business, where the mission is established, I have found that, often, the mission steers the vision statement and the other strategies for the future.

GUIDELINES TO FORM COMPANY VISION STATEMENT

> *"The future belongs to those who see possibilities before they become obvious."*
>
> John Sculley, the former CEO of
> Pepsi and Apple Computer

You can carry an individual survey of the staff members in order to identify the guiding principles for treating each other and the customer. I am sharing with you simple guidelines to build a vision statement for your company.

1. Analyze your mission statement and see the core values and develop shared values.
2. Where do you see your company within 3 years from now?
3. Imagine you are delivering a lecture on 3rd Annual Celebration. What will you say in that lecture?

4. What future plans do you have to attract new customers and to have people contact program?
5. Envision your future in full details.
6. If your company or you are on a magazine cover, what it will say about you and your company?
7. Commit to your vision statement to keep it alive: Share it with potential partners, staff and employees if you have them.
   The vision statement of Tata Motors Limited, India's largest automobile company, is to be "Best in the manner in which we operate, best in the products we deliver, and best in our value system and ethics."

HOW TO FORM PERSONAL VISION STATEMENT?

"The greatest danger for most of us is not that our aim is too high and we miss it, but that it is too low and we reach it."

Michelangelo (1475–1564)

With the dawning of another year, there is no better time to evaluate who you are and where you are going. Take a few hours and work through the creation of vision and mission statements with the help of words defining action and values. Your value, ethics and mission statements will play a major role in crafting personal vision statement or PVS (2). It's a thought-provoking exercise and well worth the effort.

1. Let us start with a look at the location of your Home. Where do you want this to exist? What kind of landscapes and yard should your home have? Do you want a swimming pool for you and a stable for your horses? Imagine the colours and design, furniture and interior decoration (paintings and hangings) of each room starting from drawing room to your master bedroom at last. When you are planning to get the possession? Just appreciate your dream home in full details with sense intelligence.

2. Secondly, visualize your dream car(s), Business Office(s), Training Centre(s) and any other important possession(s) that money can provide. Just believe, you are having them already and feel them in full details through your total senses with sense intelligence.
3. Thirdly, imagine your relationships. How many candid friends do you possess? What about your family atmosphere, are you doing fine with all your family roles? What changes do you want in all relationships? How much time do you look to maintain your relationships and friends for fun and recreational activities? What kind of friends you are looking to have?
4. What job or profession you are into? Are you satisfied with current role? If yes or no – then why? Are you planning to have your own business? If yes, then in what sector and why? What changes do you see in your income after that business?
5. What about personal growth? How many books do you want to study per week? What good habits do you own? Have you left all the bad habits, if no then why? What kind of training and workshops do you want to attend to enhance your skills and knowledge? What instrument do you want to play? Do you like to sing? What countries are you looking to visit in next thirty years?
6. What health state are you having? What dream shape you are looking for? Do you exercise regularly? What physical ailments and diseases do you have? Have you undergone any correctional therapy for them? If no, then at what time are you planning to have? What food habits do you have? Do you eat seasonal fruits and dry fruits? Have you crafted your balanced diet with the help of a good dietician?
7. What locality are you presently living? What can you do to improve state of affairs in your locality? Are you participating in social activities? How many memberships do you have of groups and clubs? Are you doing your best to make your residing place a dream place?

8. What image do you want to have in public at large? What are you doing to eradicate social evils? What programs are you looking to organize to be called as "Best Citizen of Country?" Do you support any national campaign?
9. What about your dream projects? Have you planned the locations you will work in? Have you started people contact program for that? What steps do you need to take and when to realize your dream life?
10. At last comes your financial abundance. How much money do you want to save and invest to generate your total net worth to enable you to materialize your breakthrough goals and other dream goals? What is your annual income? How much money do you want to earn? Divide and aim that money in months, weeks and then to daily income.

IS YOUR VISION STATEMENT THE RIGHT ONE?

> *"Peak performers want more than merely to win the next game. They see all the way to the championship. They have a long-range goal that inspires commitment and action."*
>
> Charles Garfield, *Peak Performance*

It isn't hard to write a vision statement. But it is sometimes difficult to write a vision statement that truly summarizes your vision for yourself or your company. When you write your vision statement, make sure that you have chosen the vision that is most vital to you. In this process, it is imperative to visualize the answers with closed eyes and then write these on a paper. What's more important is that you must revise vision and mission on daily basis to make it in alignment with your value system. You must share vision, mission and values with people because if you don't fully believe in your vision statement, you won't be able to fully commit to it and writing a vision, mission and value statements that you can't or won't fully commit to is a waste of time and energy. When you share what you hold in your brain some people come forward to help you in making it happen and that exactly you want. By being enthusiastic to share your experiences, you are putting out to the universe that you are in quest of answers. The Nestle Cocoa Plan launched in 2009 in Africa is the best example of shared values with a view to help cocoa farmers to have a better quality of life.

SUGGESTED STRATEGY

> *"Vision without execution is hallucination."*
>
> Thomas Edison (1847–1931)

Each part of your life must be examined in the background of what really matters most to you. You should begin each day with the Big Life-Image as the standard by which everything else is scrutinized. I advise you to have a tagline for yourself also like Mr. X – "The Best Student of the College" Mr. Y – "The Best Teacher in the World" Mr. Z – "The Best Businessmen in the World." Write it on your photograph and paste it on your wall to keep yourself motivated.

By keeping that Big Life-Image in mind, you can make certain that whatever you do on any particular day is in keeping with the PVS (2) you describe as extremely significant, and that each day contributes in a significant way to the vision you have of your life as a whole.

ASSIGNMENT

1. Develop a Vision Statement for your life.
2. Try to live, love and laugh to inspire others through making your daily decisions and choices on your PVS (2).
3. Listen to the Audio program *Live With Passion* by Anthony Robbins. You can also search www.audiobooks.com for other motivational audios.

VISUALIZATION

When you get up, visualize yourself making your daily decisions and choices on the basis of PVS – Personal Vision Statement. Knowing your destination is half the journey. Remember: As Stanfords envisioned a university and they established it. You ought to have your big projects so as to realize them.

SELF SUGGESTION

My future appears great. I'm dedicated to my passions in life.

Bear in mind: Super achievers always keep their commitments.

[*Promise & Put Your Signature Here With Date*]

5

Who Do You Want To Be?

OBJECTIVES

- To learn the "Law of Desire Oriented Profession",
- To find out your "Dream Profession", and
- To seek "Pleasure and Prosperity" from your passionate profession.

GOLDEN GUIDANCE

"Your profession is not what brings home your weekly paycheck, your profession is what you're put here on earth to do, with such passion and such intensity that it becomes spiritual in calling."

Vincent Van Gogh (1853–1890)

ONLY 5% PEOPLE ACHIEVE SUCCESS

"The job is what you do when you are told what to do. Someone can always do your job a little better or faster or cheaper than you can. Your art is what you do when no one can tell you exactly how to do it. I call the process of doing your art 'the work.' It's possible to have a job and do the work, too. In fact, that's how you become a linchpin. The job is not the work."

Seth Godin, *Linchpin: Are You Indispensable?*

A turning point comes in everybody's life. I had the fortune of reading and listening many superb thought-provoking works. I am reminded of an instance that was mentioned by Earl Nightingale in his outstanding book and audio *The Strangest Secret*. The late Dr. Albert Schweitzer, the man who received the 1952 Nobel Peace Prize for his philosophy of "Reverence for Life" was once asked: "Doctor, what is wrong with men today?" The great doctor was quiet a second, and then he whispered, "Men simply do not think!" Do you know what happens? Nightingale then mentions his observation: Let's take 100 individuals who start even at the age of 25. Do you have any idea what will happen to those men and women by the time they are 65? These 100 people, who all start even at the age of 25, all believe they're going to be successful. But by the time they are 65, only one will be rich, four will be financially independent, 41 will still be working, and 54 will be broke – depending on others for life's necessities. The great Nightingale concludes with an imperative fact: Out of the 100, only five make the grade. It is one of the most powerful and inspiring messages I've ever heard.

Moral of the story:

1. Common behavioural patterns conform to wrong percentile 95% group.
2. The prize of conformity: Everybody is pleased with you except yourself.
3. Conformity makes earth a miserable place and takes life out of society.
4. Never fear to be eccentric from fear of conformity.
5. Majority of us set easy goals out of conformity.
6. Surrender to conformity is the easiest cowardice.
7. Conformity kills freedom and hampers growth.
8. Most people are happier with old problems than with new solutions.
9. Opposite of courage in our society is not cowardice, it is conformity.

BROAD-BASED EDUCATION v. INNATE INTELLIGENCE

> *"Often, it's not about becoming a new person, but becoming the person you were meant to be, and already are, but don't know how to be."*
>
> Heath L. Buckmaster, *Box of Hair: A Fairy Tale*

Most of the people look for a broad-based education that is contrary to the traditional rote learning. High scores alone do not make a good student in today's highly competitive society. Holistic education is a necessity, which aims to train a jack of all trades and attaches equal importance to physical, mental and other aspects of health. An interesting story is coming to my mind. Some animals got together in the forest one day and decided to start a school of all-rounders. There was a panther, a hawk, a squirrel, a dog, a fish, and an eel, and they formed a board of directors. The panther insisted that running be in the curriculum. The squirrel emphasized that perpendicular tree climbing would be must for everyone. The hawk insisted that flying be in the curriculum. The fish insisted that swimming had to be in the curriculum, and the dog said that barking was completely indispensable to the curriculum. They put all of these things together except barking and framed a curriculum manual. Then they insisted that all of the animals would take all of the subjects to get a broad-based education. All the animals got A grades in their innate jobs and poor grades in others' works. Finally, the animal who ended up being valedictorian of the course was a mentally retarded eel who did everything half way. The dog was still struggling to get barking included in curriculum. This story has diverse versions. But the message is quite clear in all of them.

Moral of the story:

1. A true education prepares students for life without losing their areas of interest and ability.
2. Everything in the universe has a purpose.
3. You are here to manifest your God-Gifted strengths.

4. The innate potentials in present education system are killed because faculties become blunted, and paralyzed due to overload and overstuff.

WHY DO SOME PEOPLE RISE TO TOP?

"All human actions have one or more of these seven causes: chance, nature, compulsions, habit, reason, passion, desire."

Aristotle (384 BC–322 BC)

Broad education story is an example of law of desire oriented profession and an answer to the questions you probably hear/think a lot. So what do you want to be when you grow up? How can I get work that fits me completely? Can I have a career I'm passionate about? Can I get a job that's not a big compromise? Can a job be realistic? Is there any job that uses my talents fully? Can someone tell me a job that fits my personality? Is there a job doing which I enjoy? Many people find themselves in hard times when they are asked to answer this question. May be you do too? These questions reflect the choice of profession as a means of our livelihood. Mr. Anubhav Arora is Director of Universal Law Publishing Co Pvt. Ltd. which is a prominent law books publisher in India. He is an intellectual member of my resourceful psyche group. He opines: "Life can get so busy that we don't have time to really think about what we want to be in our life. And when we do find what we want to be, it may look impossible to accomplish it. Choosing a job or career is one of the crucial decisions of our life. It requires courage plus desire. It's hard to march alone than to join the big parade."

Have you ever noticed that some people just stand out? Regardless of their industry or profession, they rise to the top. They are "living certificates" of the fact that when it comes to success, it's not *what* you do, but *how* you do it that counts. So, *here is the golden tip*: "Successful people are plugged into their passion. They chase significance and success chases them. The top guidance is by Oscar Wild: "Be yourself; everyone else is already taken."

MARY KAY ASH—AN INSPIRATION

> *"The difference between a job and a career is the difference between forty and sixty hours a week."*
>
> Robert Frost (1874–1963)

Mary Kay Ash was born in Hot Wells, Harris County, Texas. She was the daughter of Edward Alexander and Lula Vember Hastings Wagner. Her mother was trained as a nurse and later became a manager of a restaurant in Houston. She attended Reagan High School in Houston, and graduated in 1934. She got married at a tender age of 17 and got 3 children. She used to sell books door-to-door. She obtained a divorce in the intervening time. She also worked for Stanley Home Products but retired in 1963 because her trained junior was given preference in promotion. She wrote a book to assist women in business and the book turned into a business plan for her ideal company, and in the summer of 1963, Ash and her new husband, planned to start Mary Kay Cosmetics. Though, one month before opening of Beauty by Mary Kay, as the company was then known, her second husband died of a heart attack. On September 13, 1963 when she was 45 years old Ash started Mary Kay Cosmetics. The company started its original storefront operation in Dallas. Her slogan "God first, family second, career third" kept her company and family in good balance. She remained active in business until suffering a stroke in 1996. She authored three books, all of which became best-sellers. She died on November 22, 2001. At the time of her death, Mary Kay Cosmetics had over 800,000 representatives in 37 countries, with total annual sales over $200 million. As of 2008, Mary Kay Cosmetics has more than 1.7 million consultants worldwide and wholesale volume in excess of 2.2 billion. Mary Kay is considered as a foremost female entrepreneur in American history and stands as glaring illustration of law of desire oriented profession.

Moral of the story:

1. Your dream job does not exist. You have to create it.
2. Passion is the difference between having a job and having a career.
3. Our calling is inherent in ourselves.
4. Family is as important as your career.
5. Family circumstances can't stop a man on mission.

DECIDE AND DESIRE

> *"In order to succeed, your desire for success should be greater than your fear of failure."*
>
> Bill Cosby, an American actor

The important question is not whether you will succeed or not, the question is how single-mindedly do you want to succeed? You will not be what you want to be unless you decide what exactly you want to be. Simply wanting success isn't enough. After all, *WANT*, as Marshawn Evans says, just means *Waiting, And Nothing Transpires*. You must develop a burning desire for your desired dream-goal. Live with it. Eat with it. Sleep with it. Be thankful for the nights that turned into mornings.

Rajnarayan Panghal, a journalist and a social thinker, is one of the selected personalities in my resourceful psyche group. He had all the adversities in his life. He got failed in High School examination three times—in 1994, 1995 and 1997. He qualified in Senior Secondary examination out of his determination and got admission in five-year law programme. His success story interested me because he got 23rd position in law entrance examination in general quota among 1200 students. When I asked him about this achievement, he said politely, "I had no option but to study sincerely since my parents didn't have the money to get me a seat on paid quota." He became a certified lawyer by completing his law graduation in time with average scores. Once again a turn came in his life and he got admission in post graduation but in a diverse field – mass communication. I became curious again and asked him,"Why did you shift your interest to mass communication leaving your good base in law?" He replied,"I saw many government officers during my young days. I noticed one thing common in all of them. All of them were law graduates." He further asserted,"We choose our professions not out of our passion but out of compulsions by parents, suggestions by friends or out of our own observations.""My observation was wrong in the sense that law was not my prime interest. I have always loved to have a talk with people. I got that satisfaction from my law career but I realized later after persistent subconscious confrontation that I was born to advertise, and then I chose to study mass communication because it's never too late to become who you want to be." Rajnarayan is a satisfied journalist now and derives full pleasure in reporting the events of public concern. When VVS Laxman, the Indian cricket player was young, he wanted to be a doctor. Both of his parents are doctors and his father was his role model. Like any young kid in India, he played cricket but never thought that he would play it as a professional. So friends! Let me tell you that it's a high time to find out, what's your own success, in other words, what does success mean to you?

LAW OF DESIRE ORIENTED PROFESSION

> *"It's hard to tell with these Internet startups if they're really interested in building companies or if they're just interested in the money. I can tell you, though: If they don't really want to build a company, they won't luck into it. That's because it's so hard that if you don't have a passion, you'll give up."*
>
> Steve Jobs (1955–2011)

What do you think? Do you have ideas about what you might want to be when you grow up? If you're lucky enough to have an obsessive interest, online career test is a good place to start discovering the options. And even if you are grown up already, it's never too late to think about what you want to do next in your career. Although, you are not sure what type of job you want or what you want to do next with your career, a career test can help you to precise your job choices and help you choose an accurate career that is well-suited with your interests. Passion liberates tremendous energy and power. Dr. Ashok Kumar, one of my good friends in law teaching fraternity, stands as an example of living the life by a feeling of happiness. He became a teacher of law from a peon. He was so determined to become a teacher that he improved his grades in study and did Ph.D. in law. He has also authored three books on law. He also confirms: "A profession based on passion can give you an eternal satisfaction inside and excellence outside." Do you agree? Our miseries and troubles are not going to end by our casual agreement. We can end our miseries and troubles only when we become mindful of the threat of imposed profession.

We need to promote our children's interest from their childhood. A psychologist Erik Erikson opines that a child of 5–12 years begins to show his interest in special activities like sports, music, etc. and if the child is denied this opportunity he may develop lack of motivation, low self-esteem or inferiority and lethargy.

I strongly believe that all the incarnations like Krishna, Jesus, Buddha, Nayagar, Nanak, Mahavir, Osho and others were sent on this earth with a purpose. Similarly, I believe you are also sent here with a unique purpose. It is rightly said: "You are a masterpiece. Your master's piece. Celebrate your uniqueness." The twist is that personality tests and career aptitude tests can give you ideas about what you probably should do rather than you simply thinking what you want to do. I ask you to chase your passion and you will see that success will chase you. But most of the people chase their pension. When you are looking for pension, Chrissy Greig, a personal development coach asserts: JOB becomes *Just Over Broke*.

YOUR TWINKLE CAN BECOME A FULL MOON AND LIGHT EVERYTHING

> *"What can one person do? Here's the answer: Throughout your life there's a voice that only you can hear. It's a call to make a difference that only you can make. If you never hear it, something magical will be lost. But if you hear it and heed it, your life will become a wonderful romance and adventure."*
>
> Dan Zadra And Kobi Yamada, *1: How Many People Does It Take to Make a Difference?*

Our world needs more passionate people than ever before, and more you in it. But, how many people does it take to make a difference? The answer is: Only One—You. The mission of our life is to discover our God-Gift. The meaning of life is to give our gift away to other people. Dr. George W. Truett, an American pastor who was invited by Woodrow Wilson to address Allied Forces once said: "Man's greatest knowledge is to know the will of God. Man's greatest discovery is to find out the will of God. Man's greatest achievement is to do the will of God." The world, country, state, district, locality and the place you are in needs you today. As an alternative of asking an egotistic question: "What can I get out of this world?" You ought to find answer to a philanthropic question: "What can I give to this world?" We all come into the world with Individual God-Gifts intended to make the world a superior place. Your twinkle can become a full moon and light everything.

DO WHAT YOU LOVE

> *"Most people have no idea of the giant capacity we can immediately command when we focus all of our resources on mastering a single area of our lives."*
>
> Tony Robbins, an American self-help author

How will you know your calling? I would like to offer an advice: Don't aim for success, just do and believe in what you love, success will come sooner or later. If you feel happiness while doing the work, take my word, you are on a right track. And, if you start to make people feel happy due to your work, it means that your success is nearby. And, if people expect happiness from you and your work, it means you have become significant. Rather than focusing on trying to make money, put your time and energy into finding your happiness. Listen to your inner voice and not the noises of the world outside. Believe in self suggestions and not in hetero-suggestions. Learn by heart that money is simply a medium for exchanging value. Stop focusing on the effect: Receiving money and start focusing on the cause: *Be The Best.* I am a strong advocate of "The Best Me I Can Be" approach in loving and doing the work. Use an affirmation: I will only give attention to being the best me I can be.

SUCCESS v. HAPPINESS

> *"Happiness is inward, and not outward; and so, it does not depend on what we have, but on what we are."*
>
> Henry van Dyke (1852–1933)

You need to combine confidence and compassion for happiness. I always say, success is not the key to happiness. Happiness is the key to success. You need to maximize the happiness and then money and status etc. will grow naturally. In fact, this is the criteria, if you are doing something happily for last ten years although you never made any money from it, you should continue that thing as your calling.

My friends constantly ask me, "Why do you get what you wish for?" I always reply, "I know how to make a wish." I have followed, follow and will follow my heart in my entire life and that passion, I think, has made all the difference. You must experience the energy that comes from enjoying the things that excite you; I call this excitement "Power of Passion." There is only one thing, focus on passion, which will lead you ahead and make you happy besides. Herman Cain, an author and a candidate for the 2012 US Republican Party presidential nomination affirms: "If you love what you are doing, you will be successful."

BETTER TO BE A FAILURE

> *"It is better to be a failure at something you love than to be a success at something you hate."*
>
> George Burns (1896–1996)

I honestly believe: "It is not a failure if you enjoyed the process." I call them: "Successful Failures." Sticker of crackpot is better than disgrace of conformity. I mean, even if you fall down, don't worry. Have a fresh view. The world looks different not only from top but from the ground also. You can take from every experience what it has to offer you. Do better the second time. You never know when you success is at threshold. Why I am stressing on the factor of passion is due to the fact that it's very difficult to come up with new, creative, and novel ideas unless you are passionate about your work. So, my boy! Leave your reputation and invest in your character. Know your hidden craving and put a bet on it.

DREAMS OF OTHERS v. YOUR OWN DREAMS

> *"You taught me to be nice, so nice that now I am so full of niceness, I have no sense of right and wrong, no outrage, no passion."*
>
> Garrison Keillor, an American author

Most people are not living their dreams. The society teaches us to be nice and modest. I make this little simpler, How will you ask from your father? Generally, a child plays with a small ball and asks for a football because he/she wants to play with a bigger thing. When you grow up, you ask for a different thing and your interests are different.

Suppose, you always take interest in clicking the pictures with your private camera but your father, in the name of family honour, put you in engineering. Your father asks you, "What do you want to do?" You choose engineering out of peer pressure because everybody in the class was doing the same thing or your family wants you to join engineering. What one can expect as far as your engineering prudence is concerned, yes, you thought it right; you will not become a good engineer. Equality, if erroneously implemented, can lead to conformity and then to tyranny. You could have been a good photographer.

We do this often in our society: marrying with mother's wish; studying with father's wish; children with family's wish and doing expected things all the time. A man generally lives his fears. We never ever think of living our lives in the way we want to live. Life is meant to be lived and not to be passed. Live, love and laugh to inspire others and more importantly yourself first. Give yourself a round of applause whenever you achieve even a smallest victory.

WE ARE ALL GOD-GIFTED WITH SPECIAL TALENTS

> *"Free yourself from the complexities and drama of your life. Simplify. Look within. Within ourselves we all have the gifts and talents we need to fulfill the purpose we've been blessed with."*
>
> Steve Maraboli, *Life, the Truth, and Being Free*

I believe that we are all blessed. My firm conviction: We are all God-Gifted with some strength. It's our duty to find that only. Vance Ferrell in his book *The Wonders of Nature* Vol. 1 & 2 illustrates that everything in nature is unique. The tiny size of the hummingbird, weighing only a tenth of an ounce, gives it the elasticity to do complex maneuvers, such as beating its wings 50 times a second. This enables the hummingbird to sip nectar from flowers while hovering but it cannot soar, glide or hop. The ostrich, at 300 pounds, is the largest bird but it can't fly. Nevertheless, its legs are so strong that it can run at up to 50 miles per hour, taking strides of 12–15 feet. There are over 2,000 different kinds of shrimp. As with all other species, each shrimp reproduces only its own kind. We all have something in-built quality and if we recognize and nourish that special quality we will become successful.

DETECT YOUR PASSIONATE PROFESSION

> *"Your calling is already within you. It is an integral part of you, a part of your DNA – Destiny Now Activated. You do not get it, you grow it. The challenge is not acquiring it, the key is accessing it."*
>
> Marshawn Evans, the Founder of ME Unlimited

The Law of Desire Oriented Profession asks you to opt for that means of livelihood, doing which you enjoy. Do your work with love. Since our childhood, we have felt motivated, to select different jobs. We have tried and tested them and ultimately failed, but ever we tried to see the inspiration that comes from within. I say it often: I can motivate you, but you have to seek inspiration from within. Napoleon Hill, an American self-help author, was one of the greatest and earliest writers on success and self-help books. His book *Think and Grow Rich* is a 1937 motivational personal development and self-help tome that has been a touchstone for many thinkers. He quotes: "Success in its highest and noblest form, calls for peace of mind, enjoyment and happiness which come only to the man who has found the work that he likes best."

INFUSE YOUR WORK WITH LOVE

> *"Choose a job you love, and you will never have to work a day in your life."*
>
> Confucius (551–479 BC)

There's a novel by Mexican novelist Laura Esquivel *Like Water for Chocolate* published in 1989 in which the protagonist, Tita de la Garza, is a woman who longs her entire life to marry her lover, Pedro, but can never have him because of her mother's upholding of the family tradition of the youngest daughter not marrying but taking care of her mother until the day she dies. Tita has a love of the kitchen and a deep connection with food, a skill enhanced by the fact that the family cook was her primary caretaker as Tita grew up. Her love for cooking also comes from the fact that she was born in the kitchen.

When she cooks, her emotions become infused into her cooking, affecting all those who eat it. One of the incident from the novel is exemplary: After one particularly rich meal of quail in rose petal sauce flavoured with Tita's erotic thoughts of Pedro, Tita's older sister Gertrudis becomes inflamed with lust and leaves the ranch making ravenous love with a revolutionary soldier on the back of a horse before being dumped in a brothel and subsequently disowned by her mother.

Moral of the story:

1. Infuse your work with love.
2. Just as resentment poisons your work, doing your work with love adds more value to it.
3. Pleasure in the job puts perfection in the work.
4. A job becomes a career when you work as if you're the boss.
5. We have to apply best of ourselves to the job at hand.

ENJOY AND YOU'LL NEVER WORK FOR A DAY

"I am focused on the work. I am constantly creating. I am a busy girl. I live and breathe my work. I love what I do. I believe in the message. There's no stopping. I didn't create the fame, the fame created me."

Lady Gaga, an American singer

Hard work has never been a key to success. It is when you enjoy, you grow. Work without love is nothing but another form of slavery. No sports player works hard. He enjoys and loves to play. I would like to take you back in our childhood, when we used to play cricket for hours and hours. Our mother used to call us but we wanted to play more because we had interest in playing. We never got tired while playing, watching a cartoon show and travelling etc. Most of the people, when they are asked to do a thing, start with enthusiasm, but constantly loose the interest. Why? It's simple. They lack commitment. Martin H. Fischer quotes: "A doctor must work eighteen hours a day and seven days a week. If you cannot console yourself to this, get out of the profession." Interest goes hand on hand with convenience. But once you become committed, nothing satisfies you except the results. We often miss the blessing because it looks like work.

WHO DO YOU WANT TO BE?

> *"There are two things people want more than sex and money ... recognition and praise."*
>
> Mary Kay Ash, the founder of
> Mary Kay Cosmetics, Inc.

I consider the often asked question "What do you want to be when you grow up?" is unwise. Instead, we should ask, "Who do you want to be? What legacy do you want to leave in this world?" From there, you will have your answer as to what you should "do". "All the big businessmen, big stars, big cooks and famous personalities did achieve prosperity, recognition and praise but in their chosen field of activity. It is a fact more than an advice: "To do something well you have to love it."

TAKE UP ONE IDEA

> *"There is only one success, to be able to spend your life in your own way."*
>
> Christopher Morley (1890–1957)

Swami Vivekananda was a key figure in the introduction of Indian philosophies of Hinduism, Vedanta and Yoga to the western world, and he still inspires Indian youth a lot. He once asserted a quote that I constantly cite as a technique to get success. He said: "Take up one idea. Make that one idea your life—think of it, dream of it, and live on that idea. Let the brain, muscles, nerves, every part of your body, be full of that idea, and just leave every other idea alone. This is the way to success." I often use a line of Jim Rohn who was America's foremost business philosopher. He presented seminars, worldwide, for more than 40 years. This line is more a law to me – a law of getting success. He quotes: "Success is not to be pursued; it is to be attracted by the person we become." I think now the idea is crystal clear. "You personify the success."

OPPORTUNITY IS ALWAYS UNDER YOUR FEET

> *"We don't have to go anywhere for seeking an opportunity. It is always within our surroundings. All we need to do is recognize it by making a right decision at a right time."*
>
> Bhagavan Nayagar (1951–2001)

You can say: Okay, I know my passion but what about the opportunity. There is a well-known adage: A talent without opportunity is nothing. You must be having this maxim as an excuse in your mind. There is a story in Russell Conwell's famous book, *Acres of Diamonds* (1921). He founded Temple University based on this lecture. The story is about a farmer who lived in Africa and through a visitor became tremendously excited about looking for diamonds. He sold his farm to head out to the diamond line. He wandered all over the continent, as the years slipped by, constantly searching for diamonds, wealth, which he never found. Eventually he went completely broke and threw himself into a river and drowned. Meanwhile, the new owner of his farm picked up an unusual looking rock about the size of a country egg and put it on his mantle as a sort of curiosity. A visitor stopped by and told the new owner of the farm that the funny looking rock on his mantle was about the biggest diamond that had ever been found. The farm turned out to be the Kimberly Diamond Mine...the richest the world has ever known. The original farmer was literally standing on "Acres of Diamonds" until he sold his farm.

Moral of the story:

1. Opportunity is always under feet.
2. Grass looks greener on other side.
3. Opportunity never knocks.
4. A decision can turn your life upside down.

INNER VOICE v. OUTER VOICE

> *"If you chase two rabbits at the same time, you won't catch either of them."*
>
> Armenian Proverb

Since our childhood, we are taught what is right and wrong. We are programmed about social interaction, work, and what to believe in. This Childhood Programming put hindrances in our way to find our true desires and often we get entangled in the world-web.

I have a big mouth and give away secrets. What qualifies me blah blah? Only Common sense, My Friend! If you love talking to people, see Oprah Winfrey, if you love to laugh and crack jokes see Lenny Bruce, if you want to keep your mouth shut and enjoy see Charlie Chaplin, if you want to play cricket see Sachin Tendulkar, if you want to act see Amitabh Bachchan, if you want to dance see Michael Jackson and if you want to do politics see Nelson Mandela.

Examples are too many to cite. Therefore, let me cite the law once again in simple words: "Make sure that you chase one rabbit at one time." Life is too short to be an all-rounder. World belongs to specialists. Listen to your inner voice and never pay much heed to outer advices by the world people. (Refer to Step 1 of Self-Exploration Procedure in Chapter 3 for more insights.)

WANT v. DESIRE

"Successful and unsuccessful people do not vary greatly in their abilities, they vary in their desires to reach their potential."

John Maxwell, an eminent author on leadership

I want to earn money vs. *I desire a passionate profession from where I can earn my livelihood to my entire satisfaction.* I want to get married vs. *I desire a good human to be my partner to share my life with.* I want to live in that posh area vs. *I desire a home and society that nurtures plus enthuses me.* Can you *experience* the distinction? A want is an endeavour to "cap" a (wrongly supposed) place of blankness or have-not within yourself while a desire is your real and candid potential craving to be articulated through you, as you, with you and for you.

SUGGESTED STRATEGY

"Whatever one does for a living, three questions need to be confronted before it is too late: What really matters to me? What price do my spouse and kids pay for my career success? What price does my soul pay?"

Dennis Prager, *Think a Second Time*

Cheers to New Year! It's another chance for you to get it right with a new resolution. Make a list of 10 to 15 probable job or profession options based on your interests. Now organize the list by placing your most passionate job or profession at your first choice, and for your first five favourite jobs, examine the pros and cons. Be honest and complete this exercise.

I suggest having minimum five positives and five negatives on each option. For example, if you want to go for a big business, positives will be: 1. Working for yourself; 2. Own Boss; 3. More Money; 4. More Independence and 5. Living the life in full enjoyment. Now let us look at the negatives: 1. Less chances of success; 2. Less time for fun; 3. Less time for family; 4. Less security and 5. Unexpected changes in law, costs and competition. After Risk Analysis, ask yourself, are you ready to put up with negatives in order to have positives. If, yes, then go for the decided option with your full dedication.

ASSIGNMENT

1. There are a variety of online free career tests you can take, so spend a few minutes and see what could be your interest oriented fresh career!
2. Try to figure out different options within your single interest. For example, if you are interested in music: options can be – music teacher, music band, music instruments shop, a singer, instrumentalist, music event organizer, musician biographer, talent show organizer and music learning centre etc.
3. Ask your mentor/teacher. A good counsellor can help you in setting your dream profession.
4. Listen to Audio program *The Power of Purpose* by Les Brown. You can also search www.nightingale.com for other superb audios.

VISUALIZATION

When you go to your bed visualize yourself living, loving and laughing your dream profession to inspire others. Use your all senses. Don't worry about "How", just imagine "What" and "How" will be taken care of by the existence itself, sometimes just when you need it, even not before a minute. So go for more. Remember: Think of the work and do in Tita's way, and make sure that you infuse it with love.

SELF SUGGESTION

I derive pleasure and prosperity from my dream profession.

Bear in mind: Super achievers always keep their commitments.

[*Promise & Put Your Signature Here With Date*]

6

What Kind Of Life Do You Want To Live?

OBJECTIVES

- To learn the "Law of Accurate Aim",
- To decide accurately what we want in this life, and
- To set time bound measurable objectives.

GOLDEN GUIDANCE

"An average person with average talents and ambition and average education, can outstrip the most brilliant genius in our society, if that person has clear, focused goals."

Mary Kay Ash, the founder of Mary Kay Cosmetics Inc.

WHAT DO YOU WANT?

"There is a gold mine, in your goal mind. Focus always precedes success. What you get is what you set!"

Denis Waitley, an American writer

When asked the question, "What's success for you and how will you attain it?" nearly all the people fail to reply confidently. Samuel Langhorne Clemens, better known by his pen name Mark Twain, was an American author and humourist. He is most noted for his novel *Adventures of Huckleberry Finn* that is also called Great American Novel. He claims: "I can teach anybody how to get what they want out of life; the problem is that I can't find anybody who can tell me what they want." On April 12, 1961, Soviet cosmonaut Yuri Gagarin became the first person to fly in space, There was a space race at that time. JFK was eager for US to take the lead in the Space Race. Prestige of America was in question. He announced the goal of landing a man on the Moon in the speech to a Joint Session of Congress on May 25, 1961. He said: "First, I believe that this nation should commit itself to achieving the goal, before this decade is out, of landing a man on the Moon and returning him safely to the Earth." On July 20, 1969, almost six years after Kennedy's death, Apollo 11 landed the first manned spacecraft on the Moon. Please mark: Decide what exactly you want before you get what you don't want.

When you consider the question, "What do I want?" or "What do I want from my life?" your first answer may be that you want to change some aspect of the past. But changing the past is not within your power, you can change your future by visualizing future and not past.

This is a law of science of success, "paradigm shift" i.e. a change from one way of thinking to another. Once you have worked on personal mission statement, established your vision, articulated your desires, the next step is to convert them into achievable accurate goals. So, *here is the golden tip*: "Many people in this world behave like brainless creatures and pursue meaningless goals. Whereas, key to success lies in setting the smart goals." Brain Tracy suggests: You have to "become the kind of person on the inside who can achieve any goal on the outside."

MEANINGLESS GOALS

> *"Fill your mind with the meaningless stimuli of a world preoccupied with meaningless things, and it will not be easy to feel peace in your heart."*
>
> Marianne Williamson, a spiritual author

Unclear goals promote unclear results. There is a short story on meaningless goals. It's a popular one. Every day, on their way to meet the Spiritual master, the disciples saw a farmer's dog chasing passing vehicles. It was in habit of sitting by roadside waiting for vehicles to come around. As soon as one came, it used to run down the road, barking and trying to overtake it. One day, a disciple asked the Spiritual master, "Do you think the dog is ever going to catch a car?" The Spiritual master replied, "That is not what bothers me. What bothers me is what it would do if it ever caught one." Many people in life behave like that dog – pursuing meaningless goals.

Moral of the story:

1. Most of people are chasing wrong things.
2. To exist just for yourself is meaningless.
3. One must set realistic and achievable goals.
4. Everything that glitters is not gold.
5. Material possessions, winning scores, and great reputations are meaningless.

OTTO VON BISMARCK—DREAM BIG AND AIM HIGH

> *"If you want your life to be a magnificent story; then begin by realizing that you are the author, and every day, you have the opportunity to write a new page."*
>
> Mark Houlahan, a New Zealand writer

All the big achievements you dream can only be achieved when you aim high. Go for a big try. The way to live your day: Live as if you'll die today.

Therefore, do the maximum you can. The way to dream: Dream as if you have to live for 100 years. I think that we should try to fulfill the dream by working constantly. Otto von Bismarck (1815–1898) is considered the founder of the German Empire. Germany had existed as a collection of hundreds of separate principalities and Free Cities since the formation of the Holy Roman Empire. Over the centuries various rulers had tried to unify the German states without success until Bismarck. He was a conservative German statesman who had a goal to unify most of the German states into a powerful German Empire under Prussian leadership. The German victory in the Franco–Prussian War won over the southern German states, and in 1871 they agreed to join a German empire. Wilhelm I of Prussia became emperor. In 1890, Bismarck resigned after disagreeing with the new emperor, Kaiser Wilhelm II. He retired to his estate near Hamburg and died there on 30 July 1898. Bismarck's final years were devoted to writing his memoirs. Vallabhbhai Patel (1875–1950) guided India into a united, independent nation by integrating 562 princely states. He is often known as the "Iron Man of India" or "Bismarck of India" or "Sardar" (Chief) out of respect. He is also remembered as the "Patron Saint" of India's civil servants for establishing modern all-India services. I treat Bismarck and Patel as two of the greatest examples of goal-setting. I always employ a quote when I set a target. The quote is: "Shoot for the moon. Even if you miss, you'll land among the stars." At any cost, accepting below what you want is nothing but a compromise. The higher your aspirations are, the better will be your successful failures. You will achieve new heights each time, even if there is a failure.

ZIG ZIGLAR—NO. 1 SALESMAN

"Building a better you is the first step to building a better America."

Zig Ziglar (1926–2012)

Zig Ziglar is a best-selling author and one of the well-loved motivational speakers in the world. Yet he grew in poverty. He was the tenth of twelve children. And to make things worse, his father died of a stroke when he was 6 years old. His younger sister died two days later. Zig wanted to become the No. 1 Salesman. And life was very hard. As a small child, he had to work. He worked in a grocery store from 4:30 in the morning to 11:00 near midnight every day. In case you can't do the math, that's an 18-hour workday. He lived with a modest income in his young days. When Zig got married, he applied as a salesman. But for the first two years, he couldn't sell his products. So he had to sell his furniture just so he and his wife could survive. It is said that when his daughter was born, the hospital bill was $64. He didn't even have $64—and had to go out and sell something so he could take his family home. It was these hardships that fueled his desire to succeed in life. And succeed, he did. In one year, he became the number one salesman of his company. His greatest success came in 1975 with the book *See You at the Top*, which had been rejected by some thirty publishers previously. And later on, he set up his own company. Ten of his 25 books have been best-sellers. He has been a very successful author and motivational speaker.

Moral of the story:

1. Family circumstances don't hamper your goal achievements.
2. You must have a burning desire to be successful.
3. You have to perspire before attaining the comfort of success.
4. Always and forever set highest goal.
5. Obstacles strike every human being.
6. The finest angle to approach any problem is the try-angle.

BE SELFISH TO ASK

"Without goals, and plans to reach them you are like a ship that has set sail with no destination."

Fitzhugh Dodson, a clinical psychologist

There is a twist in our society. Your blood relations, your friends, and your society have taught you that it is self-centredness to ask for what you want. Certainly, imbibing equanimity toughens you when employed in spiritual quest. But if your "equanimity" is shaded with anger or fear, then you are deceiving yourself. You would help yourself and others by believing in your experience (that comes from bad experiences) and asking for what accurately you want. There is one quote of Albert Einstein that has been a law of happiness for me. Einstein quotes: "If you want to live a happy life, tie it to a goal, not to people or things."

DECIDE! DECIDE!! DECIDE!!!

> *"Whenever you want to achieve something, keep your eyes open, concentrate and make sure you know exactly what it is you want. No one can hit their target with their eyes closed."*
>
> Paulo Coelho, *The Devil and Miss Prym*

There are no jumps in capability. First deserve then desire. In the journey of success, you have to decide, what do you want to achieve? What do you want to do? What do you want to be? What do you want to have? Decide your long-term (Up to 10 years), mid-term (up to 3 years) and short-term goals (up to 1 year) in the realm of reality. Decide what qualification will you need? What training you have to go for? A thousand-mile journey begins with the first step and you can only take one step at a time, there are no short cuts. Suppose you are at level 2 on a 10-point scale then for reaching at 10 you have to cover 3 to 10. Let us have a look at differences between some terms in order to appreciate the art of goal setting. It may look boring but these differences will make you absolutely clear in setting your goals.

OBJECTIVE v. SUBJECTIVE

"Give me a stock clerk with a goal and I'll give you a man who will make history. Give me a man with no goals and I'll give you a stock clerk."

J.C. Penney, the founder of J.C. Penney Department Stores

This difference can help you to choose and decide. You should be objective, and try to look at object only, I mean you become quite emotional when you are reading a book, interacting with new friends and enjoying entertaining activities like watching a movie. You know that scientific facts are objective facts backed by data whereas opinion, statements and speeches are subjective and art oriented involving thinking colour of the subject. I advise you to choose subjectively and decide objectively. You must work in the same manner i.e. with passion. Set and achieve targets objectively. Your goals create your career.

QUALITATIVE v. QUANTITATIVE

"They have succeeded in accumulating a greater mass of objects, but the joy in the world has grown less."

Fyodor Dostoyevsky, *The Brothers Karamazov*

The quality and quantity of success also make a difference. What is quality? A quality is property of a thing like, good, bad, beautiful, ugly, useless, fascinating, boring, filthy, sparkling, pale, dark, soft, hard, wonderful, colourful, evil, angelic, etc. and can't be measured but only can be experienced. How will you define quantity? A quantity is a number, the objects which can be measured like hot, cold, short, fast, slow, large, small, many, few, heavy, light, near and far etc. You come to know two thinking patterns when you apply this distinction. A scientific man remains objective to measure his targets whereas an artistic man like a poet has to be subjective. What's practical implication? People will see your success by your possessions but you can enjoy your life only when you see your success by your contentment. People will measure your success in quantitative way whereas you'll cherish your life when you enjoy success qualitatively.

GOAL v. AMBITION

"Big results require big ambitions."

James Champy, a business issues expert

Success requires a success consciousness or a success thinking pattern. You must be determined to achieve success. You must be ambitious. Ambition involves determined action to achieve success in achieving your goals. The word 'ambition' is derived from the Latin *ambitio*; has its other adjective form as *ambitious,* adverbial form in the word *ambitiously* whereas the word 'goal' is often used only as a noun. Goals are your destination and ambition is the way. Goals are objects of your ambition. Ambition pertains to a particular or a chosen field. To win the finals of cricket league is the ambition of a cricket team whereas being champion of the league is itself a goal. Ambition requires a verb like 'to win' in its formation whereas goal is expressed in nouns. All this words research leads to one conclusion: "You've to be ambitious first and then set goals to be successful."

GOALS v. OBJECTIVES

"A goal properly set is halfway reached."

Abraham Lincoln (1809–1865)

Goals are less precise whereas objectives are more accurate. Goals are long-term whereas objectives are with deadlines and help us to realize our goals. I want to be slim is my goal and loosing 5 kg per month is my objective. Objectives are small steps to realize your goals.

ACCURACY v. PRECISION—ART OF GOAL SETTING

> *"You can't hit a target you cannot see, and you cannot see a target you do not have."*
>
> Zig Ziglar (1926–2012)

Think of shooting at a target: Being accurate means you hit the bull's eye. Being precise means you hit near bull's eye every time. Accuracy is one attempt precision is many. You can be accurate every time when you train yourself from precision to accuracy. This is art of converting practice into perfect practice. Goethe (1749–1832) prescribed the law of perfect practice: "It is not enough to take steps which may someday lead to a goal; each step must be itself a goal and a step likewise."

An ancient Indian sage was teaching his disciples the art of goal setting. He asked all his pupils to be ready with their bows and arrows. "There is a bird perched on that branch of the tree," sage said pointing his finger in the particular direction, "and I want each of you to shoot the eye of the bird. Each of you will have your chance as your name will be called." Many disciples were asked to describe what they saw. Each one of them said, "I see the trees, the branches, the leaves, the sky and the bird." The sage asked all these disciples to wait. Then he asked hero of our story the same question and he replied, "I only see the eye of the bird." The sage said, "Accurate! Then shoot." The eye and only the eye had been shot. The head and the body of the bird were intact. For a hasty spectator it appeared as though the bird was still there, perched on the bough as before. Only a microscopic look revealed that the eye of the bird was missing. This famous Indian sage was Dronacharya and the hero of our story was Arjuna, a much loved student of Dronacharya among all the pupils of Kauravas and the Pandavas.

Moral of the story:

1. You must be absolutely certain of the target you want to hit.
2. Set a goal that commands your thoughts.
3. The art of goal setting is in establishing clearly defined goals.

4. In all things that you do, consider the end.
5. A good archer is known not by his arrows but by his aim.

WHERE DO YOU WANT TO GO?

"Focus on the journey, not the destination. Joy is found not in finishing an activity but in doing it."

Greg Anderson, a personal trainer

In 1994, by chance, I had the good fortune of learning the most fundamental law of success. I have learned from my life a lot. It happened with me when I was in tenth standard. I was standing at a bus stand. There was no direct bus at that time of the day. The only option was to cover the distance by covering in-between places one by one. Suddenly I saw a bus that looked like the one I was waiting for. I jumped in. I asked the bus driver, "Where is this bus going?" The bus driver questioned me, "Where do you want to go?" I replied, "Delhi." The bus driver advised, "Then take the accurate bus and please ask the bus driver "Is this bus going to Delhi?" instead of "Where is this bus going?" "Gentleman! You have to take an accurate bus to reach to your destination." He further counselled. This incident taught me the lesson of setting accurate aims.

Moral of the story:

1. If you don't know where you're going you'll end up somewhere else.
2. The going is the goal in itself.
3. Well begun is half done.
4. Reaching at one goal is the preparatory point to another.
5. The path is not as essential as the direction.
6. The distance between you and your success is your ignorance.
7. A genuine guide really helps a lot to achieve success.
8. You must have a roadmap to your destination so as to get it.
9. Success is not a destination but more of a journey.
10. Doing is more important than outcome.

LAW OF ACCURATE AIM

> *"Goals are dreams with deadlines."*
>
> Diana Scharf Hunt, a time-management expert

Aims give a sense of direction. Aimless person is often compared with a rudderless ship; nobody can predict where it will go. Would you sit in a plane or a bus without knowing where it was going? The clear answer is no. Then, why do people go through life without having any aims? You must set yourself a clear, specific and accurate target and also a deadline to accomplish it.

If you ask most people what is their one major objective in life, they would probably give you a vague answer, such as, "I want to earn lot of money, be married to a dream partner and make a good name and live quality life," and that is it. They are all wishes and none of them are clear goals. For example, "I want to earn 1,00,000 Rupees per month." This is wishful thinking. It becomes a specific time bound goal when I pin myself down to "I will earn 3333.33 Rupees per day and that will make 1,00,000 Rupees per month." I will lose 20 kgs till 12.12.2012, 5 p.m. Every goal should have a starting and a finishing date.

HOW TO SET SMART GOALS?

> *"I recommend that you focus on both substance and process of your goals. I believe that both are equally important: by setting a high-quality SMART goal you will enable yourself to be conscious and your actions will carry more meaning; meanwhile, it is the execution of the SMART goals strategy that separates achievers from the rest of the people."*
>
> Anna Stevens, *Turn Your Dreams And Wants Into Achievable SMART Goals!*

Do you have an important personal or professional goal that you really, really want to achieve? If yes, then here is SMART that is a mnemonic less and more of a technique that has been used by management experts for many years throughout the world. SMART Goals are based on Neuro-linguistic programming. This SMART Goal Setting Technique can make a huge difference in business and personal growth. In 1981 George T. Doran published an article *There's a SMART way to write management goals and objectives* in November issue of Management Review. SMART – stands for Specific, Measurable, Attainable, Realistic/Relevant and Time Bound goals. Some experts has enlarged this acronym with the addition of the words Evaluate and Reevaluate used in more recent works making it SMARTER. Gwenn Clayton, the author of *Smartest Goals Formula* has added Ecological (count the negative points), Steps (mini goals/action steps) and Tools (resources and tools) to make it SMARTEST.

I call it as an art of setting clear goals and objectives. Smart goal sentences always begin with "I". They are very specific and can be felt, seen and heard with your senses. NLP was talked by Bandler and Grinder in 1970. It has become a global subject now. One of the concepts in Neuro-linguistic programming is to form well thought and structured end results that enhance the chances of success to a great extent.

A well-set goal should meet the following criteria –

1. S – Specific. A specific goal will usually cover the five Ws – What, Why, Who, Where & Which. For example take this un-smart and unspecific goal, "I want to be successful" and now look at this smart and specific goal, "By the end of 2020 (When), I (Who) will be the most successful salesman (Why) in XYZ Company (Where). I will earn 1 lakh rupees per month (What) and be the head of my unit through my honest work (Which)."
2. M – Measurable. How will you know when it is accomplished? The goal sentence is specific as a result of determining the following visible measures.

- ✓ Checks of 25 thousand rupees per week are deposited into your bank account each week making it one lakh rupees per month.
- ✓ You are most successful salesman of your company.
- ✓ You're working in XYZ Company as a head of sale unit.

3. A – Attainable. How can the goal be accomplished? The best goals call you to stretch a bit to realize them, but they are not impossible to achieve.
4. R – Relevant. Does it support other goals? For example, being the successful salesman will inspire you to work more. Promotion of head of sales unit will make other staff motivated to work also. Honest work will set an example in the organization. The reputation and profits of company will grow by increased sale.
5. T – Time-bound. What & When – There is a sense of urgency in time-bound goal. For example, I'll be the most successful salesman (What) by 2020 (When).

In business and personal life goal setting is inevitable because having a goal is a preliminary step to achieve success but this art is often not used well.

FIND OUT YOUR BREAKTHROUGH GOAL

"The achievement of one goal should be the starting point of another."
Alexander Graham Bell (1847–1922)

Generally, people tend to have only incremental goals, which add to your current reality like reading a book each month, attending seminar and hobby classes etc. Setting a breakthrough goal requires a skill.

Do a "Mind Map" exercise to get from where you are to where you want to be. It will require devoting extra time on learning and training in new activity. It can be one of the biggest like creating a killer website, a live show and as small as taking a leap in social media sites etc. But these goals put you into realm of a whole new world. They are out of your comfort zone and stretch you. They require passionate dedication and change you forever. You have to stay on road (work on this each day) and avoid distractions until you achieve the "Dream." You have to "Plan and Prepare" for them. One of the motivating exercises to keep you motivated is to revise your goal 5 times a day.

MEASURE YOUR SUCCESS

> *"Anyone can count the seeds in an apple, but only God can count the number of apples in a seed."*
>
> Robert H. Schuller, an American televangelist

Success is a numbers game; so check your numbers. A very remarkable and efficient technique is "Ask Yourself", it will reflect many things. For example, just ask yourself and write the answers in a notebook—How much money have you saved and invested in the last 5 years? Did you exercise regularly in the past month? Did you write in your journal this week? There are some things that you must check every day; there are some things that you need to check once a week; there are some things that you need to check once a month; and so on. As an illustration, if a salesman is supposed to sell ten items a day, his supervisor can ask him once a week how many items he sold that week. Measuring your results objectively, quantitatively and accurately allows you to take corrective action. It looks everybody just counts his troubles. No one count his pleasures. I have advised many people to count their pleasures and each one of them was amazed to see that every set has sufficient joys to be happy and live appreciatively.

WRITE GOALS ON PAPER

> *"Cherish your visions and your dreams as they are the children of your soul, the blueprints of your ultimate achievements."*
>
> Napoleon Hill (1883–1970)

You must treat your goals like your children. Write your short- and long-term goals down on paper. However, live your life by heart. I have observed and I am still continuing to observe that putting your dreams and goals down on paper, improves your belief, that they can be achieved – although you have to take a course adjustment in achieving your goals, time after time. Realize: If you don't know where you are going, any bus will get you there.

SUGGESTED STRATEGY

> *"Shallow men believe in luck. Strong men believe in cause and effect."*
>
> R.W. Emerson (1803–1882)

Whatever you think can build or tilt your progress. The future you perceive is the future you find. How? Simple. The answer is: Master Law of Cause & Effect. The thought is the cause of which circumstance is the effect. You can't think low inside and have good circumstance outside. Can you? Similarly when you think positively inside, the outer circumstances have to be equally good. I am theorizing: "Your outer circumstances are the outcome of your inner thoughts." In computer language, you call it *GIGO – Garbage In Garbage Out* and *I call it PIPO – Positive In Positive Out*. Do an exercise if you are feeling not enough enthusiasm in your life. Make a list of 30 things that (1) You can at least aspire *to have* in next 30 years, for example 30 things you want to possess (have) like, a good branded car, a big home in posh area etc.; (2) 30 things you want *to do* like world tour, rock climbing, fast driving and other adventures etc.; (3) 30 things you want *to achieve* like salvation, businessman of the year, 70% marks and first position in final year etc. and (4) 30 things you want *to be* like, a good father, a good husband, a good son and a good brother etc. Total 120 things – 4 things per year. Decide which year – which goal. How will you prepare this list? Keep in mind: Every top, when reached, becomes a bottom.

ASSIGNMENT

1. Take your journal and start writing your 120 goals.
2. Try to figure out how much money will be needed to materialize the goals.
3. Ask yourself how to multiply your income from your dream profession.
4. Find out your breakthrough goal – What and How.
5. Listen to the Audio program *Goals* by Zig Ziglar.

VISUALIZATION

When you go to your bed, relax and visualize yourself living, loving and laughing your dream "haves, dos, achieves and bes" like a Mercedes Car, Big Villa etc. to inspire others. Use your all senses and feel, see, hear, taste and touch it in full details. Don't worry about "How", just imagine "What" (cause) and "How" (effect) will be taken care of by the existence itself, sometimes just when you need it, not even a minute before. So go for more. Remember: You can hit the target only when you have the clarity of goal as Arjuna.

SELF SUGGESTION

I remain focused on what matters most.

Bear in mind: Super achievers always keep their commitments.

[*Promise & Put Your Signature Here With Date*]

7

Are You Ready To Enter Into The World Of Possibilities?

OBJECTIVES

- To learn the "Law of Positive Believing",
- To understand the theory of double work, and
- To believe in yourself and in your positive doings.

GOLDEN GUIDANCE

"One person with a belief is equal to ninety-nine who have only interests."

John Stuart Mill (1806–1873)

YOU CAN DO IT IF YOU BELIEVE

"It's not who you are that holds you back. It's who you think you're not."

Hanoch McCarty, a famous keynote speaker

Belief philosophy is expressed in inspiring and sometimes valid maxims such as "Whatever the mind of man can conceive and believe it can achieve." Majority of people say that the phrase "You can do it if you just believe" has become so common to the point that people just make their faces when they hear it. "I've tried it and it just doesn't work for me" is their common answer. I have found that the people generally never really go through the exercise of creating their own beliefs, because they've been spoon-fed from day one. Learning is a many-sided process. Synaptic pruning or neuron generation in human brain is influenced by environmental factors and is generally thought to represent learning. Everybody is extraordinary. You are the single you. I am the single me. God does not create nonsense. Each person is only one of his kind. Each one is special. Believe: You are masterwork and have all the stuff you need to excel in your God-Gift. Know: The real difference maker is the belief.

NURTURE FROM CHILDHOOD

"Find out what your gift is and nurture it."

Katy Perry, an American singer

A great psychologist Erik Erikson in his book *Identity, Youth & Crisis* explains eight stages (0 to death) through which a healthily developing human should pass from infancy to late adulthood negotiating his or her biological forces and socio-cultural forces. One of the significant things he shows is that a child of 0–2 years imbibes the qualities of trust or mistrust through his interaction. He defines trust as "an essential truthfulness of others as well as a fundamental sense of one's own trustworthiness." This thesis shows that proper nurturing of an appropriate belief system right from childhood is essential for a future successful life.

YOU ARE ALWAYS TOLD LIES

"One believes things because one has been conditioned to believe them."

Aldous Huxley (1894–1963)

Our environment, education and experience shape our beliefs. Shiv Khera calls it triple E's of attitude. Suppose you want to do business but if you hail from a family of service people, your family will criticize you. Whenever you decide, you challenge a belief outside or inside. You are always told only lies. The biggest lies of your life told to you by your parents, friends and society:

1. Money doesn't grow on trees.
2. Getting success is not a child's game.
3. Hard work is the key to success.
4. You have to study to get a good job.
5. Circumstances, caste and class play roles in success.
6. We need to see what people think.
7. One person can't move the mountain.
8. We need resources to achieve something big.
9. One alone man can't sustain for long.
10. Love is a filmy concept as it can't motivate the person.

I don't agree with any of them. There are many more to come if you don't watch these with sense intelligence. Roman Rolland, Nobel Prize Winner for Literature in 1915 once said, "A hero is a person who does what he or she can." Therefore, I see you as a hero of your life story. You can and must do what you can.

Money can grow on trees. Yes! Tree of Success. You can succeed if you behave passionately like a child who turns everything into a game. He runs one day but he improves step by step from crawling. Hard work has never been a key to success. It has always been a burden. When you enjoy, you succeed. So, enjoyed work is the key. There is no connection between qualification and success. Education is different from qualification. Success comes from education and not qualification. Most of the great businessmen were educated but not highly qualified. Paper degrees are not going to do any wonders. I will deal with these white lies in this Bible of Believers and break them once for all and in fact, in every chapter you'll find that white lies are being broken.

HAVE REASONS FOR YOUR DECISIONS

"Whatever you decide, collect reasons for sticking with it."

Brian Kim, a globally known motivational author

Simple decisions become powerful beliefs when you have reasons. You can find these reasons in perfect examples of perfect people – they exemplify what and how. It is very easy to quit if you don't have reasons for sticking with what you want to be/have/do. You must also have reasons for your "how" also. I mean you must have reasons to support your plans. Surround yourself with believers of you and limit your contact with disbelievers of you.

So, *here is the golden tip*: "Human beings are psychological organisms. Everything we are or ever will be is the direct result of the way we think. If we improve the quality of our thinking, we'll improve the quality of our lives." You must know that it is a world of belief systems. Whatever you think and believe you experience. By learning how to use your thinking system through this book lessons, you'll start to think differently about yourself, about others and about each situation. And there is no other way to do it. Sounds Great!

GOODBYE TO IMPOSSIBLE "WORLD AND WORD"

"There are two ways to face the future. One way is with apprehension, the other is with anticipation."

Jim Rohn (1930–2009)

Warren Buffett once said: "I always knew I was going to be rich. I don't think I ever doubted it for a minute." So friends, are you ready to enter into the world of possibilities? Are you ready to say a final and one time goodbye to the world of impossibilities? This is the end you must accept in order to build your new world. So join me in giving a farewell to "The world of impossibilities." We will say goodbye in loud words:

"GOODBYE! Impossible—World and Word."

WELCOME TO WORLD OF POSSIBILITIES

CONGRATULATIONS!!!

Now, since you have said goodbye to world of impossibilities, let me welcome you to a new world of possibilities.

WELCOME—MY FRIEND!!!

You know the difference between convincing yourself and believing yourself. Do one thing, take your dictionary and cross the ten letters word *Impossible*. Make the other ten letters word *Confidence* your companion. Let us now simplify what are the implications of your action. Can you imagine what have you done? You have said goodbye to "I can't" and from now on, there are three words that will govern your mind while doing any activity. You will say to yourself loudly and your confidence should also be manifested in your action. "YES, I CAN."

I CAN IF OTHERS CAN – THE CAN ATTITUDE

"Only as high as I reach can I grow,

Only as far as I seek can I go,

Only as deep as I look can I see,

Only as much as I dream can I be."

Karen Ravn, the author of *Little Seeds of Wisdom*

Where there is a will there is always a way. It's all about TCA – The Can Attitude. Disbelief can happen with anybody. In great Hindu epic *Ramayana*, Lord Hanuman was to be told his glory, and only then he was able to cross the sea. In the same way, we have forgotten our real powers and need to be told our glory. The first best way remains to believe in ourselves first. And, the second best way is to look at others. If other people can be in excellent health, I can also be; if my boss can earn in six digits, I can also earn; if my neighbour can have a big house, I can also have; if any member of parliament can have many people behind him, I can also have cordial relationships in my family and in my society; if any celebrity star is popular in people, I can also be equally popular and enjoy same status among my friends; if chairman and managing director of my company can lead the company executives, I can also lead and be a powerful leader of a social cause; if a saint can live a satisfied life, I can also be satisfied in and with my life; if my friend can enjoy the life, I can also enjoy the life and if a religious devotee can excel in his spiritual life, I can also excel spiritually.

I AM IMAGE OF GOD

"The way you treat yourself sets the standard for others."

Sonya Friedman, a theatre producer

It's good if you look at others for motivation but the inspiration is the game changer and that my friend comes from inside. The most important belief: "I can do whatever I want because I am created in the image of God." Yes, this is true. The Holy *Bible* claims: "Both male and female are created in the image of God." Yes, I believe and ask you to believe that every human is made in the image of God, so everyone should treat oneself with proper respect and honour because he/she reflects God. Of course, many people are full of evil and hatred and we must guard ourselves and others against them. Still, we must treat others and ourselves with respect. Certainly, the earth and animals too have a place in God's world, but basically, the world was created as a place for man/woman to try to live, love and laugh.

ATTITUDE=ALTITUDE

"You have brains in your head. You have feet in your shoes. You can steer yourself any direction you choose. You're on your own. And you know what you know. And YOU are the one who'll decide where to go ..."

Dr. Seuss, *Oh, the Places You'll Go!*

Your "I Can" is more important than your "IQ." "Yes, my dear! There is a difference between will and wish. The level of your success is fixed by the level of your belief. Negative or reactive people choose to be driven by feelings, by circumstances, by conditions and by their environment. Positive people prefer to respond with a positive action instead of a hasty reaction. Positive people use their potential talents and resources and prefer to take positive steps instead of thinking positively only.

What I am suggesting is that if you work on your inner world, you will definitely get breakthroughs in outer world. I tell you, the most unattainable thing in the world is to have quality changes in the inner world without an equivalent quality changes in the outer world. So, I tell you, for the first time in the history of mankind: "If you are working on yourself, you are doing an exemplary work. Even if people say you are doing nothing."

BEHAVIOUR v. ATTITUDE

"Nurture your minds with great thoughts. To believe in heroic makes heroes."

Benjamin Disraeli (1804–1881)

Your actions reflect your attitude. Behaviour is external whereas attitude is internal. Attitude is what you think and behaviour is what you do. Therefore attitude can shape your behaviour. Big success lies in big change. Big change comes through big opportunity. Big opportunity comes from big creativity. Big creativity comes from big idea. Big idea comes from bold thinking.

HABIT v. BEHAVIOUR

"People are always blaming their circumstances for what they are. I don't believe in circumstances. The people who get on in this world are the people who get up and look for the circumstances they want, and if they can't find them, make them."

George Bernard Shaw (1856–1950)

A behaviour when becomes a repeated action is called a habit. In every action you will find the hidden beliefs. Everybody acts according to his beliefs. Habit is result of subconscious mind whereas behaviour is also controlled by endocrine and nervous system, and often learned through external resources. The success secret is success habits. You can learn and unlearn the habits by imbibing a correctional behaviour in your daily routine. One such habit is thinking positively followed by positive doing. Dr. Norman Vincent Peale sums the formula in three words: Believe and Succeed. Dorothea Brande (1893–1948) was the outstanding editor and writer who had a philosophy: Act as if it were impossible to fail. Charles F. Kettering (1876–1958) who was an American inventor, engineer and the holder of 186 patents uttered an improved version: "Believe and act as if it were impossible to fail." Positive believing is a mind-set of self-confidence that comes with preparation. Having a positive thinking without making the positive effort is nothing more than having a wishful daydream.

IT IS THE STUFF INSIDE THAT MAKES IT RISE

"Your inner world creates your outer world. You become what you think about. Your thoughts make your world."

Buddha, the founder of Buddhist religion

I am reminded of a story that is cited by various authors too often because of its simple words yet powerful message. There was a man who made his living selling balloons at a fair. He had all colours of balloons—red, yellow, green, blue, orange. Whenever business was slow, the man would release a helium filled balloon into the air and when the children saw it go up, they all wanted to buy one too. They would come up to him, buy a balloon and his sales would go up again. He continued this process all day.

One day, he felt something tugging his jacket. He turned around and saw a little boy. The little boy asked, "If you release a black balloon, would that also fly?" The man replied, "Son, it is not the colour of the balloon; it is what's inside that makes it fly." I love the simplicity of this story as a reminder that it is your inner circumstances that determine your progress, not just your outer circumstances. Let me prescribe a success formula: "If you are not getting what you have thought then redefine your life concepts, toughen your attitude and put more life-skills in your activities."

Moral of the story:

1. It is not your race, religion or creed that determines great heights.
2. It is what's inside that matters—your attitude, your beliefs and values.
3. People always find justifications of success in superficial things.
4. You'll fly when you're filled with flying material.

PMA IS RMA

> *"Close the door to fear behind you and you will quickly see the door of faith open before you."*
>
> Napoleon Hill (1883–1970)

Now, since you believe that "I can do whatever I want because I am created in the image of God." "What if I believe I CAN?" This is the next question that must be bubbling in your mind. I want to tell you the power of belief. "You will be able to do it, if you believe you can." This statement is the guiding star of many people with whom I have shared my success consciousness. I want a promise from you before I share the power of

"IBIC – I Believe I CAN" and that is: If at the end of story you feel that I have lighted your beacon of possibilities, you will pass on this beacon by sharing this story with other people and tell them about "PMA (Positive Mental Attitude) is RMA (Right Mental Attitude) in any given situation."

THE STORY OF MOUNTAIN MAN

> *"If you are not the hero of your own story, then you're missing the whole point of your humanity."*
>
> Steve Maraboli, an internet radio commentator and author

Generally, the love stories are narrated orally. But I am going to share with you a story of a mountain from India, which has become a place to view. Our hero of the story was born in 1934 into a poor labourer family in Gahlour village near Gaya in Bihar. His village was surrounded by rocky hills. The villagers had to travel more than 50 km to reach the nearest town, which was only five km away but the path blocked by a rocky hill. His wife was seriously injured while crossing the hill to bring him water.

That was the day that he decided that he would cut a pass through the hill. He sold his goats, bought a hammer and a chisel, and started hammering away at the hill. Everyone made fun of him. They laughed at him, discouraged him, and told him it was not achievable. He refused to be influenced and kept at it. One stone at one time was his motto. It took him 22 years (from 1962 to 1984) to cut a 300-foot high mountain of Gehlour hills single-handedly and carved a 360-foot-long (110 m), 25-foot-high (7.6 m) and 30-foot-wide (9.1 m) road through the hill.

Moral of the story:

1. One can really move the mountain if he believes he can.
2. Every success demands persistent work and strong determination.
3. Slow and sure progress is the best way to achieve any success.

4. You have to live each day as a separate life.
5. You shouldn't bother too much about what others say.
6. Multi-tasking is a bad habit and hampers growth.
7. You can cover miles by taking one step at one time.
8. Any big accomplishment requires a lot of courage and a lot of sacrifice.

THIS IS A REAL STORY

"A pessimist sees the difficulty in every opportunity and an optimist sees the opportunity in every difficulty."

Winston Churchill (1874–1965)

Our superhero is none other Dashrath Manjhi who believed that he could do it and he did it. This passage reduced the distance between Atri and Wazirganj blocks of Gaya district from 75 km to just ten km, bringing him international acclaim. This is the true story of Dashrath Manjhi who is popularly known as mountain man. He died on August 17, 2007 at the age of 73 years. He was given a state funeral by the Government of Bihar. His wife Falguni Devi was not there to see all this in 1984. This pass is often compared with Taj Mahal, because both took 22 years to complete and both are outcome of love, although Taj Mahal was created with the help of 20,000 labourer and this pass was made single-handedly by our hero of the story. Our hero's story is subject of many upcoming films and writings. Amir Khan wrote an article "The Power of One" in the *Hindustan Times* dated 29 July 2012 describing our hero's achievements. Manjhi was also a subject of famous TV Indian Talk Show "Satyamav Jayte". You can search him on YouTube also.

MINDSET OF WINNERS

> *"My formula for living is quite simple. I get up in morning and I go to bed at night. In between I occupy myself as best as I can."*
>
> Cary Grant (1904–1986)

Let us imagine the mind of our hero Dashrath Manjhi at the very first day … "I can do it" could only be the guiding force in his mind. Even though he could have broken few cubic inches of rock on the first day and this task would have seemed even more promising at the end of the first week. As, time after time, year after year, I feel, the broken stones would have kept him going for 22 long years. If you want to be a wealthy, powerful, sophisticated, healthy, influential, cultured and unique individual, first you must believe it's feasible, secondly you must also believe that it is feasible for you, thirdly set goals, fourthly act to achieve goals and the most important and fifth one, at the end of the day don't forget to write a note.

DO YOU WANT TO BE A BELIEVER OR DISBELIEVER?

> *"Some people want it to happen. Some wish it would happen. Some make it happen."*
>
> Michael Jordan, an American
> former professional basketball player

So, may I ask you "Do you want to be a believer like Dashrath Manjhi or do you want to be a disbeliever like villagers who laughed at him?" Each one of us has to put this question to ourselves, and in our response vests our future and the future of our family, our society and our country. In our response vests the reply to the following questions also: Do you want to pursue your dreams determinedly like Dashrath Manjhi or do you want to be a cynical naysayer like villagers? And, I think choice is crystal clear.

BE LIKE DASHRATH MANJHI

"Knock the 't' off the 'can't.'"

Samuel Johnson (1709–1784)

Each one of us (including me and you) would like to be "Dashrath Manjhi." Each one of us can stand with a hammer of belief and a chisel of work against a mountain of difficulties. If Dashrath Manjhi could do it, we can also do it. This is the power of belief, believing in oneself, believing in one's aim even if people may not support your activity and may even laugh at you, still it is the thought of I CAN that will do it. You can do it if you believe you can. Our hero knew what he had to do. He had a plan. While doing, he must have used the power of auto-suggestion by saying "I CAN" to himself and he did it. Believe, really believe, you can move a mountain, and you can. Not many people believe that they can move mountains. So, as a result, not many people do.

SUPREMACY OF ONE

"When there is no enemy within, enemies outside can't hurt you."

An African Proverb

Disbelief is depressing command. When the mind disbelieves or doubts, the mind magnetizes various reasons to carry the disbelief. Suspicion i.e. disbelief is the main factor that leads the subconscious mind to wish for failure, and that to me is responsible for most failures. Imagine hesitation and fail. Imagine success and succeed. What can one man do single-handedly? I am just one among many a billion. Even if I transform, what good will it do? What about the other people? Who will revolutionise everyone? First get everyone else to transform then I too will transform. These are some of the most cynical thoughts I have heard throughout my life. The story of Dashrath Manjhi is a fitting reply to all these statements.

It demonstrates us what one man can accomplish. It demonstrates us the supremacy of one. It demonstrates us that one man can definitely move the mountains.

SECOND-BEST ATTITUDE

"It's me who is my enemy
Me who beats me up
Me who makes the monsters
Me who strips my confidence."

Paula Cole, "Me" *This Fire*

Everybody knows about the first climber of Mount Everest. Everybody can tell about the first man to land on moon. The reason is quite simple: human memory takes an enormous effort to remember the second. Why? I tell you the reason: for the reason that he has done something next to the first one. The best has already done it. Benjamin Disraeli was a British Prime Minister, parliamentarian, statesman and literary figure who once asserted: "Life is too short to be little." I think you've got the concept. One must learn from the leaders, but, one should not follow them too long. Believe you can surpass the best in the business. Those who harbour the second-best attitude are invariably second-best doers. Who cares about the second one?

YOU ARE YOUR THOUGHTS

"When you're 18, you worry about what everybody is thinking of you; when you're 40, you don't give a rip about what anybody thinks of you; when you're 60; you realize nobody's been thinking about you at all."

Dr. Daniel Amen

You should not be much concerned with what others think of you. People really care about themselves. What to talk of others, even when a parent is sending you to pay the electricity bill, the concern is self-interest. Everybody is concerned about oneself. In fact, I always say: "Nothing in this world is personal except you." Therefore keep cool and understand: A few believes in you. The problem starts when you don't believe in yourself. Your disbelief in yourself shows in your all activities, in your walking, talking and in doing almost anything. We think limiting thoughts and engage in self-defeating behaviours. We defend our self-destructive habits (such as drinking and smoking) with rude logic. If you treat yourself with little respect, others will do even worse i.e. not respecting you at all. So, this is my one time conclusion: "A man is a product of his thoughts." Thoughts become things. I strongly believe that when our mind is astonishingly strong then we do feel first class in our all activities, good things start to happen in our life automatically. Robert Schuller, an American televangelist, who is best known for weekly TV program *Hour of Power* affirms: "Every achiever I have ever met says: My life turned around when I began to believe in me."

SUGGESTED STRATEGY

> *"Our remedies oft in ourselves do lie,*
>
> *Which we ascribe to heaven."*

William Shakespeare,
All's Well That Ends Well

You should begin each day with the imagination of whatever you are going to do in the next 24 hours. A work is done twice, firstly in the mind and secondly in reality. This is also called "Double Work Theory".

ASSIGNMENT

1. Write down the hours, in which, you have worked for yourself.
2. Try to live, love and laugh to inspire others through your "I CAN" Attitude.
3. Make a list of things you fear to do and then do the listed things.
4. Listen to the Audio program *The Psychology of Achievement* by Brian Tracy. You can also search www.openculture.com for other audiobooks.

VISUALIZATION

Visualize the things that you already have done and then imagine finishing the untried. Remember: Be like Dashrath Manjhi as he is the superstar of winning attitude.

SELF SUGGESTION

I stand firmly in my belief: I can do whatever I want.

Bear in mind: Super achievers always keep their commitments.

[*Promise & Put Your Signature Here With Date*]

8

Have You Progressed From Belief To Faith?

OBJECTIVES

- To learn the "Law of Good Luck",
- To convert belief into faith, and
- To have and derive full faith in and from God and Spiritual Master.

GOLDEN GUIDANCE

> *"There are only two ways to live your life. One is as though nothing is a miracle. The other is as though everything is a miracle."*
>
> Albert Einstein (1879–1955)

BE A GOOD FINDER—DO GOOD AND FIND GOOD

> *"Expect a miracle in everything, even in small things, because it is in them your strength lies."*
>
> Mother Teresa (1910–1997)

The finest approach to live a good life is to have a good heart. You should and must start from the hypothesis: All people are good at their heart. They can really improve if proper guidance is given. I am a great believer in Zig Ziglar pursuits. He often mentioned about Andrew Carnegie (1835–1919) who was America's first great industrialist. He led the enormous expansion of the American steel industry in the late 19th century. Nearly 100 years ago he had 43 millionaires working for him – an unheard-of occurrence in those days. A reporter asked Andrew Carnegie how he managed to hire 43 millionaires. Carnegie responded that none of them were millionaires when he hired them but observed: "You develop millionaires the way you mine gold. You expect to move tons of dirt to find an ounce of gold, but you don't go into the mine looking for the dirt—you go in looking for the gold."

Moral of the story:

1. Even the millionaires are unable to motivate themselves.
2. Even a great leader needs support from other good leaders.
3. You can find good in everything when you look for it.
4. A rich man puts his all eggs in one basket and watches it.
5. No man becomes rich unless he enriches others.
6. Great wonders can happen with a good teamwork.

WHAT IS FAITH?

> *"Desperation is the raw material of drastic change. Only those who can leave behind everything they have ever believed in can hope to escape."*
>
> William S. Burroughs (1914–1997)

You will not find good things unless you have faith. You'll not dare to take any risk unless you have faith. You'll feel safe when you submit yourself to your faith or God/Guru. Martin Luther King Jr. was an American clergyman and a leader in the African-American Civil Rights Movement. He had full faith in using non-violent civil disobedience. He defined faith once: "Faith is taking the first step, even when you don't see the whole staircase." Faith is, to hope for things which are not seen, but which are true. To have faith is to have confidence in something or someone. You have to have faith that what can go right will go right. When we watch Cricket, we pray to an unseen force. Cricket is a game of uncertainties but still we expect certain certainties from our team and if our favourite team performs poorly we pray in faith so that those certainties may happen in the favour of our team. Our anticipation that something miraculous will happen generally comes true when a bowler hits a six at the last ball. Everything gets all right. What could go right went right. Faith is kindled by hearing the testimony of those who have faith. Miracles are God's Gifts. You are child of God and you've every right to receive God's gifts. Miracles do not produce faith but miracles often confirm one's faith.

So, *here is the golden tip*: "You must have a belief to have a faith. I ask you to believe in yourself first and out of this personal belief you will do well. But, if you want to do it in a great way, I ask you to have faith in God." You always have an option as R.W. Emerson says "to put creed in every deed."

GOD GIVES BEYOND EXPECTATIONS

> *"I don't think anyone in business had a tougher time than I had. My faith sustained me when we had internal problems with franchises, when the media would write nasty things."*
>
> Tom Monaghan, the founder of Domino's Pizza

Most of the people predict what they will get and when. I have full faith in one philosophy: We get little when we take; but, when God gives, He gives us more than our expectations. I would like to share an inspirational story on God's Gift. I read this story somewhere. Once a boy named John went in to a shop with his mother. The shopkeeper showed him a jar full of toffees and said, "Dear John, you can take the toffees." But John didn't take. The shopkeeper was surprised. Again he told John to take the toffees. Now the mother also heard that and said, "John! Take the toffees dear." Yet John didn't take. The shopkeeper seeing John not taking the toffees, he himself took the toffees and gave it to John. The child was happy to get two hands full of toffees. While returning home the mother asked the little John,

"Why didn't you take the toffees when the shopkeeper told you to take?" Can you guess the response: The little John replies, "Mom, my hands are very small, and if I take the toffees, I can only take few. But, now you see – when shopkeeper gave with his big hands... how many more toffees I got?"

Moral of the story:

1. God never does injustice with anyone.
2. God gives much beyond the expectations.
3. Miracles happen when you have faith, hope and love in God.
4. Humans have restricted reach but God has infinite.
5. God doesn't do what you fancy. He does what is right.

FAITH v. BELIEF

> *"Promise yourself to be so strong that nothing can disturb your peace of mind. Look at the sunny side of everything and make your optimism come true. Think only of the best, work only for the best, and expect only the best. Forget the mistakes of the past and press on to the greater achievements of the future. Give so much time to the improvement of yourself that you have no time to criticize others. Live in the faith that the whole world is on your side so long as you are true to the best that is in you!"*
>
> Christian D. Larson, an American author and educator

In my view, faith is a misused word. And so is belief. Let us understand the difference between these two terms. What's the distinction? You must have seen that belief is pretty much based on the fact when you're convinced that you will achieve your goals. You base your belief on past experience, logic, or just the fact that you know somebody who achieved a similar goal. Faith, on the other hand, usually brings along with it the implication that it's needed to achieve those goals that seem out of reach, hence phrases like "taking a leap of faith" are used when it comes to those types of situations. In other words, faith is usually used in the context of achieving extraordinary goals to overcome feeling of inferiority complex or self-doubt. Faith is needed when you want to do something beyond the reach of believing.

FIRST BELIEVE THEN HAVE FAITH

> *"You can't believe in God unless you believe in yourself."*
>
> Swami Vivekananda (1863–1902)

Faith is a verb chiefly. Belief is a system. Several people use "faith" as a noun for certain. Faith is a belief, as I call it, in something for which there is no evidence. Faith is universal; all men have faith. Sometimes, the misbelief is that any faith is good enough proves to be good enough for unseen situations. Belief comes from your mind. Faith comes from your heart all the way to your gut. Here is an example to distinguish between the two. The first scientists to invent something new like flying machine with humans inside (airplane, as we call it) – Wright Brothers had faith. The subsequent scientists who created the shuttle, helicopter, jet, etc. – they had belief. Now, you know the tool to set new records, every now and again the records are being broken by persons who have faith. Average beliefs will solve average problems, but you will need a great faith for bigger problems.

EARTH—IT DOES REVOLVE

> *"None of us knows what might happen even the next minute, yet still we go forward. Because we trust. Because we have Faith."*
>
> Paulo Coelho, *Brida*

All the researches come out of doubt. Doubt and faith can't co-exist together although they are twin brothers as I call them. Faith does not call for proof generally, but when proof is there against the faith, it breaks easily. Italian scientist and philosopher Galileo was a true Renaissance man who brought changes in the record by stating that earth revolves. The disagreement between Galileo and the Catholic Church began back in the 17th century when Galileo began offering observations that supported Copernicus's theory that the planet earth was revolving around the sun rather than the sun revolving around the earth. Although the church had long since accepted the Copernican system it wasn't until 1992 that Pope John Paul II officially apologized and set the record straight. In his statement, although, he used Galileo's defense saying that the scriptures were not wrong, they were just mistakenly interpreted by the theologians, surely to maintain the faith.

WHATEVER HAPPENS, HAPPENS FOR THE GOOD

> *"Faith is not the belief that God will do what you want. It is the belief that God will do what is right."*
>
> Max Lucado, the preacher at
> Oak Hills Church in San Antonio, Texas.

An old story is told of Akbar, a king in India who had a very intelligent minister, Birbal. The minister had a habit of looking at every situation that ever occurred in his life (positive or negative) and remarking, "Whatever happens, happens for the good!"

One day Akbar and Birbal were out on a hunting expedition. The minister would load and prepare the arrows on the bow for the king. Birbal had apparently done something wrong in preparing one of the arrows, for after taking the arrow from Birbal, the king shot it and his thumb was blown off. Examining the situation the minister remarked as usual, "Whatever happens, happens for the good!" To which the king replied, "No, this is not good!" and proceeded to send Birbal to jail.

About a year later, the king was hunting in a tribal area. Tribal captured him and took him to their place for sacrificing before a deity of their

Goddess for worship. They tied his hands and body to the sacrificing pole, celebrated with foods and wine and as they came near to cut off his head before the deity, they noticed that the king was missing a thumb. Being superstitious, they never sacrificed anyone that was less than whole. So untying the king, they sent him on his way.

As he returned home, he remembered the event that had taken his thumb and felt remorse for his treatment of his friend. He went immediately to the jail to speak with his minister. "You were right," he said, "It was good that my thumb was blown off." And he proceeded to tell Birbal all that had just happened. "And so I am very sorry for sending you to jail for so long. It was bad for me to do this." "No," his minister replied, "Whatever happens, happens for the good!" "What do you mean, 'Whatever happens, happens for the good'? How could it be good that I sent my minister to jail for a year?" Birbal, the intelligent minister answered, "If I had not been in jail, I would have been with you."

Law of Good Luck

"If there are a hundred steps
In thy path to success
And ye have not reached it
In ninety-nine of them
Do not conclude
That the journey is a failure.
Press on and up...
The prizes are generally at the end of an effort,
Not at its beginning ...
And not to go on
Is to miss them.

Be valiant ... have faith in yourself.
Success belongs to him
Who dares to win it."

George S. Forest (1924–1990)

This law takes to your divine self. Just for a split of a second when you believe you are an expansion of God, you believe also that you are successful beyond any hesitation; the whole thing around you will transform to reveal this reality. Believe that you are a son or a daughter of Heavenly Father, that He loves you. God although do not make any discrimination, however diverse devotees come with diverse purposes and consequently they get the same from Him as a result. The great Hindu Holy Book *Bhagvad Gita* has defined four different types of devotees depending on their approach to God. *Arta* are the distressed devotees who approach God to get liberated from their pains either at physical level or at mental level. *Artharti* are devotees with certain wishes who approach God with the desires of material wealth, kids, name and fame. *Jigyasu* are knowledge seekers who read scriptures and meet saints to know more about God. *Jnani* are self-realized gurus who have finally realized God and have true knowledge of Him. You must have faith that you are here for a glorious purpose. Our inner voice is God's voice. Christ said: "Faith comes by hearing by the word of God."

Gail Devers was training for the 1988 Summer Olympics when she started experiencing health problems. She was suffering from among others migraine and vision loss. She qualified for the Olympics 100 m hurdles, but she was eliminated in the semifinals. Her health continued to deteriorate even more. She was diagnosed with Graves' disease in 1990. She underwent radioactive iodine treatment followed by thyroid hormone replacement therapy. She began to develop blistering and swelling of her feet during radiation treatment. Eventually, she could hardly walk and had to crawl and or be carried. A doctor considered surgically removing her feet. She recovered miraculously as soon as the radiation treatment was stopped. She resumed training. She is a three-time Olympic champion in track and field for the US Olympic Team. It's not what other people believe you can do, it's all about what you believe. She affirms: "Keep your dreams alive. Understand to achieve anything requires faith and belief in yourself, vision, hard work, determination, and dedication. Remember all things are possible for those who believe. Faith makes all things possible, but it is love that makes all things easy." Lance Armstrong had won the Tour de France a record seven consecutive times between 1999 and 2005. In October 1996, Lance was diagnosed with testicular cancer that had spread to his brain and lungs. His cancer treatments included brain and testicular surgery and extensive chemotherapy. He recovered and came back more strongly.

There is nothing more important than the goal you strive to attain. When you trust God you trust the old adage "Everything happens for the good" and that means there is no such thing as bad luck and there can be only one type of luck as I say and that is GOOD LUCK. When you want to achieve success, change your thought and feeling. Think positive. Feel positive. Believe that you are lucky. When you do so, you sleep in peace and get up in joy. Every moment becomes a new beginning to start with. You will pursue your passion with enthusiasm and successively, your career will overflow with success.

HUMAN INTELLIGENCE CAN'T COMPREHEND DIVINE WILL

> *"Faith is a reasoning trust, a trust which reckons thoughtfully and confidently upon the trustworthiness of God."*
>
> John R. Stott (1921–2011)

Be positive. Look for the hidden messages in the events. Jesus said the words, "If it be thy will" during one of His prayers, to seek the will of God. This "if" is of future not of doubt. Saint Augustine once rightly said: "He who created us without our help will not save us without our consent." I believe: Faith begins when will of God is known. There is an interesting joke that helps to understand how God works. A heavy flood came in a village. All the people gathered in a temple due to its elevated base. The rescue team came in a boat and took all the people in small groups except one man. He was not ready to get into boat. When all the people asked him to hop in, he said: "My God will save me." As the water rose he entered in the temple-core and hugged the statue and waited to be rescued. He was murmuring: "My God will save me." The floodwaters kept rising. After some time, a rescue helicopter came and the pilot shouted at the man and asked him to get in but the man said: "God will save me." The floodwaters rose increasingly higher, and at last, floodwaters ran over the temple and the man drowned. When he went to heaven, he met God and asked furiously: "O God, why didn't You save me?" God replied: "O King of Fools! Did your father send that boat and that helicopter?"

Moral of the story:

1. Faith without logic becomes superstition.
2. We should interpret the events in a divine way.
3. A little doubt makes the faith stronger.
4. Finite intelligence can't interpret infinite will.
5. You can't have faith without hope.
6. Faith is a loving and logical intuition.

I AM THE DIVINE RADIANCE AND I AM SHINING ON ALL THE BEINGS

> *"I am receiving God's Gifts of love, happiness and prosperity from everywhere and from everybody. I believe I love everybody, everybody loves me and I am loveable. I believe that God cares for me and He protects me."*
>
> Bijan Anjomi, *Absolutely Effortless Prosperity*

All Indians are familiar with the fact that in *Bhagwat Gita* (Holy Book of Hindus), Lord Krishna asks Arjun to surrender completely. In the same way, I ask you to submit yourself to infinite intelligence and believe that you are born lucky. Think success and you will be a success because the universe will provide you everything you want. The infinite intelligence will help you in realizing your goals. Everything you need will come to you in rich abundance. I believe that our prosperity is tremendous and is in the offing and is waiting to be received by us. You are very rich. You have to believe that you have plenty of money and prosperity. Just do not think future but live it. When you act as if your prayers have already been answered, you will become walking example of God's love and you will be highly favoured by the universe because you are child of God. Wherever you go, people will be drawn to your dynamic personality and in this whole process, you will become irresistibly attractive. Wherever you will be, you will be surrounded by the friendliest and most helpful people because the universe will favour you.

You must bear in mind: "God loves you more than you love Him." Your evil-self will try to dissuade you. Most of the times, evil-self distracts you and convinces you, more often through foolish logics, that you should not trust God absolutely. Instead it will say, trust yourself, and soon it'll ask you not to trust anybody, not even yourself.

In fact, all the negative things are absence of positive things. For instance, poverty is absence of prosperity. All the negative waves are illusions created by evil-self i.e. ego. Take another example, you are sitting depressed and suddenly you receive a phone call that you have qualified a test and you have stood first in merit, what will happen to you. You will "Jump & Enjoy" in excitement. This means that if you can maintain a positive atmosphere in your whole existence, you can be happy all the times.

In Hinduism, our soul is said to be a part of God, and it is always shown in form of light, taking a lead from this fact, I suggest you to assume yourself as the "Walking Sun", and using the auto-suggestion, "I am the divine radiance and I am shining on all the beings." Repeat this magic sentence all day during all the activities. The impact, this magic sentence generates is awesome, and you will be amazed to see the results. Commit to memory one quote of John Lilly: "In the province of the mind, what one believes to be true either is true or becomes true."

TRANSITION FROM BELIEF TO FAITH

"Do not be afraid; our fate
Cannot be taken from us; it is a gift."

Dante Alighieri, *Inferno*

A desire is when you wish to receive something in future. A desire ripens into a hope when you have strong reasons for expecting it. A strong hope when established in your conscience becomes a belief and when a belief becomes mature it is called faith. You can have hope without faith, but you cannot have faith without hope. In common world, you believe when you see. In belief, you see what you believe. There's no such thing as "immediate faith." Lots of people put their faith in lots of different things. Faith comes from a background of your culture, beliefs and your programming since childhood. It takes a century to build faith but it takes a second to break that. Like we, now, have belief or faith that earth revolves around the sun. You must not doubt in surrendering your unknown future to a known God because when you have full faith in God, your plan will be merged in divine plan. Prof. (Dr.) Afzal Wani who is best known for his contribution to Islamic Jurisprudence affirms: "No prayer of any level of poetic composition can help you unless you have the faith. I believe with my heart what I say with my mouth in prayer. The solo lively component in prayer is faith. Prayer of full faith will bring spiritual gifts and graces." Your belief will become faith. Promises of belief become guarantees of faith. Faith to me is: believing and trusting in my Guru. I often say: My Guru/Spiritual Master is my hope for which I am in faith. Faith is a way of living, tried, tested and true. Memorise: Faith is required: to please God and to receive from Him. Belief is required: to have confidence in yourself. Faith is the vision of a holy heart, as a faithful heart can see the unseen and achieve it.

GREAT FAITH COMES FROM GREAT FORCE

> *"Faith that it's not always in your hands or things don't always go the way you planned, but you have to have faith that there is a plan for you, and you must follow your heart and believe in yourself no matter what."*
>
> Martina McBride,
> an American country music singer

Reality will forever remain the exception to faith. However, the record-breakers continue to break the records by ignoring the "Doubt Element" in faith and opting for "Trust Element". And, because reality lives alone in the brain, you can create your own reality. Why the devotees are able to cross hard ways and hard times for reaching a holy place and to meet holy people. The reason is simple: they are blessed with infinite faith that comes from infinite intelligence. Faith in eternal forces like God or Guru removes your ANTS as Dr. Daniel Amen abbreviates *Automatic Negative Thoughts*. There lies a paradigm shift. "Once you do that you believe, you develop genuine faith to do that you don't believe." Your outer results are product of your internal beliefs. Your thoughts create your world.

SUGGESTED STRATEGY

> *"A man of courage is also full of faith."*
>
> Cicero (106 BC–43 BC)

Write down your beliefs every day in your life journal and you must drill the beliefs into yourself by constant hammering of auto-suggestion and visualization that your trusts and beliefs are already being achieved every day. This is called law of attraction, and you can use it to transform your beliefs into trusts. The reality is that you take in all the information from your environment by the use of your five senses and process that in your brain and in there, your experience is created. What I mean to say is this: "You can create your own reality."

ASSIGNMENT

1. Write down your beliefs every day in your life journal and paste them everywhere you can see; on your refrigerator, study table, mirror, walls, door, computer, TV, wall, bathroom, front door, screen door, everywhere.
2. Try to live, love and laugh to inspire others through your rock-solid faith in your God and Guru.
3. Try to develop a ritual like touching your locket etc. to initiate feeling of faith before doing anything important.
4. You can also submit to a Living Guru i.e. Spiritual Master, if you like.
5. Listen to the Audio program *Jump and the Net Will Appear* by Robin Crow.

VISUALIZATION

When you do your ritual, visualize yourself doing all day activities with full power and divine support. You can use Mary Baker Eddy's quote for guidance. Know that: "Today my soul can only sing and soar. An increasing sense of God's love, omnipresence, and omnipotence enfolds me. Each day I know Him nearer, love Him more, and humbly pray to serve Him better." Remember: The little John has full faith in God so he gets two hands full of toffees.

SELF SUGGESTION

I succeed effortlessly because I am connected to my Guru/God: the resource of strong, supportive and soaring energy.

Bear in mind: Super achievers always keep their commitments.

[*Promise & Put Your Signature Here With Date*]

9

How Do You Know Which Is The Best Choice?

OBJECTIVES

- To learn the "Law of Proportional Exertion",
- To realize the difference between choice and decision, and
- To master the art of perfect decision-making.

GOLDEN GUIDANCE

"In any moment of decision the best thing you can do is the right thing, the next best thing is the wrong thing, and the worst thing you can do is nothing."

Theodore Roosevelt (1858–1919)

DOCTRINE OF ELECTION

"The measure of choosing well, is, whether a man likes and finds good in what he has chosen."

Charles Lamb (1775–1834)

We decide every day. In fact, all we say and do is the outcome of a decision. Whether we make the decision consciously or not, that is totally a different issue. The point is: We decide. Just imagine a situation. It is quite interesting and really gives us an insight into decision-making. Which one will you opt? You are going somewhere by your car. Suddenly, you see that a group of eight or ten children is playing on the road and two children are playing on the side of the road. You are driving the car on full speed and car can't be stopped suddenly. You have two options either to hit the group of children and killing all of them or you can choose to hit two children who are playing on the side of the road. Let us pause for a minute to think before you respond with your decision. Majority of people will decide to sacrifice two children. You might think the same way, I presume. I would have chosen the same alternative to be honest. Of course, this decision looks a rational decision to most of people on all levels be it ethics or emotion. But, have you ever considered that the two children were right because they opted to play at a secure place? Even so, they had to suffer because of the wrong choice of their friends. As the proverb guides: "He who walks with the wise grows wise, but a companion of fools suffers harm."

Moral of the story:

1. The marginal is often sacrificed for the interest of the majority, without having any regard to the righteousness of marginal.
2. Life is full of hard-hitting decisions.
3. Quick decisions may not always be the right one.
4. Right things are not always well-liked.
5. Generally, accepted things are not always right.
6. You have to pay the price of keeping foolish friends.
7. Decision is choice of lesser evil between two evils.

We find ourselves in these types of situations every day. Doctrine of election is referred as doctrine of necessity in law books.

Section 81 of Indian Penal Code, 1860. *Act likely to cause harm, but done without criminal intent, and to prevent other harm.* – Nothing is an offence merely by reason of its being done with the knowledge that it is likely to cause harm, if it be done without any criminal intention to cause harm, and in good faith for the purpose of preventing or avoiding other harm to person or property.

We have to exercise doctrine of election in every situation. We have to choose between two alternatives in friendship, relationships, family, politics, office and society. Each decision leads to some consequences.

LIFE IS THE SUM OF YOUR CHOICES

> *"It is our choices that show what we truly are, far more than our abilities."*
>
> J.K. Rowling, the author of Harry Potter fantasy series

The process of decision calls for consideration of choices. "Life is the sum of your choices." This quote by Albert Camus, a French Nobel Prize Winner, author and a contributor of Absurdism Philosophy is vividly brought to life in the autobiographies of every great person we know. Every success is a story of achievements, a process of good decisions; the summation of smart choices. We, as leaders, in various capacities like parents, managers, students and house-wives of present era, are making decisions every second. But are we making right choices? A good decision is a good choice. But are all good choices good decisions? The answer is an obvious no. So, *here is the golden tip*: "Every small choice is counted. You make thousands of tiny choices in a day. Success calls for a change and you can create change just by choosing to choose. The definite difference, between people who succeed in their lives – continuously – and people who don't, is of choice. It's about creating a pattern of success."

DECISION-MAKING

> *"You must be careful never to allow doubt to paralyze you. Always take the decisions you need to take, even if you're not sure you're doing the right thing. You'll never go wrong if, when you make a decision, you keep in mind an old German proverb: 'The devil is*

in the detail.' Remember that proverb and you'll always be able to turn a wrong decision into a right one."

Paulo Coelho, *Brida*

A decision is the final determination (final choice) or I would say a final opinion that you hold about a certain thing. Decision-making is commonly considered as a mental or cognitive process. It's that when you say "I have made up my mind." You keep on waiting, when you don't make up your mind, for right person or right thing and more often than not, later becomes never. Most of the people are happy to live with their grievances. They have not decided for a change yet. Know: Indecision and procrastination are good friends and they attract each other.

Most of the people act on wishes or directions of other people. I call these directions as hetro-suggestions. You cannot live your life to please others so the choices must be yours. Unless you exercise your freedom to choose, you will not be able to capitalize the opportunity and there is every possibility that you will end up as a prisoner of indecision. Niels Bohr was a Danish physicist who made foundational contributions to understanding atomic structure and quantum mechanics, for which he received the Nobel Prize in Physics in 1922. I would like to use his lines to say my thought. Yes, my dear friend! Are you thinking? "No, no you're not thinking, you're just being logical." This chapter, if truth be told, guides you in the art of making better decisions to all kind of problems that someone could face in life; it shows you a way to face it more methodically as well as more logically.

IMPORTANT DECISION v. DIFFICULT DECISION

"A true hero is not someone who thinks about doing what is right, but one that simply does what is right without thinking!"

Kevin Heath, CEO, More4kids

Life is full of hard and easy decisions. Decision-making is based on your value system. You can make hardest decision in no time if you know your values. You need to learn spending more time on important decisions rather than on difficult ones. It depends on your values. Save your time and energy for breakthrough decisions. Choosing a style and set of clothes for a party can be a difficult decision to make but it is not an important decision at all. However, preparing your speech at the same party is more important than selecting the clothes. This is known as theory or law of proportional exertion. You devote your time as per the importance and not as per difficultness of task. You'll make some bad decisions. It's okay. It's good for next good decision.

THE GODS DO HELP THE DOER

> *"Remember, if you ever need a helping hand, it's at the end of your arm, as you get older, remember you have another hand: The first is to help yourself, the second is to help others."*
>
> Audrey Hepburn (1929–1993)

There were many red and yellow fishes in a pond. They were friends with each other. One day, two fishermen passed by that pond, and considering the number of fishes in pond, one fisherman said to another fisherman, "There are many fishes in this pond ... we will catch them tomorrow." One red fish overheard this conversation and intimated this danger to all the fishes. All the red fishes decided to leave the pond in the night and advised the same to yellow fishes but the yellow fishes said, "This pond has been our home. We are born here. We will not leave it at any cost." The red fishes left the pond in the night. The next day, the fishermen came, spread out their nets and caught all the yellow fishes.

Moral of the story:

1. God help those who help themselves.
2. An emotional decision often leads to troubles.

3. The opportunity is a God-Gift in itself.
4. Self-help is the best help God can offer.
5. One must accept the danger and prepare accordingly.
6. You can only advise a person to do the right thing.
7. A foolish man does what he likes not what the wises advise.

THE RIGHT CHOICE

> *"You have only always to do what is right. It will become easier by practice, and you enjoy in the midst of your trials the pleasure of an approving conscience."*
>
> Robert E. Lee (1807–1870)

We know that decision-making is an indispensable art. All high achievers make right decisions. In 1932 presidential elections, Franklin Roosevelt wanted to really help the country because America was in dire economic crisis. He made powerful speech during his inaugural address. He said: "I pledge myself to a new deal for the American people. This is more than a political campaign. It is a call to arms." Guess what? His cabinet was sworn in at afternoon of the same day. The next day, he issued two proclamations, one to convene a special session of Congress and the second to declare four days holidays for banks so that in the mean time the laws can be made to control the banking crisis. He started with agriculture. He decided to motivate the farmers first. So, in the second week of his assuming office he sent Farm Relief Bill to Congress. He was leading the country in a new direction. So, next he took a decision to establish the CCC – Civilian Conservation Corps, which offered work for 250,000 young men between the ages of 18–25. After this, he decided to establish the FERA – Federal Emergency Relief Administration to help states in establishing their own relief projects. He went into a kind of reformative mood. He had already decided to oppose the Herbert Hoover's concept of "Help Oneself" or privatization and tried to give maximum help from the federal setup. Hydro-electric power, soil conservation and flood control to seven southern states were major issues so he established the TVA – Tennessee Valley Authority for these states. He addressed the home mortgage foreclosures which had led Americans to lose homes. He helped the real estate and construction markets in their revival. He decided to discard the gold standard to evade the gold runs from foreign nations. He controlled the rise in inflation. He passed the National Industrial Recovery Act in order to encourage industry and ascertain labour standards. He also enacted the Farm Credit Act and the Railroad Coordination Act. He enacted Glass-Steagall Act, which established the FDIC – Federal Deposit Insurance Corporation. He lifted the prohibition and legalized the sale and production of liquor. In these "Hundred Days," he got all the support from Congress and the press. FDR was under immense pressure during his first hundred days. He passed fifteen major laws, given fifteen messages to Congress and ten speeches. He held press conferences and cabinet meetings twice a week. He also sponsored an international conference. He made all major policy decisions, foreign and domestic in this time of 100 days. What was the impact of these 100 days? Walter Lippmann famously noted: "At the end of February we were a congeries of disorderly panic-stricken mobs and factions. In the hundred days from March to June we became again an organized nation confident of our power to provide for our own security and to control our own destiny."

Decision-making ability derives its ability from attitude. However, we learn the art of making decision through experience. We never receive any training in our whole life except when training is a job compulsion. I often say, self-interest and compulsion move a man. No doubt we learn better through experience but it is an expensive and incompetent teacher also. We use hit and trial method and consequently we are susceptible of getting used to wrong things that often get converted to bad habits. Obviously, we learn many good things along with bad ones. Experienced man can beat any newly trained man, that's a fact. But at the same time this life is too short to live it by experience only. The circumstances and situations in each decision greatly differ. Therefore, experience, to me serves little purpose. It's always a new experience. I am in favour of getting training and guidance for each and every thing. I believe there is always a right way of doing the things. Edward de Bono defines an expert as "someone who has succeeded in making decisions and judgments simpler through knowing what to pay attention to and what to ignore." Experts guide us to do the right things in less time and with less worry. You become an expert by taking expert coaching.

IMPORTANCE OF DECISION IN LIFE

> *"It is in your moments of decisions that your destiny is shaped."*
>
> Tony Robbins, an American self-help author

You decide at your home, at your workplace and in your life. There are certain decisions that you have to make every now and then. And, there are crucial decisions to be made, that can change your life. Cassius Clay, the famous boxer decided to become Muslim although after that he had to face all the bans, agitations and disliking but he did what he want. He changed his name to Muhammad Ali. Napoleon lost the battle of Waterloo because of his decisions. His decisions in leadership and communication contributed to his downfall. His judgments on important issues at critical times were not up to the mark. He chose wrong leaders and used old horse-men method of communication. A good decision is always planned. Many experts opines that John F. Kennedy in 1961 made Fidel Castro a hero by attacking Cuba. It is known as Bay of Pigs Failure. In 1962, during Cuban Missile Crisis, he went through process choices. There were two proposals, one for military action and the second for a naval blockade. JFK chose the second option to end the crisis. A decision can be like a billiard ball that caroms many times before it hits the target. Decision can have an indirect route. John D. Rockefeller wanted to have monopoly on the oil but he was facing opposition from smaller companies. So, what he did? He purchased the railways and therefore he was able to persuade the opponents because railways were the carrier of oil. We all make decisions from buying home, car, mobile phone to eating next dish or taking next cup of tea. We take on, deal and accept new problems and challenges in life by taking decision. You will get what you want once you decide what you want. When Christopher Columbus went to the Americas, he demanded and got the title of "Grand Admiral of the Ocean" along with the funding from the Spanish Government. Almost anything that a person does attracts decisions. A study of all the decisions in the life of a person is the study of his activities. The first female prime minister of Britain, Margaret Thatcher (1925–2013) was well-known for firmness to her decisions. When entered into 10 Downing Street, she introduced a series of political and economic programs intended to reverse high unemployment and to fight discontent and an ongoing recession. A Soviet journalist called her the "Iron Lady", a nickname that became associated with her unbending politics and leadership style. As Prime Minister, she implemented policies that have come to be known as Thatcherism. Have you ever sit down on your study table with a pen and a paper, to think about the effect your choices have had, or are having, on quality of your life? If not, I urge you to stop here and undergo this exercise. It is a great learning experience and a fun also.

IMPORTANCE OF DECISION IN BUSINESS

> *"Most discussions of decision-making assume that only senior executives make decisions or that only senior executives' decisions matter. This is a dangerous mistake."*
>
> Peter Drucker (1909–2005)

Making good decisions is an essential ability at all levels. In business, a manager faces new problems and challenges every now and then. A good manager tries to solve them by taking quick and correct decision that results in better exploitation of available resources in form of 6 Ms i.e. men, money, materials, machines, methods and markets. An average manager bets on better time. Although deciding not to choose has always been a best choice. Is it not? We time and again do so. We often rarely choose and live our lives by not to choose. We are acted upon. Most of the administrators if they are given two tough choices, they develop the third choice: not to choose. A manager is faced constantly with many choices and the great manager who knows the art of decision-making, picks the right choice. The ability to take "QRCD—Quick, Rational and Correct Decision" is the highest paid ability in world today. A good decision helps in better deployment of the resources. It helps the organization to realize its objectives. It leads to higher returns at low cost. It helps to develop new ideas, new products, and new processes and thus promotes innovation. All the employees and workers are motivated to participate in implementation of QRC decisions. Management is all about decision-making in all departments of business. It's because of the above reasons, I think the coaching of what to choose, and how to choose is the most important learning one can ever get. It's the choice to decide that will take your life beyond survival into thriving.

DECISION AND CHOICE

> *"What's right is often forgotten by what is convenient."*
>
> Bodie And Brock Thoene, the authors of more than 65 works of historical fiction

The word "Decision" comes from Latin *decidere*, literally, to cut off and the word "Choice" has its roots in Latin *gustare* i.e. to taste. Decision is when you think back and use the past whereas you take a chance when you choose. It's your choice to do one thing or another, but you haven't made your decision yet. With choice, there are still options, but your decision is final.

DECISION PROCESS

"Stay committed to your decisions, but stay flexible in your approach."

Tony Robbins, an American self-help author

There are prescriptive or should standards available for decision-making but we tend to decide really or descriptively. There are two sets of theories available for decision process. The first set of theories, called as sequential theories, includes Dewey, Simon, and Brim et al, who are of the view that decision-making process consists of various stages to be performed in a sequence whereas the other set of theories known as consecutive theories includes several authors, notably Witte who are of the view that stages are performed in parallel rather than in sequence. I am not presenting all the theories but my view is that it all depends on the nature of problem, whether to go for sequential or consecutive approach.

PLANNING AND SPONTANEITY

"When air conditioning, escalators, and advertising appeared, shopping expanded its scale, but also limited its spontaneity. And it became much more predictable, almost scientific. What had once been the most surprising became the most manipulated."

Rem Koolhaas, a Dutch architect

Creativity comes from spontaneity of a passionate leader because in spontaneity you can be who you really are, for example humour is always spontaneous. There is always a conflict between planning and spontaneity. Some say success happens. Others say success is planned. A person loses spontaneity as he grows older but he gains maturity in this process. Analysis kills spontaneity but in absence of planning, decisions become adhoc choices. Nevertheless, spontaneity is still the best rated quality of a great leader. This spontaneity is not foolishness but it is supported by keen observation, mental alertness and creative intelligence. You can look in leadership chapter for proper planning method and explanation of spontaneity.

THE ART OF DECISION-MAKING

> *"Human decision-making is complex. On our own, our tendency to yield to short-term temptations, and even to addictions, may be too strong for our rational, long-term planning."*
>
> Peter Singer, an Australian moral philosopher

The art of decision-making is not as effortless as it looks on the face of it. Research in psychology has revealed that our decisions are disrupted by an array of biases and irrationalities. Human decisions are brilliant combinations of emotions and reasons. A decision involves head or/ and heart. What's right for most people in most situations isn't right for everyone in every situation. I am suggesting you certain things, to make things easy, in form of a structured approach that will help you in taking a decision about a thing and in addition these steps will also enhance your decision taking ability. During the process, don't forget to take deep breaths in order to get relaxed. The seven steps to a good decision are:

1. Identification of the Problem: The first step towards good decision-making is to decide the problem. You may want to take a decision about your car, home, family, business, money, savings, love, health and so on.
2. Definition of Problem: Most of the people take things too much personally. They make big things out of tiny issues. Emotions are short-lived so a long-term decision can't be based on emotions alone. You should imagine a situation to solve this anxiety. Just imagine what would you suggest to your client in this situation? You will see the problem looks bigger when you are too near.

Majority of problems get resolved at this step. Decide what are not the problems? And then go for problem. You should begin with an end in the mind. Decide the outcome you are looking for when you make a decision to act or omit. Describe your problem in details. What do you need? Why do you need? When do you need? Write down all the specifications and get to the exact picture that lies in your mind. A problem clearly stated is problem half solved.

3. Making List of Possible Alternatives: Most of the people think within a restricted frame. They have limited alternatives. So, you need to work on the area of alternatives or options. Look for more options. I suggest crossing the available options. More options will definitely appear in your mind when you trust your brain and think creatively. Expert advice is always the last option in finding more options. Let the ideas come in from all the directions. Don't care of their relevancy. Creativity may come in form of a crazy idea. Moreover, you always have the option to cross it later on, if the idea doesn't click your intelligence. Every choice has a corresponding consequence that has an impact on our lives. This is known as brainstorming in business studies.
4. Evaluation of Possible Alternatives: After finding few right options, the next step is examining your options in real life situation. There is VIP—Verification Idea Prejudice: Most of us think that we pick the right choice. But this VIP thinking often does more loss. You need to consider the exact opposite of possible outcome and in this process you should constantly challenge the authority of your chosen option in solving your problems. You must look out for evidences and support material for each option. You will need proper research for this, on each option and should consult the experts of that field. You need to know philosophy, professional practice, theory and methodology in each option for proper decision on options.

5. Making the Decision: This step involves selection of a strategy for performance. You can select one option or combine more than one option to make it suitable for needs. You should always set a deadline for making a decision. Don't be overconfident. Prepare to be wrong: Prepare yourself for both the outcomes.
6. Executing the Decision: All the best decisions in the world will not work unless you work the decision. Every good decision calls for a good action. A good idea is a like a seed, unless you sow, it will not grow into a tree.
7. Supervising the Decision: You need to check and recheck from time to time the follow up actions on the decision and if there is a variation in the results from your visualized reality or decision is not working fine then change or alter the decision. Revisit the past decisions also.

It's certainly not the *practice* alone that makes a man perfect but the *perfect practice* makes a man perfect. You may need diverse thinking *moods and modes* for each step. So keep practicing perfectly. Take perfect decisions regularly. There is no single magic method that will solve your all problems in all situations, but following the structured method suggested in this chapter will at the very slightest facilitates you to focus on the right things. You will be able to ask the right questions at the right time during the process. In the end you can clarify your decisions better to others as well as to yourself for sure. At the end of the day, everybody will blame the decision. Yvonne Wood once said: "There are no such things as curses, only people and their decisions."

SUGGESTED STRATEGY

"When you see how the President makes political or policy decisions, you see who he is. The essence of the Presidency is decision-making."

Bob Woodward, an American investigative journalist

Govern your choices in order to govern your life. Life is a continuum of choices, and believe me you have the greatest God's gift to manage your outcomes—by managing your choices. I suggest you to select your options one by one and then if you want to spend some time on decision-making, you can assign the marks out of ten for every option or you can prepare merits/demerits list instead. You can also put plus and minus sign on each option branding them positive or negative option for quick decision. For more elaborate decision-making, select each option and then visualize your future, say for one or two years with full use of all senses in full detail. You have to always pretend that you have accomplished that envisioned future already to exert a pull on the actual reality.

ASSIGNMENT

1. Write down the important areas in your professional and personal life.
2. Take perfect decisions in above areas.
3. Make a list of perfect decisions that you have already made and try to visualize the situation at those times to get motivated.
4. Listen to the Audio program *Nudge* by Ricahard Thaler and Cass R. Sunstein.

VISUALIZATION

Albert Einstein, a German-born theoretical physicist who developed the general theory of relativity once gave a law of problem-solving: "No problem can be solved, from the same level of consciousness that created it." Using this inspiration, and to continue on this line of reasoning, I suggest you to visualize your future with your chosen reality, by using sense intelligence in full details and by being at different level of consciousness. Remember: You must be logical, correct and rational like red fish. Yellow ones will always be killed.

SELF SUGGESTION

I always make the correct decisions at correct time.

Bear in mind: Super achievers always keep their commitments.

[*Promise & Put Your Signature Here With Date*]

10

Have You Chosen To Wait?

OBJECTIVES

- To learn the "Law of Prepared Action",
- To become skilled at the art of task management, and
- To overcome procrastination.

GOLDEN GUIDANCE

"Knowing is not enough; we must apply. Willing is not enough; we must do."

Johann Wolfgang von Goethe (1749–1832)

TO BE SITTING IDLE, SIT HIGH

"He knew now that it was his own will to happiness which must make the next move. But if he was to do so, he realized that he must come to terms with time, that to have time was at once the most magnificent and the most dangerous of experiments. Idleness is fatal only to the mediocre."

Albert Camus, *A Happy Death*

Most of the people want to take rest. Look around yourself. See your boss, your colleagues, your friends, your relatives and yourself also. Majority of people look lethargic, tired and unenthusiastic. All of us want to relax too much. Charles Darwin (1809–1882) said: A man who dares to waste one hour of time has not discovered the value of life. I found an interesting story while I was reading a newspaper. It is an oft-told story.

A crow was sitting on a tree, doing nothing all day.

A rabbit asked him, "Can I also sit like you and do nothing all day long?"

The crow answered: "Definitely, why not."

So, the rabbit sat on the ground below the crow, and rested.

A fox jumped on the rabbit and ate it.

Moral of the story:

1. Idleness never brings any glory.
2. Troubles spring from idleness.
3. Many people are trapped in the web of enforced idleness.
4. Idleness is the beginning of all vices.
5. To be sitting and doing nothing, you must be sitting very high up.

PREPARATION LEADS TO SELF-CONFIDENCE

> *"Success depends upon previous preparation, and without such preparation there is sure to be failure."*
>
> Confucius (551–479 BC)

Most of the people are timid. We want to avoid unnecessary tension and worry but we want to be respected by all. Even, Napoleon had to cultivate the habit on the battlefield. Winners don't become winners by winning titles only. Winning is an attitude that is built in the preparation hours. They prepare on constant basis for years. Winning in the events is simply an evidence of their perfection in preparation. You must have observed the hawk. It is an ideal of decision and action. It circles in the sky. It is never impatient and noisy. It keeps calm and cool. It is silent. The preys on the ground don't have any idea that they are being watched. Suddenly, when the right moment comes, it decides and swoops with a swift speed that a prey can't defend against. Before the prey calculates what has happened the prey finds itself in the claws of its hunter. Final performance is the reflection of winning habit and more importantly of winning attitude. Idleness leads to low confidence and preparation leads to high confidence. One of the most ordinary ways people avoid success is by saying "NO" to take action. Bo Bennett said: "A dream becomes a goal, when an action is taken towards its achievement."

Self-confidence is one of the most critical components of success. What leads to self-confidence? Arthur Ashe (1943–1993) was one of the best world professional tennis players. He won three Grand Slam titles, ranking him among the best tennis players from the United States. He quotes: "An important key to self-confidence is preparation." Preparation builds the necessary courage, the courage to act. Inaction builds fear and doubt. I often say in my classes: The people don't realize that success comes before work only in the dictionary. Your chance will definitely come if you are preparing seriously. Say "YES" to action. Say "YES" to success.

Lou Holtz, an American football coach, active sportscaster, author, and motivational speaker advises us to act more and say less. He says: "When all is said and done, more is said than done." Remember those times, when the opportunity came to your door-steps, you wanted to grab that, but you chose to wait due to many justifications you had in your mind at that time.

People have the habit of pleading excuses, for example, insufficient education, inadequate money, physical disability/disease, bad luck, age and the list never ends and in fact, the list can never be full stopped, just because, thoughts as time goes by, become a part of subconscious mind, and ultimately, the person who pleads excuses becomes convinced that the real reason for his failure is pleaded justification. He misunderstands often, by habit of repetition, excuse for reason, of failure. Wayne Gretzky, a Canadian former professional ice hockey player and former head coach rightly said, "You miss 100 percent of the shots you don't take."

But there is a problem: As long as you keep choosing to wait, you will never move forward with your dream. So *here is the golden tip*: "A true visionary shows his vision with his actions. Action is the key to success. If there is no action, you have not actually decided." We have to convert high-quality knowledge (personal philosophy) and high-quality feelings (positive attitude) into high-quality activity i.e. positive doing.

PERSISTENCE AND PROCRASTINATION

> *"Procrastination is the bad habit of putting off until the day after tomorrow what should have been done the day before yesterday."*
>
> Napoleon Hill (1883–1970)

Do you know the difference between Persistence and Procrastination? When Poor Fellow says, "I am waiting for the right time to start" at the same time the Rich Fellow is working, even though his business may not be that sound. Wilfred Peterson, an American author once said: "Success comes in cans, failure comes in can'ts." Persistence comes from your good-self and the procrastination reflects through your evil-self.

Vic Johnson describes Napoleon Hill's Classic book *Think and Grow Rich*, a pyramid of three principles—Desire, Faith and Action. Look at success. Success is a pyramid of three principles—Desire, Faith and Action. Newton's law also endorses it. A body at rest tends to be at rest and a body at motion tends to be at motion. It means a lazy person will not do any action and an active person will continue to do action after action. Your desire to be rich or successful will feed your faith and your desire and faith together will feed your action and then your action will re-feed your desire and all these three will continue to get strong day by day. Most of us know what we need to do, it's doing it, and that's the question, we should ask ourselves, what I can do I know I need to do.

TEN YEARS RULE

> *"In fact, researchers have settled on what they believe is the magic number for true expertise: ten thousand hours."*
>
> Malcolm Gladwell, *Outliers*

Preparation is the basis of success. Practice makes a man perfect. It often takes years to get ready for success, there are no sudden successes. Jim Rohn, an American entrepreneur, author and motivational speaker quotes: "We have to put our assets to work." What appears to be sudden success is generally the consequence of at least 10 years of preparation. Colin Powell, an American statesman and a retired four-star general in the United States Army puts it in an emphatic quote: "There are no secrets to success; it is the result of preparation, hard work, and learning from failure." I wish to put "enjoyed work" in place of "hard work" and the rest of quote is superb. You need ten years of enjoyed work to get success. You need to prepare yourself at least for ten years before you succeed. Robin Sharma, the propagator of LWT – Lead Without Title philosophy, asserts: "If you aren't over-prepared, you're under-prepared. To double your results, double your level of execution. You don't get lucky. You create lucky." I call them "GOP – Genius Of Practice" and believe me they stand above all others. Success is as the old adage goes, "95% work and 5% talent."

You need 10,000 hours of practice of a specific task to become an expert so start putting in that time now. 10,000-Hour Rule was originally formulated by Dr. K. Anders Ericsson, professor of psychology at Florida State University. It is notable that in normal course it takes exactly 10 years to meet the 10,000-Hour Rule.

Is 10,000-Hour Rule applicable to all the top artists, musicians, writers and business leaders? Yes it is. Does 10,000 hours of practice make one the master of any chosen pursuit? Yes, it does. If one spends an average of 40 hours per week on carrying out a preferred pursuit that comes to 2,000 hours per year. Accordingly, you can become a leader in the field in coming five years provided you work 40 hours per week. I am in favour of spending 10 years instead of 5 years because success comes from perfect practice and not mere practice. If you are spending 10,000 hours practicing how to do something and you are doing it wrongly, you'll still be terrible, so you have to spend 10,000 hours expertly, practicing how to do something the right way each time, every time.

LAW OF PREPARED ACTION

> *"You have to be perfect in practice also before being perfect in final act. You've only one option of 'zero mistakes' to get dream score of 'hundred marks' and there's no other way to improve your greatness."*
>
> Bhagavan Nayagar (1951–2001)

It is the discomfort of psychological pain that a runner experiences when he undergoes stress of daily training before he runs the final race of his life, a student avoids all pleasures and studies daily before he becomes his man of dreams. Failures and wins are a part of success journey. There will be a constant rise in expectations of your boss, your friends and your family and importantly of yourself. In journey of success, discomfort comes first before you feel the comfort of success.

In this regard only, I am the glass half-empty kind of guy, because I strongly believe that pious hopes don't produce results because they may be only good enough to step into your greatness. In terms of practice and preparation, I am a strong believer in negative thinking that calls for fewer mistakes with improved performance each time.

STUPID CREDIT CARD

> *"Inaction will cause a man to sink into the slough of despond and vanish without a trace."*
>
> Farley Mowat, a Canadian author and environmentalist

The habit of postponing or delaying needlessly out of subconscious laziness is known as procrastination. Procrastination is the assassination of our destination. Procrastination is like a credit card, as Christopher Parker, an English actor and television presenter calls it. It is lot of fun until you get the bills. Everybody knows that sweet procrastination has a bitter taste. There are many old people who now regret not having used the time they had before their feet grew numb. Today is the tomorrow you talked about yesterday. You can keep waiting, but it never happens. Later may be better but generally it is never.

PLEASURE PRINCIPLE OF FREUD

> *"You can't just turn on creativity like a faucet. You have to be in the right mood. What mood is that? Last-minute panic."*
>
> Bill Watterson, the author of *The Complete Calvin and Hobbes*

The human beings like to enjoy but doing a good thing is not an easy task. You can sleep all day but you can't afford to work all day. It takes a great belief to rise early. You can indulge yourself in all the bad habits but installing good habits is a tough task. Psychological pain is the price you have to pay for accomplishing your goals. I always advise my students to stay away from procrastination by quoting this quote of Olin Miller: "Procrastination is an art of making an easy task looking harder." Most of the students fall in the category of procrastinators. In psychology, they call it a natural behaviour to postpone stressful times to cope with anxiety. Sometimes it becomes a grave in which opportunity gets buried. Edward Young, an English poet, best remembered for *Night Thoughts* calls procrastination, a thief of time.

PROCRASTINATION SYNDROME—JUSTIFICATIONS

"The thing all writers do best is find ways to avoid writing."

Alan Dean Foster, an American author of fantasy and science fiction

Out of "Procrastination Syndrome" people choose to wait until deadlines arrive because affected people believe: "A person concentrates more near deadlines." I tell students to study in the exam-mode: "Tomorrow is your exam day." And, trust me this approach has made a huge difference in their lives. Dr. Yogender Singh is one of my resourceful psyche group members. He has been an excellent student. He is a teacher of law now. He has the unique ability to crack any exam easily. I asked him, "What's the secret?"

He confidently replied, "Continuity with positive thinking."

I said, "I didn't get you?"

He explained, "A student who studies regularly will beat the student who tries to complete everything in one-go. This is the effect of continuity. I use positive thinking to answer the questions. I don't explain the answer with any negativity. Almighty has been kind to me. This approach clicks each time."

"Paralysis of Analysis" is the root cause of procrastination. Ask these procrastinators and they have a readymade answer, "I have gone through many self-help books and I am thinking to plan." What a great perfectionist! Stop thinking, you are over-motivated now, just take inspiration from within and start your work.

Trivialization is another reason. We take many things lightly till they become a big problem. Little things when accumulated make big difference. The most ignorant part in our life, I feel, is our health and then our family. Just stop for a moment and have a look at your health and the family relationships.

Mood factor is no factor. Stop telling yourself that you have to wait until you're "in the mood" before you take action. You can defer all the priority work and engage yourself in less priority deeds but trust me they are only distractions. If you put off doing what you ought to do, you will end up not having enough time to do it properly. So, make it a habit of doing it now.

SATISFACTION COMES FROM ACTION

> *"Laziness may appear attractive but work gives satisfaction."*
>
> Anne Frank, the most discussed Jewish victims of the Holocaust and author of *The Diary of a Young Girl*

Jack Canfield is an American motivational speaker and author. He is best known as the co-creator of the Chicken Soup for the Soul book series, which currently has nearly 200 titles and 112 million copies in print in over 40 languages. He asserts: "Satisfaction (Satisf+action) includes and comes from action." The ultimate goal of all learning is action. Do you learn for knowledge? It's good to get knowledge but a little action is always better. Satisfaction comes from a sound work ethic and confidence comes from being prepared. All the actions come from a sound attitude. Mahatma Gandhi worked day and night. He used to sleep only for four hours. Benjamin Franklin was the 15th of 17 children born to father Josiah Franklin, a candle-maker. He got only two years of formal schooling. He was an action oriented men. All his life he read. He learned and implemented. He became one of the Founding Fathers of the United States. A noted polymath, Franklin was a leading author, printer, political theorist, politician, postmaster, scientist, musician and inventor. Muhammad Ali, the great boxer trained six days a week. On schooldays, he woke early in the morning so that he could go running and then would go workout at the gym in the evening. When gym closed at 8 pm, Ali would then go train at another boxing gym. Ross Perot is an American businessman best known for being an Independent Party Presidential Candidate in 1992 and 1996. He founded Electronic Data Systems (EDS) in 1962, sold the company to General Motors in 1984, and founded Perot Systems in 1988.

Perot Systems was bought by Dell for $3.9 billion in 2009. He achieved this height only because of his action approach although his father was a cotton broker of French-Canadian ancestry. John D. Rockefeller (1839–1937) revolutionized the petroleum Industry by setting up Standard Oil Company. Rockefeller is also the founder of both the University of Chicago and Rockefeller University and funded the establishment of Central Philippine University in the Philippines. He excelled in his life by doing work although his father was only a salesman. Harry S. Truman was born into a farming family in Missouri. He became 33rd President of the United States although he couldn't complete his education due to his poor eyesight. He achieved highest position by his action orientation. Sam Walton (1918–1992) was an American businessman and entrepreneur born in Kingfisher, Oklahoma best known for founding the retailers Walmart and Sam's Club. He attained the success by his action moves although his family moved from one small town to another for several years for farming and mortgage profession in his younger days. Abraham Lincoln was one of the greatest presidents in United States history. He lacked connections, charisma, good looks and formal education. Famously born in a one-room cabin to uneducated farmer parents, he is well-known for his story of log-cabin to the White House. The key to his life was his attitude. He took action when it was required. He continued to believe in action although he lost in his life and career many times. Ask anyone and he will say: "I want more satisfaction in my life." So friends, let us have a look at the roots of word *satisfaction*. It comes from two words in Latin: *satis*, which means enough, and *facere*, which means to make. Thomas Edison filed more than 1500 patents during his lifetime and founded 14 companies including General Electric although he received only 3 months of formal schooling and lost his hearing capacity at a young age. Do you know his secret? Action. He worked 12 hours a day, 6 days a week. What's the conclusion: Enough making produces satisfaction. Frederick Douglass (1818–1895) was an American social reformer, orator, writer and statesman. He rose from slavery to become one of the well-respected black men in the United States. All his life can be described in one word: work. Please honestly observe: It's not too much making, the workaholic approach, but it is enough. Consequently you have to take enough action if you want satisfaction. The last six letters in satisfaction spell what it takes to get satisfaction? Action. Accordingly, action is the key.

HABIT—"DO IT NOW"

> *"My philosophy is that not only are you responsible for your life, but doing the best at this moment puts you in the best place for the next moment."*
>
> Oprah Winfrey, best known for *Oprah Winfrey Show*

We are each responsible for our own life – no other person is or even can be. Understand that the right to choose your own path is a sacred privilege. With every experience, you alone are painting your own canvas, thought by thought, choice by choice. So, be more splendid, more extraordinary. Follow your instincts. That's where true wisdom manifests itself. Prof. (Dr.) KPS Mahalwar has been an ideal who has inspired many individuals. He is a reputed law professor in India. He told me secret to his achievements. He says, "Time is the essence. You must make each second count, otherwise at every 60th second you'll lose a minute. And for that, I see the habit of 'Do It Now' as the only approach." Use every moment to fill yourself up. Gentleman! Use every moment to paint the canvas of your life; otherwise people will fill it up. Learn by heart: Either you act or you will be acted upon.

BEST TIME MANAGEMENT TECHNIQUE

> *"Managing your time without setting priorities is like shooting randomly and calling whatever you hit the target."*
>
> Peter Turla, an internationally known time management expert

I call it "Golden 5" or Most Important Five Tasks (MIT–5) method. Make a list of your five top priorities a night before and start your day by doing first priority and forget the rest. Take ample time to complete it, with your full satisfaction and justification. Whatever you do, just for a moment stop and visualize that you are going to do that work in the best way you know. The golden 5 can turn out to be your best time management strategy.

STORY OF INCANDESCENT LIGHT BULB INVENTOR

"Focused action beats brilliance."

Mark Sanborn, the author of *The Fred Factor*

Our superhero is famous as inventor of the Incandescent Light Bulb and The Phonograph Player. He was 12 years old when he begun printing his own weekly tabloid newspaper which he named *The Grand Trunk Weekly*. He was at the ripe old age of 10 when he set up his own laboratory in the basement of his home. He developed the flat disc, created the first fireside record player. His other inventions include searchlight, talking doll, dc alkaline batteries and then he made the electric car. Now in this time of the 21st century the electric automobile has become a part of our everyday life! It was our superhero who encouraged his close friend Henry Ford to get into motor car manufacturing.

Apart from his many inventions, he was the owner of several business companies. He was also instrumental in helping the United States of America in tracking down German Submarines during World War I. He produced the Edison Universal Stock Printer, the Quadruplex, as well as other printing telegraphs, such as the Replicating Telegrapher. I am talking about Thomas Edison, who was the originator of the General Electric Company. Learn more about his explosive life experiences, his trials and tribulations. His most famous quote has been: "Genius is 1% inspiration and 99 % perspiration." He will remain the great American inventor of the

19th century, whose inventions shaped our future. The key to his success was action. He was always at his work.

TASK MANAGEMENT—"TIPS FOR TASKS"

> *"Those who make the worst of their time most complain about its shortness."*
>
> La Bruyere (1645–1696)

I am sharing with you one of the greatest techniques to achieve success in your actions. Placed below are ten steps to master the art of task management:

1. Decide the importance of taken task in your life. Are you the best person to do this task? Is this the right time to start this task? Am I not deferring any other more important work? Before you agree to do anything that might add even the smallest amount of stress to your life, Oprah Winfrey suggests ask yourself: What is my truest intention? Give yourself time to let a yes resound within you. When it's right, I guarantee that your entire body will feel it. If you feel, you are determined to take up the task, then proceed and take next step.
2. Divide into subtasks. One of the main reasons that people procrastinate is because the project that they need to tackle is so big, that they don't know where to start. This makes them feel weighed down. What you need to do is break the project down into small pieces, so that they feel manageable, for example, the task you have been given to complete is supposed to be completed in three months, so I'd advise you that instead of focusing on three months deadline, break the task into subtasks, say one task per week.
3. And then, each subtask can further be subdivided. Like into day-tasks, and day-tasks into mini-tasks, taking one mini-task per hour. If you break down your tougher goals into smaller bits, it is

easier to manage them. In this fashion, you can have objectives to be achieved and a task at one time can make the whole task look easy. Visualize in mind the start and end of each step. Life is hard by the yard, but by the inch, said Gean Gordon, it's a cinch.

4. Go ahead with the mini-task with whatever resources you have. Start wherever you are. Never go for the complete picture of task. Just concentrate right in front of you like we drive our car. Imperfect action is better than perfect inaction. Avoid all or nothing attitude. You can have it all but you just can't have it all at once. This is law of natural growth. You were a child once. Go step by step. Live one day at a time and learn from your experiences. Tomorrow is the new door that God has opened, when the last door (yesterday) was closed.
5. You have to turnoff all the probable distractions. You must have seen the children especially when they watch television, when they don't understand what they're watching, they look away. We, adults do the same thing when we are confused: if we don't know how to start a project, we'll "look away" and start searching for a distraction or something else to do. You need to switch off your cell phone first and then take care of social media sites, email accounts and regular overlong friends etc. You should fix the hour of play and fun. Too many distractions lead to interruptions.
6. Awards and Penalties. Set awards and penalties for completing or not completing the task on the deadlines. Suppose you sit for more than one hour on your study table, you can reward yourself with a good branded chocolate that you have put for the success and if you don't keep your promise you have to give that delicious chocolate to your neighbour's little daughter.
7. Begin with an end in mind. When you find yourself deferring any work, always concentrate on the end result and the positive feelings that you will have at the completion of a task. For example: you

will feel proud that you are able to complete the task on deadlines. Your self-worth and self-image will grow and you will feel ready to take on new challenges.

8. Keep a track record of your progress. How much time have you spent on your main task? How much time can you save to invest in the task? How can you accomplish the task before deadline?
9. You can use Alarm Method. Keep alarms in your cell phone. For example: Mini-task 1 @ 6 a.m. Mini-task 2 @ 7 a.m. etc.
10. Avoid being in mood. Just do it every day, every hour and every second. Just think of it, sleep with it and eat with it and stop not till you achieve what you have thought of. Don't forget to be thankful for dreams that turned into reality.

Only one idea will be enough to get you rich. Once you have it, you need to act upon it. Nothing is accomplished without taking action and keep taking action persistently and adapting yourself to the new challenges until you get it.

WHERE DO YOU BEGIN?

"Action expresses priorities."

Mahatma Gandhi (1869–1948)

How do you put "first things first" when it seems that everything needs to come first? Where do you begin? What can be done later? And what doesn't need to be done at all? So before doing anything make a list of the steps in serial numbers you need to take for achieving the results you imagine and then decide the importance. Circle or tick the indispensable 5 steps and mark them A1 A2 A3 A4 A5. Now mark the 5 steps you can defer as D1 D2 D3 D4 D5. Now identify the distracting things, mark them F1 etc. Now you have your plan to succeed. Start with A1 and so on. Defer D1–D5. And, always try to avoid F1 and so on.

SUGGESTED STRATEGY

> *"For better or worse, about one-fifth of everything in your life produces about four-fifths of the results."*
>
> Paul And Sarah Edwards, the authors of *Working From Home*

Vilfredo Pareto (1848–1923) was an Italian engineer and economist. He found that 80% of the land in Italy was owned by 20% of the population. He coined 80–20 rule. 80% is achieved simply by doing 20%. That 20% is working your plan. A small proportion (20%) of any activity produces the majority (80%) of the results. You have to accept the fact that you stopped yourself by one reason or another. Don't worry. You always didn't know what it takes to make a start or keep working. For many reasons – ignorance, low self-esteem, sense of security, fear of failure – you chose not to act but to be acted upon. You had the power, but you chose to wait and not to exercise the power.

Whatever happens, it happens for the good. Who knows why? Past is history, future is mystery and present is the gift of god, so make it a habit of doing it now. Past doesn't matter, what matters most is that from now on you will act as if you are 100% responsible for whatever does happen or doesn't happen to you.

It is not the external stimulus but your response, your choice that makes all the difference. Circumstances can never ever stop you – it is you! You stop yourself.

Do it now in "do it anyway" style. Do it anyway even if you fear or you are not in mood. Go for it. Give it a true try. "Be a Super dad/mom to your child."

It is the strategy of "to act as if" that makes you to "do it now". And "do it anyway" makes all the difference. It is the choice to act and not to be acted upon. After all, life is sum of choices.

ASSIGNMENT

1. Decide what you really want to "be/have/do" and then act as if you already had your goal.
2. Note improvements in your personality day by day to get motivation.
3. Listen to the Audio program *The New Dynamics of Winning* by Denis Waitley.

VISUALIZATION

Shakespeare (1564–1616) was an English poet and playwright, widely regarded as the greatest writer in the English language. He has given a powerful suggestion: "Assume a virtue, if you have it not." "WTSB – Walk–Think–Speak–Behave" = visualize yourself in WTSB mode as if you were already the person you would most like to be. If you want to be an actor, visualize and act now as if you are an actor. Remember: The inactive and idle rabbit is always attacked by an active fox and often gets killed by the fox and a patient but a decisive hawk catches its prey.

SELF SUGGESTION

I always act whether I am happy or not.

Bear in mind: Super achievers always keep their commitments.

[*Promise & Put Your Signature Here With Date*]

11

Do You Doubt Your Ability To Perform?

OBJECTIVES

- To learn the "Law of Persistence",
- To treat a failure as a step forward, and
- To stick with your idea till you succeed.

GOLDEN GUIDANCE

"Making your mark on the world is hard. If it were easy, everybody would do it. But it's not. It takes patience, it takes commitment, and it comes with plenty of failure along the way. The real test is not whether you avoid this failure, because you won't. It's whether you let it harden or shame you into inaction, or whether you learn from it; whether you choose to persevere. Change is never easy, but always possible."

Barack Obama, the 44th American President of the United States

BORN TO WIN BUT CONDITIONED TO LOSE

"You were born to win, but to be a winner, you must plan to win, prepare to win, and expect to win."

Zig Ziglar (1926–2012)

You should keep yourself on track even if you fall few times. You should not let people discourage you. You should not allow situations to lower your self-esteem. You ought to be careful that you should not permit even yourself condition you to lose in life. There is an oft-told story which is one of my favourites. Once there was a wandering man who found an eagle's egg. It was a pretty big egg. He put it in the nest of his hen along with other chicken eggs. The young eagle grew up with all the other chickens. Whatever the chickens did, the eagle also did. He was trained to cluck, cackle, scratch in the dirt for grits and worms. The young eagle was brought up like a chicken. All his life he lived like a chicken. He scratched the earth for worms and insects. He clucked and cackled. And he would beat his wings and fly a few feet into the air a little better than his fellow friends.

Years passed and the eagle grew very old. One day the eagle saw a magnificent bird flying high above him. He was very intimidated and also inquisitive so he asked the hens around him, "Who is that great creature?" He asked once again, "Can I fly like him?" The hens told him, "No, You can fly better than us but that is the eagle, the emperor of the birds, eagles fit in the sky and hens feel right on the earth." Consequently, the eagle lived and died as a chicken because that is what he thought he was.

Moral of the story:

1. You should widen your boundaries and try new things.
2. Listen to your heart and try.
3. Don't listen to negative people.
4. Be all that you are meant to be.

Law of Persistence

"A little more persistence, a little more effort, and what seemed hopeless failure may turn to glorious success."

Elbert Hubbard (1856–1915)

You must have made out that, the life you have led so far, was not the one which you had expected to live when you were young. You must have also seen that when you try numerous times and get failed, your best friends often tell you that "You have no talent or X factor" or "You aren't born for this business" or "You can never be successful in this work" and similar sentences. Well don't be disheartened and go for persistence instead. Please mark: You will achieve new heights when you derive enjoyment from your commitment to work. It's just a matter of having positive attitude. Gulbir Chauhan, a Civil Engineer friend rightfully prescribes a formula of 3S – Single-mindedness, Studiousness and Strict discipline. You can overcome any problematic situation in your life by being persistent. The habit of persistence is the habit of success. Persistence is a winning blend of decisiveness, dedication and discipline that result in distinction. I call perseverance as the strong side of persistence. Walter Elliot (1888–1958) who was a prominent Scottish politician once said: "Perseverance is not a long race; it is many short races, one after the other." Failure is not a person with any name, it is an occasion.

One of my motivational friends, Rajnarayan Panghal has been successful in imbibing his enthusiastic approach in his wife Reena Grewal's life also to whom he got married in 2005. Although Reena was a topper of her PG batch and cleared national teaching eligibility test in the stream of physics in 2003. She couldn't secure a settle teaching career for a long time. She was sinking in herself. I told Raj to counsel her and only in 2012 she was able to become an assistant professor in a government institute. She stood first out of 235 candidates in Haryana. Reena also owes all her success to his husband because it was his counselling that convinced her that she can really achieve what she aspires.

Another good friend, Hardesh Goswami cleared the prestigious National Eligibility Test, to become eligible to teach in a college or university. He was the first student in his city to clear this test in journalism. Before that, during his academic career also he topped the entrance exam of Mass Communication post graduate course and got third rank in law-entrance course. People criticized him for not getting success at one point in his life. All his success came as a result of the favourable motivation that he got from his "friends and family" and the way of success became easier. Please mark: You can afford to have better choices in case of an occasion. You can choose better response. You will always have enough when you do enough. So *here is the golden tip*: "Most of us are good starters but poor finishers. Mediocre people make fewer mistakes and great people make many mistakes for they do new things. Quitters never win. Winners treat failure as another stepping stone to distinction."

There are many factors and forces to keep you doing the common things. Everybody has DNA of his success. Nonetheless, you may have your version of success in form of a vision of a new product or new service. I always say that someone somewhere is looking for exactly what you have to offer. Colonel Sanders (KFC) was having an idea to help the restaurant owners in increasing their sales by his chicken recipe and showing them how to cook chicken properly and then getting a percentage out of their increased sales.

BE DEAF TO NEGATIVITY

> *"The average person puts only 25% of his energy and ability into his work. The world takes off its hat to those who put in more than 50% of their capacity, and stands on its head for those few and far between souls who devote 100%."*
>
> Andrew Carnegie (1835–1919)

Quit-thinking is a common thing in society. Instead of changing the things, people wait for the things to change. Look at a situation wherein someone is sailing. The worrywart will always find fault in the wind. The hopeful God-believer will pray to God to change the wind. But the pragmatist will correct the sails first.

I want to share with you a frequently told short story. Once upon a time there was a bunch of frogs who arranged a running competition. The goal was to reach the top of a high tower. A big crowd had gathered around the tower to see the race and cheer on the contestants. The race began. No one in crowd really believed that the tiny frogs would reach the top of the tower. The audiences shout out comments like: "Oh, it is really too hard!" "They will never make it to the peak." "Not a possibility that they will make it. The tower is too tall!" The frogs gave up, one by one. The crowd continued to shout: "It is too difficult! No one will make it!" More frogs got exhausted and gave up. But one continued higher and higher and higher. This one wouldn't give up! At the end, everyone else had given up, apart from for the one tiny frog, he was the only one who reached the top! A journalist asked the tiny frog how he had found the power to achieve something and get to the top. They found out that the tiny frog was deaf! Since he couldn't hear the negative comments he kept going and won the race.

Moral of the story:

1. Listen to your inner voice.
2. Never ever listen to negative comments.
3. People respect the winners.
4. People never expect commoners to reach at the top.
5. Quit-thinking is the biggest negativity.

IDEA WORKS IF YOU STICK WITH IT

> *"You must try to live a life by design, not default. You can achieve anything you set out to achieve with the three p's – patience, persistence & perseverance."*
>
> Dr. Eric Shoars, *Triumph*

Once in a while an idea comes that is so simple yet so powerful, that compels people to think: Why hasn't anyone thought this before? Do you know the power of an idea? Some people say business is about idea of power. I believe business is all about power of an idea. Bisleri has 36% market share in packaged drinking water in India. Bisleri was originally an Italian company created by Felice Bisleri, who first brought the idea of selling bottled water in India. I strongly trust that though no one can go back in his past and make a new start, nevertheless anyone irrespective of his caste, creed, colour or religion can begin now and make a new ending. An idea can change your life and provide you the breakthrough you are looking for, provided you stick with that idea and have the willingness to fail again and again without being defeated.

"A lie can get halfway around the world before the truth can even get its boots on." This observation of Mark Twain rings true. All the filmy chit-chat, celebrity's marriages, heinous crimes and statements of idiots travel easily. However, people with important ideas – business people, teachers, politicians, journalists, and others – struggle to make their ideas stick. Why do some ideas flourish while others die? And how do we improve the success chances of precious ideas? People believe and circulate only those things which are sudden, emotional or reliable. Popular things travel from mouth to mouth and become a story. All you have to do is to bring a new thing suddenly and attach the thing to people's emotions. You will get an added advantage if you provide a reliable stuff. You can apply this method in any situation where persuasiveness is an asset. Chip and Dan Heath credit six key principles: simplicity, unexpectedness, concreteness, credibility, emotions and stories. The initial letters spell out "SUCCESs" – well, approximately.

SHAKE IT OFF AND STEP UP

> *"There is nothing in this life that can destroy you but yourself. Bad things happen to everyone, but when they do, you can't just fall apart and die. You have to fight back. If you don't, you're the one who loses in the end. But if you do keep going and fight back, you win."*
>
> Alexandra Monir, *Timeless*

People will always throw stones in your way. You can make a wall or a bridge out of them. A story is told often of a farmer who owned an old donkey. One day a farmer's donkey fell down into a well. The donkey cried for hours but the farmer was not able to find out what to do. Finally, he decided, the donkey was old, and the well also needed to be covered up anyhow; it just wasn't important to rescue the donkey. He called all his neighbours to come over and help him. They all grabbed dirt and began to shovel dirt into the well. At first, the donkey didn't realize what was happening and cried badly. Then, to everyone's surprise he calmed down. A few shovel loads later, the farmer finally looked down the well. He was surprised at what he saw. With each shovel of dirt that hit his back, the donkey was doing something remarkable. He would shake it off and take a step up. As neighbours of the farmer continued to shovel dirt on top of the donkey, he would shake it off and take a step up. Everyone was stunned as the donkey stepped up, in next to no time, over the edge of the well and joyfully trotted off.

Moral of the story:

1. Nothing can destroy you; you destroy yourself.
2. You should not quit when bad things happen.
3. You must fight back even in a dead end or no-win situation.
4. You will always win if you refuse to give up.
5. Patience, Intelligence and Persistence bring glory.

TEMPORARY FAILURE—DO NOT QUIT

"When things go wrong as they sometimes will,

When the road you're trudging seems all up hill,

When the funds are low and the debts are high

And you want to smile, but you have to sigh,

When care is pressing you down a bit,

Rest, if you must, but don't quitz.
Life is queer with its twists and turns,
As every one of us sometimes learns,
And many a failure turns about
When he might have won had he stuck it out,
Don't give up though the pace seems slow,
You may succeed with another blow.
Often the goal is nearer than,
It seems to a faint and faltering man,
Often the struggler has given up,
When he might have captured the victor's cup,
And he learned too late when the night slipped down,
How close he was to the golden crown.
Success is failure turned inside out,
The silver tint of the clouds of doubt,
And you never can tell how close you are,
It may be near when it seems so far,
So stick to the fight when you're hardest hit
It's when things seem worst that you must not quit."

Author Unknown

I can introduce to you the people from all walks of life who will not only inspire you but give you an idea about you how to overcome any obstacle between you and your goals. Some of the big successful persons failed temporarily. Nobody can be winner all the times. There is a poem "Don't Quit" which stands as an anthem for people who believe in law of persistence that I greatly appreciate. The highlight of this poem is: Temporary beat is not permanent defeat. It means there is something incorrect with the plan. F.W. Woolworth was not allowed to wait on customers in the store he worked in because he was told that didn't have enough sense. Producers told Marilyn Monroe that she was unattractive and could not act. Julia Roberts was auditioned for *All My Children* and got rejected. Walt Disney was fired from a newspaper because people thought that he lacked imagination and had no original ideas.

There are some notable characteristics of High-Achievers. They take complete responsibility of their actions. They know themselves inside-out. They devote themselves to purpose of their lives. They pursue their passions. They set SMART goals. They chase significance and success chases them. They believe in themselves. They believe in their ideas. They make good decisions. They constantly prepare themselves for new problems and challenges. They find their freedoms in doubt, uncertainty, fear and anxiety. They fight with their guilt and shame. They have big disciplines even in small things. They have winning habits. They laugh and enjoy their failures and successes. They always buy assets and never act reach. They are life-long learners. They are passionate with their profession. They value relationships. They have sound personal philosophy. They exercise and meditate daily. They are super-leaders. They are always grateful in each situation. They have a proper self-esteem. They constantly read motivating books, meet motivating people and watch motivating movies. They have sense-intelligence and visualize before they act. They have a well-balanced life. They take help of people and make a resourceful psyche group. They look for creative and permanent solutions to the problems. They always begin from an end meaning thereby, they persevere, regardless of the size and number of challenges. In my own view, all the traits of High-Achievers reflect in their one trait—perseverance.

FAILURE—A STEP FORWARD

"Winners never feel discouraged and treat every wrong attempt discarded as another step forward."

Thomas Edison (1847–1931)

Every time leaders do something, they learn from it, and they find a way to do it better next time. Winners would not accept no. Opening point of all great achievements is desire. Feeble desire brings pathetic results. Strong desire leads to extraordinary results. Winners would not allow anything to stop them from making their vision, their goal and their dream—a reality.

J.K Rowling, the famous author of *Harry Potter,* didn't magically become rich overnight. She wrote the first Harry Potter book on an old manual typewriter. Her manuscript was rejected by twelve publishers. After a year, she was given the golden opportunity by Barry Cunningham from Bloomsbury, who agreed to publish the book but also advised her to get a day job because there was no money in children's books.

HOW MANY TIMES HAVE YOU TRIED?

"Defeat doesn't finish a man, quit does. A man is not finished when he's defeated. He's finished when he quits."

Richard M. Nixon (1913–1994)

Many people ask for advice from me by saying that, "I have tried millions of ways to be successful with zero results!" or, "I've tried thousands of ways!" Think about it. They, in all probability, haven't tried even in dozens. Most people have tried five, six or ten (to be maximum) ways to make a change, and when it hasn't worked out, they've left. Every man who is trying, is sure to face a lot of temporary defeats and, possibly a few failures. Failure is a normal thing before success. When you face failures after failures in a line, the most convenient and the most consistent thing to do is to quit. This is just what the most people do.

Winners never give up. The book "Carrie" by Stephen King received 30 rejections and the author threw it in the trash. Luckily his wife took it out again and encouraged him to resubmit it. The book "Jonathan Livingston Seagull" by Richard Bach was rejected 18 times before it was published. It then sold over one million copies in the first year. John Grisham's first book was rejected by 12 publishing houses and sixteen agents.

QUITTERS NEVER WIN

> *"I have missed more than 9,000 shots in my career. I have lost almost 300 games. On 26 occasions I have been entrusted to take the game winning shot, and I missed. I have failed over and over and over again in my life. And that is why I succeed."*
>
> Michael Jordan, a renowned American basketball player

Thomas Edison was told by a teacher that he was too slow to learn anything. He failed ten thousand times before he finally made an incandescent electrical bulb. He did it out of his persistence. The people mentioned in this chapter hail from around the globe. The present book is also filled with inspiring stories of ordinary people who achieved extraordinary results because they overcame their obstacles with faith, determination and persistence. We have to believe that we are exceptionally talented for something, and that this God gifted something, at any price, must be achieved. In fact, lack of this trait is responsible for failure of over 90% of people in the world.

I always say that the seeds you have planted will give you a huge harvest in due season. The Vice President of Columbia told Harrison Ford that he was never going to make it in the business of acting. So even if you fail, tap yourself on the back for trying and try better and harder next time.

When Michael Jordan was cut from the high school basketball team, he went home, locked himself in his room and cried. He turned out to be the greatest basketball player and never let failure deter him. I love his one quote … "If you're trying to achieve, there will be roadblocks. I've had them; everybody has had them. But obstacles don't have to stop you. If you run into a wall, don't turn around and give up. Figure out how to climb it, go through it, or work around it."

THE POWER OF DECISIVENESS

> *"For all the sad words of tongue or pen,*
> *The saddest are these: It might have been!"*
>
> John Greenleaf Whittier (1807–1892)

I believe that you act according to your belief. Henry Ford was an American industrialist who is famous as the founder of the Ford Motor Company. He asserts: "Whether you think that you can, or that you can't, you are usually right." I have seen that persistence is the quality behind all great leaders. It is the quality that makes a person to confront new challenges and look for the new solution even when there is a constant failure of earlier analogous solutions. Winston Churchill failed in the sixth grade. He was defeated in every public office role he ran for. Then, he became the British prime minister at the age of 62. The story of Harland David Sanders is an example of law of persistence and is a fitting reply to all the lame excuses you think before you act. Oftentimes we say things like "I will try my level best" or "I will try" or "I hope I can" and so on. But, I tell you the real words of decisiveness: "I will" nothing less nothing more.

THE STORY OF COLONEL SANDERS

> *"Did you hear about the rose that grew from a crack in the concrete? Proving nature's laws wrong, it learned to walk without having feet. Funny, it seems to by keeping it's dreams; it learned to breathe fresh air. Long live the rose that grew from concrete when no one else even cared."*
>
> Tupac Shakur, *The Rose That Grew from Concrete*

Troubles and rejections come in everybody's life. One who keeps going ultimately wins. Always remember a quote of Henry Ford that is more of a law of success: "If you can't fight and you can't flee, flow." I would like to share with you another story. The hero of our story is Colonel Sanders, Yes, the founder of KFC i.e. Kentucky Fried Chicken Corporation. Can you make guesses for the reasons of his success? I would like to suggest a few: he was born in a rich family, he had a management degree from a world class university like Harvard, he started his business from his young age, and this was his family business.

To your surprise, he was a school dropout at the age of 12 and thought of this dream at the age of 65 and talking of his wealth, he got a social security check of only $105 and was angry but he activated his good-self and prepared a chicken recipe and went around the country knocking doors of restaurants, in hope that restaurant owners would love his fried chicken recipe, sleeping in his car, wearing his characteristic white suit and black western string tie, and all he got was 1009 times "No" for two years and then one "Yes".

Just think, Sanders must have used a better version of his plans each time. Normal man could have tolerated ten or twenty noes but it takes "Confidence of Colonel Sanders" to be "Colonel Sanders." Do you want to know his background? Well you can search it and you will find that he had all the difficulties and adverse circumstances but he pursued his idea with few failures temporarily without being a failure permanently.

YOU DON'T HAVE TO BE PERFECT?

> *"Success consists of going from failure to failure without loss of enthusiasm."*
>
> Winston Churchill (1874–1965)

Here are few more success stories for your motivation and to make you persistent enough to continue with your vision. Albert Einstein didn't speak till he was four and didn't read till seven. His parents and teachers thought he was mentally handicapped. His teachers said he would never amount to much. He turned out to win a Nobel Prize and still is the face of modern physics. Beatles were turned down by a recording company because of their sound and guitar music. Charles Darwin was told by his father that he would amount to nothing and be a disgrace to himself and his family. Beethoven was told by a music teacher that as a composer he is hopeless. Enrico Caruso was told that he couldn't sing at all. Isaac Newton did poorly in school and failed at running the family farm.

ARE YOU READY TO FAIL?

> *"When the weather is stormy and the waters are rough*
> *In the moment of peril the strong gets tough*
> *Whenever life presses you down a bit*
> *Stand up and shout I will not quit!"*
>
> Ann Nixon, an outstanding poet

I have narrated a few success stories as an example of law of persistence, in brief, in this chapter, and I hope that these stories will continue to motivate you each day. These stories include some of the big names and I am using their names with a few harsh words (sorry for that) to encourage you. I feel this is the only way to inspire. These stories are of positive people who were told some of the most negative things or something similar but they went on to be big successes.

Winners always have this motto: Winners don't quit, and quitters don't win. This quality of persistence demands full commitment without any doubt on your ability to perform. Nothing worth having comes easily. In 1962, John F. Kennedy gave his famous speech at Rice University on September 12, establishing the national dedication to go to the moon by saying: "No nation which expects to be the leader of other nations can expect to stay behind in this race for space. ... We choose to go to the Moon in this decade and do the other things, not because they are easy, but because they are hard." And, rest is history.

SUGGESTED STRATEGY

> *"Only a man who knows what it is like to be defeated can reach down to the bottom of his soul and come up with the extra ounce of power it takes to win when the match is even."*
>
> Muhammad Ali, a great American boxer

Winston Churchill was a British politician and he is best known for his leadership of the United Kingdom during the Second World War. His one quote is my strategy – "You can't reach your destination if you stop and throw stones at every dog that barks." As you can see, the people mentioned in this lesson are the people who refused to listen to the criticism or the experts. If they could do it – so can you. The key to success is to decide what's indispensable to you and then make the most out of each day to make it superior, yet when it doesn't look as if it's working.

ASSIGNMENT

1. Make a list of successes that you have accomplished and then try to visualize the mindset at those times.
2. List the failures at those successful times and then see the weaknesses in the idea and improvement you made.
3. Listen to the Audio program *Pure Genius* by Dan Sullivan. You can also search www.librivox.com for more audios.

VISUALIZATION

You should and must visualize yourself as a man of your dream in whatever activities you do and whatever situation you are in. The idea is fake it till you make it. Remember: You are born as an eagle but you are among chickens. It depends on you whether you will fly like an eagle in the sky or cackle like a hen on earth. It's all a matter of shaping one's life.

SELF SUGGESTION

I am a go-getter in my goals accomplishment.

Bear in mind: Super achievers always keep their commitments.

[*Promise & Put Your Signature Here With Date*]

12

Do You Fear From An Uncertain Future?

OBJECTIVES

- To learn the "Law of Exposure Therapy",
- To understand the neurobiology of fear and fear conditioning, and
- To learn how to embrace fear, anxiety, uncertainty and doubt.

GOLDEN GUIDANCE

"The trouble with the world is that the stupid are so confident while the intelligent are full of doubt."

Bertrand Russell (1872–1970)

DOUBT v. CONFUSION

"If you are not confused, you are not paying attention."

Tom Peters, a business management writer

During or before the journey of success, there are many times or situations, when you feel that you are in some kind of fears, uncertainties and doubts, and in result you may be in a state of unhappiness for not making any significant progress. William S. Burroughs, an American novelist, who was a great spoken word performer once stated: "A paranoid is someone who knows a little of what's going on. A psychotic is a guy who's just found out what's going on." Doubt is often said to be a tool of science in higher form and confusion in degraded state. I see uncertainty as an essential feature of living things but it should not be mixed with insecurity. It can be minimized with knowledge and application of laws of nature. Andre Gide (1869–1951) was a French author and winner of the Nobel Prize in literature in 1947. He had a profound impact on many writers including Jean Paul Sartre and Albert Camus. He gave a law of achieving success: "He who wants a rose must respect her thorn. One does not discover new lands without consenting to lose sight of the shore for a very long time. Work and struggle but never accept an evil that you can change. Only fools don't contradict themselves but be faithful to that which exists nowhere but in yourself – and thus make yourself indispensable."

OPPORTUNITY v. SECURITY

> *"Fear is the father of courage and the mother of safety."*
>
> Henry H. Tweedy (1868–1953)

A priest was walking when he saw a remarkably good-looking garden. A lot of people were in queue waiting to enter into the garden. The priest stood gently with many people at the gate of garden, who were appreciating the neat order of beautiful flowers, plants and trees. The gardener was watering the plants when he saw the priest. He came to the gate, out of respect, where the priest was standing. The priest said to him: "God is great. He has blessed you with a beautiful garden. You should be grateful for it." The gardener replied: "You should have seen this place when God had the whole land to Himself."

Moral of the story:

1. Super achievers look for opportunity whereas the average people look for security.
2. There are no securities in life but only opportunities to explore.

3. The single genuine security that a man can boast in this world is a reserve of information, practice and skill.
4. Life is either a courageous expedition or nothing.

FEAR OF UNKNOWN

"Fear is the needle that pierces us and it may carry a thread to bind us to heaven."

James Hastings (1852–1922)

We do not try new things because of the fear of the unknown. We have fear of death, fear of not being good enough, fear of failure, fear of not getting success, fear of not paying our installments, fear of accident and other fears. Human mind is full of fears, anxieties, uncertainties and doubts. Erik Erikson, a researcher, highlights that during the age of adulthood, 20–24 years, a young person interacts with other people. He shares his intimate emotions like love and pains, if there are successful interactions, and, unfortunately if there is a rejection, the young one may develop a feeling of isolation, fear, anxiety and doubt.

So, *here is the golden tip*: "If you are ready to exercise your doubts on existing hypothesis to search for truth in the realm of uncertain reality, then you can set the ground for revolution. Revolution necessitates stepping from the misery of known to the paradise of unknown."

DO THEY EVER GO AWAY?

"Courage is resistance to fear, mastery of fear, not absence of fear."

Mark Twain (1835–1910)

Do they ever go away? Nope! Fear, uncertainty and doubt never go away. Only really stupid people never get scared. The key is learning how to embrace them. You can find your freedom in fears. The present book is all on the inevitability to perform in an uncertain or unknown reality and to recommend strategies for using the anxiety in the region of the unknown and as a clinical psychologist Harriet Lerner says, "to be the best and bravest self you can be." You are all you can be. Go on and be it. Therefore, let us first understand these three concepts in some detail.

WHY DO YOU DOUBT?

"Our doubts are traitors,

And make us lose the good we oft might win,

By fearing to attempt."

William Shakespeare, *Measure for Measure*

Doubt is a state between belief and disbelief and involves uncertainty in which mind remains in confusion of picking between two or more than two alternatives. Doubt is based on what you know. Doubt is double mindedness. You tend to base your doubts on your personal fears. You look for faith, clarification and guidance to clear and overcome your personal fears; you look for truth based on research and updation of information or knowledge. In every faith, deep down there is a doubt. Go and be whatever you want to be but first beat the doubt that you can't be.

Some try more, some less, but all people have their doubts. It is a natural thing. Doubts unite people. Once you master the art of listening to your inner voice, you can overcome your fears and doubts. I will doubt something only if it cannot probably be true. In doubt you delay your decision to know the truth or reality. I will doubt only if it goes against the known laws of science and/or if it challenges itself. Truth never challenges itself. That's why all the adversarial legal systems in world like India, ask to prove the contentions beyond all reasonable doubts in criminal cases. So, doubt is a positive concept that involves zeal for thinking to know and reach the truth.

UNCERTAINTY BREEDS PROCRASTINATION

"Doubt ... is an illness that comes from knowledge and leads to madness."

Gustave Flaubert (1821–1880)

Everybody looks uncertain about uncertainty. But every religious believer is quite certain of his faith in uncertain God. What to do next? This is the question that bubbles in the mind of an uncertain person. Uncertainty means lack of certainty. Uncertainty never leads to a quick decision and hence raises procrastination. It is a negative concept for many scholars. You are uncertain when you are not sure because the thing is beyond your imagination and knowledge, for example, the universe, life after death and mysteries etc. I believe, it is uncertainty that single-handedly forms fear in the mind, in its diverse types.

I consider absolute certainty as a moral death. If everything is uncertain, then the future will not be open to creativity, not only for human creativity but also for the creativity of the entire nature. Uncertainty throws a challenge to human will and ignites our creativity. It's the reason why there have been so many inventions. It seems easy to blindly move down a beaten path. It seems only suitable at this time to mention Steve Jobs and to ask, where would we be if he had always taken the certain route to where he was going? He revolutionized how we communicate, how we make and watch movies, how we listen to music, just to name a few marks he made on the world.

FEAR—A NATURAL DEFENCE MECHANISM

"Nothing in life is to be feared, it is only to be understood."

Marie Curie (1867–1934)

Fortunate coincidences will not happen unless you act and overcome your fears. Fear is an inborn, natural and built-in stressful defence response of "fight, freeze or flight" induced by a perceived specific stimulus of physical or emotional threat or danger. Muscle tension, narrow or tunnel vision, sweating, increased heart rate, less sleep, less concentration, irritation, anger and shortness of breath are a few of the symptoms associated with a response to danger. Peter Guber, an American film producer, says that "Fear either paralyzes or catalyzes. Leaders must tell a story that makes fear an ally, not an adversary, ultimately conveying the message that fear – F.E.A.R. – is "False Evidence Appearing Real".

He further says that a story acts like an emotional transport, because it puts facts into emotional context and if well told, can turn people into apostles. All the great leaders turn fear into positive foundation to launch their success from and one of the amazing things that inspire to overcome a fear is a great story to learn from.

Most people view anxiety and fear as very unpleasant or negative emotions, especially people with an anxiety disorder, such as permanent fear responses or post-traumatic stress disorder (PTSD). The symptoms of PTSD can be difficult to cope with, and as a result, many people with PTSD develop unhealthy coping strategies, such as self-harm, smoking, drinking and drugs.

WHAT DO YOU FEAR?

> *"Doubts are the ants in the pants of faith. They keep it awake and moving."*
>
> Frederick Buechner,
> an American writer and theologian

What is the thing that you are most afraid of happening? Some of the most common fears or panic triggers or specific phobias are existence of evils or ghosts, death, snakes, heights, water, failure, examinations, public speaking, driving, injection needles, gang violence, war, being alone and aging etc. These fears come out of a phenomenon known as preparedness or conditioning. We, human beings, are trained to fear from the above listed fears. You can easily induce these fears, for example, most of us have taken, at some point of our life, a rope for a snake in a dark night. More than 100 times in the *Bible*, God commanded people: "Don't be afraid." But the real question is whether this is fear or something else.

NEUROBIOLOGY OF FEAR

"He worked by day
And toiled by night
He gave up play
And some delight
Dry books he read
New things to learn
And forged ahead
Success to earn
He plodded on
With faith and pluck
And when he won
They called it luck."

Author Unknown

At this moment, let us understand mechanism of fear and fear conditioning. The almond shaped brain arrangement that is basically the hub of most neurobiological events related with fear is called amygdale. It is placed at the back of the pituitary gland. In the happening of a scary stimulus, the amygdala produces the secretion of hormones like Epinephrine,

Norepinephrine and Cortisol that persuade fear. Epinephrine manages heart rate and metabolism as well as dilating blood vessels and air passages. Norepinephrine increases heart rate, blood flow to skeletal muscles and the discharge of glucose from energy stores. Cortisol increases blood sugar and helps with metabolism.

NEUROBIOLOGY OF FEAR CONDITIONING

"Most men appear wiser in their doubts than in their belief."

Norman Macdonald, a Canadian
stand-up comedian

Subsequent to a fearful incident or situation, the amygdala and hippocampus record the event experience from beginning to end by synaptic plasticity. Plasticity and memory arrangement in the amygdala are formed by creation of the neurons in the area. This fact is explained in the adages, "Neurons that fire together, wire together" and "neurons that fire apart, wire apart." If there are two neurons in close proximity that frequently generate an impulse at the same time, their cortical maps become one. This plan also works in the opposite manner, i.e. that neurons which do not repeatedly generate concurrent impulses will form diverse maps. Amygdale is also involved in long-term memory consolidation through repeated behaviour.

FEAR v. ANXIETY

"To believe is to be strong. Doubt cramps energy. Belief is power."

Frederick W. Robertson (1816–1853)

The word *fear* always connotes something bigger and stronger than anxiety. The neurobiology of fear is different than the neurobiology of anxiety. You may feel a little uneasy and perhaps have a few butterflies in your stomach before making a phone call to a big officer or minister whereas when an intruder holds a knife to your back or points a gun at you, the emotion you experience is fear. There is a clear, immediate and real object of fear while anxiety comes from imagined danger. Fear and anxiety are interrelated. Fear causes anxiety, and anxiety can cause fear.

Take another example; visualize yourself going on a road two days before. And suddenly a fast and furious driven car misses you by few inches. You experienced the stress symptoms as explained above like increased heart rate etc. Next day, when you were walking on same road, all of a sudden you feel the same stress symptoms on that exact spot or near as you felt last day but there is no car to threat you. In the first scene, there is fear and in the second scene, there is anxiety and the stress symptoms are common in both scenes.

WHAT YOU FEAR WILL COME UPON YOU

"Fear makes the wolf bigger than he is."

A German Proverb

This is a reality that "Fear is attracted to itself." We put so much attention, thought and energy into things we worry about that ultimately, through law of attraction, we create them. It can be difficult to treat anxiety, because anxiety or apprehensiveness comes in response to unseen or imaginary dangers. You must be remembering the night when you were alone and the ghost you watched in the horror movie on television made you scared and you didn't dare to answer even your natural call in that whole night. You are only reaffirming and adding liveliness to a simple situation and making it a fearful situation by being nervous.

I have come to the conclusion that most of us hesitate to go in dark places in fear of ghosts, we look for snakes in our toilets and we assume many things and feel the stress symptoms out of anxiety and not fear. Most of the women and old age persons hesitate to drive because they visualize many dangers and threats while driving and in result they don't drive, not even in their dreams.

GO OUT AND GET BUSY

"Whenever you fear choose action over inaction."

Dale Carnegie (1888–1955)

The good news is that you can train yourself in coping with your fears and more importantly with your anxieties. Courage comes when you master your fears. You have to get going even though thumping in your heart and shivering of your body tell you to go back. So, go out and get busy. Don't fear mistakes. Act because action is the engineer of confidence that in turn builds the courage, and the courage is the biggest among weapons required to grow personally as well as professionally.

FUD TRAP

"There lives more faith in honest doubt
Believe me, than in half the creeds."

Alfred Tennyson, *In Memoriam*

FUD is a sales and marketing acronym which stands for Fear, Uncertainty and Doubt. Many people cite Amdahl as coining the phrase when he left a big computer company to start his own company thus making himself a FUD target. Most of the Big Brands use this tactic to overpower the whole market and kill other small or equal competitors by attempting to instil a sense of fear, uncertainty or doubt in the minds of consumers regarding a competitor's products or services. This concept means stick with us; don't go anywhere else because we are too big to match.

I am applying this concept to our fears or anxieties. We are all applying FUD to our growth. In the real world, fear can be acquired by a frightening traumatic real or imaginary accident. For example, if a child falls or visualizes himself falling from a height in dreams, he may develop a fear of wells and heights known as acrophobia. Whenever, this child looks or steps up a high structure like multi-storied buildings, mountains and tall trees or poles, he will fall into FUD trap and will suspect his ability to cope with things he panics from, for example height in this case.

DOES FEAR MOTIVATE YOU?

> *"The cave you fear to enter holds the treasure you seek."*
>
> Joseph John Campbell (1904–1987)

The trinity of FUD can give us pain, anxiety and suffering. However, accurately valued and controlled, fear, uncertainty and doubt can become a platform to be our best and bravest selves for creativity and productivity. Inaction breeds doubts and fears. Action breeds confidence and courage. The all time remedy remains the same: Go out and get busy. Your body begins to generate certain chemicals in your body such as adrenaline when fear is motivating you. Much of scientific progress has been made by working in the realm of uncertain reality, by overcoming fear of failure and most importantly by having a doubt on previous hypothesis.

SUGGESTED STRATEGY

> *"Expose yourself to your deepest fear after that fear has no power."*
>
> Jim Morrison (1943–1971)

Never fight with anxiety as fighting with anxiety makes it stronger. Henry Drummond (1851–1897) correctly opines: "Christ never failed to distinguish between doubt and unbelief. Doubt is can't believe. Unbelief is won't believe. Doubt is honesty. Unbelief is obstinacy. Doubt is looking for light. Unbelief is content with darkness." Replace anticipations with plans and focus on the things you can control. Accept that you are feeling anxious and use this auto-suggestion: "I am feeling anxiety but I will get through this feeling as this feeling will pass." The anxiety will go away in no time. Never get lost in feeling of fear.

You can use the distraction technique also by doing your favourite routine or habitual work. We can confront our fears in a positive manner and one day we will be able to suppress the fear-triggering memory or stimulus. You can make the present moment a hell by converting fear into depression or you can build a new tomorrow out of present day by treating uncertainty as a motivation.

Military commanders use military drills or battle cry in order to induce trance-like psychological state of the battle trance in their units. Battle trance is a term coined by Joseph Jordania for behavioural activation that turns into behavioural consolidation with repeated induced behaviour.

I suggest one strategy. Make a list of things you fear from. Choose one fear for one month. Do that thing. Look at others in your age group who are doing same things with ease. This is known as exposure therapy that is response conditioning to anxiety-provoking situation often termed Pavlovian extinction. This is a journey from frightened to fearless. Start using this strategy with the easiest one then move to harder one and at last the hardest one from diverse fields. Put focus on your work not on your fear. Choose action over inaction. What's the worst that can happen? Answer to this question can help you to take on the thing you fear from. So, before appearing for any interview or exam, before any public speaking, before any phone call or before any fearful thing, just ask this question and accept the worst outcome, chances are that you and the world will live to tell the tale. The heavy breaths, sweating and increased heart rate will come down to normal. Finally, remember to reward yourself with a treat for the progress that you make.

ASSIGNMENT

1. Make a list of things you fear from. Choose one fear for one month. Do that thing.

2. Try to catch yourself when you are afraid. See whether it is fear or anxiety. Get relaxed and let it pass. Focus on things you can be in command of.
3. Listen to the Audio program *Turnaround* by Dr. David A. Russ and Christopher McCarthy. You can also search www.gutenberg.org and www.emusic.com for more audios.

VISUALIZATION

To foster real motivation, you must visualize what matters most to you instead of what matters to others. Engage yourself completely into the activities you fear most with sense intelligence. Remember: The gardener turned a useless land into a beautiful garden by treating this as an opportunity whereas an average man would have fallen into FUD trap.

SELF SUGGESTION

I live by faith. My life functions by faith. Everything I do I do by faith.

Bear in mind: Super achievers always keep their commitments.

[*Promise & Put Your Signature Here With Date*]

13

What Can You Do To Conquer Guilt And Shame?

OBJECTIVES

- To learn the "Law of Divine Humanity",
- To understand the difference between shame and guilt and
- To master the art of apology.

GOLDEN GUIDANCE

"Unhappiness is fueled by three key emotions: anxiety, fear, and shame. They are the uninvited guests in our lives. When tragedy or hardship hits, they may become our constant companions."

Harriet Lerner, a clinical psychologist and feminist theorist

GOD HAVE MERCY ON ME

"Shame isn't a quiet grey cloud, shame is a drowning man who claws his way on top of you, scratching and tearing your skin, pushing you under the surface."

Kirsty Eagar, *Raw Blue*

Jesus told a story about two men, a Pharisee and a tax collector, each one extremely overloaded with guilt and shame. The Pharisee along with his tax collector friend went to the temple every day. He used to pray: "God, I thank You that I am not like other men – extortioners, unfair, adulterers, or even as this tax collector. I fast twice a week; I give tithes of all that I possess." But the tax collector stood at a distance. He would not even look up to heaven, but beat his chest and said, "God, have mercy on me, a sinner." The tax collector went down to his house justified rather than the other. The English writer and preacher John Bunyan wrote a book *The Pharisee and the Publican* based on this parable in 1685. This parable helps us in understanding the behaviour of guilty and shamed people. Two people go to pray to lighten guilt and shame. One goes home still guilty and ashamed. One, who relies simply on God's mercy, goes home justified. Which one are you?

Moral of the story:

1. Everybody finds a place or a way to justify himself before the God.
2. Shamed and guilty people are confident of their own righteousness and treat themselves at a higher level but look down at everyone else.
3. Everyone who exalts himself will be humbled but he who humbles himself will be exalted.
4. One who recognizes his state of unworthiness before God and confesses his need for reconciliation and comes to God in humility, receives the mercy and reconciliation he asks for.
5. People seek positions and proud titles and feel appreciation when people admit their outer actions and activities.
6. Shamed people try to become a perfectionist to stay away from doing anything that will produce more off-putting feelings about themselves.
7. Shamed and guilty people always blame others so as to keep their list of sins short.

8. Shamed and guilty people prefer to hide themselves and are powerless to deal with.
9. The arrogant does not receive any mercy from God.
10. One should pray humbly to seek mercy from God.

SHAME IS MORE DESTRUCTIVE

> *"One unconsciously takes it for granted that doer and sufferer think and feel alike, and according to this supposition we measure the guilt of the one by the pain of the other."*
>
> Friedrich Nietzsche (1844–1900)

We hurt many people in our life, home and workplace through our actions. When we do something wrong and thereby inflicts pain on others, we feel guilty. Sometimes, we hurt others while doing honest deeds also. Majority of experts are of the view that guilt, if not properly dealt with, turns into a stronghold called shame or humiliation out of affect theory wherein an emotion is called as an affect that is observed through display of its typical response – eyes lowered, the head down, averted and blushing. Gershen Kaufman and Donald Nathanson both are also of this view. Kaufman wrote a classic on a fundamental aspect of all emotional suffering i.e. *Shame: The Power of Caring* which is an excellent study of how shame occurs, develops, and takes hold of a life. Nathanson in his book *Shame and Pride: Affect, Sex, and the Birth of the Self* shows how nine basic affects – interest-excitement, enjoyment-joy, surprise-startle, fear-terror, distress-anguish, anger-rage, dissmell, disgust, and shame-humiliation – not only determine how we feel but shape our very sense of self. Silvan S. Tomkins (1911–1991) authored *Affect Imagery Consciousness* in four volumes and propounded the affect theory.

Shame says you deserve bad things. "I am good for nothing" concept is a self destructive shame tendency. Bad guilt breeds hate and blame, firstly for out world and eventually settles into shame wherein a person feels comfortable in one's own personality by blaming himself. You treat others as perfect and end up feeling bad for who you are. You end up feeling pain and cringing with remorse.

So, *here is the golden tip*: "You must have the strength of character in journey of success meaning thereby, you must learn to conquer animosity against others, you must become skilled at concealing your guilt feelings, and you must train yourself to forgive quickly because when you attempt new things competition, failure and hurt happen and if you don't possess a strong character you can do the worst thing that is not to try." Sir Ahmed Salman Rushdie (born 19 June 1947) is a British Indian novelist and essayist. His second novel, *Midnight's Children*, won the Booker Prize in 1981. Much of his fiction is set on the Indian subcontinent. He once said, "We all owe death a life." The advice is clear: We should give a well lived life to our death.

IT ALL STARTS FROM CHILDHOOD

> *"The Negro needs the white man to free him from his fears. The white man needs the Negro to free him from his guilt."*
>
> Martin Luther King, Jr. (1929–1968)

Guilt and shame are with us from our childhood age. Leonard F. Peltier, author of *Prison Writings* has rightly said: "We each begin in innocence. We all become guilty." Psychological researches have shown that the emotion of guilt has been found in the children of age three to six, whereas the feeling of shame begins a lot sooner – from fifteen months to three or even earlier corresponding to some hypothesis and theories. Over the years, shame has been used as a tool by many perpetrators of genocide and hatred. Authoritative people used it to remain authority over few species by making them feeling lower. I love one quote of Robert D. Caldwell: "All the people live their life in order to heal the shames they experienced in their childhood." Understand: We surround ourselves with friends, clubs and families in order to generate a feeling that we are loveable. Your parents shamed you for your bad conduct and not doing what they wanted. In this process, you end up feeling ashamed about yourself. Actress Jane Fonda in her book *My Life So Far* wrote that her mother, Frances, suffered from a severe mental illness which would in time result in her suicide. As a child, unaware of the depth of this anguish, her mother's frequent absences from home were both hurtful and frustrating. In time, this turned into anger. Thus, on what was to be her final visit home, Jane refused to come out of her room to say goodbye. Regret for this will wound the adult Ms Fonda throughout her lifetime. Singer Ray Charles (1930–2004) in his book *Brother Ray* with commendable frankness, wrote, "I didn't use drugs because I was black or blind. The fact is, I used them because I liked how they made me feel." He decided to end his addictions when he found himself arrested during one of his sons' Little League games. If his drug abuse had reached the point where its results had become a source of humiliation to his children, it would need to be halted. Worldwide respected child star Shirley Temple in her 1988 book *Child Star: An Autobiography* does state that she kept a journal. She describes her life in details stating all the professional cheatings with her, relationships, facing sexual advances and the wrong operations by a surgeon. She was so popular that President Franklin Delano Roosevelt called Temple "Little Miss Miracle" for raising the public's morale during times of economic hardship, even going so far as to say that, "as long as our country has Shirley Temple, we will be all right." TV Presenter Jeremy Kyle in his book *You Couldn't Make It Up* wrote that while deciding whether to undergo laser surgery or begin wearing spectacles, he imagined that, if such glasses were broken during a night out with friends: "Would I stumble around blindly for the rest of the evening or would I have to go home straight away? No fun, game over, sent home like a blind Billy No Mates? Boo." Writer David Nobbs in his book *I Didn't Get Where I Am Today* recalls with regret: "I was ashamed of the cozy unpretentious simplicity of my parents' lives, ashamed that we had tea instead of dinner that we never went abroad. I'm more ashamed of this than anything else in my life. Oh, not that we weren't sophisticated. That doesn't matter a hoot. Ashamed of how much I must have hurt my dear parents." Did you get any idea about what I am trying to suggest? A man draws shame and guilt by looking backwards and hope by looking forward. Erik Erikson opines that a child of 2–4 years is quite prone to develop doubt and shame in taking new challenges if not properly nurtured. A child of 4 to 5 years can feel guilt if his act does not produce the desired results. This is the age where a child engages himself into risk taking behaviour and learns goal setting and leadership traits. And, if unfortunately the adults discourage the child's activities, the child can develop a feeling of guilt.

GUILT v. SHAME

> *"Guilt has very quick ears to an accusation."*
>
> Henry Fielding (1707–1754)

The crux is we feel guilty for what we do and we feel shame for what we are. Merle A. Fossum, author of *Facing Shame: Families In Recovery* define shame as "a painful feeling about oneself as a person." Whereas Helen B. Lewis, author of *Shame And Guilt In Neurosis* asserts "In guilt, the thing done is the focus."

In guilt a person feels uncomfortable because he has done something wrong as per his moral code. You feel guilty for committing crimes, for taking the prohibited drugs and for enjoying sinful wishes. Guilt is followed by punishments. It can be temporary in which the action that inspires guilt generally involves the infliction of pain, either deliberately or by mistake, upon another person. It can be permanent also where we feel guilty about things we feel obsessively responsible for no rational reason. It becomes a pity party.

In shame, a person feels embarrassed and humiliated when he doesn't live up to the expectations of others. We trust in others rather than in ourselves. In shame, one tends to divide oneself in-to two selves—Internal and external. Shame can be momentary because of self-awareness when we see ourselves as others see us. It can be permanent in form of neurotic or toxic shame where a person tends to keep himself away from society because of low self-image like we wish to better in terms of caste, class, colour, creed, sex, family, status and beauty etc. There is no shame in being poor, black and low caste etc. but being ashamed of it is. Shame can be described as a belief that one is not loved because one is not lovable. Understand: Love is the internal experience of being *wanted* whereas shame is the internal experience of being *unwanted*. In shame you feel that you can't do anything. One thing with shame, I have found, is that it can only be endured and can't be cured. However, one thing is certain that you can always pull yourself from it. One of the ways to heal shame is to replace shame with good guilt where you can do something about unacceptable things. I have looked in all standard books on psychology shelves in libraries and talked to psychologists on this issue, and all I can say is that healing the shame is a long hard work and not an instant cure. We will never be free of guilt and shame as they will always be there and we can simply learn to live more comfortably with them. This will bring us peace and free us from guilt and shame.

GOOD AND BAD GUILT

> *"Whoever has done harmful actions but later covers them up with good is like the moon which, freed from clouds, lights up the world."*
>
> Buddha, the founder of Buddhist Religion

Good guilt is feeling sorry for something you did. It can really act like a moral compass and can be a very positive emotion to effect positive behaviours or social change. It happens when you feel bad about your actions and want to make amends. I always say that those who have shame have grace as shameless people are graceless people. William Blake

(1757–1827) has rightly called Shame as pride's cloak. Blaise Pascal (1623–1662) who was a French mathematician, physicist, inventor, writer and Christian philosopher asserts: "The only shame is to have none." Ann Patchett, an American author who received the Orange Prize for Fiction and the PEN/Faulkner Award in 2002 for her novel *Bel Canto* suggests: "Shame should be reserved for the things we choose to do, not the circumstances that life puts on us." I am asking to have sense of shame and not to feel ashamed. Bad guilt comes as a feeling of depression when we expect too much from ourselves and from our friends, relatives and family. It is all about setting unreasonable high standards and then failing to achieve them. Some people feel entitled to get something when there is no sensible explanation why they should get it. This type of guilt leads to anger. Another type of conduct that leads to anger is to avoid taking responsibility for your actions. This is anger based on trying to avoid feeling guilt and shame. Benjamin Franklin (1706–1790) who was one of the Founding Fathers of the United States also said: "Whatever is begun in anger ends in shame." Depression is the rest between anger and anguish. Both these anger based behaviour are called bad guilt and over the time, if not taken care of early, tends to convert itself into shame by lowering the self-image. You can also feel guilt when you stop your child for not demanding ice cream, but this is false or fake guilt that is totally different from bad guilt.

ART OF APOLOGY

> *"Would 'sorry' have made any difference? Does it ever? It's just a word. One word against a thousand actions."*
>
> Sarah Ockler, *Bittersweet*

We all make mistakes in life, at home and at work. To err is human and to apologize is humanity. And, I would like to add further, to forgive is divinity. Apologies hold great prospective for individual development. Through them we learn self-reliance, accountability, understanding and integrity. In real meaning, we highlight our own character when we make an apology. Always keep in mind: It's never too late to say I am sorry.

However, a badly structured apology can do more damage than the original offence. The words "I am sorry" can stuck in the throat of a person with low self-image. A good apology at a bad time can sink any ship of relationship. If apologizing has become your habit then it's time to do some introspection. A good or genuine apology includes the true responsibility for the actions and injuries done. Whereas, a bad apology keeps the actions and injuries in doubt because of the use of "Ifs & Buts", in other words, apology is an acknowledgement of guilt and regret on your side. Try to keep it simple and straight like I am sorry. Describe your wrong exactly you did it. Do not use sophisticated words for the wrongs. Your apology must not include excuses but you can explain your behaviour why you did that. You must show true regret and take positive steps towards serious restoration.

A psychotherapist Joseph Burgo suggests that we must not go for forgiveness straightway and instead wait for apology to sink in. The logic he puts forward is that at that time victim is not ready to forgive and we are demanding once again from him in form of forgiveness. In other way, we are shifting the responsibility off our own shoulders. You must be ready to live with the guilt and regret despite having apologized. It depends on other person. I said it earlier, to forgive is divinity.

After apologizing, you should feel excellent about yourself, because you are committed to your honesty. You acted courageously and rendered your apology by taking full responsibility of your actions and injuries. And, always remember you can't please everybody.

DIVINITY AND HUMANITY

"Humanity seeks to gather and divinity seeks to distribute."

Neale Donald Walsch, an author of *Conversations with God*

One should also understand the difference between divinity and humanity. The holy experience is when you know the difference between these two and when that difference disappears. They become one when you enter into holy moment.

All the divine or human traits for instance forgiveness can be seen in the life of Jesus. He was amazingly divine and at the same time he was a simple human being too. The Ten Commandments are a perfect definition of sin and can be summarized as follows. The greatest commandment summarizes the first four commandments well, Man's duty to God. Love your neighbour as yourself summarizes the last six commandments, Man's duty to his fellow man.

The law of divine humanity calls to forgive the sinner and forgive ourselves too. By this divine humanity, we control our guilt from converting into shame. The sacrament of confession in the Catholic Churches is reflection of this divine humanity. All the true saints enjoyed their life because they confessed their sins and their difference between divinity and humanity disappeared. When we put God first and obey His commands, we will love and respect our fellow man. Stop sinning! And let us forgive ourselves and others.

SUGGESTED STRATEGY

> *"He declares himself guilty who justifies himself before accusation."*
>
> Thomas Fuller (1608–1661)

You need to stop focusing on the problem, and begin to look for the solution to the problem. I suggest you to imagine yourself in the shoes of another person and mend your action. But watch that you must not cringe with remorse feeling the more pain (more than victim) as it can turn out to be a shame. Making an apology is an essential stride in releasing guilt for past and recent misconduct. Learning how to apologize perfectly is a vital skill at work, at home, and in life. Understand the difference between what

I did and who I am. There is an art to apologizing! Knowing how to do it right is a life skill.

ASSIGNMENT

1. Make a list of the wrong deeds that you did in past and say sorry to all those persons immediately on whom you inflected pain and agony.
2. List those persons who have done something wrong against you, call them and forgive them all by blessing them.
3. Listen to the Audio program *End Shame, Blame and Guilt* by Sprudio.

VISUALIZATION

Whenever you do something wrong, imagine yourself saying sorry to yourself and to your God or Guru and visualize yourself taking a pledge of not repeating this conduct again. Imagine that you have gone deep inside your body and mind and collected all the guilt and shame, and after collecting that scrap, put it in a bag and then send it to Pluto or bury and burn in a volcano or dig it in some unknown place. You must feel relaxed after releasing this guilt and shame. Remember: You always have the option of being the tax collector and consequently you will go to your home justified.

SELF SUGGESTION

I love myself and everybody loves me.

Bear in mind: Super achievers always keep their commitments.

[*Promise & Put Your Signature Here With Date*]

14

Do Little Things Make Big Differences?

OBJECTIVES

- To understand the "Law of Accumulation",
- To learn the seven daily habits of the winners, and
- To use Pavlov's Concept in habit (de)formation.

GOLDEN GUIDANCE

> *"Excellence is an art won by training and habituation: we do not act rightly because we have virtue or excellence, but rather have these because we have acted rightly; these virtues are formed in man by doing his actions; we are what we repeatedly do. Excellence, then, is not an act but a habit."*
>
> Will Durant, *The Story of Philosophy*

SOW AN ACT, AND YOU REAP A HABIT

> *"Some rules are nothing but old habits that people are afraid to change."*
>
> Therese Anne Fowler, *Souvenir*

There is panchtantra story of one man who had many donkeys. He used to take all the donkeys to bring sand in the morning. He was in the habit of taking rest in the afternoon under a tree. He used to tie all the donkeys to the same tree while relaxing. One day when he went to bring the sand, the tying rope of donkeys fell short. He tied all the donkeys but one donkey remained untied. He took a seat and held the donkey by its ear. Neither the donkey nor the man was feeling comfortable. A saint who was passing by saw this scene. After knowing the problem of the man, the saint suggested: "Pretend to tie the donkey on the regular spot." The man did what he was told to do. The donkey stood still on its spot. After relaxing for a while, the man untied all the donkeys and started to walk but the donkey which was falsely tied refused to move. The man did all things possible to make it move it but it didn't move. By chance, the same saint was coming back from the same way. The man stopped the saint and said: "My Lord! The donkey is not moving." The saint asked: "Is this the same donkey which you tied falsely?" The man said: "Yes, My Lord." The saint replied: "O King of Fools! Will you release the donkey?" The man said: "The donkey is already free." The saint said: "No, this donkey is tied in the same way as you tied it earlier. Now pretend to untie it in the same manner." The man did the same. The donkey moved.

Moral of the story:

1. We are tied to our habits by our minds.
2. Your actions become your habits by way of repetition.
3. We become what we repeatedly do.
4. The chains of habit are too feeble to be sensed until they are too tough to be broken.
5. You have to sow an act in order to reap a habit.

UNDERSTAND HOW HABITS WORK

"If you diagnose the habit you can really change your behaviour."

Charles Duhigg, *The Power of Habit*

Success is a byproduct of success habits. Winning habits are must in order to win. Old habits die hard. Sometimes even winners have strange habits. Gail Devers was notable for having exceptionally long, heavily decorated fingernails. One of the fastest starters in the world, she even had to alter her starting position to accommodate her long nails. Her long nails came as the result of a contest her father devised to get her to stop biting her nails as a child. There is also a story from my personal life. This is about how I uninstalled my habit of wasting my time on internet and social web-sites every evening at 8 p.m. By learning how to investigate habit, I discovered that this activity happened on a definite time of the day i.e. at 8 p.m. and the purpose I worked on internet each day wasn't because I was longing a time pass activity. It was because I was longing socialization, as each time I used to make a good friend also but I got lost in social media sites overdoing it and consequently wasted my time. Criss Jami rightly says, "An over-indulgence of anything, even something as pure as water, can intoxicate." So, I reorganized the habit, and after that, between 8 p.m. to 8.30 p.m. each day, I invest my time on socialization on social media sites. Instead of contacting too many new people from my side, I try to focus on consolidation of relationships by answering the mails and messages only that too within the time frame of 8 p.m. to 8.30 p.m.

DEFINITION OF HABIT

> *"The chains of habit are too weak to be felt until they are too strong to be broken."*
>
> Samuel Johnson (1709–1784)

"A habit is the intersection of knowledge, skill, and desire." Stephen R. Covey further explains his definition. He says knowledge is the theoretical paradigm, the what to do and the why. Skill is the how to do. And desire is the motivation, the want to do. In order to make something a habit in our lives, we have to have all three. All the big companies study the consumer habits to sell their products. Your life, presently, is a result of your current habits. Have a look at your thinking habits, eating habits, money habits, working habits, etc. and you'll know whatever I am saying is right or wrong, for example, if you are overweight, look at your life style and eating habits.

I define a habit as a *persistent pattern of behaviour*, a sequence of recurring actions. A habit is something we repeat; means repeat the repeating to form a habit. So, *here is the golden tip*: "Success is a matter of installing the good habits and uninstalling the bad ones. It's not just what we do, but what we do repeatedly that certainly settles as our future." One has a good character if he has good habits and if he has bad habits, he certainly has bad character. Character is sum total of habits. Lao Tzu was a philosopher of ancient China who is best known as the author of the *Tao Te Ching*. I admire him for his association with the Tào Té Chīng that has led him to be traditionally considered the founder of philosophical Taoism. He once said: "Our thoughts lead to actions, actions lead to habits, and habits form character." Why Character is so important? The answer is simple. Character leads to destiny. This statement emphasizes the importance of thinking right. Excellence, then, is not an act but a habit.

PAVLOV'S CONCEPT

> *"Motivation is what gets you started. Habit is what keeps you going."*
>
> Jim Ryun, a former American track athlete

Ivan Petrovich Pavlov was a famous Russian Physiologist. He made a discovery regarding the mind's ability to learn information through associating connections between things that are separate but connected. The theory for which Pavlov is well-known is the "conditional reflex" that he developed together with his assistant Ivan Filippovitch Tolochinoy in 1901. Pavlov's experiment with his dog involved ringing a bell whenever food was present so the dog would eventually connect the bell with food and thus produced saliva at the mere sound of the bell. On the same pattern, we can condition our waking up with sound of alarm in the morning.

Charles Duhigg, a habit expert, is of the view that there is a three step loop within our brains to frame a habit. First, there is a cue, a trigger that tells your brain to go into automatic mode and which behaviour to use. Then there is the routine, which can be physical or mental or emotional. Finally, there is the reward. Duhigg aptly opines: The key to exercising on a regular basis, losing weight, raising outstanding children, becoming more productive, building revolutionary companies and social movements, and achieving success is about understanding how habits work. You should try to cultivate good habits as early as possible. Memorize an advice of Aristotle: Good habits formed at youth make all the difference.

LAW OF ACCUMULATION

> *"Enthusiasm is the electricity of life. How do you get it? You act enthusiastic until you make it a habit."*
>
> Gordon Parks (1912–2006)

You don't have to set an inaccessible target to be victorious. Between December 26th (the day after Christmas) and January 1st (New Years Day), many people over the planet earth take what they call New Year Resolutions. But just stop and ask yourself will you wait for a year to change, certainly not. Instead, you just need to keep doing the small things – even when the immediate results aren't obvious. Experts like Darren Hardy calls it compound effect for which I use the term "Law of Accumulation" and rightly so. Small things are taken too lightly but when accumulated little things produce huge difference.

The "Law of Accumulation" is the law of reaping massive rewards from a sequence of small and smart choices. For instance, most of us have given up the hope of being in shape after the tenth day of running because we were still overweight at the tenth day, although, deep inside we knew that little by little we accumulated the fat and the way to lose fat is the same—little by little. You can learn a good habit and unlearn the bad ones through this method.

PERSISTENCE IS THE KEY

> *"H is for Habit, winners make a habit of doing the things losers don't want to do."*
>
> Lucas Remmerswaal, *The A–Z of 13 Habits*

Winners have a habit of winning. Lucas Remmerswaal asserts that H stands for habit in winners' dictionary. All the great empires like Egyptians, Greeks, Romans, Spanish, Portuguese, French and English collapsed just due to complacency. I always say this "Nothing fails like success" by citing these great empires as an example. When we have prosperity, health and wealth, consequently, we become complacent as a result. Experts emphasize the power of little incremental improvements over time to create considerable effects in life. Most of us have a tendency to get too comfortable when we get a certain level of comfort in terms of income and wealth. We stop doing what we did to get us there.

A leadership specialist David Cottrell reveals the eight basic truths of success, including: No Matter What: accept your responsibilities, maintain focus, and move forward, And Then Some: give a little more than people expect, Above All Else: know what is non-negotiable at work and in life, From Now On: earn from your failures and refuse to make the same mistake twice, Consider It Done: deliver on your word, without fail.

SUCCESS: RESULT OF HABITS

> *"Once you learn to quit, it becomes a habit."*
>
> Vince Lombardi (1913–1970)

Successful people and winners mesmerize every one of us. We always speculate what makes them so special that they look different from others. Consequently, we read books on the subject of "SSP – Success and Successful People" and make an effort to detect what are the winning habits that winners have. One such success was Vince Lombardi (1913–1970) who was an American football player, coach and executive. He is best known as the head coach of the Green Bay Packers during the 1960s, where he led the team to three straight and five total league championships in seven years, including winning the first two Super Bowls following the 1966 and 1967 NFL seasons. The National Football League's Super Bowl trophy is named in his honour. He was enshrined in the Pro Football Hall of Fame in 1971. He once said: "Winning is not a sometime thing; it's an all time thing. You don't win once in a while, you don't do things right once in a while, you do them right all the time. Winning is habit. Unfortunately, so is losing." Aristotle is also an inspiration who was a Greek philosopher and polymath, a student of Plato and teacher of Alexander the Great. He asserts: "Quality is not an act it is a habit." Successful people are very much similar *in terms of their habits* regardless of what profession they work in or what passion they are pursuing. There are some daily habits that almost all successful people have. Here are the seven of them that I have discovered, these are: waking up early, working on priorities, keeping same spot for daily items, being in perfect shape, living in present, eating healthy food and reviewing the day. Let us have a brief discussion on all these habits.

INDUCTION HOURS

> *"It is well to be up before daybreak for such habits contribute to health, wealth, and wisdom."*
>
> Aristotle (384 BC–322 BC)

Do you wake up each morning and ask yourself, "What good shall I do this day?" Most of us do not. I am also a big fan of getting up at 5 a.m.

because I complete my winning habits like exercise and meditation before 8 a.m. and it gives me a competitive edge. We all accept as true that getting up early is a good habit. How to achieve this success? You should avoid sudden changes in your waking time like an hour or two because it will not last too long since the body will try to fill the deficit next day because of biological clock system. The best method to change your waking time is to do it *slowly but surely*.

It's not that you're not a morning person but the problem is that you tried to change too quickly each time. You have to leave the evening person image and work on maintaining relations otherwise. Maintaining a regular sleep pattern is the vital factor. The key is to avoid CAS – Caffeine, Alcohol and Sugar in evening because these three things affect soundness of your sleep and make you restless. After winding up all day's work, I advise you to read few pages of a book on bed because it's not good to go to bed with active mind.

All the success coaches tell you to wake up early and deal with the day before or at sunrise, but the common man timetable may vary depending on the circumstances. When the schedule is hectic, you put your best, and the next morning you keep on pressing snooze button in mobile again and again. At that time your effort is to get out of the bed at last feasible minute. Consequently, the morning becomes the part of the day you hate most. Why? You chase the things in a hurry. The bath is taken in a rush. The breakfast is generally not eaten fully. You reach your office late. You have to win the battle of bed. You can't allow the mind to rest too much on mattress.

You have to makeover your morning routine. When you have ample time in your hands you will enjoy doing the things. During the morning hours you will feel to have maximum clearness and creativeness. This is when I habitually do my planned belief by revising my statements after a little bit of meditation. I visualize what I believe. I call these "Induction Hours" because these hours set the pace to your whole day with endless possibilities. You should watch News Headlines on television and read newspaper quickly in order to be generally aware. I deal with news when I take my breakfast. You can also listen to motivational podcasts and audio books in this hour or you can do it my way, I prefer to listen during the commute to my workplace.

PUT FIRST THINGS FIRST

> *"Character is a habit, the daily choice of right over wrong; it is a moral quality which grows to maturity in peace and is not suddenly developed on the outbreak of war."*
>
> Charles Wilson (1933–2010)

Winners believe that life is too short to waste on small things; therefore, they invest their precious time only on their priorities and not on obligations. If you find yourself in the middle of uncertainty or doubt, ask yourself: "If I could only finish one thing today, what would it be?"Is this the best use of my time right now?" This is the best formula to prioritize. You must learn to say no to trivial tasks, in spite of fear of losing the friendship. People who achieve big success have an end in mind. They recognize what they want and they commit themselves to attain it.

Winners don't oblige anybody except themselves because they are not over-ambitious. I spend my precious time on what I love most, which is improving myself and my relationships. So I say "I love you" to my family members twice a day at least and appreciate my friends. I make an effort to send a quick email or text to a friend each day. It's a great way to stay in touch with friends when I am exceedingly full of activities.

All the successful people prefer to complete today's work on today itself. They have a big engine. They work hard and are not lazy. They try different ideas so they fail often. They try fast so they fail fast without being a failure. They address each paper, letter and complete their "TDL – To Do List" on daily basis. They keep their inbox clean whether it is inbox of their phone, or inbox of their email id or inbox of their day. They save the important ones and trash the others. They are ever ready for learning new things by keeping their inbox clean.

Another thing, I have seen in nearly all the successful people is that they switch off their phones when they are in important meeting or while sleeping or having fun because they know how to relax. Therefore, I say successful people have an on–off switch.

SAME SPOT THEORY

> *"Less is more."*
>
> Wieland (1733–1813)

I have seen it in my father's life that he used to keep his wallet and other daily articles like cell phones, car keys, hand watch and handkerchiefs at the same place. I have a favourite spot too for these items and I have never been late for work wondering where my keys or cell phones are hiding. I prefer to declutter my wallet on daily basis in the morning. I love one quote of Jean Fleming: "Life is simplified when there is one centre; one reason, one motivation, one direction and purpose.""Daily De-Cluttering" is the master key whether it is your daily work, your cell phone inbox, your wallet or your life.

SHAPE PLAYS ITS ROLE

> *"For too long, and despite what people told me, I had fallen for what the culture said about beauty, youth, features, heights, weights, hair textures, upper arms."*
>
> Anne Lamott, an American writer

Your body shape does play a unique role in treating yourself; you respect and love yourself more when you are in shape. Rajnarayan Panghal, a journalist and a social thinker has developed what he calls as formula of *NDS – Nomination, Driving and Swimming.* You will be amazed to see his thinking. He says, "In India, a child can get admission in swimming classes at the age of seven, and if he gets that admission and continues with swimming, he can keep his body in great shape. Stamina is an added advantage." What about Driving? I asked him. He replied, "In India, a person can get a driving license at the age of 18 and if he gets that license and knows driving skill, he will excel in his life because he can go wherever and whenever he wants to go. He can maintain his social circle. He will learn to value the time." I was inquisitive on another one. I threw my question at him, "What is this nomination?" He answered, "One can get different jobs and positions at a specific age, and if you continue with a little watchfulness, no one can stop you. In spite of everything, at least in theory one can become President of India at 35." He laughed. I endorse his thoughts fully especially the swimming and driving parts.

Being in shape affects the way others treat you and more importantly people develop a perception by your first look before they get to know you further. At workplace, successful people are treated as a constructive force who acts from authority. Why? For the reason that they put into effect what is known as *Halo Effect* by being physically attractive and by this effect they fetch more assignments than others. Thin waist in woman and huge biceps in man attracts. Successful people exercise in gym to stay in shape or at least they find a cardio activity as a habit like swimming, running, cycling or playing volleyball etc. that challenges and increases heart rate. Being physically fit gives you extra confidence to put more energy in your work and thereby you increase your chances of success.

LIVE IN NOW

"The living moment is everything."

D.H. Lawrence (1885–1930)

Neither the past is real nor is the future. You look at past and future through mind's eye with the help of thinking. When you think back, it is called past and when you think ahead, it is known as future. The past is a memory you re-experience in the present, therefore, past leads to proud or guilt. The future is a projection you create in your mind; consequently, it leads to fear, uncertainties, doubts and anxieties. Past is no more and future is not yet. Both are process of disturbing the mind except when it is intentional in the induction or review hour. All the successful people have mastery over the art of living, that is, they live in the present and they think right now and they act right now. Moreover, you reconnect with nature when you live in present frequently or rather I would say you exist in nature when you live in present.

EAT HEALTHY

> *"He that takes medicine and neglects diet, wastes the skill of the physician."*
>
> Chinese Proverb

All winners plan their diet. Make the habit of drinking one glass of water after you wake up in the morning. When you wake up, your body is dehydrated and needs water. Diet is only one part of the equation apart from exercise and sleep but for me it is the most important. You are what you eat. La Rochefoucauld has rightly said: "To eat is a necessity, but to eat intelligently is an art." Therefore, I suggest you to plan your daily meal well in advance. I also recommend you to substitute the chips, candy and chocolate with fruit, vegetables and nuts. You can have a preference to take at least one glass of juice and one glass of milk per day. I advise you to have a balance between protein, fats and carbohydrates. I believe in eating more vegetables and fruits – the more colourful and wide-ranging, the better. I limit salt and sweet intake in my foods. I always take and advise food supplements as I think normal foods are not good in terms of nutrition.

REVIEW HOUR

"Every day we need to ask ourselves the question: Am I getting any closer to my purpose in life? Am I making this a better place to live? If the answer is no, then I have just wasted a day of my life."

Shiv Khera, *You Can Win*

At the end of the day, you should visualize your day ahead. Close your eyes and visualize what you want to happen in the upcoming day. For this, first you can prepare a to do list of Most Important Five Tasks (MIT–5) and then you have the liberty to dive deep into imagination and see what you want to happen next day. This is known as "Law of Attraction".

You should review your day activities in review hour. Life will reward us in proportion to our contribution. You can use time log to get a clear picture of how you are spending your time and make the necessary adjustments. I find this is a great technique to get nearer to accomplishing my goals. If there is a gap between promise and performance, you can analyze and improve over that. You should develop a habit of rewriting your short, medium and long term goals in the review hour. Eliminating the non-priority tasks is important part of target setting. As one task is finished I put a cross against the task. So easy, yet so useful. You must fix the time to go to bed with at least six to eight hour to sleep with. I go to bed at 10 p.m. and I try to sleep at 11 p.m. after reviewing my whole day for an hour. You can read one book per week, as I do, if you just read few pages per day in this hour. I prefer to lay out my clothes for the next day and pack my bag the night before.

SUGGESTED STRATEGY

"Only a habit can subdue another habit."

Og Mandino, *The Greatest Salesman In The World*

It took me a number of months to set out from waking at 7 a.m. to 5 a.m. The key was to improve it slowly by chipping away at 10–15 minutes at one time and then conditioning the body for a week or so. The strategy is to take small steps and be patient. You focus on one change for thirty days. After that time it becomes a habit. Multitasking often means none becomes a habit. Making a public commitment to everyone can compel you to stick with it. I always offer myself a reward if I make it a month. You must have reasons to support your goals. For instance, it is quite easy to lose weight and to get in shape when you are getting married in next three months.

ASSIGNMENT

1. Prepare your daily meal plan on calorie intake in consultation with nutrition expert.
2. Fix your exercise routine in consultation with fitness expert.
3. Fix your waking up and sleeping time.
4. Listen to the Audio program *The 7 Habits of Highly Effective People* by Stephen Covey. You can also search www.librophile.com for more audios.

VISUALIZATION

When you do something, visualize what you want to happen day after day. Remember: Even the donkey couldn't move just due to a simple yet powerful feeling of knotting. Success is built on each day. "Success is", asserts Jim Rohn, "a few disciplines repeated on a daily basis."

SELF SUGGESTION

Every day, I am developing new and positive habits.

Bear in mind: Super achievers always keep their commitments.

[*Promise & Put Your Signature Here With Date*]

15

Are You Too Afraid To Laugh?

OBJECTIVES

- To learn the "Law of Laughing Success",
- To understand that "successful people laugh", and
- To become expert at the art of crafting the fun.

GOLDEN GUIDANCE

"I love people who make me laugh. I honestly think it is the thing I like most, to laugh. It cures a multitude of ills. It's probably the most important thing in a person."

Audrey Hepburn (1929–1993)

GOD DISPOSES WHAT MAN PROPOSES

"That which we expected is not accomplished. While for the unexpected, God finds a way. Man thinks, but God decides."

Euripides, *Andromache*

Sometimes, we make a plan and leave no stone unturned to realize it, but many times our well premeditated plans also fail at the last minute. That's why we say: Man proposes but God disposes. I am sure God laughs when we tell Him our plans. I am double sure God laughs even louder when we tell Him how much we know. Understand: God will not allow Himself to be barred from the workings and devices of His creation. I read a story somewhere. Three women died in an accident and went to heaven. When they arrived Saint Peter warned: "Here is only one rule: Don't step on the ducks." They made the promise. Consequently, they came in but they saw that there were ducks all over. It was nearly impossible not to step on one of the ducks. Three women tried very hard. One day, the first woman had an accident and stepped on one duck. Saint Peter came with the ugliest man ever seen, put them (The 1st woman and the ugliest man) together in chains and said: "That's your punishment for stepping on a duck, and forever you'll be chained to this ugly man." Next day, the number two woman stepped on a duck. The man who misses nothing, Saint Peter came with an another ugly man, put them (The 2nd woman and the ugly man) together in chains and said: "That's your punishment for stepping on a duck, and forever you'll be chained to this ugly man." The third woman had seen what happened to two women, and didn't want that to happen to her, so she walked very carefully. She managed not to step on the ducks for some months. She forgot to laugh in this pursuit. One day Saint Peter came to her with the most handsome man ever seen. Saint Peter put them (The 3rd woman and the most handsome man) together in chains without a word. The happy woman said: "I wonder what happened, since I should be chained with you forever." The man said: "I don't know what you did, but I stepped on a duck." The woman laughed with all her heart.

Moral of the story:

1. Life is very tough even in heaven.
2. You can't avoid the unavoidable with utmost care.
3. People forget to laugh even while doing day to day works.
4. One should laugh because in the end God disposes what man proposes.
5. You should do the best you can but you can't control everything.
6. There are certain things in our life that will happen like old age, illness, stress, etc.
7. You can plan out and think up whatever you like, but, in the end, it will be God who will decide the outcome of it.

HUMOUR IS THE GREATEST ASSET

I Know 10 Facts About You

Fact 1 : You are reading this.
Fact 2 : You can't say the letter "m" without touching your lips.
Fact 3 : You just tried it.
Fact 4 : You're smiling.
Fact 6 : You're smiling/laughing again.
Fact 7 : You didn't notice I missed fact 5.
Fact 8 : You just checked it.
Fact 9 : You're smiling again.
Fact 10 : You like this.

Did you smile or laugh at duckland story? Having a sense of humour is the greatest asset a person can have, because it can diffuse difficult situations. The observance of Law of Laughing Success can be found in the life of Navjot Singh Sidhu, former Indian cricketer. In fact he has a larger than life image because of his language and sense of humour. I have also found that group laughter can make you interact with people in a great way and lessen your stress level. Humour is a multi-disciplinary field of research. People have been working on humour in many fields of research like psychology, philosophy and linguistics, sociology and literature. William Makepeace Thackeray was an English novelist of the 19th century. He was famous for his satirical works. He has gone to the extent of calling "a good laugh as sunshine in the house." Fortunately, just about everybody can laugh. So, *here is the golden tip*: "Laughing is a celebration of good. Laughing is what makes life fun. When you laugh, you release your good-self." Eyes moisten during laughter as a reflex from the tear glands. I would rather say you reveal your good-self. Enjoy your life, regardless of how tough it may appear. When life gives you a hundred reasons to shed tears, be an evidence for the world that one can always have a thousand reasons to smile.

MAGICAL TALISMAN

"Laughter is the remedy for 1001 illnesses."

An Azerbaijani Proverb

This magical talisman, which I am going to share with you, has done miracles for many. It is the ability to laugh, play, and have fun with others. "The more you laugh, the more prosperous and successful you will be." Andrew Carnegie puts the law in better words: "There is little success where there is little laughter." Laughter is a sign of progress, because at the end of day, if you cannot laugh, how can you say that you are successful. Humour is a natural stress-reducer and best medicine. Sigmund Freud opines that laughter releases tension and psychic energy. I often remember Prof. (Dr.) S.S. Sheelwant who taught me during my college days. He was fabulous in one aspect. He has the unique ability to tell the difficult things in the easiest of ways. You will never find him sad. He always looks energetic and pleasing simply because of his attitude towards the life. He asserts: "You can treat any given thing as hard as you want but at the same time you can also treat a hardest thing as simple as you want." Sir William Osler was a Canadian physician. He was one of the Big Four founding professors at Johns Hopkins Hospital, located in Baltimore in Maryland. He has called laughter as the music of life. Understand: Laughter reduces stress hormones such as cortisol and epinephrine. It helps you keep a positive, optimistic outlook through difficult situations. Laughter is critically important to successful social interactions. Humour and shared laughter strengthen our relationships.

GOD IS A COMEDIAN

A guide was explaining the uniqueness of Niagara Falls to people: "I welcome you all to Niagara Falls. These are the world's largest waterfalls and the sound intensity of waterfalls is so high that even 20 supersonic planes passing by can't be heard. Now, may I request the awesome ladies to keep quiet so that we can hear the Mighty Niagara Falls?"

The law of Laughing is indispensable to be successful. When you laugh, your pure presence do miracles, I mean everybody will look at you as a source of happiness, joy and love. There are thousands of languages, hundreds of thousands of dialects, but everyone laughs in pretty much the same way. François-Marie Arouet, known by his nom de plume Voltaire, was a French Enlightenment writer, historian and philosopher famous for his wit. He once said: "God is a comedian, playing to an audience too afraid to laugh."

Ella Wheeler Wilcox (1850–1919) was an American author and poet. Her best-known work was *Poems of Passion*. Her most enduring work was *Solitude* which contains the lines: "Laugh, and the world laughs with you; Weep, and you weep alone." Her autobiography, *The Worlds and I*, was published in 1918, a year before her death. I am sharing few inspiring lines from solitude:

"Rejoice, and men will seek you;

Grieve, and they turn and go.

They want full measure of all your pleasure,

But they do not need your woe.

Be glad, and your friends are many;

Be sad, and you lose them all.

There are none to decline your nectared wine,

But alone you must drink life's gall."

From the poem *Solitude*
written by Ella Wheeler Wilcox

LAUGHTER—TRUE JOY

Interviewer : "To whom do you own your success as a millionaire?
Millionaire : "I owe everything to my wife."

Interviewer : "Wow, she must be some special woman.
Interviewer : "What were you before you married her?"
Millionaire : "A Billionaire."

Laughing is an involuntary reaction to certain external or internal stimuli like jokes, stories or thoughts. It is a regular series of short vowel-like syllables usually transcribed as ha-ha, ho-ho or hee-hee. It is very hard to have a laugh structure of ha-ho-ha-ho but ho-ha-ha or ha-ha-ho laughs are possible. The sound of roaring laughter is far more contagious than any cough, sniffle or sneeze. Laughter can never be induced, it comes from within. But I am a great believer in the concept of Laughter Yoga which is based on a scientific fact that the body cannot differentiate between fake and real laughter. One gets the same physiological and psychological benefits. Laughter is also extremely difficult to control wilfully. Try asking your good friends to laugh on your wish, for instance. Most will say, "I can't giggle or chuckle on command." We are not sale guys who are perfect in giving fake smiles. Thomas Carlyle (1795–1881) was a Scottish philosopher, satirical writer, and teacher during the Victorian era. He gave a law of smile: "A laugh, to be joyous, must flow from a joyous heart, for without kindness, there can be no true joy." Know: Genuine people laugh not only with mouth but from eyes as well—from their whole existence.

EMULATE CHILDREN

Teacher : Correct the sentence, "A bull and a cow is grazing in the field."
Student : "A cow and a bull is grazing in the field."
Teacher : "How?
Student : "Ladies first."

Laughter is our birthright. Infants start smiling during the first weeks of life. According to some studies, infants as early as 17 days old have vocal laughing sounds or laughter. Researchers have also shown that an average baby laughs around 300 times a day compared to an average adult, who laughs only around 20 times a day. The new baby when he laughs looks like that he is saying to the world: "I am all set to mingle." Children are the experts on playing, taking life lightly, and laughing. They have the ability to live, love, laugh, play and have fun with people and things. One of the techniques they innocently resort to is that they convert their problems into games.

GELOTOLOGY

> *"I made the joyous discovery that ten minutes of genuine belly laughter had an anesthetic effect and would give me at least two hours of pain-free sleep."*
>
> Norman Cousins (1915–1990)

Norman Cousins developed a recovery program incorporating megadoses of Vitamin C, along with a positive attitude, love, faith, hope and laughter. He found that laughter has painkilling effect and induces a sound sleep also. When you laugh the brain releases endorphins that can relieve some physical pain. Laugh and it will detoxify your whole existence. How important is it for us to laugh about our health and fitness? There is a separate discipline Gelotology (from the Greek *gelos*, meaning laughter) which is the study of laughter and its effects on the body, from a psychological and physiological perspective. Research suggests that laughter really may be the best medicine; laughter provides a vigorous workout to tighten your tummy and strengthen your heart, and regular laughing may boost your immune system. Laughter boosts the number of antibody-producing cells and enhances the effectiveness of T-cells, leading to a stronger immune system. In 2005, researchers at the University of Maryland Medical Center found that laughter causes the dilatation of the inner lining of blood vessels, the endothelium, and increases blood flow. There is no known laugh centre in the brain. Neurophysiology indicates that laughter is linked with the activation of the ventromedial prefrontal cortex that produces endorphins. Scientists have shown that parts of the limbic system are involved in laughter. This system is involved in emotions and helps us with functions necessary for humans' survival. The structures in the limbic system that are involved in laughter: the hippocampus and the amygdale.

GO FOR MORE

A man at art gallery: I suppose this horrible looking thing is what you call modern art?
Art Dealer: I beg your pardon sir, that's a mirror.

Smiling is the beginning of laughter. Like laughter, it's contagious. Smile and laughter both involve 15 facial muscles. William Penn Adair "Will" Rogers (1879–1935) was an American cowboy, vaudeville performer, humourist, social commentator and motion picture actor. He was one of the world's best-known celebrities in the 1920s and 1930s. He remarked: "There's never a vegetable that can make people laugh." So go for more ... don't smile, laugh instead and prosper. Laughter is a powerful antidote to stress, pain and conflict. You can afford to be funny with sense of humour but without sense of humour, laughing looks silly. You must be able to laugh at or at least see the humour in difficult situations of life. Humour is all about finding the correct pauses to laugh. "Forever, at start or at last, never in between" is the golden rule.

THE TALENT OF BEING FUNNY

A teacher asked her class for sentences using the word "beans".

"My father grows beans" said one student.

"My father cooks beans" said another student.

Then little boy stood up and spoke: "We are all human beans."

The art of telling the funny story or funny jokes is a unique endowment of a successful person. Most of the authorities are of the view that anyone can acquire this ability and be the master of crafting fun. "Comedy Nights with Kapil" – An Indian Television show has become success because of Kapil Sharma's talent of being funny. Being funny does not mean that you are bad-mannered and disrespectful to others. It means you share a laughter together. High-quality delivery, accurate timing, precise words can make the situation memorable. All successful people plan and prepare their funny stories or funny jokes. The amateur does the opposite. He spoils a really good story or a joke with poor delivery, inaccurate timing and needless words.

ART OF CRAFTING FUN

> *"Laughter is a mechanism everyone has; laughter is part of universal human vocabulary."*
>
> Robert Provine, a laughter expert

According to Nietzsche, humour can be used for both positive and negative roles. A thinker when uses humour to get relaxed is using humour in positive sense but in social conflicts humour can be destructive. The old wise saying "it's not *what* you say but *how* you say it," makes the quality of voice very important part of communication, be it funny stories or amusing anecdotes. High-quality deliverance attracts and holds the concentration of people. Pantomimists like Charlie Chaplin, Buster Keaton, Stan Laurel and Marcel Marceau show the emphasis of gestures in what you are saying. Dorothy Parker, one of our wittiest writers of the twentieth century, was brilliant with one-liners.

I mean you should take extra care of your gestures, facial expressions, vocal varieties, timings, pauses and punch lines while using humour. You should never rush for the punch line and instead should use pregnant pauses to generate the curiosity. You can start by being a clown in your family. You should stay in highlight as far as possible and learn to be comfortable with people.

STUDY FUNNY PEOPLE

A teacher broke traffic signal. Police officer arrested her.

Teacher : "Please let me go, I am a teacher."

Police officer : "Oh ho! I have waited this moment whole year." Now write 10,000 times that "I will never break Traffic signal again."

I advise the readers to study the funny people. I would strongly recommend you to study the works of Mark Twain, Robert Benchley, James Thurber, Dorothy Parker, George S. Kaufman, George Bernard Shaw, Henrik Ibsen, Nikolai Gogol, Oscar Wilde, P.G. Wodehouse, Stephen Fry, Kaz Cooke, Sarah Silverman, Woody Allen, Bill Bryson, Bill Watterson and Doughlas Adams. You can also look for Shaun Micallef, Groucho Marx, Zach Galifianakis, John Cleese, Maria Bamford, Stephen Colbert, Bill Cosby, Danny Kaye, Dame Edna Everage and Tina Fey for more inspiration in laughing. One of the greatest comedic geniuses was Steve Allen who wrote forty-one books and nearly 5,000 songs and won many awards. Steve Allen's *The Funny Men, Funny People, More Funny People* and *How To Be Funny* are great works. Gene Parrot's *How To Hold Your Audience With Humour* is indispensable. Mel Helter's *Comedy Techniques for Writers and Performers* can also be a great aid around.

PARADISE v. HELL

> *"Life is the definition you give to events that occur. This life is for loving, sharing, learning, smiling, caring, forgiving, laughing, hugging, helping, dancing, wondering, healing, and even more loving. I choose to live life this way. I want to live my life in such a way that when I get out of bed in the morning, the devil says, 'aw shit, he's up!'"*
>
> Dr. Steve Marboli, a Behavioural Scientist

Life is a living paradise where successful people live, love and laugh to inspire and they eventually make it a celebration i.e. laughing success. Thomas

Hobbes (1588–1679) was an English philosopher, best known today for his work on political philosophy. He said: "The passion of laughter is nothing else but sudden glory arising from sudden conception of some eminency in ourselves, by comparison with the infirmity of others, or with our own formerly." For the unsuccessful people, life becomes a living hell where they cry and complain and make it a price tag and eventually a nightmare. Scratch the shining surface, you will find the hardest rock inside. Louise Olmwake conducted a research and found that factors such as age, gender, education, language and culture are determinant factors as to whether a person will experience laughter in a given situation. My point is this: One should try to laugh even in angry or sad mood and that to me is the sign of a real successful man.

LAUGH AT YOURSELF

> *"There is nothing that feels as good as standing on stage and hearing the laughter and applause of an audience."*
>
> George Burns (1896–1996)

Share your awkward moments. Most successful people in every walk of life are those who have learned to laugh at themselves. Finding humour in stressful moments allows you to separate who you are from what you do. Remember a quote of McElravy: "It's not just what you do that defines who you are." You may have done something stupid, but you're not a stupid person. The ability to laugh at yourself develops your self-acceptance and elevates your personal esteem to higher levels. *All My Best Friends* by George Burns is a treasure trove of hilarious anecdotes.

William Arthur Ward (1921–1994), author of *Fountains of Faith*, is one of America's most quoted writers of inspirational maxims. He quotes: "To make mistakes is human; to stumble is commonplace; to be able to laugh at yourself is maturity." I believe that laughing at yourself is the best way to take yourself less seriously. It is a fun to speak about times when you took yourself too seriously and became the problem yourself. Mature people laugh at themselves and make other people feel special and important too.

NEVER LAUGH AT OTHERS

> *"Laugh at yourself first before anyone else can."*
>
> Elsa Maxwell (1883–1963)

Laugh at yourself and at life. I am not asking you to laugh in the spirit of contempt or self-pity. You can always use laughter as a remedy. Laughter as a miracle drug will relieve your pain. It will heal your depression. It will help you to put in the perception of thinking clearly towards the solution even in a likely defeat. Never take yourself too seriously. You must never laugh at others. You have to become able to laugh at yourself. I think people see the human side of you when you do that. You become mature, the day when you have the first real laugh at yourself. You should be more about "laughing with" than "laughing at." When you become subjective in humour, it breeds contempt. It is advisable to stay objective. You should not take it otherwise when people laugh at you. I tell you why because people will laugh with you and not at you. People laugh at you because you are different; you laugh at them because they're all the same. All the same people will laugh at special people like you.

ABRAHAM LINCOLN

> *"Gentlemen, why do you not laugh? With the fearful strain that is upon me day and night, if I did not laugh, I should die."*
>
> Abraham Lincoln (1809–1865)

Something that has always inspired me about Abraham Lincoln is his sense of humour. "I laugh because I must not cry, that is all, that is all." He often said this line. As far as I can see, he's the first American President to have ability to laugh, play, and have fun with others. The one reason, I found is that the term "sense of humour" really wasn't in common practice at that time and it was called "the sense of the ridiculous." In the well-known Lincoln–Douglas debates, when Douglas accused Lincoln of being two-faced, Lincoln replied, referring to his homeliness, "Honestly, if I were two-faced, would I be showing you this one?" Abraham Lincoln used the method of laughter as his campaigning tactics. He said, "My father taught me how to work, but not to love it. I'd rather read, tell stories, crack jokes, talk, laugh." He used to keep jokes books in his table drawer. Many books have been written on his love for funny stories and jokes. One of the latest is a picture-book biography "Lincoln Tells a Joke: How Laughter Saved the President (and the Country)", by Kathleen Krull and Paul Bremer.

LAUGH AND THE WHOLE WORLD LAUGHS WITH YOU

"To truly laugh, you must be able to take your pain, and play with it!"
Charlie Chaplin (1889–1977)

Always remember golden words of Ella Wheeler Wilcox: "Laugh and the whole world laughs with you, weep and you weep alone." People like to be around optimistic people who make them laugh or make them happy. It's contagious. People who laugh usually smile a lot. They are positive and are usually surrounded by friends who enjoy their company. Shared laughter is one of the most effective tools. When laughter is shared, it binds people together. When we laugh with one another, a positive bond is created. It's much more fun to laugh though and most people would rather laugh with you and are just uncomfortable with a person who cries. People can laugh when they can work together and share an experience together.

ORIGINALITY IN LAUGH

Teacher : "Laziness is the father of all bad habits."
Student : "We should respect laziness; after all he is a father."

Marilyn Manson (born January 5, 1969) an American multi-media artist once remarked: "The burden of originality is one that most people don't want to accept." People would rather sit in front of the TV and let that tell them what they're supposed to like, what they're supposed to buy, and what they're supposed to laugh at. You have to find out what is best for you. It is for you to choose the things you like at your original level. Certainly, this is not for the comedians of laughter show to suggest you the ways to laugh, if you can find your own ways.

LAUGHING BUDDHA

"Always laugh when you can. It is cheap medicine."

Lord Byron (1788–1824)

The celestial Buddha named Hotei or Pu-Tai is best known as the jolly Laughing Buddha. He is based on an eccentric Chinese Ch'an (Zen) monk who lived over 1,000 years ago. Because of this monk's benevolent nature, he came to be regarded as an incarnation of the bodhisattva who will be Maitreya (the Future Buddha).

Laughing Buddha is a symbol of joy and wealth. In China, he is known as the Loving or Friendly One. He has become a significant part of Buddhist and Shinto culture. His large protruding stomach and jolly smile have given him the common designation "Laughing Buddha." The Laughing Buddha's image graces many temples, restaurants and amulets, as he has become a deity of contentment, happiness and abundance.

HALO EFFECT

"One can know a man from his laugh, and if you like a man's laugh before you know anything of him, you may confidently say that he is a good man."

Fyodor Dostoevsky (1821–1881)

I have seen laughing buddhas, light up the whole atmosphere just by entering in the room. Laughing buddhas are amazingly magnetic and have halo effect. Laughing buddhas build and maintain large relationships, always influence (in a high-quality way) the people around them, again and again make people feel better about themselves. Scientists have found that mutual laughter helps people feel at ease around each other.

SUGGESTED STRATEGY

> *"Anger and laughter are mutually exclusive and you have the power to choose either."*
>
> Wayne Dyer, an American self-help author

You must try to say the "Exact Opposite" of what you are feeling when something goes wrong. Once a student came late in my class, instead of rebuking him, I allowed him calmly. Later on in the lecture, I deliberately raised the issue of punctuality and said: "If we can reach the PVR well before the time to see 'Spiderman 3', we can easily make it in the class. A class is more important than a movie." The whole class (including the boy) laughed and the atmosphere again lit up. The impact was magnificent and the student never came late in my class afterwards.

But then there's this difficulty – what if nothing seems very humourous and you can't find anything to laugh on? I always believe that we can essentially "fake it 'til we make it"—in another words, we can pretend to laugh quietly. Watch comedians objectively to absorb and adapt the techniques. Practice gestures before the mirror. Read a joke ten times and tell the same joke to at least ten people and notice how you get perfection in delivery and other areas each time. Get into habit of developing your own jokes and stories.

ASSIGNMENT

1. Learn the "Laughter Meditation" and "Laughter Yoga" from a trained trainer.
2. Watch, read and collect the humourous material like movies, shows, jokes and stories book.
3. Dance on your favourite song at least once in a day, ideally before going to work place.
4. Bring a Laughing Buddha and place it on your table.
5. Maintain a 'Laughter Journal' and record the funniest stories and jokes therein.
6. Go to a comedy club.
7. Host game nights with your friends.
8. Listen to the Audio programs on jokes and laughter. Play in car music system. You can also search Lit2Go for audios.

VISUALIZATION

Whenever you enter in your workplace or in your home, just stop for a moment, imagine something funny. Remember: Visualize yourself as Laughing Buddha, who makes people laugh and dance. You will definitely step on a duck one day but till then don't stop laughing.

SELF SUGGESTION

I am the living Laughing Buddha. My life is full of joy, laughter and happiness every day.

Bear in mind: Super achievers always keep their commitments.

[*Promise & Put Your Signature Here With Date*]

16

Why Are You Not As Wealthy As You Should Be?

OBJECTIVES

- To learn the "Law of Wealth Accumulation",
- To analyze and increase your earning ability, and
- To promote and sell yourself more.

GOLDEN GUIDANCE

"Money may not buy happiness, but I'd rather cry in a Jaguar than on a bus."

Francoise Sagan (1935–2004)

RICH THINKING

"The key to attaining great wealth begins with thinking like rich people do."

T. Harv Eker, *Secrets of the Millionaire Mind*

Rich people always have a schedule. Benjamin Franklin explained this ancient wisdom in form of a maxim "Early to bed, early to rise, makes a man healthy, wealthy and wise" although since then things have changed a lot. But what exactly do rich people know that others don't? Believe me! It's a mystery to rich people also why others don't get rich. Often rich people attribute richness to thinking. As Napoleon Hill said, think and grow rich. Poor people attribute richness to luck. Harlan Coben, an American author of mystery novels and thrillers quotes: "Writing my first book, I think in hindsight I went into it saying, 'It's gonna sell.' I was earning enough to scrape by sometime around a book or two before 'Tell No One.' I moved up from $50,000 to $75,000, then $150,000 for each book. I had never thought I would be doing anything else. I had enough encouragement." Hindsight is accepting a situation or event only after it has happened. This acceptance comes from understanding the reasons and followed by doing of things. Hindsight has 20/20 vision, meaning that you can clearly see after the fact what you should have done. Hindsight is always better than foresight but hindsight bias is not. Hindsight bias is a tendency of people to overvalue their skill to predict an outcome that could not have been predicted in any circumstance. In essence, the hindsight bias is sort of like saying "I knew it." An example of hindsight bias would be: a person places a bet on a horse, but when their horse loses, they look at the winner and think, "I knew it. I should have listened to myself and bet on that horse." Hindsight bias is not rich thinking, hindsight is. In this chapter, you are going to experience and have a powerful piece of information that can make you to think rich and help you get rich overnight. I will talk about important theories or secrets of money-making and wealth accumulation that will solve this mystery and by implementing them you can succeed in getting all the wealth and income you dream.

DO YOU WANT SUCCESS BADLY ENOUGH?

> *"Concentrating means sacrificing all other activities. It means directing all your thoughts, all your emotions, all your energy, all the force in your body, nerves, and hormones – everything towards that ONE single goal. It means making your*

> *entire being ardently desire the same things, and sustaining that desire for days, months or even years. That is what Sacrifice is. I call this, present moment living."*
>
> Mark Fisher, *The Instant Millionaire*

Often we take high standards and confidence of leaders as cockiness but these are necessary. As said by Matthew Lush, if you want something bad enough, you can achieve it. Billy Strayhorn puts it: If you want something hard enough, it just gets done. As Napoleon Hill also said, when your desires are strong enough you will appear to possess superhuman powers to achieve. I have a great story about the desire for success. You might have heard this before. It goes like this: Mohan Singh approaches his spiritual master in the village to teach his son Ram, the secrets of success. The master tells the man to send his son tomorrow near the river at 4 a.m. Mohan Singh showed his inability to send his son the very next day due to some work at home. The master said, "A day lost is an opportunity to be successful." Mohan Singh agreed to send his son the next day at 4 a.m. The next day Ram arrives at 4 a.m. near the river. The master says, "If you wish to learn, you must do accurately what I tell you, agreed?" Ram replies, "Yes, agreed!" The master speaks, "I want you to walk into the river." Ram walks into the river until the water is up to his knees. The master utters again, "Further ... Walk further." Ram goes further until the water is at chest level. The master, having walked with him, takes Ram by surprise and dunks him under the water. Ram tries to rise above water but the master holds him down. Just when it seems like Ram is out of breath, the master pulls him out of the water. The master says, "I have only one question for you: What did you want the most when you were under water?" Ram replies, "I wanted to breathe!" The master says, "Did you want family, food, fun, sleep, friends, comfort, money or anything else?" Ram answers, "No. I wanted some air only at the cost of anything. I could sacrifice everything for a little air." The master says, "That is the secret to success. You may think you want it so bad, but do you really? When you want to succeed as bad as you want to breathe, then you become superhuman and only superhuman gets successful. There is no other secret."

Moral of the story:

1. The whole point is that: since all of us would do anything to keep breathing to live. We can make ourselves successful if we have the same inspiration and determination as we would if we were under water trying to breathe and get some air.
2. You may think you want it really bad, but are you willing to give everything you've got?
3. You must succeed more than anything else and that is how you should live your life.
4. You need present moment living for success.
5. Be a superhuman. Don't let a day go by when you don't work hard or study or practice on your skill or ability.

WHY AM I NOT AS WEALTHY AS I SHOULD BE?

> *"Self-made wealth isn't magic; in fact it is largely the result of routine and mundane work. It's just that wealthy people are willing to step out of their comfort zone to follow the money."*
>
> Lewis Schiff, *Business Brilliant*

Why I don't have money all the times? Why there are so few rich people. "I am hardworking, educated and dedicated." Then, "Why am I not as wealthy as I should be?" This question comes to the minds of many people when they look a school dropout taking their job interview or a sweet shop owner opening any educational institute or a non MBA as the CEO of a company or an illiterate person becoming a minister. I choose to listen to the Winners not the Whiners. One such winner is American comedy writer Robert Orben. He has written multiple books on comedy, mostly collections of gags and one-liners. He has been Director of the White House Speechwriting Department during the presidency of President

Gerald R. Ford. He was head speechwriter during his vice-presidency also. He affirms: "Every day I get up and look through the Forbes list of the richest people in America. If I'm not there, I go to work."

A million dollar advice from a reputed career counsellor starts with getting an appropriate degree and then choosing the right profession in right place and looking for a change of jobs and employers continuously. High-achievers ask you to invest in education first and then in real estates and stock markets.

The reason for mediocrity or richness lies in the money plan. The money thinking that we have in our subconscious mind is manifestation of many factors and influences since our childhood. We have been trained subconsciously that "It's very difficult to earn money." I would like to offer an advice: "If you are not doing as well monetarily as you would like, you will have to change your money plan." There is no secret which only rich people know. I have watched many common people attaining great wealth. It all lies in thinking and doing like rich people do. Rich people have proper planning about their money and poor don't. A rich person gets richer because he is devoted to being rich. A rich man creates life of his dreams. The common poor person wants to be rich but believes life happens to him.

DID YOU ANALYZE YOUR EARNING ABILITY?

> *"Your greatest asset is your earning ability. Your greatest resource is your time."*
>
> Brain Tracy, a motivational speaker and author

All these pre-earning investments increase your most valuable asset in terms of cash flow and that is your ability to earn that depends on your ability to apply your knowledge and skill in a timely fashion to get results for which others will pay. You have to exploit this ability. If you're like many people today, financial concerns top the list of worries. You have to sell your time. Invest your time and money.

WHO IS A MILLIONAIRE?

"If you want to be a Millionaire, start with a billion dollars and launch a new airline."

Richard Branson, a British business magnate

So, what do you want to be? A Millionaire. Let us see who is a millionaire. In US, a millionaire is a person whose total assets, if sold off in a non-fire-sale situation, would bring (after tax obligations – if any) a net minimum of $1,000,000.

1 US dollar = 54.5300 Indian rupees (On 14th April, 2013)

1 British pound sterling = 83.6763 Indian rupees (On 14th April, 2013)

1 million is 10 lakhs units (10,00,000 US dollars = 5,45,30000 Indian rupees and 10,00,000 British pounds sterling = 8,36,76300 Indian rupees).

Richness in America is different from India and vice versa. Ask any millionaire, who is rich? According to him, a rich has at least 10 millions. So, no absolute number can be fixed to define richness. It is always relative.

HAVE YOU CALCULATED YOUR NET WORTH?

"Bottom line is, I didn't return to Apple to make a fortune. I've been very lucky in my life and already have one. When I was 25, my net worth was $100 million or so. I decided then that I wasn't going to let it ruin my life. There's no way you could ever spend it all, and I don't view wealth as something that validates my intelligence."

Steve Jobs (1955–2011)

The above pound–dollar–rupees exercise will reveal the actual image you must see before you decide to be a multi-millionaire. Now, take your notebook and calculate your total of your realizable net assets right now. Don't make a rough estimate. Take a notebook, write your assets and their market value. Now, assess your liabilities like bills, instalments and commitments. Then, subtract liabilities sum from your assets sum. Divide the resultant value by the active working years. What you are left with is your net worth. How will you increase your net worth? Understand: Work on your self-worth and your net worth will definitely increase. As said by Mark Victor Hansen, when your self-worth goes up, your net worth goes up with it.

HAVE YOU DECIDED YOUR VALUE?

> *"Your net worth to the world is usually determined by what remains after your bad habits are subtracted from your good ones."*
>
> Benjamin Franklin (1706–1790)

When we ask ourselves why we aren't rich already. Then, our subconscious mind will supply a list of limiting beliefs, excuses and false reasons. George Carlin aptly says: Most people work just hard enough not to get fired and get paid just enough money not to quit. Experts of abundance theory say that people become wealthy because they decide to become wealthy. I see only one reason why a poor person is not wealthy. He is poor he has not yet decided to be rich.

Gentleman! You have to decide, "Where you are right now" in order to decide, "Where you want to be." Now, are you pleased with your net worth? If not, start today to do something about it. First thing is to feel tired of your present situation so that you can put the effort to change the whole scenario. There are two types of Pain in this world: Pain that hurts you, and Pain that changes you. Feel the pain that changes you. Stop looking at yourself as "the type of person who makes $20 or 1100 rupees an hour", and give yourself approval to start looking yourself as "the type of person" who makes ten times that. If you make 20 dollars an hour, how much do you make a year if you work 40 hours a week? 20 dollars per hour × 40 hours a week = 800 dollars per week, 800 dollars per week × 52 weeks in a year = 41,600 dollars yearly. Did you get this?

It is all about increasing the self-worth. This is about making your conscious mind believe that figure in order to make your subconscious mind to have faith that you deserve that. Create a goal to double your income by the end of this year and then to triple your income by the end of next year and then figure out what you'll have to do to achieve it. This is called millionaire mentality.

Successful people think of long-term goals to be a multi-millionaire. Decide your net worth year by year and visualize at what value you are going to end yourself? Can you dare to say "I am worth over $100,000,000!"

DEFINITION OF WEALTH

"Wealth takes sacrifice, discipline, and hard work."

Thomas J. Stanley And William D. Danko,
The Millionaire Next Door

You need to understand money in order to make, and keep it. The word wealth can be defined as the "abundance of valuable resources or material possessions." The word "wealth" is derived from the old English *weal,* which is from an Indo-European word *stem*. An individual, family, community, organization, region or country that possesses an abundance of such possessions or resources is known as wealthy. One interesting research that I came across is by Stanley and Danko who talk about three categories of people—average accumulator, under accumulator and prodigious accumulator. Average Accumulator of Wealth (AAW) have a net worth equal to one-tenth their age multiplied by their current annual income from all sources. E.g., a 50-year-old lawyer who over the past twelve months earned income of 12 lakhs rupees and investment income of 30,000 rupees should have an expected net worth of 61,50,000 rupees. An Under Accumulator of Wealth (UAW) would have half that amount. A Prodigious Accumulator of Wealth (PAW) would have two times.

MY NOTION OF BEING WEALTHY

"Life's a garden, dig it and you make it work for you. You never give up man, that's my philosophy."

Joe Dirt, 2001 American film

There are different options available to a person for making money. You can earn money by working as an employee in an organization and in that case you have a job. You can go for self-employment and in that case you own a job. You can be business owner wherein you have a system (such as a franchise like Domino's Pizza) that generates cash flow for you and there is an added satisfaction that others work for you. But I always advise the fourth option and that is being an investor because in that case your money works for you. The key point, I highlight in my writings and speeches is that rich people are getting more than 50–70 percent of their cash flow and income by having money work for them. Believe me! I am not exaggerating.

The simple rule to be wealthy is: "Money must work for you." Yes, I hope you read it right. It is not "You must work for money." You have to acquire money and then put that money to work for you. You become wealthier when money works for you. Rich people treat time in a different way. They buy it, while poor people sell it. Poor people do the jobs while rich people hire the jobs like unproductive time consuming household works.

In physical world, North Pole attracts South Pole and vice versa. My thesis: In behavioural world money is the universal magnet which pulls everything and everybody irrespective of polarities. Money is the exchange force. Making money is not as a sin, which is generally propounded by so called saints, but as a form of power which can make one's life highly comfortable e.g. a 100 rupees note contains in it all things of the world which cost 100 rupees. But, at the same time, one must be master of money and should not get victimized by its hypnotism.

HOW TO BE WEALTHY?

> *"Wealthy people don't employ business-as-usual practices; they adopt a business brilliant mind-set."*
>
> Lewis Schiff, *Business Brilliant*

Are you going to inherit from your father? Are you going to become a big professional like a doctor, engineer, accountant, lawyer or an architect? Can you become a chief executive officer of a huge company? Have your astrologer guaranteed a lottery win? Are you looking to win in a reality show? According to a research, 10% of world affluents are senior executive people, 10% of world richest people come from professionals, 5% are top sales guys and 1% comes from top people in different fields like sports stars, singers, musicians, inheritances and authors etc.

If your answer to the above six questions is in negative, then the one and only way left – seventh and self-made way – is to start your own business. This research concludes that self-made or business way is the reservoir where from 74% of richest people spring. Wealth is, more often than not, acquired in the course of investment strategies that capitalize on unrealized (nontaxable) income and lessen realized (taxable) income.

I was on a constant observation during the writing of this chapter and I found only few people (one in twenty people) dare to step out of comfort zone to follow money. It means only five out of hundred become wealthy. Wealthy people ask for money in circumstances wherein ordinary people habitually don't ask. They don't follow the common business patterns rather they have a business approach with unique vision. Wealthy people have a business thinking and do only business. They make money by creating circumstances to make more. In short, they follow money and successes follow them. So, where do you start? Get your corporate entity registered whether company or partnership. Get your letterhead and business cards printed. Open a business account. Build your opportunities and see other opportunities will come from all directions.

WHAT DO YOU NEED TO START?

"If you have ideas, you have the main asset you need, and there isn't any limit to what you can do with your business and your life. Ideas are any man's greatest asset."

Harvey S. Firestone, an American businessman

What is it you need to do to get rich? The answer is an idea to add value to people's life. "There is no substitute for knowledge. To this day, said Eli Broad, I read three newspapers a day. It is impossible to read a paper without being exposed to ideas. And, ideas more than money are the real currency for success." So, find a real need (its real need and not need only) of the people and then be a brand name to fill that name. People want it; need it; can use it; can afford it and are willing to buy it now. Who is the customer and why will he or she buy from you? Why will he or she switch from their current supplier to buy from you? Ideas often come from clients. Charge reasonably for providing that extra value. All the great salesmen, sports star, businessmen and successful persons offer that extra. Customers get extra value for money; the same money that your counterpart charges but you offer extra value for their money. And if there isn't, find a different product or a different market. You have to be busy with your passion. That's it. This is business.

OVERNIGHT SUCCESS OF FACEBOOK

"The biggest risk is not taking any risk... In a world that changing really quickly, the only strategy that is guaranteed to fail is not taking risks."

Mark Zuckerberg, the co–founder of facebook

Mark Zuckerberg was the Harvard computer science student who along with a few friends launched the world's most popular social networking website called Facebook in February 2004. Mark Zuckerberg also has the distinction of being the world's youngest billionaire, which he achieved in 2008. He was named "Man of the Year" by *Time* magazine in 2010. Zuckerberg currently is the chief executive and president of Facebook. The idea is that you can build something really good in a night. What Zuckerberg created in his college dorm room at the tender age of 19, was nothing short of a worldwide phenomenon that changed the way people and businesses interact forever. It is an observance of the thesis that wealthy people don't follow the common business patterns rather they have a business approach with unique vision.

STORY OF DOMINO'S PIZZA

> *"I was distracted by some of the rewards of success, which was hurting my business. I put all of these distractions aside, and focused solely on Domino's Pizza."*
>
> Tom Monaghan, the founder of Domino's Pizza

Domino's Pizza is an international pizza delivery corporation headquartered in Ann Arbor, Michigan, United States. Founded in 1960, Domino's is the second-largest pizza chain in the United States (after Pizza Hut) and has more than ten thousand corporate and franchised stores in seventy countries and all fifty U.S. States. Domino's Pizza was sold to Bain Capital in 1998 and went public in 2004. Do you know the founders were dealing in a common food (Pizza) offered by many of restaurants? So what he did. He added extra value to his food by making it available more quickly than his counterparts. This idea made Domino's founder Tom Monaghan one of the wealthiest man in the world. An idea can change your life. An idea can do it overnight. An idea of adding that extra can be the breakthrough you are looking for. This example is an observance of thesis that wealthy people create opportunities to earn money wherein ordinary people habitually see them as problems.

DON'T LOSE MONEY

> *"Rule No. 1: Never lose money. Rule No. 2: Never forget Rule No. 1."*
>
> Warren Buffett, an American business magnate

There is always a before and an after. You remember the old proverb: A fool and his money are soon parted. There is another one: When a man with experience meets a man with money, the man with the money is going to end up with the experience and the man with the experience is going to end up with the money. Yes, there is serious gold in these words. The advice is deceptively simple. As Steven J. Lee said, "the first rule in making money is not to lose it." The only thing easy with money is to lose it. Even a small leak in the ship can sink your whole ship. So, think twice before you part with your hard earned money.

FINANCIAL SECURITY

> *"If you want to rear financial blessings, you have to sow financially."*
>
> Joel Osteen, an American lay preacher

The financial security that you are looking for will come through three sides: (i) Saving (ii) Insurance and (iii) Investment. You must save to feel secure. You must insure adequately to provide against any emergency that you cannot pay for out of your bank account.

You must invest to earn until your money is paying you more than you can earn at your job and then you can manage your assets. Keep a strong hold on your numbers. Rich people are always in great control of their finances. They maintain good budgeting, accurate book-keeping and accounting. Cash is the blood of business. They practice penny-pinching. Positive people always make an analysis by very careful budgets, week by week, month by month, and year by year.

HOW DO I GET RICH?

> *"Dare to be different! You'll never get rich doing the same things as the poor majority."*
>
> Author Unknown

How do I get rich? What makes a man rich? What do you have to do to be one of the wealthiest and most powerful people in your city? The answer is in form of an advice: "Buy assets" because assets plus your money and put money into your pocket and liabilities take money out of your pocket. A large portion of *Rich Dad Poor Dad* author Robert Toru Kiyosaki's wealth came from real estate investing. Golden guidance is to "choose freedom over comfort". Avoid "Better Off" and "Better Than" approach in your life.

Delay your gratification and never fall in trap of cycle of debt. Rich people don't spend; they invest. Rich people buy shops; poor buy homes. Riches sell shops every year and poor pay installments every year. Poor people buy private cars; rich people buy cars for their companies. This law of delayed gratification asks you to choose permanent fortune over temporary gratification by avoiding the urge to spend in a hurry.

Temporary comfort can never give permanent freedom. You may be tempted to spend the profits or unexpected income generated from investments but instead deposit in investment account and wait and plan to reinvest. Living on credit cards and loans won't make you rich. Choose good debt over bad debt. This is cycle of reinvestment which is better than cycle of debt.

Just do what you want and judge yourself with inner scorecard and never do what others expect you to do. Go and do it and avoid unnecessary sitting and thinking. Warren Buffett calls it "thumb sucking".

So, *here is the golden tip*: "To be above average do what average people never do i.e. think differently and do that after assessing the risk. Yes, risk will multiply your money. Take risks on the advices of your millionaire friends and not the ones who think twice before betting on a card game.

Surround yourself with self-made millionaires. Learn from them. It's been said that like attracts like. People like to be around and to promote people they like."

Go for giving your "best value" instead of your "best time". What's the alternative to getting a job? Plant a tree that grows inspite of the time you give. Didn't get me? Start a work that generates 24 × 7 incomes. Never worry what people say. Choose business over job and prefer to stay jobless instead of choice less. Don't worry about the cliché that 9 out of 10 businesses fail in the first five years. Start a killer website, a business and be an entrepreneur.

SAVING IS A DISCIPLINE

> *"Saving regularly is important, no matter how little."*
>
> Jean Chatzky, *Make Money, Not Excuses*

You need to invest the money you don't spend so that it can work as strong for you as you are working to earn it. You can become financially independent when you develop a habit of saving from each payment made it to you. Saving and investing a certain amount of money will grow to in 20 or 30 years. Some of the amounts, an American financial journalist Jean Chatzky mentioned in her book are really amazing. For example, start investing 10% of a $35,000 income at 30 years old and you will have $457,254 at retirement, if the employer gives a 5% match it will be $685,881 at 65 years old.

The Law of Conservation says the accurate assessment of how rich you are really becoming is how much you keep out of the amount that you earn. May be you don't want to be rich. But do you want to be poor? It's so important, as a matter of fact, as Brian Tracy asserts: "Saving is a discipline, and any discipline affects your life."

CONFIDENCE ACCOUNT

> *"The 8th wonder of the world is the magic of compound interest, which is, simply put, interest on principal and interest, not just simple interest on principal."*
>
> David Chilton, *The Wealthy Barber*

It's not how much you make; it's how much you save. David Chilton in his book explains the maxim: "The best time to plant an oak tree is twenty years ago" by an example: "If you had started putting $30.00 a month away, the equivalent of a dollar a day, at age eighteen and you continued until age sixty-five, averaging a 15% annual return, how much would you end up with?" Someone in the story hazards a guess and says $70,000? The barber tells him the correct answer... (Are you ready for this)? It is approximately $2,000,000. Save first before you spend. Pay yourself first. This is the law that has been taught by our elders. The law is to pay yourself first. Go in your favourite bank and open a "Confidence Account". And, take a pledge to never touch it. I ask you to save 10% of your each payment. Put that money in the confidence account and each time when any payment is made to you, contribute 10% of each payment in the accumulation account with the same respect as pay your rent or loan installments.

The Law of Accumulation says that every great financial achievement is an accumulation of hundreds of small efforts and sacrifices. Learn to live on the rest 90%. Soon you will develop a life style to excel on the remaining 90%.

"By the yard it's hard, but inch by inch, anything's a cinch." The cumulative effects can be enormous. All the excuses creep in to your mind when you decide to do anything. It's hard to make a start but once you do your momentum takes you further. Nothing succeeds like success. This is called law of attraction or momentum. Money attracts money. A simple habit of emptying all of your spare change (coins in particular) into a jar can make you realize the power of accumulation.

SPEND WISELY WITH BOXES

"A part of all you earn is yours to keep, and if you cannot save money, the seeds of greatness are not in you."

W. Clement Stone (1902–2002)

Some of the experts recommend a 50–30–20 budget. It means that if a salaried person goes to the ATM he can divide the money. He can keep half into his account for the online payments of rent, installments and utility bills etc. Transfer 20% into his savings account. And the rest he can take out in cash for the daily spending in whole month.

However, you can also opt for my spiritual master's advice. After paying yourself first divide your 90% income into five parts. First part is to spend on yourself like on your personal promotion, insurance for car, health, family and home etc. I spend 3% of this part (and daily 1 hour reading) on my personal and professional development. You should spend second part on your parents. Third part is meant for your spouse and children. Fourth part is a tribute to your parents. Divide the fifth part into two parts i.e. first part is to be spent on blood relatives like brothers, sisters, friends and guests. Second part is a charity fund. You can have labeled boxes for this purpose.

This division is the advice of my spiritual master. If you are in heavy debt, then adjust the percentage accordingly. Create a monthly budget that covers all your basic expenses and leaves a little bit of "fun" money aside. Do not go over this. Just separate the wants from the needs. Beware of little expenses. Don't save what is left after spending. Instead, spend what is left after saving.

INVESTING ACCOUNT

"If you took away all of Donald Trump's money, he would be right back to where he is today because of the way he thinks."

Scot Anderson, *Think Like A Billionaire, Become A Billionaire*

We think a better job will make us wealthy. Billionaires know that a job will never make them wealthy; investments will. After my research for this chapter was over, I came to a conclusion. Billionaires think differently than the rest of us. It means if one can change his thinking, he can change his net worth ten times. Scot Anderson in just one year took a net worth of maybe $250,000 on a good day, to a net worth of over $3,000,000 in just one year by changing his thinking. That's a net worth more than twelve times where he started, with an additional $15,000,000 in current projects. Save and invest the additional income apart from your income throughout your working lifetime, and you will become rich. Billionaires get ready today for the chances of tomorrow. Just deposit 25% of each additional payment in this account and invest it wisely until your money is paying you more than you can earn at your job.

Make a decision to choose long-term financial independence over short-term pleasures. From now on, think every day about how you can put more money into that account. With remaining 50% you can enjoy the life and do adventurous things you always hunt in your dreams.

Take advantage of tax deferred savings and investment plans. I have also observed that self-made millionaires are almost obsessive about accumulating their funds in assets. Generally wealthy people prefer to invest in assets such as real estate; self-owned businesses and equities. There is only one reason for this approach because these increase in value without triggering tax liabilities.

FREE WILL ACCOUNT

> *"Insure a future income – do work that you love to do. Become excellent at it."*
>
> George Samuel Clason,
> *The Richest Man in Babylon*

You must have noticed that I have left 25% in above division of additional income, now I ask you to deposit that amount in a separate account. Your aim is to collect salary/income of 6 months in this "Free Will Account". This liquid savings equal to 6 months income of this account will give the courage to listen to your self-call and leave the job or group you are not interested into and respect your self-image.

LIVING COSTS REDUCTION

"I'd like to live as a poor man with lots of money."

Pablo Picasso (1881–1973)

Our elders often say that "Expenses usually rise to match income." My proposal: "If your income increases, don't adjust your expenses accordingly. Instead, invest the additional money in your future. Control thy expenditures." Our wise old men give us a solid suggestion: "Always live well below your means." But, do we really observe this golden guidance? A massive portion of our society stays in deceptive society of wealth. Most of the people want to look rich. The less rich people have fallen into hyper-consumerism that keeps them from getting wealth. "It is easier to look rich than to become really rich." All we have to do is to buy the luxury goods/services like shoes, suits, watches, wines and cars that we think the rich buy and we get the feeling that we are rich. But this kind of excessive consumerism or brand consciousness is injurious to our net worth. Most rich people become wealthy and stay that way by being economical and by being investment oriented as opposed to expenditure oriented. I am simply asking to cut off your unnecessary expenditures, for example – you can go for a children insurance plan with the money spent on their chocolates, cold drinks and video games. Aim for a minimum of a 10 percent reduction in your living costs over the next three months. Deposit the reduction difference in investment account.

WORLD IS DIVIDED IN TO TWO CLASSES

"History is written by the rich, and so the poor get blamed for everything."

Jeffrey D. Sachs, an American economist

The world is divided in to two classes – Creamy and non-creamy layer. Creamy layer people are first class people and at minimum they are millionaires. The non-creamy layer is again separated into middle class and lower class. The middle class people have an illusion of upper middle class and lower middle class. You must have seen that these non-creamy layer people have a prescribed lifestyle; they act rich and have all the things on loans. Most of the alcoholics and smokers are from this group because they can't match to expectations of themselves and their friends and family members. Banks are their real parents. "A bank lends money to those who don't need it." When there is any rise in income of non-creamy layer people they spend on possessions as a manifestation of better than and better off theories. The first thing a young boy from non-creamy layer does, when he gets a high salaried job, is to get a big car on bank loan. Most of non-creamy layer people spend on the education of their children, possessions, home EMIs and car loans. The high earning professionals are more susceptive to have low net worth. They require a costly degree and often get a delayed start. These professionals often lack behavioural skills also because of their early involvement in technical studies. This loan inheritance is carried forward to their children also.

SELF-PROMOTION

"Heroes must see to their own fame. No one else will."

Gore Vidal, *Julian*

Self-promotion is the business of getting ahead more rapidly in your life by selling yourself more effectively to more people, in more places, more often. I have also found that rich people constantly try to learn and grow because they want to promote themselves and their value. I often say to my students that you have to decide to be best expert in your field. Do your very best at everything. Put the "best foot forward." "The final key to the way I promote is bravado. I play to people's fantasies," said Donald Trump, "people may not always think big themselves, but they can still get very excited by those who do. That's why a little hyperbole never hurts." Pay any price and make every sacrifice to know your product and service inside out.

A jack–of–all–trades is also a master of none. Specialization or personal excellence is the key. You must not only be different but also be better than your competitors in the same field. Upgrade your work-related special skills, knowledge and make sure that your superiors know about it. This is called law of high visibility. When your boss feels that you are eager to learn and grow, often he or she will become a mentor to you.

Develop a sense of urgency. Two important qualities that can make you rich are: "Set priorities and do things quickly." Always work on the task that your boss considers to be the most important, and stay with it until it is done.

You have to develop a reputation for competence and capability. There's always something more you can do to add value to areas your bosses, your customers or you think as important. The law is "Exceeding the expectations".

Human beings are creatures of perception. You must be perceived as being very competent at what you do. It is not what they see but what they think they see that determines how they think and act. Set high standards for your appearance. Look, act and dress the part. Become knowledgeable about styles, colours and fabrics. Dress better than your co–workers. Never take anything for granted. Dress, walk, talk and act as if you are going somewhere with your life.

Develop your contacts, both inside and outside the company. The most successful men and women in any community are those who are known by the greatest number of other successful people. Enthusiasm is communicable and it can be the stuff you are looking to begin. Begin with your professional association or club, and join a reputed charity that you care about and that also has a prestigious board of directors. However, the poor people would still think they already know everything. Ask them why didn't you implement these things if you knew them? They would say, "I think selling and promotion are not good things." Another common reply is: "Sun needs no introduction." This book is for the high achievers and not for complainers and worrywarts. These nitpickers often ignore their friends and family in the race of money. It's good to earn money but take care of your family also.

HOW MUCH DO YOU MAKE AN HOUR?

"A wise man should have money in his head, but not in his heart."

Jonathan Swift (1667–1745)

Wealthy men have enough acumen to be financially secure. They realize that money is compulsory for a secure existence; however they don't let money rule their life. As put by Benjamin Franklin, money has never made man happy, nor will it; there is nothing in its nature to produce happiness. Take my advice: Money should not be the love of your life. Warren Buffett has also said: "It's nice to have a lot of money, but you know, you don't want to keep it around forever. I prefer buying things. Otherwise, it's a little like saving sex for your old age." There is a short story on time versus money. A little boy asked his father, "Daddy, how much do you make an hour?" The father said: "Don't trouble me now, I'm exhausted." "But Daddy, just tell me please! How much do you make an hour," the boy insisted. The father finally replied: "Twenty dollars per hour." "All right, Daddy? Could you lend me ten dollars?" the boy asked. The father yelled: "So that was the motive you asked how much I earn, right? Go to sleep and don't trouble me anymore!" After an hour the father thought, "Perhaps there is something he truly needs to purchase with that 10 dollars and he actually doesn't ask for money very frequently." Finally, trying to lighten his mind, the father went to his son's room. "Are you asleep son?" asked the father. "No, Daddy. Why?" replied the boy partly asleep. "Here's the money you asked before," the father said. "Thanks, Daddy!" delighted the son. "Wow! I have a sufficient amount! Now I have twenty dollars!" the boy said to his father, "Daddy could you sell me one hour of your time?"

Moral of the story:

1. It's good to earn your money per hour or per minute but you must spare some time for your family also.
2. The more of money one has the more one wants.
3. Don't let money rule your life.
4. You must live a balanced life.

SUGGESTED STRATEGY

"The man who does more than he is paid for will soon be paid for more than he does."

Napoleon Hill (1883–1970)

The key to be wealthy is a simple rule i.e. to add extra value. You have to add something special, something useful and something unique that brings smile in many lives. Yes, all the successful people add extra value to the products, services, persons, companies, business, society and country etc. They always look for an occasion to add extra value every time, every day and in every transaction.

Excellent performance comes from your passionate calling. Excellent performance leads to excellent financial freedom. Many local shopkeepers in India buy a thing and make it available for the locals at a higher price. Importers and exporters do it at big level. The income tax lawyer or charted accountants who save money of their clients are adding extra value. The doctor who has changed the fate of surgery has added extra value in the life of his patients.

They are highly speculative. Whatever job you are doing, you should be preparing for your next job. And the key question is always, where are the customers? Which businesses and industries are growing in this economy, and which ones are declining? They all are bringing more happiness in the life of people. People are bigger assets than money. More importantly, positive people treat adding extra or best value as their duty.

ASSIGNMENT

1. Open your confidence account.
2. Open your free will account.
3. Have a brainstorming session on value added business.
4. Open your investing account.
5. Label boxes to spend from.
6. Cut your living cost.
7. Decide your self-promotion strategy.
8. Analyze your net worth.
9. Analyze your earning ability.
10. Watch out your saving, insurance and investment.
11. Listen to the Audio program *The Automatic Millionaire* by David Bach.

VISUALIZATION

Visualize yourself as the top businessman who is managing all things in a nice way. Imagine yourself giving a lecture on this chapter to students. Remember: The master asserted: When you replicate the same level of desire, as you want to breathe, in anything, then you can be successful.

SELF SUGGESTION

Wealth and money flow to me easily, frequently and abundantly.

Bear in mind: Super achievers always keep their commitments.

[Promise & Put Your Signature Here With Date]

17

Are You Ready To Learn Lifelong?

OBJECTIVES

- To learn the "Law of Continuous Learning",
- To improve on your weak areas, and
- To achieve all round development with "Researched Effort Approach".

GOLDEN GUIDANCE

"Leadership and learning are indispensable to each other."

John F. Kennedy, the 35th U.S. president

PRINCIPLE OF CONTINUOUS LEARNING

"The illiterate of the 21st century will not be those who cannot read and write, but those who cannot learn, unlearn, and relearn."

Alvin Toffler, *Revolutionary Wealth*

Life-Long Learning (LLL) is the self-motivated pursuit of knowledge for either personal or professional reasons. Generally, only a quarter of our lives is devoted to learning, and then we simply rest on our achievements for the remaining three quarters of it. My advice: If you want to become the greatest person you can be; you have no other option but to adopt a mindset of lifelong learning. All the great leaders have a habit of continuous learning. Louis L'Amour (1908–1988) is a perfect example of the charming life one can create for himself when he makes the promise to be a lifelong learner. L'Amour dropped out of school when he was fifteen and spent the next eight years travelling around the American West working odd jobs on cattle ranches, farms, lumber mills, and even mines. He was in love with books so much that he skipped food often so that he could purchase the books with that money. He was in habit of taking notes. He became an established writer. Many of his stories were made into movies. It is said that at the time of his death some of his 105 existing works were in print – 89 novels, 14 short-story collections, and two full-length works of non-fiction. He was considered one of the world's most popular writers. Our life is constantly at "Challenge of Comfort" by the technological innovations every minute. You must know how to operate the computer in order to have the comfort of computer. Denis Waitley, an author, consultant and speaker named to the International Speakers Hall of Fame asserts: "Your formal education has a very short shelf life. Lifelong learning, once a luxury for the few, has become absolutely vital to continued success. Continue gaining expertise and avoid thinking like an expert."

A powerful leader constantly tries to improve business, people and results. Learning is an essential part of leadership. You have to get that information which is required to be successful and happy in any field. A person can do what he wants provided he is willing to learn. Leadership is not only a title but a system of life. Leadership is all about leading yourself inside out. I believe that learning is one road that leads to a successful life. So, *here is the golden tip*: "All the successful people are great learners and interestingly they learn by their choice not under any compulsion. They possess a deep emotional desire to learn. Learning is the winners' winning or competitive edge. They get success after success because they learn to do things in a better way or learn to do new things on an on-going basis." They improve constantly by constant learning. They practice what is called by experts as "Personal Leadership" and one of the attributes of personal leadership is the continuous learning by choice for a change.

THERE IS SO MUCH TO LEARN FROM

"Success depends on the ability to think critically."

Vincent Ryan Ruggiero,
Becoming A Critical Thinker

Learning opportunities are all around you. Learning is not confined to what's found in books. As said by Albert Einstein, learning is not a product of schooling but the lifelong attempt to acquire it. Any fool can know. The point is to understand. Just look around in your room, the fan can teach you to stay cool; the calendar can teach you to be up-to-date; the floor can teach you to kneel down and pray; the door can teach you to push hard for your goals; the clock can teach you that life and time are precious; the roof can teach you to aim high; window can teach you to see the world and spread the fame and the mirror can teach you to reflect before you act. I read the above idea at someplace but the message is clear: This universe is reservoir of knowledge and if you have quest to learn, you can learn from the smallest of things. Nature is a great teacher. You can learn discipline from sun, patience from earth, purity from water, flow from air and vastness from sky and so on. Your complete life is learning. You are perpetually learning – all time, all places and in all circumstances. A little is being added to your previous experiences each day. Good days give you joy, bad days give you experience, and the worst days give you lessons. All individuals are learners despite of difference in their occupation, whether they work in the office, kitchen, school or college. Be grateful for each day of your life because the fastest way of learning is little by little and day by day.

SUPER LEADERS—MULTI-DIMENSIONAL PERSONALITY

"A human being should be able to change a diaper, plan an invasion, butcher a hog, conn a ship, design a building, write a sonnet, balance accounts, build a wall, set a bone, comfort the dying, take orders, give orders, cooperate, act alone, solve equations, analyze a new problem, pitch manure, program a computer, cook a tasty meal, fight efficiently, die gallantly. Specialization is for insects."

Robert Heinlein (1907–1988)

Benjamin Franklin (1706–1790), the great American intellectual and author, was most successful statesman of his time. He is a great role model to be followed. He had constant desire to personal development and lifelong learning. Franklin's success is all the more beyond belief, given the fact that, his father was a soap maker, who could not afford education for his 17 children. The super leaders are multi-dimensional. They don't let their work define themselves. Their profession is not their identity. A profession is not who they are, it's what they do.

Learning is one road that leads to success eventually. Super leaders constantly work and always find a way to maximize their potential. Learning is a form of meditation. Stephen R. Cover calls it "Sharpening the saw" that relates to overall development. Sharpen the Saw means preserving and enhancing the greatest asset you have – YOU. It means having a balanced program for self-renewal in the seven areas of your life: family, finances, career, friends, social life, health and spirituality. You can get training programs and courses on better spiritual health. You can join the gym or get a good dietician to plan your diet. You can learn the art of influence in a workshop and can make better friends. You can improve your social communication skills. You can learn any new game. You can join the hobby classes. You can learn to swim. You can improve your confidence in any of the games by playing with the experts in those games. You can ask for professional advices in finances and career. You can enhance the employability and competitiveness in professional life by completing various technical and academic diploma and degree courses. I mean there is so much to improve provided you accept your ignorance in an area and be willing to improve in that.

The world's leading authorities and constant research on creative thinking, accelerated learning and innovation have shown that lifelong learning is valuable more than ever. It has become essential for personal and professional achievements. I consider Aamir Khan, an Indian film actor as one of the greatest models of lifelong learning. He is known for his intense performances. Look at his films. In *Lagaan,* he played the role of Bhuvan and studied colonial rule in India, in historical drama *Mangal Pandey* he played the title role and studied Indian Freedom Struggle, in *Ghajini* he exercised for 13 months to get an international body with eight pack abs, in the comedy *3 Idiots* he played a role of a college boy with a lean look and in *Talaash* he was seen in a police uniform doing scuba-diving and swimming. In *Dhoom 3,* he is playing a role of circus acrobat. In April 2013, he was among TIME magazine's *100 Most Influential People* in the World List. Whatever he touches turns into gold. The Government of India honoured him with the Padma Shri in 2003 and the Padma Bhushan in 2010 for his contributions towards the arts. There are certain attributes in him which are responsible for his powerful performances. He has a never-ending curiosity that's why he generates curiosity among viewers also through his multiple roles. He also checks and verifies his ideas through experts' and others' practical experiences. You must have seen that he always takes the help of experts in the field. He has a perfectionist temperament so he constantly renews and improves his sense intelligence and that develops his analytical skills. He keeps himself open to fresh ideas during the project. He is also ready for contradictions and doubts in old and new ideas. He tries to involve his whole brain. Watch any of his film carefully, you will find a combination of science, art, logic and imagination. He has a balanced approach in his life and business. He also tries to establish some kind of connections as conclusions between different systems. My point is that winners try to be creative and productive at all levels. They extract maximum out of themselves. Only the leader who learns constantly will survive the tough challenges of life in this competitive world. I have learned so much just from reading a book cover to cover than most ordinary people learn in a lifetime. All the super leaders are perpetual learners. In fact, they are "Learning Leaders." Not all the good learners turn out to be super leaders but all super leaders are very good learners for sure.

Successful people are lifelong learners. They constantly work at educating themselves. You can see these persons getting formal academic degrees in different disciplines. They are equally good at informal mode of learning also. They are student of life and continuously learn from watching, listening, reading and asking. They also try to verify the truth of their findings by doing at experimental level. They learn all at these three levels. They learn all they can so that they can contribute all they can. Franklin sought out the knowledge wherever he could. He once said, "If you empty your purse in your head, no one can take it away from you. An investment in knowledge always pays the best interest." "Tell me and I forget." He further said, "Teach me and I remember. Involve me and I learn."

WORK ON YOUR WEAK AREAS

"What you do today can improve all your tomorrows."

Ralph Marston, a writer and motivator

"Improvement begins with you." There is neither a trick for getting success nor it is a hereditary trait that passes on to generations, rather, it is a way of life, it is choosing action over procrastination. Success lies in being on the driver seat rather than putting life on autopilot, it is a matter of learning the winning habits and unlearning the habits of failure. Successful people accept that they don't know everything and hence they try to improve the areas of their weakness. It is also necessary to maintain and enhance the employability and competitiveness in professional life. The art of reading is part of my life's journey. I read both fiction and non-fiction. Mainly, I read non-fiction for one fundamental justification – knowledge. I read fiction to nourish my imagination and it is often very greedy. I can escape into another world with a book. I find a wonderful world in each book wherein everything is achievable and I become a part of it. I make profound connections with the characters if it's written well.

Lifelong learning makes you a better thinker in every aspect of your life: in your career, and as a consumer, citizen, friend, parent, and lover. You must find out the core skills of effective thinking; then analyze your own thought processes, identify weaknesses, and overcome them. You have to translate this critical and effective thinking into better decisions. You will have greater satisfaction levels when you make good decisions. Most of all, you will have a bigger self-confidence to chase and attain your most essential goals in life and business. In any case, success is all about trying new ideas and new things. I always say that failure is a great teacher, if we have right attitude. All the winners learn from their mistakes. There is a science of success and you must learn and apply the law of success to get it. Success is achieved through the hard way and there is no shortcut to success.

BEST-CUT TO SUCCESS

> *"A coach is someone who can give correction without causing resentment."*
>
> John Wooden (1910–2010)

There is a shortcut and I call it Best-Cut to the process of achieving success. Get yourself a mentor or a trainer in the area of your chosen field. There can be three types of mentors. Trouble-Solver is the person you meet or call when you are in trouble. Advice-Giver is an expert who is good at analysis so he advises on a problem. Promise-Binder constantly reminds you of your promises. I prefer personal coaching because a perfect mentor combines all the above three functions of three mentors at a personalized level. Whether you want to lose weight, learn guitar or launch your own business, a guru who has been there can help you to move in quickest and safest way towards your target. In view of the fact that they had already reached where you want to be, they are acquainted with the challenges that you will face and what will work for you in a particular fix. Pay them for their knowledge and have access to their wisdom.

A GOOD ADVICE CAN SAVE YOU

> *"It takes a great man to give sound advice tactfully, but a greater to accept it graciously."*
>
> Logan P. Smith (1865–1946)

The folk tales have a great wisdom in them. Confucius once said: "By three methods we may learn wisdom: First, by reflection, which is noblest; second, by imitation, which is easiest; and third by experience, which is the bitterest." I tell you a famous folk tale on wisdom. An intelligent man came to a city from his village to earn his living. He read only books in his young days so he took a shop on rent and decided to sell the wisdom. He hung a board – "Wisdom for Sale" on his shop. He stood in front of his shop and started to call out at the top of his voice, "Come, Wisdom for sale." All the other shopkeepers made fun of him but the man did not pay any attention to their gesture and comments. One day a rich man's son came to this man and asked, "What is the price of 1 kg wisdom?" The wisdom-seller replied, "Wisdom is not sold as per weight but by quality." The son of rich man said, "O.k., Give me wisdom worth one rupee."

The wisdom-seller took one of the sheets of paper and wrote: "Don't stand around and watch two people quarrelling." The son when told his father about this bargain, his father got angry. They went to the wisdom-seller immediately. The rich man said to wisdom-seller, "You have taken advantage of my son's foolishness. Return our money otherwise I will complain before the king and have you punished for befooling people." The wisdom-seller said, "Return my wisdom and take back your money." "Here it is! Take your wisdom back," the rich man said and threw the piece of paper on his face. The wisdom-seller spoke, "No, this piece of paper is not the wisdom. It is the idea that makes the difference. Your son must promise not to use the wisdom I have given him and should always stand and watch people quarrelling. So, the man promised that his son would not use the wisdom that wisdom-seller had sold him and took one rupee back. The king of that kingdom had two queens who constantly quarreled with each other. Each one had a maid and the two maids were also quarrelsome. One day, as rich man's son wandered around the market, he saw that the two maids were fighting on the same fruit. Rich man's son kept his father's promise to the wisdom-seller and stood by to watch the fight. Both of them noticed him and said: "You're our witness as to who started this whole fight?"

So, the king called rich man's son in order to sort out the matter. The rich man was scared. Anyway, finding no other solution, they went to wisdom-seller. The wisdom-seller charged one hundred rupees and told rich man's son to pretend to be mad. Rich man's son followed the advice and the king dismissed the case finding the witness of unsound mind. However, the rich man soon realized that if the king came to know about this trick, they would be in deep trouble. So, back they went to seek another advice about this issue. The wisdom-seller this time charged five hundred rupees and told the rich man to tell the truth when the king was in a good mood. The rich man did so. The king laughed and forgave them. The king was also curious about this young man who sold wisdom and next day the king called for wisdom–seller. The king asked, "I have heard that you sell wisdom. Do you have something special for me?" The wisdom-seller replied boldly, "Yes, My Glorious King! I have a special advice for you. It will cost one lakh rupees." The king gave the money and the wisdom-seller gave him a note on which it was written: "Think deeply before you do anything." The king made this printed on almost everything he used. Once, the king fell ill. One of the ministers conspired with elder queen to kill the king. The royal physician was bribed and the physician offered a medicine mixed with poison. Before drinking the medicine, the king started to see the instruction written on that glass: "Think deeply before you do anything." The physician thought that the king had caught him. He told the king about the conspiracy. The king banished the doctor, queen and the minister from the country. The king made wisdom-seller his minister. The wisdom-seller helped the king rule the kingdom wisely and well for many years.

Moral of the story:

1. A good consultancy is always costly.
2. A good advice can save you from many troubles.
3. Everybody from layman to king needs advice.
4. A good advice becomes effective only when it is implemented.
5. A minister should always be a good consultant.

KNOWLEDGE IS POWER

> *"Human behaviour flows from three main sources: desire, emotion, and knowledge."*
>
> Plato (428 BC–348 BC)

Reading gives you "Knowledge to excel" and exercise gives the much needed "Energy to excel" to put that powerful knowledge into action. You must develop a habit of giving mind and body an exercise. The key lies in regular exercising and reading. Plato said: "Knowledge is the food of soul." Learning is the greatest thing in life that can keep your mind young. The purpose of any education is the knowledge. This knowledge is not of facts but of values. William Shakespeare has compared knowledge with the wing wherewith we fly to heaven. It makes sense, doesn't it? After all, knowledge is power when it is applied. So, you are getting both good health and sound mind through exercise and reading. But remember information is not knowledge. Real knowledge is to know the level of one's lack of knowledge. To know that we know what we know, and to know that we do not know what we do not know that is right knowledge. Right knowledge will make you imaginative and will give you the vision to see the unseen because imagination is and will remain more powerful than knowledge.

RESEARCHED EFFORT APPROACH

> *"Knowledge has to be improved, challenged, and increased constantly, or it vanishes."*
>
> Peter Drucker (1909–2005)

You must focus on all-round development of your personality. You should read on the area of concern, the area of biggest effect, and then start reading on that area. Robert Feldman, a professor of psychology, prescribes a formula for success and that is POWER – Prepare, Organize, Work, Evaluate and Rethink. Consult the people and take guidance from coaches. For example, if you are getting overweight the best way will be to look for a good coach and to work out at a good gym. I will also advise you to read some good books and writings on this subject. The approach is whatever you do, make it a habit to read, surf, search on that area and keep trying new things. I call it "RE Approach—Researched Effort Approach." Aamir Khan is one of brightest examples of this approach. B.R. Ambedkar – chief architect of the Indian Constitution, Dr. A.P.J. Abdul Kalam – 11th President of India, Martin Luther King Jr. – First president of Southern Christian Leadership Conference are known for their learning abilities. Theodore Roosevelt read a book every day before breakfast. He was known for defeating the scientist, technicians and others with his knowledge. Henry Ford said: "Anyone who stops learning is old, whether at twenty or eighty." Napoleon Bonaparte spent hours with his books. Winston Churchill once said: "I am always ready to learn." Abe Lincoln plowed with a book in his back pocket for reading during frequent breaks. Kay Winters wrote for Lincoln: "He loved books. They changed his life. He changed the world." Adolf Hitler had a personal library. August Kubizek once wrote for Hitler: "I just can't imagine Adolf without books. He had them piled up around him at home. He always had a book with him wherever he went." Hitler said: "Reading is not an end to itself, but a means to an end." Mahatma Gandhi also had a love for lifelong learning. He said: "Live as if you were to die tomorrow. Learn as if you were to live forever." I try to make an effort with proper prior research. But when I don't have time to take on research, I prefer to take action with proper guidance and study during the process of making an effort.

LEARNING—A CONTINUOUS PROCESS

> *"The more I live, the more I learn. The more I learn, the more I realize, the less I know."*
>
> Michel Legrand, a French musical composer

Your learning will show its effect in your thinking patterns, your attitudes, your behaviours and in your lifestyle and more importantly in your personal philosophy. There are people like Carlos Ruiz Zafón who once said, "Some like to believe it's the book that chooses the person" however I believe no designation or post, howsoever high, it may be, is good enough to stop learning.

We are moving from Information Age to Conceptual Age. Future of global business belongs to the right-brainers. According to Daniel H. Pink, the keys to success are in developing and cultivating six senses: design, story, symphony, empathy, play and meaning. For the age that we are in, we need a whole new mind. Creativity and innovation like iPhones design emerging from right brain is going to dominate the world in coming future. I recommend a blend of critical and creative thinking, a combination of left and right brain, a winning strategy.

You create relevant things when you create after learning. My civil engineer friend, Gulbir Chauhan justifies studiousness: "There is nothing like the smell of books. Learning is a continuous process. In fact, one is expected to learn every moment. In that case only, you can be called as – Learned Person." We should learn new knowledge and skills. We should acclimatize to positive learning (good things) and avoid negative learning (bad things). You can opt for personality development course, a fitness program, a financial training session, etc.

SUGGESTED STRATEGY

> *"Reading is to the mind what exercise is to the body."*
>
> Sir Richard Steele (1672–1729)

Surround yourself with successful people, motivational books and more importantly imbibe winning habits through positive learning. You can also set goals for yourself on skills and knowledge you want to attain every month or year. All true book-lovers employ the method of reading in bed because no book can be understood until it has been slept with and dreamed over. I personally choose to keep one book in my attention till I finish it. I carry it to office; keep it in my car and near the bed. The motto is: I read whenever I get the time. I really scratch my head in puzzlement when I hear people say they don't like reading. My belief is that they just haven't found the right book yet. Make it a habit of reading a book or surfing internet before you sleep and set a target to complete the topic or book. Then, you can record the observations in your notebook or on your blog. Soon, your observations will take a form of a book. Every page of my book, I write, is like a painting to me – made of words.

ASSIGNMENT

1. Be a member of famous libraries or join good websites and visit at least twice a month.

2. Read at least one book per week. You can change the subject each week if you like to avoid boredom or can continue with same theme for a research.
3. Identify the weak areas in your personal and professional arena and plan the strategies for reaching your set goals.
4. Listen to the Audio program *Think and Grow Rich* by Napoleon Hill. You can search podiobooks.com for more audios.

VISUALIZATION

You must visualize yourself taking all the instructions with full intensity and being successful ultimately. It is once again "fake it till you make it" policy. Remember: Whatever Lifelong learners touch ultimately turns into gold.

SELF SUGGESTION

I do research before I act on anything.

Bear in mind: Super achievers always keep their commitments.

[*Promise & Put Your Signature Here With Date*]

18

Do You Want To Be Your Own Boss?

OBJECTIVES

- To learn the "Law of Entrepreneurship",
- To understand the desired legal form of your business and,
- To prepare your plan B.

GOLDEN GUIDANCE

> *"Business is a game, played for fantastic stakes, and you're in competition with experts. If you want to win, you have to learn to be a master of the game."*
>
> Sidney Sheldon (1917–2007)

STRUGGLE: A PART OF GROWTH EXPERIENCE

> *"To live is to suffer; to survive is to find some meaning in the suffering."*
>
> Friedrich Nietzsche (1844–1900)

The most successful people we have known are those who have undergone defeats, undergone suffering, undergone struggle and undergone loss. But they have found their way out. We should draw survival and motivation from any bad experience. Sufferings are essential part of life. I often quote:

The higher you fall from; the higher you bounce back. A little boy was playing with his mother in a garden. The boy saw a fascinating caterpillar on a tree. The caterpillar was behaving strangely. The mother explained to the boy how the caterpillar would go through a metamorphosis to become a butterfly. The little boy was thrilled to hear about the changes in caterpillar. A small hole appeared in the cocoon and the butterfly started to struggle to come out. At first the boy was excited, but soon he became concerned. The butterfly was struggling so hard to get out. He snipped the cocoon to make the hole bigger and the butterfly quickly emerged. As the butterfly came out the boy was surprised. It had a swollen body and small, shrivelled wings. The butterfly didn't fly. It was only crawling. As the boy tried to figure out what had gone wrong, his mother took him to talk to a scientist relative. He learned that the butterfly was supposed to struggle. The scientist said to the boy, "The entire world is filled with suffering. It is all about survival of the fittest."

Moral of the story:

1. Struggling is an important part of any growth experience.
2. The struggles of life are not intended to ruin you, but to make you stronger and superior.
3. You will learn how to get up when you fall.
4. The tougher the lesson, the bigger the blessing.

TANSTAAFL

> *"There is no worse tyranny than to force a man to pay for what he does not want merely because you think it would be good for him."*
>
> Robert A. Heinlein, *The Moon is a Harsh Mistress*

Nothing is free, and if something seems free, it's just that you're getting charged through a back-door means; e.g., a bar might offer you a free lunch but you pay for it in the price of drinks.

Allow me to quote a story. A spiritual master wanted to draw the final conclusion from the wisdom of the ancient texts and saints, so he ordered his disciples to spread around the world and asked them to come with the greatest wisdom of all time. After about two years they came back with a report that contained more than 10,000 pages. The master looked at the report and said, "This is far too detailed, can you reduce it down a bit?" So, they went away and came back three years later with a 1000–page report. Again, the master looked at the second report and said, "Still too much detail. Can you reduce it still further?" In about five years they came back with one simple sentence. It read, "There ain't no such thing as a free lunch." The master asked, "Why this phrase only?" The scholars explained, "Our ten-year research reveals that you have to pay price for each and everything." This phrase actually dates back to at least the 1930s. This version of the phrase is often reduced to the acronym: TANSTAAFL. Nobel-prize winning Chicago-school economist Milton Friedman is famous for saying, "There is no such thing as a free lunch." Science-fiction novelist Robert Heilein also used the phrase in his book *The Moon is a Harsh Mistress*.

Moral of the story:

1. Every business is in existence to earn a profit.
2. Business is all about: People, Product and Profits.
3. There is a price for everything: Be it business or life.
4. Banks, suppliers and other lenders will help you only when you are making profit.

MAINTAIN YOUR CREDIBILITY

> *"Think twice before you speak, because your words and influence will plant the seed of either success or failure in the mind of another."*
>
> Napoleon Hill (1883–1970)

A shepherd boy used to graze his sheep in a forest near his village. He was very foolish and a liar. One day he thought to play a joke. He started crying at the top of his voice "Wolf! Wolf!" It was a white lie. On hearing his cries, all the villagers came running with sticks to help him. On reaching there, they found no wolf. Instead the shepherd laughed at them. They understood that the boy had befooled them. They returned to their houses. One day, a wolf really came there and attacked the boy. He started shouting at the top of his voice "Wolf! Wolf!" But the villagers thought that he was trying to befool them once again. They did not come to his help. The wolf killed the boy and took away one sheep. The foolish boy was killed because he was a liar.

Moral of the story:

1. Think twice before you lie.
2. You have your success founded upon your credibility.
3. Every credibility space will have a credulity space also.
4. Credibility applies in every aspect of life and business.

WHY DO YOU WANT TO START A BUSINESS?

"A business that makes nothing but money is a poor business."

Henry Ford (1863–1947)

Are you struggling hard to make money? Are you letting your struggle to define you? Do you want to be your own boss? Do you want to become rich? There are two ways of being rich. One is to have all you want; the other is to be satisfied with what you have. Most of us are not happy with what we have; hence we look for business option to make more money. A successful business gets five times profit as compared to actual costs.

Indeed in most cases it is the dreams of great wealth or financial security that directs people to go for this option instead of job. It allows you to use your time and work towards something that is all yours. So, *here is the golden tip*: "A business is nothing but a way you opt to live the kind of life you want to live. And if you do it accurately, your business can be a way to pull the change you want to see in the world. Most of all, you want to create something you're proud of. A business is more than money."

WHO IS AN ENTREPRENEUR?

> *"New opinions are always suspected, and usually opposed, without any other reason but because they are not already common."*
>
> John Locke (1632–1704)

The word"entrepreneur" has French origin. An entrepreneur is an economic innovator or imitator who exploits opportunities to bring change or improvement. Cecil Castle affirms: "Professionalism is a frame of mind, not a paycheck." He makes the most out of readily available products and services, to generate new products and new services. He develops, organizes, manages and more importantly leads a business venture by converting sources into resources in the field of manufacturing, whole selling, retailing and service for profit. He is a sensible risk taker and is different from intrapreneur who is an entrepreneur within a previously established organization. I call an entrepreneur the economic scientist who develops the regional, national and global economy.

INTERNAL COMMITMENT

> *"You are never too old to set another goal or to dream a new dream."*
>
> C.S. Lewis (1898–1963)

The plus point of business is that old or young can do it. The only thing you need is to step forward. If you don't step forward, you will always be in the same place. If you don't go after what you want, you will never have it. You don't have to make excuses rather make changes. Always remember the golden law of growth:"If it doesn't challenge you; it won't change you."

Richard Branson, an English Business Magnet and founder and chairman of Virgin Group of more than 400 companies asserts: "There is no point in starting your own business unless you do it out of a sense of frustration." Stepping up—It's a simple concept, the first thing, an internal commitment to begin your business. I put this first, because it's the reason of passion that will motivate you the most to start a startup. A person or an organization will survive forever, if they have the 5 Cs i.e. Character, Commitment, Conviction, Courtesy and Courage.

IDENTIFY YOUR BUSINESS IDEA

> *"To turn really interesting ideas and fledgling technologies into a company that can continue to innovate for years, it requires a lot of disciplines."*
>
> Steve Jobs (1955–2011)

This is the second thing you need to consider. The business idea is the conception of business. Will you deal in objects or services? There are three ways to identify your business options.

The first way is to identify your passions. A business must involve you. It should be enjoyable and based on your creative impulses. Make a list of your interests. Look at the things you have been doing since your childhood for free or at low cost. Wrap up your skills in a package and offer that in form of your services or objects. This product (object or service) is that you always wanted to offer. The second way is to see what business other people are doing and then choosing the right one as per your choice. The experiences of previously successful and/or failed entrepreneurs are everywhere. Learn from others' mistakes and wisdoms. The third way is to identify people's demands or real needs. You can always fulfill the market gap in objects or services. The most important thing is that you must study and research on the idea and take people's advices for your business in terms of its success. "Research is the tool that you apply to your business idea to see if there's a requirement."

OVERNIGHT FAME OF FLIPKART

"It takes more than capital to swing business. You've got to have the A. I. D. degree to get by - Advertising, Initiative, and Dynamics."

Ren Mulford Jr. (1859–1932)

The overnight popularity of Flipkart, an e-commerce website was surprising for many. It was founded by Sachin Bansal and Binny Bansal in 2007. In its initial years, Flipkart focused on online sales of books, but it later expanded to electronic goods and a variety of other products. This website is one of India's top 20 websites. Sachin Bansal, the CEO was planning to get a job while he was studying inspite of the fact that he comes from a business family. After graduating from IIT Delhi, Sachin Bansal and Binny Bansal were working in Bangalore. They were not entirely happy because they wanted to do something useful. Then, they thought of their own online shopping site. They were convinced that Indian market will give them space for this website. They sensed the sweet smell of success. This website has proved to be bookworm's best friend and reported sales worth 100 core rupees a month since July 2012. A management teacher and corporate consultant, Sandeep Aggarwal affirms: "The misfortune is that a huge number of people have great ideas, but they don't make out whether there's a need for it." It is equally essential to research your contest.

BUSINESS PLAN

"Give me six hours to chop down a tree and I will spend the first four sharpening the axe."

Abraham Lincoln (1809–1865)

After determination of the business idea, third thing is to plan your business. The common nomenclature is plan B. Write down your goals, business strategies and action steps in your business journal. Develop a working name for your business even if you change it later. You need to conduct a feasibility study in terms of Strengths–Weaknesses–Opportunities–Threats, in short have a SWOT scrutiny. Business gurus call it STP – Segmentation, Targeting & Positioning Analysis.

For proper market segmentation, you must divide the market into distinct groups based on demographic, geographical, psychographic and behavioural segmentation with distinct needs that might require separate products. Geographical factors like country, region, city, density and climate; Demographic factors like age, gender, family size, income, occupation, education, religion, language, customs, race, nationality, industries, companies and locations; psychographic factors like lifestyle, social class and personality and behavioural factors like occasions, benefits, user status, aptitude towards products, loyalty and readiness play their respective roles in determining purchasing approaches.

Target market consists of a set of customers that shares common characteristics or needs that a company decides to serve. You must evaluate the size and growth of segmentation, level of competition, paying capacity of buyers and substitute products. You can also select socially responsible targeting like children or handicapped.

Positioning is all about generating the brand image in the minds of potential customers and for that you need to select appropriate positioning strategy including USP – Unique Selling Point that is point of difference from similar products.

You can offer free samples and have feedback from your prospective customers. You must assign roles and responsibilities of your staff (including you) clearly. You have to divide the tasks and assign each sub-task to a team.

The 1992 USA Olympic basketball team was a dream team and that was a collection of immortals gathered in one place at one time. The team featured the golden trio of Michael Jordan who was possibly the most notable person in the world at that time, Magic Johnson and Larry Bird as well as Patrick Ewing, Charles Barkley, David Robinson, John Stockton,

Karl Malone, Clyde Drexler, Chris Mullin, Scottie Pippen and Christian Laettner. Chuck Daly was the coach. The point that I want to make is: The greatest task is to have a dream team and the next greatest is to maintain it. You have to see that your team is not in a self-destructive mode. The five stars of team management are:

1. You should build trust among your team members.
2. There should not be any apprehension of any difference or dispute.
3. You should renew the commitment of team members towards the purpose.
4. Liability must be fixed. Who will do what?
5. Results must be examined.

Results must be carefully studied, and if there is any mistake liabilities must be seen and commitment must be renewed. One should have his trust in other and all must have trust in you and if there is any difference or dispute, the atmosphere should be cleaned to keep it tension free. The golden rule of team management: Keep team interest above the personal interest.

You should recruit staff members on the basis of reasoning ability, market capability, data interpretation, computer skills and English and other languages competence. You should make one person team leader from each team and decide the leadership style for him/her. You must provide attachment for each sub-task in form of promotional reward or punishment. I personally see only two simple disciplines of healthy organizations:

1. You should constantly work on building effective team and maintaining it.
2. You should try to maintain clarity in term of organizational goals and standards.

The important thing remains the earliest understanding: Crystal Clear Communication and Consolidation of organizational clarity. Selection of right person for right job is also must. "Hire character and Train skill."

This quote of Peter Schutz can motivate any leader in recruitment and training. A team leader has to maintain a sound corporate culture and behaviour. The principle of sound culture and behaviour: Whatever affects one directly, affects all indirectly.

As far as sale is concerned, you must determine costs and benefits to settle your price of product or service. You can begin with an end in mind. Like Tata Motors announced 1 lakh rupees car Nano first and then designed it. This is known as reverse engineering. After price, you have to decide whether you will use a distribution channel or you will approach the customers directly. You must plan your promotional strategies like media, social sites, newspapers and games etc. You can either move with push method or you can pull the customers from the first go.

You need to carry our many B2B (Business to Business) transaction before you deliver one B2C (Business to Consumer) transaction. For example an automobile manufacturing company will use many B2B transactions like buying tyres, windscreen, engines and other parts etc. before delivering the finished product transaction to the end consumer B2C.

A big change is unachievable unless you have the support of enthusiastic cooperation of a number of individuals and for that continuous motivation holds the key. Change sticks when it becomes the way we do the things. You can never promise a win, but you can always earn your right to win. Zig Ziglar said: "You were born to win, but to be a winner, you must plan to win, prepare to win, and expect to win." Preparation at physical and mental level, smart decision-making and toughness in the face of adversity are the game changers.

There are market proverbs like most of the businesses collapse during first five years. Take your chances. Look out for an incubation program or government scheme suited for your business. Be courageous, you will not see the light unless you walk through tunnel and experience the darkness.

DECIDE THE LEGAL STRUCTURE

> *"Every company has two organizational structures: The formal one is written on the charts; the other is the everyday relationship of the men and women in the organization."*
>
> Harold S. Geneen (1910–1997)

You must decide the type of business entity or legal structures. The higher your structure is to be, the deeper must be its foundation. Since each legal form has its own unique plus and minus points, your goal is to choose the form that works best for you.

Sole proprietorships are the most common – and simplest – form of business organization. A sole proprietorship is an unincorporated business organization that's owned and operated by an individual. Sole proprietors own all assets and profits of the business and also assume complete responsibility for business liabilities and debts.

When two or more people decide to join together to carry on a trade or business, their relationship is considered to be a partnership. In general, each partner contributes to all aspects of the business including money, property and labour or skill. In return, each partner shares in the profits and losses of the business. They have a formal written agreement. Partnerships come in two varieties: general partnerships and limited partnerships. In a general partnership, the partners manage the company and assume responsibility for the partnership's debts and other obligations. A limited partnership has both general and limited partners. The general partners own and operate the business and assume liability for the partnership, while the limited partners serve as investors only; they have no control over the company and are not subject to the same liabilities as the general partners. Limited Liability partnership provides all the benefits of an incorporated company as well as the flexibility of a partnership.

A cooperative society is an autonomous, jointly owned and democratic association of persons who voluntarily cooperate to meet their common economic, social and cultural needs. This is a society registered or deemed to be registered under any law relating to cooperative societies. This form is mostly used in community service. In a survey, it was found that over 800 million people are members of cooperatives around the world. The cooperatives provide 20% more employments as compared to multinational corporations.

The corporate structure is more complex and expensive than most other business structures. A corporation is an independent legal entity, separate from its owners, and as such, it requires complying with more regulations and tax requirements. A corporation can sell stock, either common or preferred, to raise funds. A corporation's debt is not considered that of its owners, so if you organize your business as a corporation, you are not putting your personal assets at risk.

HIRE PROFESSIONALS

"The executive exists to make sensible exceptions to general rules."
Elting E. Morison, the founder of MIT's Program in Science, Technology and Society (STS)

There are two professionals every business requires in the early hours: an accountant and a lawyer. The reason for hiring an accountant is crystal clear. You want someone to help you in maintaining your business accounts, review your numbers periodically, and prepare all of your necessary tax returns and other important documents. Get a good attorney to take care of all the documentation as per rules and regulations. A good business attorney will provide basic help in almost every aspect of your business, from basic local conformity and copyright and trademark suggestion to formal business incorporation and lawsuits and liability. I advise you to go for professionals in other areas too. But you can manage things in the early periods to keep the cost low. Remember what Robert Bosch said: "I have a lot of money because I pay good wages."

MARKETING STRATEGY

> *"The man who will use his skill and constructive imagination to see how much he can give for a dollar, instead of how little he can give for a dollar, is bound to succeed."*
>
> Henry Ford (1863–1947)

The concept of marketing mix (Neil Borden, 1953) was developed into four Ps of marketing (E. Jerome McCarthy, 1960) meaning thereby Product in terms of object or service; Price of product; Place of purchase and Promotion. Recently, a fifth "P" – people – has been added.

STEPPS is an acronym suggested by a marketing professor Jonah Berger in his book *Contagious: Why Things Catch On* that stands for Social Currency, Triggers, Emotion, Public, Practical Value and Stories. In his research he found that people don't listen to advertisements, they listen to their peers. But why do people talk about certain products and ideas more than others? He explains that people will share only those things that enhances their image in other's eyes, connected with other popular thing, evoke highly arousing positive or emotions except sadness, prevalent in public eye, useful and helpful things, and so narrative that it becomes a story. Experts on marketing management agree that promotion stands on four pillars:

1. Advertisement in form of audio, visual and print media.
2. Public relation in form of press releases, trade fair, exhibition, seminars and conferences.
3. Personal selling in form of mouth momentum.
4. Motivation in form of reaching the hearts of potential customers.

Marketing plan needs to be centred on customers' satisfaction. Customer is the true boss. You need to carry out a market research in order to know the customers' needs. Then, you will target the market group logically.

STRUCTURING YOUR BUSINESS FINANCE

"Money was never a big motivation for me, except as a way to keep score. The real excitement is playing the game."

Donald Trump, an American business magnate

You need start-up cash, as professionals call it, to begin your business. If you don't have enough money, there is no other option but to look for outside financial assistance. You must compose your business plan first and then make your capital search thereafter. You can choose between debt and equity, the most common financial strategies. Now the current trend is Mezzanine debt, a combine of equity and debt that is junior to traditional bank financing but senior to equity financing in a capital structure. Memorize Mike Dolan's advice: "Work as if you own the company and soon you just might." Nothing great was ever achieved without enthusiasm.

Debt financing involves borrowing the money from banks, friends or family members. The biggest profit of debt financing is that you remain the owner of your business and enjoy the freedom to do as you like. You also enjoy tax deductions on your installments. The main drawback is that the installment money including interest has to be paid regularly despite any ups or downs in business otherwise loan may ruin your prosperity permanently. You have to pay the installments out of profit or out of pocket, this thing can make your business growth slow due to lack of investments. You need to get funding loans from diverse options to keep your cash flow high and interest rate low. The other thing is that you may not own or possess collateral assets or personal guarantee to collateralize the loan amount.

In case of equity financing, you sell your part of business ownership. An equity investor makes a return on his investment when the company is sold. The most familiar types of equity investors are Angel Investors and Venture Capital firms. Angel investors are wealthy groups or individuals who invest for long-term and don't look for large returns as Venture Capitalists do. Venture Capitalists look for large return that too in short periods like five years. Equity is good option because of more cash in hands. This cash can be invested in business growth and even if there is no profit there is no accounting for equity contributions. Equity is ownership. Risk and reward (if any) are shared. In case of a company, it can sell the shares and pay dividends. In case it fails to pay the dividends, the share price may go down and shareholders can sell their shares.

STEP BY STEP PROGRESS

> *"To be successful, you have to have your heart in your business, and your business in your heart."*
>
> Thomas Watson, Sr., (1874–1956)

Start with Bootstrapping. Use your resources and your savings to begin your business. Begin at small level. At the initial level, let it be a self-sustaining process that proceeds without external help. Step by step you can make progress. After two years, you can go for a bank loan. Later on, you can opt of further investments. You can change the form of business as your business and liabilities grow. You can start with sole proprietorship and convert that into corporation later on.

You can take inspiration from Google success story. Google was first incorporated as a privately held company on September 4, 1998, and its initial public offering followed on August 19, 2004. The founders Larry Page and Sergey Brin founded it while they were Ph.D. students at Stanford University. They financed their earlier efforts through the use of credit cards and venture capital. Kevin Smith's success is another example to follow. Kevin Smith financed a black and white 1994 movie "Clerks" by using credit cards, selling a majority of his comic book collection and borrowing money from family and friends. The shoestring budget of film was low $27,000. So, the extra cost of using colour film was impossible to finance. The movie grossed more than $3 million in theatres. Mark Zuckerberg of Facebook is an example that you can build something really good in a night. Domino's founder Tom Monaghan added extra value to his food by making it available more quickly than his counterparts. The golden rule of Domino's: Treat people as you want to be treated. For every customer he lost, he gained many. Tom Monaghan articulates: "My theory is there are people who would buy my pizza because of my position." The rest couldn't care less, but the controversy was free advertising. How to generate investments? You need to prepare the list of potential known investors including personal friends and professionals and then you will discuss your business project with them. And, if there is a yes from the first line of investors go for other people, as second line of investors and so on. You must ask all of them to pay the money by a due date.

START-UP RESERVE

> *"You only have to do a very few things right in your life so long as you don't do too many things wrong."*
>
> Warren Buffett, an American business magnate

Remember my golden advice: You should have at least six months expenses; I call them Startup Reserve, in advance along with start-up capital, because you can't expect any business to generate the money from the first day. This reserve money will give you the confidence and courage to run your business.

ORGANIZATIONAL ABILITY

> *"Successful enterprises are usually led by a proven chief executive who is a competent benevolent dictator."*
>
> Richard Pratt (1934–2009)

You must have agreed by now that business is one of the main professions of wealthiest people. There are certain essential abilities that you must have for best business success. You must have P.O.E. Skills. This talent combines three into one. It consists of *Plan, Organization* and through these to get the domino *Effect* ultimately. All the chief executive officers, directors and top management officials are paid highly throughout the world because of their P.O.E. Skills. Proper business planning requires that you must understand accounting, business financing and cost controls with their theoretical and practical implications. The planning aspect has been covered in this chapter. Let us have a look at organizational aspect. The first auxiliary of the organizational skill is the skill to select the right people for right positions otherwise you will not be able to build effective teams. A greatest manager will fail without the cooperation of his fellow workers. The domino effect comes only when the whole organization works together. The second auxiliary of the organizational skill is that you must also be proficient at personal and professional communication. It means you must have the art of influence that is very much essential because at every juncture of your life and career you have to convince others to sell your ideas. The third auxiliary of organizational skill is that you must hold meetings with the staff, people, bankers, suppliers and customers. It is all about winning the confidence. A senior management teacher and corporate consultant Dr. Vijay Rathee also confirms: "You must be good enough to respond to the feedback and always be ready to do the necessary changes by getting the concerned parties in total confidence."

SUGGESTED STRATEGY

> *"To run this business ... you need ... optimism, humanism, enthusiasm, intuition, curiosity, love, humour, magic and fun, and that secret ingredient – euphoria."*
>
> Dame Anita Roddick (1942–2007)

Step by step you can get through anything – this is the truth and you have to believe it. You must treat your business idea as your baby. I mean you should love it, nurture it and give it some time to grow and mature. In the end, you're going to succeed because you're crazy enough to think you can. Get a strong hold on ABC of business –

A – Internal Commitment;

B – Business Idea; and

C – Business Plan.

The rest is a matter of time only. Jean-Pierre Garnier, former CEO of GlaxoSmithKline said: "I don't know anyone who is passionate and unsuccessful." The wealth to grow is extensively accessible if you need it for a specific mission. Nonetheless, the bottom line remains the same: "You must add value to your products." As in business alphabets Z is always Reputation. Put more concentration on serving the people and society instead of making more money. You can offer them free samples. Hire good looking sales professionals. The more you will serve, the more money you will make. Collect the support network of supporting people like investors, traders, groups and advisors around you to help and build you and your business. Join professional organizations. You must use the powerful social networking sites, emails, blogs, websites, articles, columns, speeches and internet marketing tools to dispense your news and messages but also use conventional methods like telephone, letters and mouth publicity. Avoid the biggest risk: Reputational risk. And in case of any loss or trouble always remember: The performance of an organization is entirely determined by the excellence of its employees and products.

ASSIGNMENT

1. Try to maintain a business journal. Write your goals, strategies and action plans.
2. Develop business plan for your business idea in full details.
3. Try to figure out your finance options.
4. Listen to the audio program on *The Art of the Start* by Guy Kawasaki.

VISUALIZATION

When you get up, just sit for thirty minutes and visualize yourself living your business idea with sense intelligence. Remember: Get a strong hold on ABC of business.

SELF SUGGESTION

I have the God-Gift to use my creativity, potential and charisma to make my business more profit-oriented.

Bear in mind: Super achievers always keep their commitments.

[*Promise & Put Your Signature Here With Date*]

19

How Many Genuine Friends Do You Have?

OBJECTIVES

- To learn the "Law of Persuasion",
- To offer dual gifts of care and share to people, and
- To act as a benefactor in the society.

GOLDEN GUIDANCE

"I am very fond of strawberries and cream, but I have found that for some strange reason, fish prefer worms. So when I went fishing, I didn't think about what I wanted. I thought about what they wanted. I didn't bait the hook with strawberries and cream. Rather, I dangled a worm or grasshopper in front of the fish."

Dale Carnegie (1888–1955)

WE RELY HEAVILY ON PERSUASION

"In making a speech one must study three points: first, the means of producing persuasion; second, the language; third the proper arrangement of the various parts of the speech."

Aristotle (384 BC–322 BC)

Is it possible to convince people to do whatever you want, whenever you want? I have spent many years analyzing the behaviour and mindset of most persuasive people and came to the conclusion that this is certainly not a natural gift. Yes, experts call it art of persuasion. Everybody can learn and influence people provided he is ready to learn and practice certain ageless proven techniques in his behaviour. The enforcement of "persuasion above force" is the mark of a civilized society. No social problem like dowry, corruption, abortion, malnutrition can be resolved through legislation alone. Indian Constitution recognizes no other power than except persuasion, for enforcing religious or civil liberties. Persuasion is an art of gods. Themistocles (524–459 BC) was an Athenian politician and general who was a populist, having the support of lower class Athenians. He believed that he had with him two gods, Persuasion and Compulsion. Events even in a democratic society depend on a strong leadership with a strong power of persuasion, and not on the opinion of the masses. All the freedom fighters were great persuaders. Mahatma Gandhi is one of the leading examples of persuasion. Good political leaders are persuaders. John C. Maxwell asserts: "Leadership is influence." Lenin, Stalin, Hitler, Mao, Roosevelt and Churchill were great persuaders. FDR in his four terms, held 998 press conferences, an all-time record. He transformed the face of political communication with his use of radio. He always tried to soften the public opinion before implementing any legislation. For example, he convinced the public that social security is not against the American ideals of independence and self-help. As an orator, Churchill used words to hit opponents. He said: "The nation had the lion's heart. I had the luck to give the roar." Yitzhak Shamir (1915–2012) was an Israeli politician and the seventh Prime Minister of Israel, serving two terms, 1983–84 and 1986–1992. He believed that the will of the people is resolved by a strong leadership who has perfection in persuasion. The top 10 seducers of history Giacomo Casanova, Catherine the Great, Cleopatra, Lord Byron, Errol Flynn, Wilt Chamberlain, Russell Brand, Alan Clark, Jack Nicholson and John Wilkes had this art.

I was in constant touch with many persons especially on the concept of public behaviour. Narender Rajliwal, a public relation executive in PGI Chandigarh is one of them. He is an important member of my resourceful psyche group. He deals with people and solves their problems. He affirms: "One has to acquire at least one of the four powers – punctuality (time power), physical strength (body power), money (wealth power) or status (official power) – to be distinct. I have seen that punctual, strong, wealthy or authoritative people command great respect. If you are having all then consider yourself blessed. But the game changer is the behaviour – the fifth power – the people power." Understand the law of success: Success will be after you if you behave in an EPM—Exceptionally Polite Mode. FDR was under immense pressure during his first hundred days. In these "Hundred Days," he got all the support from Congress and the press. He passed fifteen major laws, given fifteen messages to Congress and ten speeches. He held press conferences and cabinet meetings two times in a week. He also sponsored an international conference. He made all major policy decisions, foreign and domestic, in this time of 100 days. But as Arthur Schlesinger Jr. notes: "FDR never displayed fright or panic and rarely even bad temper." Master the ability to move people emotionally. What a mother does when a child cry? She feeds. When our children disturb us what we do. We give them chocolates or make them sit before TV. Do you remember the night when you got your first android phone? Did you sleep that night? It's about emotions.

Our children can be persuaded to do the right things. Terence (195/185–159 BC), a playwright of the Roman Republic once asserted: "Children should be led into the right paths, not by severity, but by persuasion." I have observed that we all depend greatly on our persuasive powers each day. You try to get people agree with you in office or at home. You want to persuade others to arrive at a conclusion and then go for a decision as per your wishes. You want to influence people to do something as directed by you. You want to change or transform the attitude or behaviour of a person in your family or office. The key: Our success depends on how persuasive we can be.

THE ART OF INFLUENCE

> *"To be persuasive we must be believable;*
>
> *To be believable we must be creditable;*
>
> *To be credible we must be truthful."*
>
> Edward R. Murrow (1908–1965)

It takes tremendous discipline to control the influence. There are many techniques and strategies for influencing in body language. You should have an influential physical look. Gentleman clothing, well-built body and a strong posture. Mark Twain said: "Clothes make man." Your pacing must be with the vibe. Pacing is not about pushing through activities but managing your physical and mental energy prudently. Your hands should be by your side and not in pockets. Your movements should be confident meaning thereby your head is up and you know where you're going. Your chest must be out and your back should be straight. My advice: Follow the leaders in your field. You should not only be able to read but also send controlling and compelling body language messages. You should have the unique ability to attract the attention of people at any given time by your pulling card like telling a story, special treatment, flowery perfumes and exciting gifts. One of the essentials of art of persuasion is that your targeted person must feel happy and comfortable while in conversation with you. The skill of conversation is completely dependent on questions.

Dr. Ajit Singh Chahal, a social thinker, opines: "The ability to ask proper questions is an art in itself. The answers to your question are helpful in understanding your targeted person." You must have a total understanding of his value–ethic system, his unfulfilled desires, his true needs, and his belief-system. You should also have the skill of generating quick reliability and then maintaining it over a long period. You should be able to influence your target in such a way that he can't say no. You must use your convincing power cautiously as pushy behaviour can be annoying. You should put in wise words and the penalties of a negative reply. You must know what the other person is thinking in his mind. What is his stand? What are the reasons for his stand? And then at a snail's pace, you have to transform "What he thinks–to–What you think." The best thing you can keep in your head while speaking to other person is – "He is interested in what he wants." One of the techniques good persuaders employ is to start by finding the common gestures or words or hobbies etc. This is what you must do although you are eternally interested in what you want. Conversation Starter: Introduce yourself. Gary Chapman opines: "People experience love most strongly through one of five love languages – quality times, words of encouragement, gifts, acts of service, and physical touch." Everybody treats his behaviour as an outcome of external forces and other behaviour as an outcome of internal factors. Sympathizing with the other person is the golden key to unlock his heart by having a heart to heart conversation. "Where are you from?" is a great ice breaker. You can also suggest an idea and let the other person feels that the idea is his or hers. Nevertheless, you must allow the other person do all the talking to make him feel important.

TRANSACTIONAL ANALYSIS

> *"The destiny of every human being is decided by what goes on inside his skull when confronted by what goes on outside his skull."*
>
> Eric Berne (1910–1970)

In the 1950s Eric Berne began to develop his theories of Transactional Analysis. He worked with Erik Erikson who is famous for his research in Identity Crisis. He said that spoken communication, mainly face to face, is at the centre of human social relationships and psychoanalysis. When two people meet each other, one of them will speak to the other. This is

Transaction Stimulus. The reaction from the other person is Transaction Response. The person sending the Stimulus is Agent. The person who responds is Respondent. The psychology of persuasion makes the top secret clear: You have to construct controlling and compelling messages and speak to person's instincts. Berne also said that each person is made up of three alter ego states: PAC – Parent, Adult and Child. Every verbal communication comes from these three states. Parent state comes from what has been taught to you from your childhood. This includes influences of your teachers, neighbours, relatives and mentors. For example, a person may shout at someone out of frustration simply because he has been taught from childhood that this is the only way of commanding respect. Child is the felt part which you develop over the time when you react to the external events. For example, a person when criticized may look sad and depicts it by shame gestures as he used to do in childhood whereas a person who gets appreciation may show his joy by jumping and clapping or simply by a smiling face. The Adult state is the thought or learned concept and develops out of your free thinking. Strengthening the Adult state is the primary goal of TA. The suggestion that comes from this research is that you must decide the stimulus and response in order to have a successful conversation. There are three conversational transactional models – Complimentary, Crossed and Ulterior.

I give you some examples:

Complimentary Transactions

Example 1:

Agent: Have you done your assigned work? (Adult to Adult)

Respondent: Yes, I have done it. (Adult to Adult)

Example 2:

Agent: Would you like to do shopping with me? (Child to Child)

Respondent: Yes, I will. (Child to Child)

Example 3:

Agent: Have you finished your home work? (Parent to Child)

Respondent: Don't bother about me. I will do it. (Child to Parent)

You must have noticed that these are reciprocal transaction in which both persons are addressing the ego state the other is in.

Crossed Transactions

Communication failure occurs when both persons address ego states other than that their partner is in. For instance:

Example 1:

Agent: Have you done your assigned work? (Adult to Adult)

Respondent: Don't bother about me. I will do it. (Child to Parent)

Agent: You are fired. (Parent to Child)

Ulterior Transactions

In this transaction the overt social exchange occurs in parallel with a hidden psychological transaction. For instance:

Agent: I will go for the late night long drive. Will you? (Adult Stimulus but body language indicates joy intent (Joyous Child)

Respondent: No problem. (Adult response to Adult stimulus) smiling face (Child accepts the hidden motive).

Eric Berne presented his groundbreaking paper *Transactional Analysis: A New and Effective Method of Group Therapy* at a conference in 1957. This paper was officially published in 1958 in the American Journal of Psychotherapy. The phrase "I'm OK, You're OK" is the basis of a good transaction. You can read *Games People Play* by Eric Berne and *I'm OK You're OK* by Thomas and Amy Harris, for further clarifications on this theory.

DO NOT USE THREE Cs

"Any fool can criticize, condemn and complain and most fools do."

Benjamin Franklin (1706–1790)

My point is that when we criticize, condemn or complain (triple C) we find faults in somebody or something in a judgmental way. These three Cs do not bring any changes in behaviour and rather fan the flames of anger in receiver because it hurts our self-importance, pride and if I declare frankly and honestly, our arrogance excessively. Constructive criticism can mend our ways and improve our personality. But my childhood friend Dr. Praveen Gupta, who is known for his gentleness opines: "Most of the people take criticism personally in destructive sense and become self-protective and begin to shield themselves, so, I see no point in criticizing anybody, because unless the criticism is sought for, nobody treats it with any value. People give the gift of their absence to those who don't appreciate their presence. Moreover, the receiver will look for opportunity to get even with sender of criticism." But at the same time, I suggest, one of the two friends should be ready to prefer relationship over the little talks and both should not get angry at the same time. The best way to restrain the temptation to criticize is to understand others. Just place yourself in the shoes of that person and be the same person with same mindset, same circumstances and same temperament and then imagine what that person did. This exercise will make you feel relaxed because you know why they behave like this.

Most of us must have felt very bad when the teacher criticized our work in front of the whole class. Just undergo that situation, once again mentally. The key idea to put you under that agony is that nobody wants to get criticized, neither you nor me. Everybody has a desire to be appreciated and criticism hurts ambitions. Criticism can affect us, so others too, in a bad way because criticism in most cases generates shame instead of guilt. Therefore, if you want cooperation from people decline to vote criticism.

BEHAVIOUR REVEALS REAL PERSONA

> *"My relationship to power and authority is that I'm all for it. People need somebody to watch over them. Ninety-five percent of the people in the world need to be told what to do and how to behave."*
>
> Arnold Schwarzenegger, the 38th Governor of California

The behaviour towards others and especially with the less powerful people is the touchstone of wisdom and maturity of a person. All the surrounding environment including the nature, people and books have an impact over human behavioural development. Warren Buffett, an American business magnate, rightly affirms: "It's better to hang out with people better than you. Pick out associates whose behaviour is better than yours and you'll drift in that direction." I tell you a story that reveals the importance of behaviour. Once there was a farmer – Parkin. He had a cow that gave lot of milk. Parkin made lot of money by selling the milk of that cow. The cow got ill one day and stopped giving milk. Parkin behaved in a selfish manner and left the cow in jungle considering it worthless. The cow went to another farmer Pat's field. Pat was a nice man. He took the cow to his home, fed nicely and got it properly treated by doctor. The cow started to give milk in few days. Pat became famous for his cow and its milk quality and quantity in the whole area. One day when Parkin was passing by Pat's field, he recognized his cow. Parkin complained before the head of community and demanded his cow on the plea of ownership. Pat refused to give his cow on the plea of care. All the village men were confused. At last, the cow was given the option to select his owner. The cow, when left open, reached near Pat and started licking his hand. All said, "The cow has selected its owner ... the cow belongs to Pat." Parkin was amazed at the behaviour of cow and thought: "What wrong has he done to his cow?" He went away thinking, "It must be a magic."

Moral of the story:

1. Good behaviour has the ability to win the heart of everybody.
2. Your behaviour shows your true character.
3. A man judges himself on his intention and others by their actions.
4. Blame is the most common excuse to own bad behaviour.
5. Blaming people indulge in selfish behaviour.
6. Selfish person takes care of the thing as long as it gives benefits.
7. Good behaviour is the magical way to attract people.

GIVE 100% IN A RELATIONSHIP

"Relationships based on obligation lack dignity."

Wayne Dyer, an American self-help author

A relationship requires a lot of work and commitment. I am reminded of a short story on relationship. Two children Ram and Geeta were playing together. Ram had a collection of toys. Geeta had some sweets with her. Ram told Geeta that he would give her all his toys in exchange for her sweets. Geeta agreed. Ram kept the biggest and the most beautiful toy aside and gave the rest to Geeta. Geeta gave him all her sweets as she had promised. That night, Geeta slept calmly. But Ram couldn't sleep as he kept wondering if the girl had hidden some sweets from him the way he had hidden his best toy.

Moral of the story:

1. If you don't give your hundred percent in a relationship, you'll always keep doubting if the other person has given his/her hundred percent.
2. One loyal friend is worth ten thousand relatives.
3. You develop any relationship by surviving difficult times and enjoying happy ones.
4. Relationship is like a book. It takes years to write it but only few seconds to burn it.
5. Choose your relationships wisely. It's better to be alone than to be in bad company.

THREE TIPS FOR GREAT RELATIONSHIPS

"Find joy in everything you choose to do. Every job, relationship, home... it's your responsibility to love it, or change it."

Chuck Palahniuk, an American novelist

During my research for this chapter, I met with many people who are good friends, good husbands–wives and good leaders. One such great person is Mr. Vinay Singhal, who is presently the Managing Director, SJV Consultants Pvt. Ltd. He has over 45 years of work experience in senior management positions with Indian and MNC organizations. He is a Mechanical Engineer from BITS Pilani and has done Advance Management Program from Harvard Business School. He currently has many assignments like Senior Advisor, Partners Healthcare (Boston), Director of Nanobiosym (Boston) & Mazzetti Inc. of USA and Director of Nanhi Chhan Foundation. He is a member of Board of Governors in J.K. Business School and is also associated with NGOs like Path and Acord etc. He has held many glorious positions in the past also for instance Country Director of Clinton Foundation, CEO of Fortis HealthCare, President of Indo Rama & J.K. Synthetics, GM of Hindustan Unilever, and Project Head of DCM. When I asked him about his success, he highlighted hard work, passionate involvement in what you do, good networking and reasonable IQ as the main principles which have contributed to his success. There are many such conversations which I had with many successful persons but based on my research for this chapter, I want to share three tips for greater relationships:

Firstly, find the things of people's interests and be interested in those things. Then, you will have common grounds and shared interests. Show true respect to their opinions and thoughts. My first tip: You should take interest in people to enhance your people contacts.

Secondly, you have to be excited and energetic throughout the conversation. You can fake the whole process till it becomes a habit. You should behave as if you're laughing when you're smiling. Smiling makes us attractive, why, because it lifts the face and makes you younger. Start with a positive thought or appreciation. Behave like his old friend. You should use more leading questions during the conversation to keep it animated and enthusiastic. Learn to agree to disagree with them as a last alternative and admit your mistakes bravely. Always say: "I am wrong and I really want to improve." My second tip: You should learn the art of apology to keep your friends.

Thirdly, good persuaders remember people's first names and important dates in their lives and continue to reconnect with people continuously on those dates. Connection, if truth be told, is the key, before and during your conversation. My third tip: You should re-connect with your friends in order to keep them interested in you.

All my friends in my resourceful psyche group agree on one thing: "It's your social circle that matters a lot." We have resolved that we will encourage the parents to train their children in the art of influence. The parents can teach their children the importance of having and holding the company of good people. Children must be guided in how to keep their relationship alive. They must strictly be told not to associate with bad children and for this I don't care whether it's your relative children or neighbour's.

EVERYBODY LIKES A COMPLIMENT

> *"Am I glowing?"*
>
> *"Like a Christmas tree."*
>
> *"Not just the star?"*
>
> *The bed moved a little, and I felt his hand brush my arm.*
>
> *"No. You're super bright. It's kind of like looking at the sun."*
>
> Jennifer L. Armentrout, *Obsidian*

Dale Carnegie's *How to Win Friends and Influence People* was the first and best self-help book on this subject. In my opinion, it is still the best. The audio version of this book is equally popular. The key point in this book is that instead of criticizing people, let us undertake to understand truly and appreciate them from the bottom of our heart. Everybody wants praise. Everybody likes a compliment. Your appreciation must be specific, immediate and sincere. You must appreciate the person for a specific thing and exactly on the moment of accomplishment not a year later. I have analyzed many happy married couples and found that what a man needs is the respect and what a woman needs is the love, but, both need appreciation from each other. My civil engineer friend Vipin Singhal asserts: "The most profound relationship I will ever have is the one with me so if someone approves of me I will appreciate him/her too." The same is true with you. You must refrain from flattery, that's not a sincere praise but cheap butter up. You can use the exact opposite technique in this case also. Whenever you feel tempted and excited to criticize try to say the best things about the beneficiary. Treat others as you want to be treated. To act as a benefactor is the best weapon you can have in your arsenal.

CANON OF COMMONSENSE

> *"In sales we jokingly say everyone's favourite radio station is WIIFM. That stands for – What's In It For Me – and it's where everyone's attention is tuned in almost continually."*
>
> Brian Ahearn, a sales trainer

People do the things because they want to. Therefore, as a replacement of threatening, nagging and yelling, if you can give people motives to listen to your advice they will get motivated to act on your advice and help you provided their interests are involved. Before you ask anybody to do any work, just ask yourself, "How can I motivate this person want to do this?" The answer is obvious when you care for his interests and share his pains. This is all common sense and I call it dual gifts – of care and share. People ask me why I feel affection for social functions. I always say I invest in relationships. These social functions grow and mature me as a professional, spread out my people contact base and raise my prospects for superior success. You should not get caught up in the moral dilemma of selfishness or real help. "Why should I" can be the biggest block in building real relationships. In my friend circle Brijesh Singhal is known for maintaining his public relations. He gives his secret: "Talking to diverse people each time is a whole new experience and I take this as an opportunity to 'Learn and Earn' that is: I earn a new relationship while learning from new person."

YOU ARE IMPORTANT APPROACH

> *"Appreciation is a wonderful thing: It makes what is excellent in others belong to us as well."*
>
> Voltaire (1694–1778)

Let the people realize that "You are important" through your conduct and words. There is an inspirational story on this subject. During Ram's last month of college, the professor gave his students a quick fire quiz. He was a hard-working student and had answered all the questions, until he reached the last one: "What is the first name of our sweeper?" He had seen the sweeper quite a lot of times. He was short, black-haired and in his 40s. He didn't know his name. He handed his sheet, leaving the last question blank. Immediately before class finished, one student asked whether the last question would count towards the quiz marks. "Of course," said the professor. "In your lives, you will meet many persons. All are important, although all you do is SASH – Smile And Say Hello." Ram learned his lesson. He also learned sweeper's name was Ajit.

Moral of the story:

1. Everyone in your life is just like the people you give importance to.
2. Everybody wants respect and appreciation.
3. Your true nature is measured by your behaviour towards a person who can't help you.
4. People ignore the supporting staff but remember seniors.
5. Everyone is worthy of your interest and concern.

SELL THE SIZZLE NOT THE STEAK

"The aim of marketing is to know and understand the customer so well the product or service fits him and sells itself."

Peter Drucker (1909–2005)

The phrase "Sell the sizzle not the steak" is an old sales aphorism. Yes, it is possible to sell the sizzle and the steak. In fact, the expression isn't meant to eliminate the steak at all. It is meant to highlight the fact that in a free-market economy, it is just as important to sell the idea of a product as it is to sell the actual product. For example, take Florida Orange Juice. There are several regions in the U.S. that grow oranges. Nonetheless, by way of vigilant marketing strategies and advertising campaigns, Florida orange growers have persuaded many people that Florida oranges are in some way bigger, juicier, and fresher than oranges grown in other places. Therefore we can say: The Florida orange growers have sold the sizzle of the steak. This expression also tells us something about human nature. You don't purchase anything but you purchase an experience. You just don't buy a car, you buy an experience. Let your customers (friends) sell for you. The most persuasive sales tool is a client (people) sharing. After a job well done, it is equally important to make a mountain out of a molehill by giving rewards, granting some additional privileges, and presenting plenty of hugs and praises. Let the other person experience the behaviour/product/service/technology through your showmanship. Tom Monaghan, the founder of Domino's Pizza, quotes: "The golden rule of Domino's: Treat people as you want to be treated. I don't believe that in 38 years that I treated anyone unfairly. That may not be true, but as far as I know it is." We all want attention; as a result, let us learn to give real attention to others as well. Avoid laconic response: Never give short or sharp answers in ordinary conversation. Ask for his progress, take interest in his hobbies and see how many times you liked your friend's facebook status. Congratulate your friend on his desire to do great things. Allow the other person to play the lead role in your interactions.

THE BEST WAY TO POINT MISTAKES

"Behaviour is the mirror in which everyone shows their image."

Goethe (1749–1832)

You should never say "You are wrong." You should talk about your mistakes first and then indicate other mistakes indirectly. You should always allow the other person to save his face because chasing the self-respect of a person is a transgression. Moliere is right when he says: "A wise man is superior to any insults which can be put upon him, and the best reply to unseemly behaviour is patience and moderation." You can use the words "We" and "I" to show shared responsibility of mistake instead of the word "You".

The best way to mention mistakes is to keep the achievements big. We must highlight even the slightest improvement. The direct implication of the first action is that we should minimize the errors by making them easy to correct. Let the other person know about the faith in his abilities. There is no need to tell a lie but we need to pick our words cautiously.

DON'T ATTACK TO WIN ARGUMENTS

"Silence is argument carried out by other means."

Che Guevara (1928–1967)

No one can win verbal fights. Most bad behaviour comes from insecurity. There is no such thing as discussion between two aggressive people. Conversation has to be one-sided at one time. One says and other listens. Argumentation comes out of natural first reaction, so from now, choose to act and omit to react. Therefore, encourage the people to talk about their interests and listen first.

Subsequently when you have an opportunity to speak – don't attack. Nobody follows orders voluntarily. One can follow orders out of compulsion. Never get entangled into arguments. Instead ask more leading questions to clarify. Accordingly, look for areas of accord and decide what incentive would motivate him, thereafter mix it up with your offer or advice or perspective to suit his judgment of just play.

TELL PEOPLE WHY OF YOUR IDEA

> *"We use our communicating processes to generate behaviours which unconsciously stand out on their own and speak for themselves."*
>
> Richard Bandler And John Lavalle,
> *Persuasion Engineering*

People often like to discuss their passions or their subjects of expertise only. My point is you have to be truly concerned in the progress of people. Dale Carnegie once said: "It's much easier to become interested in others than it is to convince them to be interested in you." If you have a brand new idea, don't be afraid to share it. Most people want you to come up with new ideas. But they also want you to tell them why they should invest their time and energy in your idea. Be the catalyst and start the conversation. Certainly this is not manipulation but the point is that you have to let people see some gain in your proposal too.

THE MAGICAL WAND

> *"I have a definite talent for convincing people to try something new. I am a good salesman. When I'm on form, I can sell anything."*
>
> Brian Eno, an English musician

Majority of experts believe that "Influence is an art." This idea attracted me to include the present chapter in my book. We are weaving the web of persuasion to urge others every day. We have to employ art of influence in each situation. The plan is to give people freedom to choose by asking leading questions. You must throw them an opening to excel in form of a challenge. The technique is to make the other person happy while doing the work. They work for their motives on your motivation. All the political parties use this method by conferring titles and authority. You are happy because the person is doing what you suggested.

When you set a target before them and let them know that others want you to achieve that, people will do their best. We need to keep reinforcing by saying it again and again. All the quotes, wall posters and movies do motivation. I had many extensive exchanges of ideas with Dr. Poonam Datta, a professor in English literature, on various aspects of human personality. She opines: "People express themselves through a challenge to conquer their fears and often become the best they can be. People feel important through a challenge because you give them a reputation to live up to. You get to close deals more often that way."

SUGGESTED STRATEGY

"Be the kind of person people want to meet."

Bhagavan Nayagar (1951–2001)

You must impersonate the person people want to see, hear and meet. Give your approbation or approval with heart and be generous when you praise someone. Take care of your friends and people like queens and kings. We must also know that people pay attention with an intention to reply. They never pay attention with an intention to understand. You should maintain a handwritten telephone directory with A to Z names with contact numbers and email addresses. You can have this directory in your computer also. Spare an hour (friendship hour) to call, email or write a letter to your friends. Trace your friends since childhood and thereafter trace friends of friends. Keep this directory updated with latest phone numbers and addresses. Give them gifts, send the greetings cards and see off and receive your friends personally and through your driver, if personally not possible. As a final point, since everyone is made in the image of God, then everyone should be treated with proper respect and honour because they reflect God. The humble man is seldom the object of envy. Try to look at the things from the mind of other person. The ultimate goal is to form a Resourceful Psyche Group (RPG) for mutual development.

ASSIGNMENT

1. Learn the art of writing and giving a thank you note.
2. Develop and implement your showmanship of behaviour to your guests, friends, customers and other people.
3. Keep a diary in your personal car or in your office, when you visit somewhere and feel good; note the behavioural traits of people.
4. Listen to the Audio program *Your Hidden Power* by Joe Navarro.

VISUALIZATION

Make it a habit to visualize your behaviour before meeting anyone. Remember: Treat people as you want to be treated.

SELF SUGGESTION

I have the talent to attract and build inspiring relationships with anyone.

Bear in mind: Super achievers always keep their commitments.

[Promise & Put Your Signature Here With Date]

20
What Do You Need To Change To Be The Best?

OBJECTIVES

- To understand the "Law of Personal Philosophy",
- To learn that surroundings build your philosophy and
- To follow great people and writings.

GOLDEN GUIDANCE

"The secret of the man who is universally interesting is that he is universally interested."

William Dean Howells (1837–1920)

HARD WORK v. SMART WORK

"I do not know anyone who has got to the top without hard work. That is the recipe. It will not always get you to the top, but should get you pretty near."

Margaret Thatcher (1925–2013)

All of your life, you've worked hard. Then why is it, that despite all of your hard work, you don't seem to realize the results you want? What has this hard work given you? Let me give you few examples to make the things clear. Most of us use computers. We did a lot of hard work when we were learning the computer. But now we know many of the shortcuts and things have become easier. Haven't they? We studied quite hard during the whole year when we were students but at exam time we used to cover the topics on priority. I learned the value of hard work by working hard. I consider hard work as the beginning step to smart work. You cannot accomplish the skill to do work smartly until you have done the hard work. Hard work involves more use of physical energy. Smart work involves a great deal of mental skills. Smart work involves analyzing, studying, planning, prioritizing and so builds success skills or personal philosophy. Both will bring you the final result but hard work takes long time and gives you the experience. Smart work means doing the things in a better way each time and more comfortably using that experience. When a woodcutter slashes the tree from top to bottom, for the first time: that is hard work. But from next time a smart woodcutter would cut the tree directly from bottom and that's smart work. In smart work, you can deal the things by the experience and do work more swiftly. Both are interrelated with each other. Both are very important to achieve an aim. There's a story about an old woodcutter, Ram who worked hard day and night. Yet despite his dedication and hard work, he was less productive than his fellow woodcutter Shyam who worked fewer hours. Ram kept falling farther behind. How could this be? Shyam didn't work such long hours, but spent some of his time maintaining his tools, sharpening his axes, and working on other equipment that increased his productivity. When Shyam invited Ram to take a moment to at least sharpen his axe, he told Shyam, "I don't have time. I have to work hard to make a living and pay my dues." Therefore, if you're like majority and feel relentlessly tired and busy, take a day off to reexamine how you're working. Make some smart choices, and see what an enormous change it makes in your life.

Moral of the story:

1. If you are not getting better at your skills, you are getting worse.
2. Success comes from working smart.

3. A smart worker is better than a hard dumb worker.
4. Hard work is the first step to smart work.

IT ALL DEPENDS ON YOUR MINDSET

"To create something exceptional, your mindset must be relentlessly focused on the smallest detail."

Giorgio Armani, an Italian fashion designer

Everyone thinks of changing the world, but no one thinks of changing himself. You can change your world by changing your thinking pattern. The most terrible disability in the whole world is a negative attitude. I am reminded of a story. Years ago two salesmen were sent by an Indian shoe manufacturer to Africa to examine and report back on market potential. The first salesman reported back, "There is no potential here – nobody wears shoes." The second salesman reported back, "There is huge potential here – nobody wears shoes."

Moral of the story:

1. Wining depends on mindset.
2. Changing the situation is a mindset.
3. Change your thinking to change your life.
4. Once your mindset changes the situation outside also changes.

EVERYBODY HAS A PERSONAL PHILOSOPHY

"Wonder is the feeling of the philosopher, and philosophy begins in wonder."

Plato (427 BC–347 BC)

Everybody believes. Do you know what you believe? The answer: Personal philosophy. Everybody has a personal philosophy. It is what you as a person value most in your lives. It is a set of your personal belief consisting of principles that you apply in living your life. It is a continuous process of critical examination of beliefs using critical thoughts and perceptions. I am an eternal idealist. I often get asked, don't you ever feel sad and I just respond with, "Yes naturally! But I get out of it quickly because of my sound personal philosophy." Your personal philosophy is your slogan of life. What do you believe in and how do you apply that. You use it as an internal guiding system and therefore your personal philosophy dictates your choices of decisions and actions.

Your personal philosophy is the most important determining factor in how your life works out. Would you like to believe? It is who you are. It is a system of values by which you choose to live your life. Our belief system affects our thinking and hence our actions. My basic conviction is that philosophy is immensely important. You will find answers of many critical questions like existence and reality, if you take an absorbing tour through thousands years of philosophy.

EVERY LEADER FOLLOWS

> *"I believe that reading and writing are the most nourishing forms of meditation anyone has so far found. By reading the writings of the most interesting minds in history, we meditate with our own minds and theirs as well. This to me is a miracle."*
>
> Kurt Vonnegut, *Palm Sunday: An Autobiographical Collage*

Have you ever wished you could revisit in time and have a dialogue with few of the greatest minds in history? You can't. They've departed. But we can still refer to the wisdom they left behind. A major English Romantic poet, William Wordsworth (1770–1850) learned basically from nature. Ralph Waldo Emerson (1803–1882), learned mainly from people, nature and books. He called nature as a language. You can find mention of Plato, Newton, Berkeley, Wordsworth, Confucianism, Hinduism, Anaxagoras, St. Augustine, Francis Bacon, Jacob Behmen, Cicero, Goethe,

Heraclitus, Lucretius, Mencius, Pythagoras, August and Friedrich Schlegel, Shakespeare, Socrates, Madame de Staël, Emanuel Swedenborg, Schiller and Thoreau in his writings. He influenced generations of Americans, from Henry David Thoreau, Herman Melville, Nathaniel Hawthorne, Walt Whitman and Emily Dickinson to John Dewey, and in Europe Friedrich Nietzsche. I am also inspired from Voltaire (1694–1778), a French philosopher who was a versatile writer, producing works in almost every literary form, including plays, poems, novels, essays and historical and scientific works. He wrote more than 20,000 letters and more than 2,000 books and pamphlets. What kind of energy he had? He once rightly said: "Every man is guilty of all the good he did not do." Plato was a philosopher in Classical Greece. He was also a mathematician, student of Socrates, writer of philosophical dialogues, and founder of the Academy in Athens, the first institution of higher learning in the Western world. He said: "Philosophy is the highest music." I have learned a lot of things from Indian philosophical heritage. Rich Indian literature has impressed many thinkers, philosophers, scientist and poets. Ralph Weldo Emerson, Mark Twain, Francois M. Voltaire, Werner Heisenberg, Albert Einstein, George Bernard Shaw, Arthur Schopenhauer, John Archibald Wheeler, Jean Sylvain Bailly, Julius R. Oppenheimer, Frederich Von Schlegel and T.S. Elliot are few of them. Voltaire was convinced that most of things have come down from the banks of the Ganga. Personal philosophy is all about building the concepts like courage, values, leadership, learning, power, responsibility—the ingredients of success. Thomas Jefferson (1743–1826) who was an American Founding Father, the principal author of the Declaration of Independence and the third President of the United States once said: "I was bold in the pursuit of knowledge, never fearing to follow truth and reason to whatever results they led, and bearding every authority which stood in their way." I have the courage to accept the genius. I am influenced by Jim Rohn's idea of personal philosophy, Zig Ziglar's concept of personal growth, Napoleon Hill's concept of burning desire, R.W. Emerson's concepts of teaching, Robert Greene's concept of power, Tony

Robbins's concept of discipline, Joseph Murphy's concept of subconscious mind, Dale Carnegie's concept of avoiding the criticism, Jack Canfield's concept of decide what you want, Shiv Khera's concept of goal setting, Lou Tice's concept of belief and Robin Sharma's concept of leadership without title. The most important lesson I learned from Stephen R. Covey is: "Seek first to understand and then be understood." Understand: Every leader follows. You will see that each chapter of this book is well referenced because I am grateful to the philosophies contained in the great works. I always follow great people. We can do wonders. But we choose comfort over courage. We have to develop a habit of book reading. We can read all the books we want on motivation, goal setting, wealth and happiness, etc., but unless the words sink in, unless we fully appreciate their meaning and are motivated to act on them, they will be worthless. That's one rationale why I advise the people to read many different authors. Though these authors may say the same things, the words of one will ring within you, while the others are shortly elapsed.

LEARN OF ME

> *"You cannot teach a man anything, you can only help him find it within himself."*
>
> Galileo Galilei (1564–1642)

The teacher is one. Everyone learns according to his or her aptitude and capacity. There is a story on the theme that everybody learns differently even from the same teacher. A merchant, an old man, and his little daughter met under a mango tree. On the side of the tree there was an inscription on a foundation stone that read, "Learn of me!" The merchant said he learned a great lesson from the tree. It gives fruits to everybody still it is humble enough to bow at the same time. We should also be humble in our behaviour. The old man said that the lesson he learned from the tree was to do the good only because it takes the carbon dioxide and return the oxygen only. The little girl said that the lesson she learned was to serve silently, friends and strangers alike as it gives shade to each and everyone.

Moral of the story:

1. Gratitude and love are two condition precedents of true learning.
2. In life-school, the day on which we have not learned something new, is a lost day indeed.
3. Experience teaches only the teachable.
4. All teachings are mere references.
5. Self-taught people excel in their lives.
6. You have to be remarkably interested to be remarkably interesting.

WHY PERSONAL PHILOSOPHY IS SO IMPORTANT?

> *"If you set a good sail, the wind that blows will always take you to the dream you want, the income you want, and the treasures of mind, purse and soul you want."*
>
> Jim Rohn (1930–2009)

Your personal philosophy is your set of sail. It is your belief system; your attitude and concepts. Franklin Delano Roosevelt (1882–1945), the 32nd President of the United States (1933–1945) who was a central figure in world events during the mid-20th century once said: "To reach a port, we must sail – sail, not tie at anchor – sail, not drift." Whenever I felt low philosophy unchained me from a series of emotional confusions during my young days. I used to spend a lot of time in library reading philosophical books. Andrew Carnegie (1835–1919) has compared a library to an unfailing spring in the desert. You will also feel mesmerized by how ideas formulated over thousands years back can still transform your lives in the present days also. Those who lack the guts will always find a philosophy to justify it. But if you are failing on regular basis and things are not working out fine for you and you want to really improve then take my advice: Work to change your mind; your thinking; your action and your personal philosophy. So, *here is the golden tip*: "You can't expect any changes if you continue with same mindset; same thinking; same action and same personal philosophy. These are the things you need to change to be better and to be successful. Your philosophy is not working. So, change it." You must start with the personal philosophy. Formal education is good enough to give you a source of income. But Jim Rohn who is considered as America's foremost business philosopher opines that it's your self-education that gives you a fortune. The circumstances can be compared with wind. The circumstances will support you if you have a sound philosophy. The present book is all about building a good personal philosophy by motivating you. Therefore, you must keep this book with you to stay motivated and inspired to (re)set a better sail to (re)commence.

If one has a good personal philosophy, he will accept the personal responsibility for his actions and decisions but the persons with unsound philosophy will criticize the people, circumstances and luck. It is the key factor to determine your success especially your financial security. Sound philosophy helps in making sound decisions. Saint Augustine sums up all, "The higher your structure is to be, the deeper must be its foundation."

IT COMES FROM MANY SOURCES

> *"He who learns but does not think, is lost! He who thinks but does not learn is in great danger."*
>
> Confucius (551 BC–479 BC)

Personal philosophy comes from many sources. It is all you know and consequently continuous learning plays an important role in developing a sound personal philosophy. Our philosophy develops right from our childhood. Our family environment, our college environment, our work environment and the kind of people we meet all play a part in forming our personal philosophy because our surroundings influence our thought process. Therefore, it is hard to teach especially the good ideas and good habits because they are alien thoughts and hence against the personal philosophy of the taught. Most of the people say that you have to choose between wealth and happiness. They can't go simultaneously. My view: They come from the same mine of abundance. Once you go through your personal philosophical transformation, wealth and happiness will come into your life.

WATCH YOUR SURROUNDINGS

> *"Be careful the environment you choose for it will shape you; be careful the friends you choose for you will become like them."*
>
> W. Clement Stone (1902–2002)

Whatever you perceive through five senses is processed through personal philosophy. Who am I around? That's a big question. Hans Hansen quotes: "People inspire you, or they drain you – pick them wisely." Personal philosophy is also root and fruit of your continuous learning. Primarily our philosophy comes from teaching. You learn from the influence of other persons like friends, relatives etc., from the books you read, from the movies you watch, from the serials you are addicted to and from the classes you take. I am reminded of Mark Twain who once said: "Be careful about reading health books. You may die of a misprint." For that reason only, you must be particular in selection of whatever you do and with whom you attach yourself.

SUGGESTED STRATEGY

> *"Self-education is, I firmly believe, the only kind of education there is."*
>
> Isaac Asimov (1920–1992)

A Life Journal is the place where we keep what we learn from the great people. Writing what you experience slows down the process of learning and makes us more analytical in our judgment and making important concrete changes in our personal life philosophy. You can also write your personal philosophy statement when you complete this book with the idea of maintaining a balance in your life. The best method is to write what you feel in your life journal when you complete a chapter. Learn by heart: Personal development is not a goal, it's a constant process. Your whole life is a series of experiments and you have to go by conclusions.

ASSIGNMENT

1. Study the works and writings referred in this book.
2. Write down in your life journal what you learn from present book so far and review the same after completing the book.
3. Write down important lessons learned in your life from different events and people.
4. Listen to the Audio program *Lessons of a Lifetime* by Jim Rohn and Darren Hardy. You can also search www.free-audio-books.co.uk for more audios.

VISUALIZATION

Whenever you meet someone or anything happens to you, you must re-live the whole scene once again and try to see the hidden messages. Remember: You have to sharp your axe to cut the maximum number of wood.

SELF SUGGESTION

I am passionately interested and focused in my personal philosophy.

Bear in mind: Super achievers always keep their commitments.

[*Promise & Put Your Signature Here With Date*]

21

Have You Started Your Spiritual Journey?

OBJECTIVES

- To learn the "Law of Daily Meditation",
- To habituate the technique of "Breathing Awareness", and
- To increase the time of meditation gradually.

GOLDEN GUIDANCE

"If every 8-year old in the world is taught meditation, we will eliminate violence from the world within one generation."

His Holiness The 14th Dalai Lama

MEDITATION IS THE HIGHEST STATE OF MIND

"Seek ye first the kingdom of God, and everything shall be added unto you."

Swami Vivekananda (1863–1902)

Silence is to mind what sleep is to body. All religions have laid stress upon meditation. The meditative state of mind is the highest state in which the mind exists. There are three stages in meditation. You're concentrating on candle fame; this is the first stage – the concentration. In second stage, your mind becomes so strong that it does not waver and stays on flame only.

In final stage, flame and you become one. Situation is same with us. The moment we fear, we become fragile. It is fear that is the big root of misery in the world. We use our mind to think backward and forward. Past is thinking towards the back and future is thinking ahead. We treat ourselves different from God (Candle Flame) and through meditation finite intelligence become one with infinite intelligence. When the Buddha began to travel around India soon after his enlightenment, he met numerous people who took him as a very miraculous individual. They asked him: "Are you a god?" "No," he replied. "Are you a reincarnation of god?" "No," he replied. "Are you a wizard, then?" "No." "Well, are you a man?" "No." "Then, what are you?" They asked, being very puzzled. Buddha simply answered: "I am awake." The word "Buddha" means "the awakened one." How to stay awakened is all he taught in his whole life.

DO WHAT YOU CAN

I am only one,

But still I am one.

I cannot do everything,

But still I can do something;

And because I cannot do everything,

I will not refuse to do something that I can do.

Edward Everett Hale (1822–1909)

Janus is the Roman god of gates and doors (ianua), beginnings and endings, and hence represented with a double-faced head, each looking in opposite directions. Hummingbird has also two unique qualities that teach us two unique behaviours. It can fly backwards teaching us that we should look into our past but fly forward also. Secondly, its ability to hover while drinking nectar teaches to take pleasure in each moment. In fact, a story is striking in my mind. Once upon a time there lived many animals in deep green forest and they lived in harmony. One day a fire raged in whole of the forest. All the animals were running away to save their life and one elephant noticed while running that a red-throat humming-bird was picking little drops of water and spraying those on to the fire. He was doing it again and again. The elephant told this thing to all other animals. They gathered at a spot and asked, "What are you doing?" The hummingbird said, "I am trying to pacify the fire with water." All the animals laughed and said, "What do you think you are doing." The red throated hummingbird said, "I am doing what I can." Don't you think that this world is like that jungle and there is fire everywhere? We can try to pacify this fire by doing daily meditation. I admire Theodore Roosevelt (1858–1919), the 26th President of the United States, who once said: "Do what you can, with what you have, where you are."

Moral of the story:

1. We each must do what we can.
2. We have to use the existing sources.
3. We have to start from the present place.
4. It is the greatest of all mistakes to do nothing because we can do only little.
5. Anyone can give up; it's the easiest thing in the world to do.

DO YOU USE YOUR DAY OR YOUR DAY USES YOU?

> *"Time = life; therefore, waste your time and waste of your life, or master your time and master your life."*
>
> Alan Lakein, a time management expert

Super leaders do whatever they believe they can. The common belief is that super leaders wisely use maximum of twenty-four hours. Take my word, it is a fact. Why shouldn't they? If you are given a bank account with the provision that 86,400 rupees will be credited in the morning and in the night your net balance will be zero. What would you do? Of course, everyone will want to spend maximum of 86,400 rupees. On similar pattern one must try to use every second because 86,400 seconds make 24 hours of a day. The message is quite important one. Everybody from president to peon has got only 86,400 seconds to live within a day to create the future and to charge mind/body batteries.

The key lies in using this time to our maximum advantage. But do we use our day or we let the day use us. Let me ask you: "What is that part of the day you hate most?" Yes, it is our morning because we have never been able to schedule it. We rush for everything and hence can't enjoy any activity. Our mornings are generally automatic. All the things get in order after we officially start our time. My point is that our morning schedule, if properly scheduled, can become our launching pad for whole day activities. After all, we have to do just what we can.

MORNINGS HOLD THE KEY

> *"Mornings hold the key to taking control of our schedules. If we use them wisely, we can build habits that will allow us to lead happier, more productive lives."*
>
> Laura Vanderkam, *What The Most Successful People Do Before Breakfast*

Meditation, if done properly, can give you the peace of mind you are looking for. Many scientific studies have shown that meditation helps to enlarge the mind to its infinite extraterrestrial potential. It improves health and reverses the aging course. It also helps in lowering high blood pressure and danger of heart-stroke. It increases intelligence and creative imagination. It improves memory and learning ability. It decreases stress, strain, and anxiety. It enhances liveliness, energy and well being. Most importantly, it nurtures the state of enlightenment – inner happiness, contentment and fulfillment. Maharishi Mahesh Yogi was the founder of Transcendental Meditation who introduced the meditation to west. Currently, there are more than six million practitioners worldwide, with TM centres in more than 108 countries. So, *here is the golden tip*: "One of the techniques to take control of your mind right at the outset of day is to do meditation. The second modus operandi is to do some physical exercise. Super leaders have the strategy to take control of their body and mind in the "Induction Hours" because they have the best of the body and mind to use throughout the day."

MEDITATION BASICS

> *"For human consciousness to be transformed something new must be introduced."*
>
> Michael Langford, *The Most Direct Means To Eternal Bliss*

The very first thing I would like to suggest you is to search for a complete meditation guide and undertake his meditation courses. To meditate under a guide is the safest and quickest way and thus the shortcut and in my language the best-cut to success. A good book can certainly help but it can't replace a good mentor. A conceptual journey is not a journey to awakening. Secondly, I am in favour of daily meditation. I don't recommend weekly meditation camps. Thirdly, a few minutes of silence each day after meditation will certainly do a world of good to your inner health. A great saint Bhagavan Sri Ramana Maharshi said: "All living beings desire to be happy always, without any misery. In everyone there is observed supreme love for oneself. And happiness alone is the cause of love. In order therefore, to gain that happiness which is one's nature and which is experienced in the state of deep sleep, where there is no mind, one should know oneself. To achieve this, the Path of Knowledge, the enquiry in the form of 'Who Am I?' is the principal means." Fourthly, I am not in support of any music during meditation because the inner sounds are sweeter. Each person's inner world differs and each person's reaction to meditation will likewise differ. Music may be used for early relaxation. However, few experts like Victor Davich prefer silence to the soft new-age music or nature sounds on some other meditation CDs. Fifthly, a quiet place is a condition precedent for a good meditation. You must switch off mobile phone, TV, radio and computer to avoid distractions. Sixthly, you should make sure that you are not tired. You should do it in Induction or Morning hours. You can also do it in review hour at bed to end the worries of whole day and induce sleep. You ought to wear comfortable and loose clothing. Lastly, one should do meditation on the same time and on same place to get maximum benefits.

RIGHT POSTURE—LOTUS POSITION

> *"Sit very comfortably in meditation with both the hands on your lap. You have to control your mind more as compared to your body."*
>
> Bhagavan Nayagar (1951–2001)

Right posture holds the master key. I suggest keeping the back straight in any posture that you select to meditate. You can naturally sit in a chair or crossed legs on floor with pillows. My spiritual master even allowed sleeping position to some disciples. It is one of position in Indian yoga also. If one can meditate without falling asleep, sleeping position can be good for the person who has some joint problems. However, one should try to sit still with crossed legs, and gradually try to sit in lotus position.

In lotus position, the feet are placed on the opposing thighs with soles facing upward and heels close to the abdomen. The knees are in contact with the ground. The torso is centred above the hips. The eyes may be closed. In the initial period, you will need a cushion to sit on forward edge in order to incline your pelvis and achieve the balance. However, if you feel any pain in knee joints or pressure on lower back, you should discontinue it and adopt other easy positions. Proper course is to attain lotus position under proper guidance and with medical advice.

MEDITATION SESSION

> *"If we know the divine art of concentration, if we know the divine art of meditation, if we know the divine art of contemplation, easily and consciously we can unite the inner world and the outer world."*
>
> Sri Chinmoy (1931–2007)

The primary aim of meditation is to get rid of our impostor self or ego by knowing that the world is a dreamlike illusion, increase our desire for liberation and ultimately to find out our real or true self or Who Am I. Osho (1931–1990) is known for his revolutionary contribution to the science of inner transformation. About his own work Osho said that he was helping to create the conditions for the birth of a new kind of human being. He often characterized this new human being as Zorba the Buddha – capable both of enjoying the earthly pleasures of a Zorba the Greek and the silent serenity of a Gautam Buddha. He quotes: "Meditation is the first and last freedom."

Here are certain useful instructions: You should do some breathing exercises to relax your mind. Close your eyes and breathe in for a count of ten and then hold it for a count of ten and then breathe out for a count of ten. You can also use alternate nostril breathing, bumblebee and kapalbhati pranyama etc. You must assume that you are the omnipresent Soul. Soul is the Essence of Supreme Existence. You can also use the affirmation: "I am neither the body, nor the mind, nor the Buddhi (decisive faculty), neither the gross nor the subtle body." Swami Vivekananda was a great believer of this affirmation. Now, focus your attention on different parts of the body and see how it feels there. Start from your head and end at your feet. Feel the coolness when you breathe in and warmth when you breathe out. See how much air you take in and breathe out. After this, allow yourself to settle down. Keep your attention to breath process, how it moves in and out. When you are settled in watching breath try to see the gap between two breaths to create a profound experience of peace. This is called as breath awareness.

You can start with fifteen minutes and gradually go ahead. You should set an alarm to alert you right at the outset. Proper medical advice and guide supervision are mandatory for any kind of meditation. Don't forget to be grateful to infinite intelligence at the successful completion of each session.

HOW TO TACKLE DISTRACTIONS?

> *"Practice meditation regularly. Meditation leads to eternal bliss. Therefore meditate, meditate."*
>
> Swami Sivananda (1887–1963)

Some experts like Starr Daily closely associates silence with spiritual healing. You will hear different sounds, experience many thoughts, bodily sensations and emotions but just don't force yourself to think of nothing. The things that you have thought too intensely, transform themselves into a subconscious command, and consequently these come up in the mind in meditation. It's a sign that your mind is concentrating. A single disturbed thought creates ten thousand distractions. Don't try to fight with anything. Don't attach yourself with any of the distractions and let it pass. You must experience the "Soul–Feeling–I am soul only" and through this process of exclusion, absorb your mind in the transcendent knowledge which is your true nature. You can achieve the state of No-Mind by dipping your mind repeatedly in this soul-awareness. You will comprehend the real meaning of Infinite-Intelligence. The termination of all phenomenal superimpositions will pursue. There is no relative or conditioned knowledge in this situation. You will be established in your true-self. Knower and known, meditator and object meditated upon, will then become one. The soul is knowledge, the soul is Intelligence, and the soul is true and pure bliss. The soul is wholeness. Don't condemn yourself if the session did not go well. Rather, make earnest efforts to find out the causes and eliminate them next time. The mind very easily attains coolness when one practices meditation with anything on which one's mind is most suitable to settle down. You can see image of spiritual master when you get distracted. Let the spiritual master be a distraction if your minds wavers. See the image and return to breathing. Avoid daydreaming, past and future are imaginations of mind. You can feel the freshness in present only. If you notice any lethargy, drowsiness or sleepiness, you can continue but it's better to stop meditation. The biggest hurdles for the beginners are the cliché like I can't meditate, I am too tired or late to meditate etc., but trust me they're just another excuse. I believe that God has made meditation mandatory for human beings. Sleep is unconscious meditation. Meditation is a matter of training and habituation so it will take a little while for the body and mind to be on the track. You can set different motivations like white light, inner sounds or gap between breaths to keep you concentrated.

NEW RELATIONSHIP WITH BRAIN

> *"All of man's difficulties are caused by his inability to sit quietly in a room by himself."*
>
> Blaise Pascal (1623–1662)

I consider, human brain is the best gift that Nature has given us. It has the potential to connect with infinite possibilities. Your mind is gifted of unbelievable healing and continuous redesigning. Your mind can get adaptable at one point, flexible few times and intelligent many a times but creativity is my concerned area. Rudolph E. Tanzi and Deepak Chopra, in their book *Super Brain* put a thesis: Your mind works at its finest level provided you balance all the things that the mind is fine at. Neocortex or reasoning brain was the last reap, and the next leap is super brain. They opine that we can lead, inspire, invent and use our brain. Mindfulness meditation is the entryway to an infinite future. You can begin to live that future today. You reconnect with your brain at a different level. My spiritual master used to say: "Self-awareness is the key. When you watch your emotions and thoughts wonders begin to happen." We need to be cautious in one way only: Training our mind with positive experiences. You become master of your brain by keeping positivity in your brain. The present book in your hands is about establishing a fresh bond with your brain and I believe through this new relationship you can change your life.

SUGGESTED STRATEGY

> *"Meditation is the dissolution of thoughts in Eternal awareness or Pure consciousness without objectification, knowing without thinking, merging finitude in infinity."*
>
> Voltaire (1694–1778)

You must habituate meditation. Do it daily. Be it Sunday or any day of the week or your anniversary or your birthday. You must not exclude the meditation from your day. Success is an outcome of few simple habits practiced day after day. During meditation, our mind gets divided into two parts—one watcher and other creator. We should cling to watcher only. Otherwise, imaginative creativeness can become an obstacle in itself. Jiddu Krishnamurti (1895–1986) once aptly defined: The flowering of love is meditation.

The big twist in mindfulness is that we are always at a lookout for wholeness. Once I asked about wholeness to my spiritual master,

"GuruDev! What do you suggest about wholeness?"

He said, "Nothing! The reality is that it is already here and already yours."

"What is your instruction for living a better mindful life?" I asked him.

He replied, "It's simple. Come back to your awareness persistently. Look! What is going on?"

I tell you from my personal experience that it's not that easy as it looks. It's really a challenge to stay in awareness and moreover it needs lot of practice. After some time, meditation will become a way of life. Spiritual or transpersonal element is important part of personal philosophy because without connection with infinite intelligence, your finite intelligence will not achieve its full growth. Realize: Meditation is not a spiritual discipline separate from everyday life. You will live in meditative state whether you walk or eat or study. As Dalai Lama prescribes, "As you breathe in cherish yourself. As you breathe out cherish all beings." "Through meditation," he says further, "we can train our minds in such a way that negative qualities are abandoned and positive qualities are generated and enhanced."

ASSIGNMENT

1. Try to learn proper breathing exercises and meditation techniques mentioned in this chapter from a qualified teacher and finally settle on your practice-posture for the meditation.
2. Ask for medical advice from your family doctor about the ways and exercises suggested by the meditation guide and then give it a shot.
3. Read some good literature on meditation and spiritual growth.
4. Listen to the Audio program *Meditations To Change Your Brain* by Dr. Hanson and Dr. Mendius. However, guidance of a meditation expert is advised.
5. You can search websites like audiocloset.com; bookrix.com; freeaudiobooks.ws; learnoutloud.com and ebook3000.com for more audios.

VISUALIZATION

Visualize that you are praying to your spiritual master or any deity and then imagine them blessing you for the successful meditation session. Remember: Like Hummingbird, you can go everywhere humming, analyzing the past and watching the future and enjoying every moment drinking the nectar in flower of each situation, remaining awake like Buddha.

SELF SUGGESTION

I do daily meditation to transcend my life.

Bear in mind: Super achievers always keep their commitments.

[*Promise & Put Your Signature Here With Date*]

22
Do You Consider Yourself A Leader?

OBJECTIVES

- To learn the "Law of Super Leadership",
- To understand ten traits of Super Leaders, and
- To manage the disasters in advance.

GOLDEN GUIDANCE

> *"It's better to lead from behind and to put others in front, especially when you celebrate victory when nice things occur. You take the front line when there is danger. Then people will appreciate your leadership."*
>
> Nelson Mandela, President of South Africa from 1994 to 1999

WHAT IS LEADERSHIP?

> *"Leadership is influence – nothing more, nothing less."*
>
> John Maxwell, leadership expert

Leadership is the hot and new world of youth today. An online search found twenty-two million websites listings for the word "leadership". Leadership is often described as the ability to dictate and be socially influential for getting aid and support to complete some task. A leader is the guiding and dictating head of a group, organization, institution, army, political movement or a country. Known for his brutal and legendary military tactics, Alexander was probably one of the best military commanders of all time. He asserts: "An army of sheep led by the lion will defeat an army of lions led by the sheep." The art of leadership is an activity performed by a person called Leader. Leadership is an art of influencing the people. As Erskine Bowles noticed, leadership is the key to 99 percent of all successful efforts. My thesis of leadership: Greater the gravitation centre a person is, he/she will be able to pull more gravitational centres towards him/her as per the capacities, for example, sun has nine planets around it and earth has moon around it. Similarly a great leader has good leaders around him. Most of us lead something at some point – whether a company, a sports team, a family, or a trip with friends. Yet most of us have no training for leadership. Our whole world is revolving around influence. A teacher influences his class, parents influence their children, neighbours influence you, what I mean, is that we influence each other in our society. I try to show my children the richness of life and be a role model. I find that my organizational and management skills are tested more at home than at work. That's why I am in favour of personal leadership. You can revolutionize your life and ultimately the whole world, when you work in leading mood.

EVERY OBSTRUCTION PRESENTS AN OPPORTUNITY

> *"I think a hero is an ordinary individual who finds strength to persevere and endure in spite of overwhelming obstacles."*
>
> Christopher Reeve (1952–2004)

A normal person who finds power to persist and bear in the face of awe-inspiring obstacles becomes a super leader. Bravery and determination have a mysterious effect before which troubles evaporate. I am always reminded of a short story. In ancient times, a king had a big rock placed on a highway. Then the king hid himself and watched to see if anyone would remove the huge rock. Some of the king's richest merchants and courtiers came by and just walked around it. Many noisily blamed the king for not keeping the roads plain, there was some agitation in groups also, but none did anything about getting the big stone out of the way. Then a farmer came along carrying a load of crops. On approaching the rock, the farmer laid down his load and tried to shift the stone to the side of the road. After much pushing and pulling, he ultimately succeeded. As the farmer picked up his load of crops, he saw a small bag lying in the road where the rock had been. The bag contained many diamonds and a note from the king indicating that the diamonds was for the person who removed the rock from the roadway.

Moral of the story:

1. Every problem presents an opportunity to improve one's condition.
2. A leader often does the things in an unusual way.
3. A leader feels for other people also.
4. People expect changes from government.
5. Nobody takes personal pain to improve the society condition.

IS LEADERSHIP FOR EVERYONE?

> *"Personal leadership is the only leadership that is going to matter in 21st Century."*
>
> Peter Drucker (1909–2005)

Most of the people in this world are doing their work in *doing* mood only whereas the world can become altogether a new place when everybody does the work in *leading* mood. For the difference between doing and leading, says Orlando, in terms of accomplishment is stock car and a formula-one racer. Just imagine, when everybody right from sweeper to minister, housewives to managers and teachers to engineers, I mean, everybody does his/her work as a leader in leading mood. "Right here and right now, I am the only person that can make a difference." As Robin Sharma, a leadership expert asserts, leadership is for everyone. Everybody can lead without any title. Abraham Lincoln's one quote "whatever you are, be a good one" defines the personal leadership. There can be diverse categories of leaders like business or corporate leader, professional leader, community leader, family leader, inspirational leader and action leader. But learn by heart: You are leader of your life. It does not matter who you are or what you do, you get to take the lead in your life.

ARE YOU A LEADER?

> *"Who is wise? – One who learn from everyone."*
>
> Jewish Maxim

In this book, and especially in this chapter, you will find prescriptions for personal and professional leadership. A leader learns from everyone. He knows traits and skills of each one. A leader uses everybody's natural talent in the best possible way. Leadership is the human personality at its best. Leadership inspires. Leadership is a magnetic phenomenon which is a hidden craving in the nature of human personality because it is a manifestation of importance.

However, the biggest tragedy is that each one of us considers himself or herself as a leader. This self-delusion is responsible for remaining a follower. When we wake up in our bed, we take our favourite blue pill – we choose to believe what we want to believe. This ignorance of learning the leadership is a state of bliss and often followers point leadership or success to an incidental breakthrough instead of persistent efforts. As David Niven says, "Positive changes in your life will not be finished today, but it can be started today." Everybody can become what he wants if he is ready to make a start and to continue with it.

LEADERS STICK TO PRINCIPLES

> *"Change your opinions, keep to your principles; change your leaves, keep intact your roots."*
>
> Victor Hugo (1802–1885)

The people anticipate and look forward to the superheroes for guarding their city or country. Whenever we watch any movie, TV serial or read a comic book or a novel we expect from the heroes, be it Superman, Batman or Spiderman. The difference between super leaders and the rest of us is that they stick to their principles at all costs. They are never indecisive even when they are not popular – a severe scarcity in any profession especially in politics. Joseph II, the Holy Roman Emperor from 1765 to 1790 was the first ruler of Austrian dominions of the House of Lorraine who is probably history's most selfless ruler. He was an exception to the phrase "absolute power corrupts absolutely". He really did what was best for his people and even abolished slavery and serfdom. His policies are now known as *Josephinism*. Joseph inspired a complete reform of the legal system, abolished brutal punishments and the death penalty. Charles Albert Coffin created the principles and mechanisms that made General Electric Corporation one of the world's most enduring and widely emulated. Mahatma Gandhi's policy of non-violence and protest through civil disobedience eventually succeeded when he led India to freedom in 1947. Jawaharlal Nehru affirms: "Failure comes only when we forget our ideals and objectives and principles." Thomas Paine also confirms: "An army of principles can penetrate where an army of soldiers cannot." What are your principles? All of us should have them, know what they are, and live our lives by them. This book is an honest effort in this direction also i.e. to offer you powerful principles to live your lives in the leading mood.

WHAT LEADER DOES?

> *"I don't know any other way to lead but by example."*
>
> Don Shula, a former American football coach

A leader leads himself first. He is the first person he leads. He inspires, cares and serves. He convinces. He is best and makes others best too. He leads other people towards success. It is absurd that a man should rule others, who cannot rule himself. This Latin proverb talks about self-discipline. Mao Zedong (1893–1976), the leader of the Chinese Revolution was the founding father of the People's Republic of China who successfully endured and repelled the invasion by Japan during the World War II. He quotes: "The people, and the people alone, are the motive force in the making of world history." He transformed the economy of China into one of the major industrialized economies of the world. Mahatma Gandhi led India through Dandi Salt March, Quit India Movement, Khilafat Movement and Non-Cooperation Movement. Napoleon Bonaparte was a French military and political leader who led wars against France by a series of alliances. Due to his success in wars against enemies he is regarded as one of the greatest military commanders of all times. He asserts: "Victory belongs to the most persevering." Prof. (Dr.) Gurpal Singh is a proficient administrator of high competence. He is Director in a reputed law college in Punjab, India. I have worked with him. He has done wonders in terms of discipline among students. I asked him, "Sir, What is that single quality that makes an ordinary person extraordinary leader?" He replied, "Discipline is my master. I never allow myself even to violate it. I do it myself first. I believe in leading by conduct. People follow your conduct, not words." Bernie Wilke also quotes: "I've found without question that the best way to lead others to a more plant-based diet is by example – to lead with your fork, not your mouth."

A true leader is a life catalyst in society who does social engineering. He minimizes the friction in society by settling the conflict between individual interest and societal interest. In an organization, he guides, directs and influences the work of others towards attainment of specified common goals by mediating between the employers and employees in such a way that both get satisfied and come out as winners.

EMPOWERMENT IS THE KEY

> *"A man who wants to lead the orchestra must turn his back to the crowd."*
>
> James Crooks (1778–1860)

Empowerment is the key. Lao Tzu, the founder of philosophical Taoism quotes:"A leader is best when people barely know he exists, when his work is done, his aim fulfilled, they will say: we did it ourselves." The better you make people feel about themselves, the better they will work. Franklin Delano Roosevelt was the 32nd President who served his term from 1933 to 1945. He is included in the list of top three U.S. Presidents as he successfully led U.S. through the Great Depression and World War II. He was a central figure in world events during the mid-20th century. He greatly expanded the powers of the federal government through numerous programs and reforms known as the New Deal. He quotes: "If you treat people right they will treat you right – ninety percent of the time." So, *here is the golden tip*: "Leaders encourage others to realize and appreciate that there is a price to pay for everything they want. The duty of a leader is to encourage and raise the standard of all his followers and not just a few of them, and he should always remember his duty. Great leaders are those who can extract extraordinary performance from ordinary men and women."

As a great leader, you combine your personal competencies with the competencies of a variety of others into a smoothly functioning team that can outplay and outperform all its competitors. And your ability to put together a team and then to lead that team to high performance will enable you to accelerate your career. A great leader is one who excites and inspires people to perform far beyond their own expectation of themselves. Therefore, a leader is one who generates leaders.

THE MAN WHO WAS FAMOUS FOR PAYING HIS WORKERS

> *"If everyone is moving forward together, then success takes care of itself."*
>
> Henry Ford (1863–1947)

The hero of our story was born on July 30, 1863, on his family's farm near Dearborn, Michigan. When he was 15, his father gifted him a pocket watch, which our hero quickly took apart and reassembled. Friends and neighbours were overwhelmed and requested that he mend their watches too. After a few trials building cars and companies, in 1903, he established his Motor Company. He introduced the Model T in October of 1908, and for numerous years, the company accumulated 100 percent gains.

Nonetheless, more than for his profits, our hero became famous for his outstanding vision: the manufacture of an inexpensive automobile made by skilled workers who earn steady wages. In 1914, he sponsored the development of the moving assembly line system of mass production.

Concurrently, our hero announced his $5-per-day program on January 5, 1914, raising the minimum daily pay from $2.34 to $5 for qualifying workers ($110 in 2011) as a technique of keeping the most excellent workers faithful to his company. He described it as six 8–hour days, giving a 48–hour week.

Simple to drive and economical to repair, half of all cars in America in 1918 were Model T's. Our hero of story is none other than Henry Ford who died of a cerebral hemorrhage on April 7, 1947, at the age of 83, near his Dearborn estate, considered one of America's leading businessmen, and is recognized nowadays for serving to construct America's economy during the nation's weak premature years. His tradition will be cherished by us on for decades to follow.

FIRST FOLLOW THEN LEAD

"A tale is told of a man in Paris during the upheaval in 1948, who saw a friend marching after a crowd towards the barricades. Warning him that these could not be held against the troops, that he had better keep way, he received this reply, "I must follow them. I am their leader."

A. Lawrence Lowell, (1856–1943), President of Harvard University, *Conflicts of Principle*

People get divided into two classes as they go ahead in this journey of life. Five percent people who have values of life like freedom, integrity etc. emerge as leaders and constitute the minority whereas ninety-five percent people who look for comfort and pleasure constitute the majority class and are known as followers.

Everybody follows and has some followers. Benjamin Disraeli, a British Prime Minister, parliamentarian, Conservative statesman and literary figure who served in government for forty years, twice as Prime Minister of Great Britain quotes: "I must follow the people. Am I not their leader?" There is no harm in being a follower but there is no glory in remaining a follower throughout the life. Every good leader is a good follower in his earlier period. Some of good followers learn from good leaders and uplift themselves into the influential category of leaders. When a follower acquires qualities of leadership, he elevates himself and become a leader. Leaders are made and not born.

BE THE CHANGE YOU WANT TO SEE IN THIS WORLD

"We must become the change we want to see."

Mahatma Gandhi (1869–1948)

During 1930's, a young boy had become obsessed with eating sugar. Totally frustrated, her mother decided to take her son to see his icon leader – Mahatma Gandhi; thinking that possibly her son would take note of Gandhi's advice. She undertook long and hot journey with her son walking many miles and hours under the scorching sun. Finally, they reached Gandhi's ashram. There, she shared with Gandhi her worry and asked Gandhi to advise his son to stop eating sugar.

Gandhi listened to the woman attentively, thought for a while and asked them to come back after two weeks. The woman was astonished why Gandhi didn't ask her son to quit sugar. Nevertheless, she promised to come back after two weeks.

The woman along with her son revisited Gandhi. This time Mahatma Gandhi looked straight into eyes of the boy and said: "Son! You should not eat sugar. It is not good for your health." The impact was magnificent and the boy promised that he would never ever eat sugar. On the other hand, the woman couldn't keep her surprise and asked Gandhi: "Why didn't you advise the same thing two weeks ago when I brought my son here to see you?" Gandhi smiled and replied, "Mother, two weeks ago I was eating a lot of sugar myself."

Moral of the story:

1. We must strictly do what we say, as a leader.
2. Don't tell everyone else how to live; live and let them watch you.
3. If you want to change the world then start with yourself first.

IS LEADERSHIP SITUATIONAL?

Honour Your People

"If You Fail To Honour Your People,

They Will Fail To Honour You;

It Is Said Of A Good Leader That

When The Work Is Done, The Aim Fulfilled,

The People Will Say, "We Did This Ourselves."

Lao Tzu, 604–531 BC, Founder of Taoism, Tao Te Ching

To lead is to deal with situation and people. In 1948, a study by Stogdill found that leadership exists between persons in a social situation, and that persons who are leaders in one situation may not necessarily be leaders in other situations. So, leadership is situational. A person who takes a bold initiative will get followers and emerge as a great leader.

But a person who has mastered the principles of leadership can handle all the situations in a better way. I predict that girls, boys, men and women will pursue different management courses in kitchen, family, life, relationship and office. The people are looking these days, for a program that can teach them overall or super leadership. I believe that a person who has leadership skills can do all things, provided he knows strength and weaknesses of his people. That's why we basically define leadership as human engineering that revolves around the ability to get followers by persuading them through personality. As Dwight D. Eisenhower says: "Pull the string, and it will follow wherever you wish. Push it, and it will go nowhere at all." Leadership calls for a creative innovation so a leader functions as a social scientist also by emerging with an idea that clicks. Eleanor Roosevelt once put it in form of law of leadership: "A good leader inspires people to have confidence in the leader; a great leader inspires people to have confidence in themselves."

HOW DO LEADERS BEHAVE?

> *"Eighty-nine percent of people learn from what they see, ten percent from what they hear, and one percent from other senses."*
>
> John C. Maxwell, a leadership expert

A true leader needs to be consistent in words and in action and behaviour. Most of the people learn from what they see and hear. All the leadership behaviour revolves around five things. These are having the vision; commanding the vision; improving the vision; testing the vision and making the vision happen. I explain these points to get a better understanding.

Firstly, a leader is supposed to have clear vision, mission and goals. Secondly, a leader makes the people concentrate on his vision, mission and goals voluntarily. Thirdly, a leader often experiments and keeps improving. Fourthly, a leader takes calculated risks. Fifthly, a leader often surprises everybody with success. In short, a leader should have a vision and be able to cast it.

LEADER v. MANAGER

"Managers are copy and leaders are original."

Warren Bennis, an organizational consultant

What is the difference between a leader and a manager? Managers do things right. Leaders do the right thing. The manager accepts the status quo; the leader challenges it. A great leader exercises acquired leadership; I call it leadership by consent. Leaders acquire greatness and on managers, greatness is imposed. We see it in politics. Legacy continues by imposed greatness. Managers or bosses exercise assigned leadership; I name it leadership by compulsion.

As Mark Sanborn affirms, "A leader develops power with followers who follow him voluntarily." A leader performs suggestive role and thus he creates the change by setting peak performance as an example. One of the marks of excellent leaders is that they never compare themselves to others. They only compare themselves with themselves and with their own past accomplishments and future potential. A true leader does not need any title or status. Leaders speak through action rather than words or titles. They listen to others' opinion carefully before sharing their views. They concentrate more on relationships. They take risks. Randy Gage opines, for leaders "Risky is the New Safe."

A manager has power over his juniors who compulsorily act as per his wishes. Subordinates report to him out of his order because he talks about performance. He reacts to change and has formal powers. They form their opinion before listening to others. They avoid or take minimum risks. Managers never work; they get it done. They sit easy and look busy. They concentrate more on tasks than people.

NOTHING WRONG CAN HAPPEN

"We can't create the future but we can event it."

Denis Gabor (1900–1979)

You, as a great or super leader, should imagine the worst that can happen in a given situation by zooming out and then make sure that worst does not happen by zooming in. Being prepared in advance with strategic planning or disaster management for the loss will not make you to suffer that loss. As Arnold Glasow observes, one of the tests of leadership is the ability to recognize a problem before it becomes an emergency.

One has to take both internal and external factors into planning. Internal premises are internal variables that affect the planning. These consist of organizational policies, different resources and the capability of the organization to endure the environmental pressure. External premises comprise all factors in job environment like political, social, technological, competitors' plans and actions, government policies and market conditions. Most important one is taking full benefit of position of law.

Prepare for the excellence even if you fail is the guiding principle of a true super leader. Prepare your best schedule based on your peak performance. Deliver your best schedule each day regardless of bad or good times will lead to best future.

Peter Drucker who was an Austrian-born American management consultant speaks out that the best way to predict the future is to create it. This creation only will improve your way and the level of working as a leader. Experts like Jim Collins and Morten Hansen call super leaders as "Productive Paranoid Neurotic Freaks". The whole point is: If you can exist in turbulent times, you can excel in peak times.

DO LEADERS BEHAVE DIFFERENTLY?

"The first responsibility of a leader is to define reality. The last is to say thank you. In between, the leader is a servant."

Max De Pree, a businessman and American writer

Yes, leaders do behave differently. We need to look at types or styles of leadership to understand behaviour application by leaders to achieve success.

Autocratic leaders like military officers are the classical example of close supervision and discipline. They make maximum suggestions and retain decision-making power with themselves. This approach is effective with trainees or new employees.

Democratic leaders are known for their participative style of working. This is a long process and a leader involves everybody in brainstorming an idea. This type of leadership is good for building team and members' satisfaction.

Bureaucratic leaders work according to the rule book and policy. Leadership is based on seniority or authority. This type of leadership is good for governmental organization that involves hierarchy of officers where working is slow and interpersonal relations are formal and depends on position rather than on personality. It is not recommended for business organization but can be effective for security units to enforce certain standards and procedures.

Free rein or laissez-faire leaders give full control to staff members when they are capable and motivated to perform the task. Generally, managers appoint committees to shift their responsibilities but leaders divide the task into groups and give free hand to a leader in these teams who is a visionary but it can be a transactional leadership that tends to be autocratic behaviour.

Paternalistic leaders generally protect and promote the loyal butters and are known for their fatherly or motherly attitude but this type of leadership can't generate innovative ideas. However, these leaders have full support because of this style.

The trend is towards transformational or super leadership that relates to choosing the right attitude and proper leadership style(s) as per situation. The office of the American presidency is a multi-faceted occupation that requires many kinds of leadership styles. Mr. Obama has successfully implemented transactional and transformational leadership in diverse areas. He has been also popular due to his cross-cultural approach.

HOW PEOPLE BECOME LEADERS?

> *"Contrary to the opinion of many people, leaders are not born. Leaders are made, and they are made by effort and hard work."*
>
> Vince Lombardi (1913–1970)

There are three basic theories or ways to explain how people become leaders.

The first theory known as great man or great event theory (Thomas Carlyle) says that sometimes a man of great character emerges as a leader out of a turbulent situation. History of the world is but the biography of great men like Muhammad, Shakespeare, Luther, Rousseau, Karl Marx and Napoleon. Although, this assumption received great criticism from another hypothesis (Herbert Spencer) that great leaders are products of their environment.

The second theory also known as trait theory attributes leadership to natural or inherent qualities. This theory says that leaders are born and not made. It was indicated by Turkheimer (2000) who found that each broad personality trait contains a significant genetic source. All personality behavioural traits are genetically heritable. Researchers taking the trait approach attempted to spot physiological, demographic, personality, intellective, task-related, and social characteristics with leader emergence and leader effectiveness.

The third theory or transformational theory makes leadership a process that can be learned by anyone. A person is not born with self-confidence. Self-confidence is built up. Integrity and honesty are a stuff of personal preference. Enthusiasm to lead comes from within the person, but the knowledge of business can be gained. Good habits can be learned. Fears and bad habits can be unlearned. The nature–nurture debate is over. While cognitive or reasoning ability has its origin partly in genes, it still needs to be built up. None of these super traits are acquired while sleeping.

QUALITIES OF A GOOD LEADER

> *"Character, clarity, courage, coach-ability and competency are the five essential qualities for those will shape the future."*
>
> Andy Stanley, *The Next Generation Leader*

Andy Stanley considers five essential qualities of a great leader. John C. Maxwell talks about 21 indispensible qualities and 21 irrefutable laws of leadership. I am a big fan of both. What about you? What do you think are the most important qualities in a leader? Who do you consider a leader and why? Some may tell you there is one characteristic more important than the rest. They'll say something like, "Oh, you have to have that 'vision thing' above all else." Not true – One can't outweigh another. Most importantly, leaders have these characteristics *in equilibrium*.

How often you have heard the comment that a leader is born not made. I have done extensive research on leadership traits including physiological (appearance, height and weight), demographic (age, education and socio-economic background), personality (self-confidence and aggressiveness), intellective (intelligence, decisiveness, judgment and knowledge), task-allied (achievement drive, initiative and persistence), and social or inter-personal characteristics (sociability and cooperativeness).

I have come to the conclusion that all leaders share some qualities or characteristics that make them look like a natural leader. I am not going to give you a list of 101 qualities or something like that. Instead, I would like to discuss ten common traits those I have seen in all great leaders. These ten personal traits act like a foundation to travel from average to super leadership. Some characteristics may be more naturally present in the personality of a leader. However, each of these qualities can also be developed and strengthened.

Good leaders whether they naturally have these qualities or not, will be attentive to time and again build up and reinforce these ten qualities in their leadership task. In fact, great leaders develop others by coaching these qualities to others. As a leader you have weaknesses that you have to overcome, and you have standards that you have to meet, if you want to survive and thrive in a competitive market or world, this is the only way to achieve human excellence for which this life is gifted by the Almighty.

Let us explore each of these ten qualities further in details.

GUARD YOUR INTEGRITY

> *"Integrity as a wholeness requires the development of six traits in the character of a man who – creates and maintains trust, is unafraid of reality, works in a results-oriented way, embraces and solves negative realities, causes growth and achieves transcendence and finds meaning in life."*
>
> Dr. Henry Cloud, *Integrity*

When we see leaders, we get impressed. "Everything is image and image is everything." because you are perceived. Yes my friend—perception is the only thing. The perception of an individual is his or her reality. People proceed on the basis of their perception of you. So, the first quality to influence is to master the art of imaging. This art includes the steps to improve intra-personal and inter-personal image. Otto von Bismarck, also known as the Iron Chancellor, was a conservative German statesman who unified most of the German states into a German Empire in 1871, leading to peace in the country till World War I. He served as the Minister President of Prussia for 28 years and ended up as the first Chancellor of North German Federation after the Treaty of Versailles. He speaks: "They treat me like a fox, a cunning fellow of the first rank. But the truth is that with a gentleman I am always a gentleman and a half, and when I have to deal with a pirate, I try to be a pirate and a half." Know thyself is the first step and then make sure that your outer appearance and behaviour support you.

Integrity requires actions and a willingness to spurn conformity. It is clear that "integrity", as professionals use the term, is much more than mere "honesty". Integrity is operationally defined by a connoisseur Stephen L. Carter as consisting of three traits: knowing the difference between what is right and wrong; acting on the knowledge of that difference; and an open and public commitment to acting on that difference.

Self-image or intra-personal image is the key. A super leader "walks the talk" means he has exemplary character. As D.L. Mody said, "Character is what you are in the dark." First lead yourself and then you lead others. To lead yourself means to lead inside out. Leaders have integrity of character that make them to live and stand rock solid in values in turbulent times. A leader who is centred in integrity will be more accessible to followers. When author and leadership expert John Maxwell titled his book *There's No Such Thing as Business Ethics,* many were taken aback. Maxwell explained that you either have ethics or you don't. There isn't one set of ethics for business and another for your personal life. Integrity is the integration of external actions and internal values.

I met with many people and had long discussion on various concepts in person and on phone. I would like to share S. Inderjit Singh Khalsa who is *Mukh Sweadar* of Baba Farid Shrines and is predominantly well-known for his honesty and truth in Faridkot, Punjab. He learned the truth and honesty from a devotee Puranmal Ji. He affirms: "Shortcuts can only bring monetary success. One must have truth and honesty towards his life, aim and success to get true and permanent triumph." It is all about having the guts to be the person you project yourself to be. There are too many hypocrites. People, who say one thing, but act the opposite.

Super leaders have a high sense of self-respect so they respect others also. Self-discipline or Self-mastery is the key to master people. Ralph Waldo Emerson once rightly asserted: "You must guard your integrity as a sacred thing." I had an opportunity of interacting with Prof. (Dr.) M.P. Singh who is the existing Chancellor of Central University of Haryana, Mahendergarh and the present Chairperson of Delhi Judicial Academy during a refresher course at Kurukshetra. A leader so great and revered, there is no two thoughts about his leadership. He is known as one of the best administrators. He has been Vice Chancellor, National University of Juridical Sciences, West Bengal. He is equally a brilliant author. He is best known for being the revising author of V.N. Shukla's *Constitution of India,* a standard textbook for lawyers on Constitution of India. I was curious about his secrets of success, so I asked him, "Sir, what are the qualities in a man that makes him successful?" He replied, "Hard work is at the root of every success. Dedication to the work comes at second place." Then, I asked him about the single quality by which an average person can reach right at the top, to this question he replied in one word, "Integrity." His success becomes an inspiration because of the fact that he was born in an ordinary farmer's family in a village, and he lost his parents at a very young age. Therefore, more than an academician, he is known for his humbleness. Your entire public image including people relationship and outer world experience is a mirror reflection of your self-image. This image comes when you convey your real and honest character in your relationships and that alone inspires others to respect you.

A leader must be reliable and responsible person in the eyes of other people. The cliché "It takes a long time to build trust and only seconds to break it" is an ancient wisdom. You must avoid breaking the promises, backbiting and gossiping to get the people's respect. People do things either out of will or compulsion so when you treat people with gentleness, good manners and politeness; you make them want to do things for you.

People show respect for powerful people due to the positioning of image in their minds. But people actually respect people of performance who have pleasing personality. Therefore, you must look exceptionally genuine and honest with your clothes, grooming and accessories and more importantly with your behaviour and thinking. Muhammad Ali Jinnah, Antony Eden, Nelson Mandela, Kofi Annan and Winston Churchill have been famous for their dressing sense.

I often advise my students to wear good decent clothes as they cover 95% part of the body, hence clothes reveal our thinking and so build our image. Most of success coaches advise to pattern yourself after the winners in your field because everything is counted by the people when they perceive your personality. It's all about how to dress, speak, behave, eat, drink, entertain, beautify and normally be better than everybody else. Dressing is all about finding the right style that's right for your body shape. You can also refer to few good authors like Clinton Kelly and Stacy London who offer spot on fashion wisdom and a solution to the dilemma, "What do I need to wear to look fabulous?" You can also refer works like *Freakin' Fabulous* to improve social skills.

COURAGE—THE FOREMOST VIRTUE

> *"The measure of your life will be the measure of your courage."*
>
> Matthew Kelly, *The Book of Courage*

The second quality of super leaders is the quality of courage that makes great leaders to stand apart. They lead others by taking initiatives for shaping a better future.

No intelligent follower will be dominated by a leader who lacks self-confidence, daring and intelligence for too long. Leaders treat fear as a great motivator. Abraham Lincoln was in office during the American Civil War where he kept the people together and is the only reason that the nation did not break into smaller parts. His greatest traits were his willpower, persistence and courage. Winston Churchill was a British politician who is best known for his leadership of Great Britain against the Nazi Germany during the World War II. He teamed up with allies and thus led to the defeat and downfall of Hitler. He was known for his fearlessness and determination. He asserts: "Courage is rightly considered the foremost of the virtues, for upon it all others depend." When people perceive you they count everything. Katharine Meyer Graham was an American publisher. She led her family's newspaper, *The Washington Post,* for more than two decades. Her greatest quality was courage and she didn't fear from anybody.

David Cottrell and Eric Harvey also state: "Courage may be one of the most overlooked virtues in leadership, but no leader can be effective without it." People follow and co-operate only the courageous initiators who take full responsibility of their actions and never play blame games. A leader has to fix problems and not blame. If it is to be, a leader says, it's up to me. This is the penalty of leadership. Phrases such as the "The buck stops here" and "If you can't stand the heat, you better get out of the kitchen" were popularized by thirty-third President of the United States Harry S. Truman.

ETHOS, PATHOS AND LOGOS

> *"The number one fear among adults is public speaking."*
>
> Tim Koegel, *The Exceptional Presenter*

The third quality of a great leader is effective public speaking. Most people agree that public speaking is one of top fears especially in adults. But in today's competitive business world, effective communication is a crucial skill, and the cost of being less than effective is quite high. It is an ability to negotiate, communicate, influence and persuade others to do things. Public speaking is absolutely indispensable to everything you accomplish in life. The key to persuasion is motivation. Every human action is motivated by something. Your job is to find out what motivates other people and then to provide that motivation. People have two major motivations: the desire for gain and the fear of loss. The winning formula to conquer the fear of public speaking is a blend of three tips given by Dale Breckenridge Carnegie. He advises: "Prepare your speech, speak on your interests and remember your audience." Many teachers of communication, speech, and rhetoric consider Aristotle's *On Rhetoric* to be a seminal work in the field. Aristotle says that the effective public speaking EPS is all about EPL—rhetorical triangle of Ethos, Pathos and Logos. Adolf Hitler's oratory skills were famous. Martin Luther King's speech *I Have a Dream* reputed him as one of the best orator.

You must be perceived by audience as genuinely trustworthy that is your ethos. CEOs of large companies have strong and credible ethos. Pathos is the quality presentation of a speaker that persuades emotions in audience like storytelling, examples and comparisons etc. Politicians have better pathos. The ability to make logical and reasoned arguments based on facts and figures is known as logos. A teacher has more of logos. A great leader has all of three EPL in balance. So we say EPS=EPL.

DO YOU HAVE 30%?

> *"An artist is not paid for his labour but for his vision."*
>
> James Whistler (1834–1903)

This 30% determines the remaining 70% of accomplishment. This 30% is clarity of vision; the fourth attribute of great leaders. This is the one conclusion that everyone agrees with. George Washington was a true visionary whose vision has endured for more than 200 years. Queen Elizabeth I set the model for a female ruler. Charlemagne was the king of the Franks who expanded and united the Frankish kingdoms into the single, powerful Frankish Empire. Fidel Castro was the leader of the Cuban Revolution who later went to become the Prime Minister and President of Cuba and endured many crisis, invasions and assassination attempts. He is well known for his vision for Cuba that still stands. Martin Luther

King received Nobel Peace Prize for standing up for racial discrimination through nonviolence. Odysseus also managed to take back his kingdom of Ithaca after it was overrun with selfish tyrants and single-handedly saved his kingdom. He shows his ability to think forward and get out of situations without just using pure power. Theodore Hesburgh who was 15th President of the University of Notre Dame once said: "The very essence of leadership is that you have to have a vision. It's got to be a vision you articulate clearly and forcefully on every occasion. You can't blow a weak trumpet." Great leaders lead by a clear, thrilling and shared vision. They have a clear idea of a thrilling prospect, and they have the class of personality that gets other people energized and devoted to the making of that potential future. A shared vision involves everyone working together. Tom Bentley, author and policy analyst, opines: "An inward understanding with an outward facing leads to a futuristic imagination." An experienced executive coach Peter Shaw says that by using the four Vs – Vision, Values, Value-added and Vitality – you can have effective vision, helping you to dream where you want to be, harness the values that drive you, release the value-added you bring to a role and grow your sources of vitality. Vision statements help a lot to stay focused. Passion fuels the rocket, but vision directs the rocket to its ultimate destination. Vision Statement of Reliance is "To be a globally respected wealth creator with an emphasis on customer care and a culture of good corporate governance." Vision Statement of Maruti Suzuki is: "The leader in the Indian automobile industry, creating customer delight and shareholder's wealth; a pride for India." The mission and vision of Amazon.com is – "Our vision is to be earth's most customer- centric company; to build a place where people can come to find and discover anything they might want to buy online." You can sense of urgency in these vision statements. As Ramez Sasson says, "The difference between can and cannot are only three letters. Three letters that determine your life's direction." The most motivational vision you can have for yourself and others is – "Be the best!"

ADMINISTRATIVE ASSERTIVENESS

"A leader is more than someone who is in charge."

Dave Dungan, *Don't Follow Me: I Am The Leader*

As an assertive administrator, a great leader makes it clear what he wants out of others that too without any misunderstandings. He also knows what others want out of him. A good leader must be an action oriented man and that calls for an administrative ability. David Packard was a co–founder of Hewlett-Packard, serving as President, CEO and Chairman of the Board. He served as U.S. Deputy Secretary of Defense from 1969–1971 during the Nixon administration. In 1949, 37-year-old Packard attended a meeting of business leaders and said: "We have a responsibility to our employees to recognize their dignity as human beings." Sam Walton, the Wal-Mart founder said: "I have the personality of a promoter but the soul of an operator." Bill Allen, Boeing's former chief said: "Don't talk too much, Let others talk." As Martin Luther King stated, "A genuine leader is not a searcher for consensus but a moulder for consensus." This fifth attribute of a great leader means that he must be able to get the work done through his followers. He must know how to plan, organize and control the work of his followers. Head of the family or team leads the action. Ross Perot is an American businessman who is best known for being an Independent Party Presidential Candidate in 1992 and 1996. Perot founded Electronic Data Systems (EDS) in 1962, sold the company to General Motors in 1984, and founded Perot Systems in 1988. Perot Systems was bought by Dell in 2009. There is a warning by Ross. He warns: "Lead and inspire people. Don't try to manage and manipulate people. Inventories can be managed but people must be lead."

Haryana Institute of Public Administration (HIPA) is an apex State Training Institute funded by the Govt. of Haryana. HIPA was established in 1983 with the objective of providing training, research and consultancy to improve efficiency and effectiveness in administration. One of my friends, Mr. M.M. Alam who is a faculty member of this institute rightfully authenticates: "A true leader is someone who understands how important it is to empower others. One of the greatest privileges you can have is the opportunity to be the leader of leaders." As Dave Dungan says, "There are plenty of bosses, but very few true leaders."

A single leader cannot do every work by himself. There has to be contribution from each one in the team. Great leaders "engage and energize" the people around them with shared values, shared objectives and shared activities. Even though you may feel you have the answers to a problem, ask for their help and advice. Thus, the best step in the technique of motivating others is to initiate with yourself; taking an intense interest in them and winning their hearts through a unadulterated concern and unadulterated smile. He coaches, guides, helps, instructs what to do, how to do and when to do it. He acts as a role model in form of coach and guide for his followers. He enjoys confidence of all the followers because of his fairness, justice and impartial stand because the moment he becomes partial to one he loses the confidence of all. He is more concerned with *what's* right rather than *who's* right.

Lenin had a watchword which he repeated frequently, it runs like an autograph through all his writings: "Patiently explain." The great leaders are best in fine-tuning when they are talking and building the relationships. They always discuss the subjects and avoid arguments. A leader controls the discussion in such a way that others don't get conscious of the degree of control which is being exercised. The people can be led easily if you can convince them that even the dullest work is part of a revolution of our time.

I think we have to try to think as the other man thinks. See how things look to him. One of the techniques can be to find out the area of accord and then to broaden that area. The people can be led easily if you can convince them that even the dullest work is part of a revolution of our time. The ball passes from one to another.

They know power lies in the relationships. People trust leaders. Warren Bennis and Burt Nauns define trust as "the glue that binds followers and leaders together." You can find manifestation of this power in all the social sites. And, all relationships begin and end with what people perceive of you. That's why leaders build power with people. People tend to lose self-esteem if they are not kept busy. Leadership calls for power, power calls for cooperation and cooperation calls for Magnanimity. Magnanimity means "To spread the fame and take the blame."

The great man never plays "I Game" because he knows that a man by nature thinks of himself first. You can look at this way that you always search for your result first before your brother's result. You will always look for your contributed article in a magazine even though you know every word of it. You look for your photograph in a group photo. Great leaders know this human nature and therefore a great leader asks what the other person wants rather than what he himself is interested in.

The option lies with us—the option to find a way. We have to find a way to get our vision set into the minds of people. If people do not take interest, it is because we have not found a way to make them interested. We can make them involved if we know how their mind works, if we value things which are important for them, make those things important to us and see ourselves with the people.

Appreciation makes people feel more important than anything else you can give them. They talk with open mind without any intolerances and prejudices which are hallmark of a closed mind. They never blow own horn and encourage others to speak and capitalize on personal strengths. "If you know what I think and act the way in which I would have acted, then you force me to act in the way you want to me to act."

The majority people consider conversation as a tennis match to be equal in terms of words. Most of the toastmasters are of view that one can speak only 60 to 180 words per minute but one can listen five times more than spoken words especially in a group. So, I will put my bet on listening more rather speaking less. Great leaders are expert in looking at things from the other person's point of view. That's why they play the game in "You" way. They use three lettered word "You" instead of a single lettered word "I" and make the conversation interactive.

COMMIT YOURSELF SINCERELY

> *"Commitment unlocks the doors of imagination, allows vision, and gives us the right stuff to turn our dreams into reality."*
>
> James Womack, founder of
> *Lean Enterprise Institute*

Do you as a leader solemnly, (which means deeply earnest), seriously, and soberly commit yourself fully to your vision? As a leader, you must answer this question by saying – Yes, I will. This sixth quality of a great leader means that you will wholeheartedly give your talent, resources and yourself totally to make your vision and mission statement a reality by doing everything humanly and spiritually possible. Leadership at one time meant muscles, but today it means getting along with people. There's a difference between interest and commitment. When you're interested in doing something, you do it only when circumstance permit. When you're committed to something, you accept no excuses, only results. The leaders like George Washington had both the qualities of perseverance and infinite courage. He was the first President of the United States (1789–1797), the commander-in-chief of the Continental Army during the American Revolutionary War, and one of the Founding Fathers of the United States. He presided over the convention that drafted the Constitution, which replaced the Articles of Confederation and established the position of President. At his death, Washington was eulogized by Henry Lee as "first in war, first in peace, and first in the hearts of his countrymen." He is consistently ranked among the top three presidents of the United States.

I would like to cite another super leader, S. Hakam Singh Jawandha who is Chairman, Bhai Gurdas Group of Institutions and is preeminently acknowledged for his leadership traits that has put Sangrur, a relatively aloof city of Punjab as a prominent place in the map of India. He quotes in a measured and sensible voice,"Consistency is the game plan. Whatever work you are doing, you should keep doing towards a particular goal, no matter how many hardships come in your way or whatever opposition you face. A great leader leads from front and will not hesitate to roll up his sleeves and get dirty because he treats himself as a part of team. He believes in leadership by example." In my view, S. Jawandha has exactly pointed one quality of a great leader. A great tells other guys through his conduct that there are not nine-to-five jobs but opportunities to cash on. A leader with passion and dedication motivates others by his enthusiasm towards his work. This ability inspires others to cooperate in getting the work done. The present time is a turning point in our history. We have been given a chance to write our history. We are scripting our own story. I am making this point because I want you to understand the importance of passion.

The basic purpose of establishing Indian Institute of Public Administration, New Delhi is to undertake such academic activities as would enhance the leadership qualities and managerial capabilities of the executives in the government and other public service organizations. One of my learned friends, Dr. Lokendra Malik who is a faculty in this Institute affirms: "I would say, beyond any shadow of doubt, one of the qualities which all great leaders have in common is their idealism – their enthusiasm to sacrifice, their passion, their perseverance, their commitment to their vision." Douglas Hyde wrote a book *Dedication and Leadership* about his experiences and the specific tactics of the Communists especially in the way that they recruited their members and built them into leaders.

One of the techniques of the Communist Party was ability to take anyone who was willing to be trained in leadership and turned him into a leader. This is the technique through which Communists capture one-third of the world's population by 1950, given the fact that Lenin had only a handful of followers in 1900. One of the points he made was that the recruiting age was 15 to 25, the age to go for idealism or dedication.

In this age period, the youth have a passion for idealism i.e. to contribute best according to his best ability. Erikson, a famous researcher, defines the age of adolescence 13–19, a period of transition from childhood to adulthood, as an age of identity crisis. In fact, Erikson is famous for coining the term identity crisis. At this age, a child develops his own ideologies, looks and determines what he is going to do with them in the future.

Due to this we saw people like Che Guevara and Fidel Castro who were communists. By 1959, they had thousands of supporters and took control of Cuba. Communists were close to the people. On October 18, 1967, more than 200,000 people gathered in the Plaza of the Revolution in Havana to hear Fidel Castro read an obituary to Che Guevara, who had been assassinated in Bolivia nine days before. Communists understood the people's language, the people's needs and preferred not to live in their own little sealed-off world like we do. I am not approving their way of life but my point is that the communists used the concept of "leaders generate leaders" to popularize their movement.

FOCUS ON CHANGE

"Innovation distinguishes between a leader and a follower."

Steve Jobs (1955–2011)

Creativity or innovation is the seventh quality of a great leader. Creativity simply means that you have the ability to think and create something new and different. Vladimir Lenin, a Russian Communist politician who studied to become a lawyer was the leader of Russia and devoted his time becoming a Marxist. He implemented several social reforms and contributed to Marxist theories, referred to as Leninism. Although sometimes called as a Dictator, he was loved by working class people for his New Economic Policy.

He quotes: "Victory will belong only to those who have faith in the people, those who are immersed in the life-giving spring of popular creativity." William L. McKnight was an American businessman and philanthropist who served his entire career in the 3M Corporation, rising to chairman of the board from 1949 to 1966. He founded The McKnight Foundation in 1953. He is known for his creativity. Charles Albert Coffin was the co–founder and first President of General Electric Corporation. Coffin oversaw two social innovations of huge significance: America's first research laboratory and the idea of systematic management development.

Creativity generates something of value or significance by experimental and energetic improvisation. Creativity requires art of right brain and logic of left brain. It is a complete brain activity that goes hand in hand with spirit of adventure. Artists, scientists and writers etc. possess this unique quality. Chip and Dan Heath in their book *Switch* cite a few metaphors. The notable of these are the Rider or mahout (i.e. our rational side), the Elephant, (i.e. our emotional and instinctive side) and the Path (i.e. the surrounding environment in which change initiatives will be conducted). The challenges are to direct the Rider, motivate the Elephant and shape the Path to make change more likely, "no matter what's happening with the Rider and Elephant... If you can do all three at once, Heaths assert, dramatic change can happen even if you don't have lots of power or resources behind you."

Take time out to ride your bike, build sand castles, fly a kite, smell a rose, walk in the woods or stroll barefoot in the sand. Denis Waitley who is an American motivational speaker, writer, consultant and best-selling author says: "We need to continually experience the world of the creative child within." This seventh quality of a leader calls for thinking outside the box whereas most of us are comfortable with our boxes.

Managers with long experience and knowledge prefer to stay in status quo or a little change. Creative leaders go for even a complete change. Dr. Martin Luther King, Jr. was a creative leader. MLK's celebrated speech "I Have a Dream" has touched the hearts of millions of Americans throughout the years. Mahatma Gandhi is also the Indian Model of servant leadership. There was nobody like him before him and there is nobody like him after him in terms of creative leadership. He was people's person. He was instrumental in getting the whole India united for the cause of Independence. He said: "Every moment of your life is infinitely creative and the universe is endlessly bountiful. Just put forth a clear enough request, and everything your heart desires must come to you." Nelson Mandela, the first South African president got elected by fully democratic elections was the main leader in the anti-apartheid movements. He is famous for his focus on change and vision. He served a 30-year lengthy prison sentence but it did not stop him and in fact motivated him to gather his people for this cause. George W. Merck was the president of Merck & Co. from 1925 to 1950. Merck served shareholders so well precisely because he served others first. But from where these leaders get all the energy? Dr. Tarun Arora, a competent administrator, and a proud member of my RPG asserts what he calls his formula of excellence: "The first thing, you need is the mental peace that comes from your lifestyle and family–office atmosphere; the second thing is focus on change that comes from dedication and commitment to your aims but that once again depends on mental peace. These two are two legs of success; if one gets broken the whole process comes at a threat." Did you get this? Super Achievers have peace of mind because of their family–office support. They are very sound in their personal philosophy because from this they get all the leadership traits.

Researchers have revealed that creativity is the quality, which is being preferred in CEOs nowadays. My point is this that even you are comfortable in the box still you can enlarge your box by being creative. You can invent anything new that can be of relevance like a product, solution, artwork, literary work, joke, a new plan, a new thought and a new way of doing things. To be creative you have to be imaginative first and then you act on that imagination. Most of us are imaginative only; because they think only but never act on that thought.

There is a technique to think which I use to create something new: Ask yourself and then ignore the first answer, second answer and so on, the later answers will open new faculties of mind. Here you have to think and not guess. Is guessing vaguer than thinking? Or is thinking more general than guessing? When you say I think – it is because you believe you know enough or have sufficient information about something – and so then you can offer an opinion. When you say I guess, you feel that you don't have enough information or none at all, so you must guess about the answer of topic. Consequently, you have to come up with new thinking patterns for creativity. Commit to memory: Nothing is perfect and it can get better in the next attempt. There is always a scope for improvement.

BE SPONTANEOUS

"Spontaneity is a meticulously prepared art."

Oscar Wilde (1854–1900)

Spontaneity is the eighth quality of a great leader. This spontaneity is not foolishness but it is supported by keen observation, mental alertness and creative intelligence. Experts like Marina Santi bestow on improvisation its legitimate role as a versatile, long-lasting creative process of knowledge and action. When you make a choice you are spontaneous. You take a decision out of your intelligence. King Bruce got inspired from a spider because of his keen observation. We require spontaneity, keen observation, mental alertness and creative intelligence in all the fields of life. Your driving is spontaneous supported by intelligence and alertness. As a leader, you have to make sound judgments out of your intelligence. In Greek mythology, Odysseus was the Greek king of Ithaca with achievements so great he was immortalized in Homer's epic *The Odyssey*. Odysseus managed to trick the Trojans during the Trojan War by building a wooden horse and hiding his soldiers in it. The Trojans took the horse into their city and into their walls, and just like that, the Greeks got past the impenetrable walls of Troy. Odysseus's renowned intelligence and cunning supplements his strong combative skills. Robert H. Schuller observes: "High achievers spot rich opportunities swiftly, make big decisions quickly and move into action immediately. Follow these principles and you can make your dreams come true." Spontaneity helps a leader to analyze and appraise a situation and then responding with a suitable plan.

Alertness helps a leader in remaining updated. Mental alertness and creative intelligence helped Newton to discover gravitational law out of falling apple. A leader has to keep his eyes and ears open. He should read all the papers carefully before signing them. He has to take care of all the activities going inside and outside his field. He must know his enemies and friends. He has to plan for any probable criticism. Intelligence is different from knowledge which is a byproduct of intelligence.

Spontaneity means acting in alignment with a natural feeling, impulse or tendency without any premeditation. Spontaneity leads to quick decision and quick action. Richard Iannelli has defined spontaneity as the quality of being able to do something just because you feel like it at the moment, of trusting your instincts, of taking yourself by surprise and snatching from the clutches of your well-organized routine a bit of unscheduled pleasure. Katharine Hepburn (1907–2003) who was an American actress of film, stage, and television said it beautifully: "If you obey all the rules ... you miss all the fun." Prof. (Dr.) Satish Arya is a Professor-in-English and Principal of an excellent college in Haryana, India. He always inspires me to look the life from a positive frame of mind. He is a gifted administrator. I often interact with him on various issues and concepts. During my recent research, once I asked him, "How do you handle people and circumstances?" He asserts: "A good administration always has a human angle. It can't be dry or tailor- made. Managers who are typical rule-book guys are not flexible. A natural leader has faith of people because of his instant flexibility and wisdom. No tree prepares for the tomorrow. No bird prepares for the tomorrow." Spontaneity is generally said to be the heart of relationships. I consider it equally good in business life also.

Spontaneity can be risky, but that's part of the fun of it. You can't have it both ways. As the saying goes, nothing ventured, nothing gained. It does not mean that I am asking you to sit easy. You have to plan and premeditate but, you have to be spontaneous. Your disciplined routine will regulate your spontaneity. If you are disciplined then you will have fewer failures. A player prepares for the final race, but, he performs in a spontaneous way. He feels, "I am done with my preparation and now I am ready to do it." You prepare for the great speech all day and night and then it goes in a spontaneous way.

Flora Colao, a social worker and therapist, utters: "It's really a lot less complicated than we usually think." Life is playfulness. Children know this. That's why they spend so much of their time playing. They are aware of wonder. Adults often need help remembering how to play. We need to play so that we can rediscover the magic all around us. "Our spontaneous action," said Ralph Waldo Emerson, "is always the best. You cannot, with your best deliberation and heed, come so close to any question as your spontaneous glance shall bring you." I always believe that spontaneity can bring great luck.

Over analysis kills spontaneity. Albert Einstein (1879–1955), a German-born great theoretical physicist, also affirms: "Our intuitive mind is a sacred gift." The rational mind is our faithful servant. Unfortunately, we have created a society that honours the servant and has forgotten the sacred gift.

PLAN THE WORK & WORK THE PLAN

"Failing to plan is planning to fail."

Alan Lakein, a time management expert

I found when I studied history that in periods, where there is no leadership, society stands still. Where there is no vision, the people perish. Leaders plan and lead the progress. "Leaders think and talk," states Brain Tracy, "about the solutions. Followers think and talk about the problems." They plan and work it. A plan is a blueprint to achieve set goals in professional life or prepare yourself for successful aging in personal life. It specifies the indispensable resource allocations, schedules, tasks and other actions. Planning is ninth quality of great leaders. Genghis Khan's brilliant military strategies and tactics made him a super-king. What made George Washington great was his foresight, vision, strategic planning and his ability to lead people to success. Fidel Castro proved to be an effective leader and commander because of traits of strategy and selecting the right man for right job. Julius Caesar single-handedly led Roman Empire to expansion. He reformed the Roman government and led several campaigns with several victories. He was the Roman general who disintegrated Roman Republic and raised the Roman Empire. His invasion in Britain resulted in him having unparalleled military control. He created the Julian Calendar and made several government and social modifications. He was a man of action and was notorious for his opportunism and strategic planning. He once said: "Creating is the essence of life." Napoleon I of France, also known as Emperor Napoleon, was a prominent military and political leader of France who dominated continental Europe through superior military tactics and intelligence. But his establishment of the Napoleon code also laid the administrative and judicial foundations for much of Western Europe. Adolf Hitler's propaganda and planning made him a leader par excellence. After becoming the chancellor of Germany in 1933, he was responsible for one of the greatest economic and military expansions the world has ever seen. He successfully invaded more than 10 countries with his brilliant strategy and meticulous planning. James Burke was the chief executive officer (CEO) of Johnson & Johnson from 1976 to 1989, a company for which he worked forty years. He was famous for his planning. Vladimir V. Putin has been Russia's leader since 2000, a strongman who has stabilized the country's economy and politics with his *Putinism* through proper planning and leadership.

In plain words, planning is deciding in advance what is to be done, when, where, how and by whom it is to be done. Effective delegating requires proper planning and contemplation, and also proper follow-up. Planning is a bridge between where we are to where we want to be. It is the route to your destination. It is organized forecasting of uncertain future.

All the management experts agree that planning is an intellectual process of thinking in advance where you envision your future on the basis of series of events to follow without any deviations. A leader who moves by guesswork, without practical and definite plans, is as good as to a ship without a rudder. Sooner or later he will land on the rocks. In absence of planning, decisions become adhoc choices. Planning leads to better control over the process. It helps to concentrate on objectives.

What are different steps in planning? The first step is set the accurate objectives or goals. Secondly, evaluate the options available in terms of merits and demerits analysis. Thirdly, plan a strategy for the predicted situations taking external and internal variables into consideration, we call it plan–A. Fourthly, plan alternative course of action, we call it plan–B. Fifthly, break the master plan into various small plans for various levels. Sixthly, assign a small plan to one team led by a good leader. Seventhly, decide the sequence for flow of work. Who will do what and at what time? Fix the starting and finishing times of each task for each of the teams. Finally, check and recheck from time to time the follow up actions on the plan and if the plan is not working fine then change the plan.

THREE ON BASIS OF ONE

> *"Great decision makers aren't those who process the most information or spend the most time deliberating, but those who have perfected the art of 'thin-slicing' – filtering the most relevant factors that matter from an overwhelming number of variables. The key is to rely on our adaptive unconscious – a 24 × 7 mental valet – and train our mind accordingly."*
>
> Malcolm Gladwell, *Blink*

Decisiveness is tenth, last and most important quality of a super leadership. One of the greatest leaders of all time, Muhammad (Peace Be Upon Him) led to the spread of Islam. He led his people to a number of migrations and successful victories in wars against armies much larger than theirs. His greatest leadership qualities were his courage, leading by example, motivational approach, determination and more notably his decision-making. S. Inderjit Singh Khalsa shared an incident when he was doing his graduation at Khalsa College, Lyallpur, Pakistan. He attended an assembly where Muhammad Ali Jinnah was addressing the gathering of over one lakh muslims. Jinnah said: "Think 100 times before you take a decision, but once that decision is taken, stand by it as one man." S. Inderjit says, "This incident has changed my life." Many experts like Michael Useem have tried to explore the process of how leaders make decisions, that is, to go or not go. Indecision and procrastination are twin brothers. All leaders fall into three broad categories on the basis of one deciding ability. An average leader tends to decide too quickly without due consideration to internal and external premises. Mediocre leaders gather data, analyze and ponder endlessly and are unable to decide due to paralysis of analysis. Making decisions too quickly or too slowly will impede your leadership effectiveness. Average and mediocre leaders struggle to decide in many areas of life and excel in one or few. We can learn the process from fire commanders, fighter pilots, paramedics, and others who make split-second decisions.

Many leadership gurus have revealed why are some people brilliant decision-makers, while others are consistently inept? Why do some people follow their instincts and win, while others end up stumbling into error? How do our brains really work – in the office, in the classroom, in the kitchen and in the bedroom? Super leaders make well considered quick decision in all areas of life. No over-caution but no under-caution too. They have courage to decide and faith to act quickly. Life itself is a chance. Prof. (Dr.) Preet Singh, an able administrator believes: "Super leaders take their chances. They stand firm in what they believe. A good leader must make proper judgments to act upon. He must have a skill to judge different situations and the performance of his followers." Napoleon Hill in his masterpiece *Think and Grow Rich* says that Henry Ford was famous for his firm and quick decisions and changing those slowly.

THE NEW BRAND OF SUPER LEADERS

"He who would be master must be servant of all."

Confucius (551 BC–479 BC)

The new brand of super leaders which the world is anxiously waiting to lead is transformational leaders (Bernard M. Bass) who use motivation to inspire the people to concentrate on goals. The originator of this concept was James MacGregor Burns who named these as transforming leaders.

These leaders can be as rare as servant leaders who contribute in team work without any recognition or title or as charismatic as top position holders. Servant leader, a type of leader, is a term coined in the 1970s by Robert Greenleaf.

These level 5 leaders, as Jim Collins calls them, are combination of personal humility and professional will. Level 5 leader looks in mirror for responsibility and look out window for credits. Collins places a highly capable individual at number one; contributing team member at number two; competent manager at level three; effective leader at level four and great executives leaders at level five. Collins wrote about level-5-leadership in a 2001 *Harvard Business Review* article, and published his research in his well-respected book, *Good to Great*. Most of good leaders end up at egoistic and autocratic level four. Both servant and charismatic leaders add value to the life of people. They are best in switching off and on the best style(s) of leadership in view of situational needs and the people they are dealing with. Guy Kawasaki quotes: "A players recruit A+ players, while B players recruit C players." The super leaders respect and hire people better than them whereas managers hire people worse than them in order to maintain their supremacy.

I call these people as total or overall or super leaders. They can lead in any situation. A transactional leader works within the structure while a transformational leader works to change the structure. They continuously work on "What they are?", "What they know?" and "What they do?" They work on themselves. They read and learn constantly. They always look for better ways of doing the things. They have a unique gift to coach i.e. teach and train the people. They act as role model and influence people through their vision and action. They look after well being of each one and stimulate his intellectual creativity and improve thinking perceptions and ultimately achieve success through shared values and shared efforts.

The first golden rule or ethics of reciprocity states that: "Do unto others as you would have them do unto you." However, other golden rule means that might is right. In the words of Thucydides, the Greek historian, "the one with the gold makes the rules." I predict that "in coming times, only golden rule is going to work not the rule of gold."

SUGGESTED STRATEGY

"Earn your leadership every day."

Michael Jordan, American former
professional basketball player

Psychologist Eric Turkheimer wrote *Three Laws of Behaviour Genetics and What They Mean*. First Law: "All human behavioural traits are heritable." Biological siblings or twins are far more similar than adoptive siblings. Second Law: "The effect of being raised in the same family is smaller than the effect of the genes." The shared environment is that which impinges on both siblings alike. Third Law: "A substantial portion of the variation in complex human behavioural traits is not accounted for by the effects of genes or families." The unique environment is everything else – that which impinges on one sibling but not another. Steven Pinker examined these and says in summary – genes 40–50%, shared environment 0–10%, unique environment 50%. Chance events lead to tiny differences. How to be a super leader? Take a red pill. There is a saying, fake it until you make it. Another way of saying that is if you want to be a super leader act like a super leader. You must fake your leadership image every day till it becomes your real self. Super leaders practice certain behaviours. My good friend Mr. Jagdish Dahiya, an executive engineer, suggests: "Assign or accept responsibility. You must delegate complete responsibility for results to your subordinates. You can discuss and agree on accurately what is to be done, when it's to be done and to what standard. Then, get out of the way and let them perform. Your role is not to challenge, criticize or argue, but to look for solutions and for opportunities to help other people make their maximum contribution as well."

One of the best ways to use this attitude in your interactions is to constantly look for ways "to say and do" positive things for people. Look for ways to do kind acts and favours for your friends and prospects. Send thank-you notes. Send birthday cards. Send clippings from newspapers about subjects you feel may be of interest to them. At the end of the breakfast or lunch or when you meet somebody under more or less every situation, one of the greatest questions you can try is this: "Is there anything that I can do for you?" This will build and increase mutual bond of trust and respect.

ASSIGNMENT

1. Study the lives and biographies of great leaders mentioned in this book.
2. Discuss each of ten qualities with your friends and team members. Ask your team leaders or friends to prepare a presentation on leadership qualities and then go for a brainstorming session to generate ideas to implement these qualities.
3. Try to live, love and laugh to inspire others through your daily activities and roles based on super leadership.
4. Listen to the audio program *Leadership 101* by John C. Maxwell.

VISUALIZATION

When you get up, just sit and visualize living in the spirit of super leadership and doing all day activities on the basis of acting on ten traits. Remember: Every leader has to remove a big rock.

SELF SUGGESTION

I am a confident and competent super leader.

Bear in mind: Super achievers always keep their commitments.

[*Promise & Put Your Signature Here With Date*]

23

Do You Thank God For What You Have?

OBJECTIVES

- To learn the "Law of Thanksgiving",
- To put into practice the art of living in present, and
- To become skilled at the techniques of relaxation.

GOLDEN GUIDANCE

"On the recollection of so many and great favours and blessings, I now, with a high sense of gratitude, presume to offer up my sincere thanks to the Almighty, the Creator and Preserver."

William Bartram (1739–1823)

GRATITUDE—MOST POSITIVE AND MOST NEGLECTED EMOTION

"Let gratitude be the pillow upon which you kneel to say your nightly prayer. And let faith be the bridge you build to overcome evil and welcome good."

Maya Angelou, *Celebrations*

All the beautiful things and people in this world are expressions of gratitude. "The essence of all beautiful art, all great art," said Friedrich

Nietzsche, "is gratitude." "Gratitude is the heart's memory." This French proverb asserts that gratitude is direct acknowledgment of a benefit that one has received or will receive. One observance of law of thanksgiving can be seen in the life of Rhonda Byrne. She began her journey with *The Secret* film, viewed by millions across the planet. She followed with *The Secret* book, a worldwide best-seller. She confirms the philosophy of gratitude. She believes: "There are no limits to the good that you can bring forth to you. By practicing gratitude daily, you will increase your magnetic power to attract a magnificent life beyond your wildest dreams." Another observance of the law of thanksgiving can be found in the life of Sarah Ban Breathnach who has appeared on *The Oprah Winfrey Show* nine times. Oprah writes in her gratitude journal nowadays. She was a freelance writer living paycheck to paycheck before writing *Simple Abundance*, a book that helped millions of women find gratitude in every moment. The book went on to sell 7 million copies. She had been on *The New York Times* Best-seller List for two years. She makes a public confirmation: "One of the most valuable lessons *Simple Abundance* has taught me is that it is in the smallest details that the flavour of life is savoured. Gratitude is the most passionate transformative force in the cosmos." Am I making sense here? Do you understand what I am trying to get at? I urge you: "Let us be thankful to the people who make us happy." No surprise, all the motivational experts advise to use gratitude, which I call as "the greatest force in our universe." It is the key to true greatness.

"Gratitude is a great way to say thank you to the people," said Den Zadra, "you appreciate so much that you just want to stop and applaud." Have you ever said one "thank you" to your mentor who taught you? Have you ever expressed your gratitude to a colleague who stood by you? Did you thank a volunteer who helped you? Did you express your feelings of thankfulness to an employee who moved mountains for you? Have you ever thought of giving a "gratitude hug" to a friend who laughed and cried with you? Gratitude is one of the most positive emotions but at the same time it is the most neglected emotion also. All of us have a caring friend or a loving parent or a gentle teacher, mentor, employee or unpaid helper who ought to have, but rarely is given, a special compliment for the difference he/she makes in our world. We must thank every day people who brighten our daily lives.

MOST THANKFUL THING EVER

> *"Even when the gates of Heaven are closed to prayers, they are open to tears."*
>
> *The Talmud*

A little girl asks her mom what her "most thankful thing ever" is, Mom turns the question into a fun trip down memory lane. Turning the pages of Mom's photo album, they discover many wonderful moments in Mom's life, from summer camp to winning a trophy in a soccer tournament, from singing on stage to her wedding day. But one event in Mom's whole life is the very best ever – the birth of her precious little girl that Mama describes holding her child for the first time, saying, "–forevermore you would be my most thankful thing." Lisa McCourt and Cyd Moore have authored this story in *The Most Thankful Thing,* a heartwarming picture book. This story reveals what every parent is most thankful for.

GRATITUDE PRODUCES FAITH

> *"Faith is born of gratitude. The grateful mind continually expects good things and expectation becomes faith. The grateful mind is constantly fixed on good things and will receive good things."*
>
> Wallace D. Wattles, *The Science of Getting Rich*

The discipline of choosing gratitude is a way for us to make a declaration of our faith to God. The God doesn't answer your prayer but your faith in Him does. You will be provided with the perfect circumstances and most helpful people in everything you do and everywhere you will go through your divine inheritance. What is my advice? The only best thing you can do to transform your life right now is to start being thankful for what you have right now. You will receive good things if you see good side of the things. You need to concentrate your mind on the subject of your desire. For example, if you want to get rich, concentrate on the money and ignore the poverty. I believe successful people have learned to welcome all the good things in their lives. If they have food, clothing and chance to learn, they are grateful to have these things because they are privileged compared to those who don't have.

GRATITUDE IS A CHOICE: THE THANK YOU POWER

> *"Gratitude is a choice. If we fail to chose it, by default we choose ingratitude."*
>
> Nancy Leigh DeMoss, *Choosing Gratitude*

By intentionally thanking God and others, bitterness and entitlement are replaced with joy and the humble realization of just how undeserving we really are. Mary Jo Leddy's life is another example of observance of law of gratitude. She is a Canadian writer, speaker, theologian and social activist. She is widely recognized for her work with refugees at Toronto's Romero House. She affirms: "We need to develop an attitude which sees God's hand in both the large and small things in life, and to realize what a wonderful miracle life itself presents to us each day." No matter whatever you receive and have at any given time, for example a difficult and tough situation, just consider it as a God-Gift. Journalist Nina Lesowitz and gratitude practitioner Mary Beth Sammons claim: "Living as if each day is a thank-you can help transform fear into courage, anger into forgiveness, isolation into belonging, and another's pain into healing. Saying thank-you every day inspires feelings of love, compassion and hope." The universe gives you an opposite reaction to your action, so whatever situation or moment you are in, be thankful, because you are reaping your sown seeds, and if you show your despair and anguish, you are sowing an action that once again be balanced with opposite misery and torture. Each day, each hour, each minute and each second is a gift that must be lived as a "Gratitude to God". You should say thank you each second. Why? You will receive a circumstance to thank in return. You can do miracles with this approach. In fact, during the writing of this book, I learned that the maximum delight and bliss comes from what we do to improve other people's lives and our own divine lives. The difference between the changes in our lives is only in the details. Everybody has his own share of bad and good phases. You have to be thankful in each and every situation, and I mean each situation. Gratitude can be the key to kicking an addiction, healing the planet, or just staying sane in a traffic jam.

You will glow with radiance and love provided you have the faith that you are child of Most High God. There is a law of gratitude and you must apply this if you want to get success. You have faith in you when you know that the supreme source has limitless supply. There will never ever be such thing which can be called as lack of opportunities. Next job will appear when you will be ready for that. You will always be safe, divinely guided and protected. You visualize what you want in your mind, then you perceive it as a reality and, that imagined reality becomes actuality eventually.

GOD'S BLESSINGS ARE NOT EXPECTEDLY PACKAGED

> *"You pray in your distress and in your need; would that you might pray also in the fullness of your joy and in your days of abundance."*
>
> Kahlil Gibran, *The Prophet*

I am reminded of a touching story that I read long back. A young man was getting all set to graduate. His father asked him, "What do you want at your graduation day?" He used to see a sports car during his study days in a dealer's showroom on the way to his college. He told his father about his wish. He knew his father could afford the car easily.

On Graduation Day evening, his father called him and handed a beautiful wrapped gift box. The young man opened the box and found an attractive, leather-bound *Bible*. He looked at his father in sad mood and said, "Dad! With all your money you give me a *Bible?*" He went out of the house, leaving the holy book. Many years passed. The young boy had become the business tycoon of the city. One day he was thinking to see his father because he had not seen him since that graduation day. All of a sudden the door bell rang, and he received a telegram that his father had died and willed all of his possessions in the name of his son. He reached at his native place in a hurry, and after funeral, began to look at his father's things. He found the same old box with that *Bible* in it. He opened the *Bible* and began to turn the pages. A car key dropped suddenly from the *Bible*. The key had a tag with dealer name and dealer signature with "Paid In Full" note. The boy looked again and he found an envelope at the back of which was written the words "A Small Gift from a Proud Father to a Son on his Graduation Day." It was his dream sports car. He felt sudden sadness and regret in his heart.

Moral of the story:

1. We miss God's blessings because they are not packaged as we expect.
2. Every parent cares for his children.
3. We should respect our parents and try to understand them.

ATTITUDE OF GRATITUDE

> *"There is much to be grateful for: the stars, the moon aglow at night, lakes and rivers, ponds or puddles, family and people we love. Each spread is a reminder of the wonders around us."*
>
> Douglas Wood & Greg Shed,
> *The Secret of Saying Thanks*

In *Bible,* we study, "In everything give thanks: for this is the will of God." Go through the works and lives of inspirational teachers and authors like

Wayne Dyer, Sarah Ban Breathnach, Mary Jo Leddy, Wallace D. Wattles, Borghild Dahl, Nancy Leigh DeMoss, Den Zadra, Nina Lesowitz, Mary Beth Sammons, P.K. Hallinan, Dr. John F. Demartini, Angeles Arrien, M.J. Ryan, Douglas Wood and Greg Shed. Study Bernie Siegel – the cancer expert, Doreen Virtue – a spiritual doctor of psychology, Shakti Gawain – a proponent of personal development, Alan Cohen – the founder of generic pharmaceutical concerns, and Dan Millman – an American self-help author. These people have demonstrated the power of gratitude in their own lives. The crux of the readings is that gratitude is an easy yet great way to stay connected with our spiritual supply. It can turn a meal into a feast, a house into a home, a stranger into a friend. It is a gift that we give ourselves and to others, for the simple logic that, a person can't be unhappy and grateful at the same time. Happiness is a spiritual experience that comes from living each second with a sense of gratitude. Wherever we go we can find something to complain about, as a normal human behaviour, but, it is very difficult to feel a sincere desire of giving something back, at least two words "thank you" to be honest. There is a word in Japanese language, *ON*, which means a sense of gratitude plus a desire to repay others for the care and support that we have received. Thankfulness is the launch of gratitude. Gratitude is the achievement of thankfulness. Thankfulness consists of words. Gratitude is revealed in acts. The highest appreciation is not to utter words, but to live by them. I encourage the readers to express their gratitude in *ON* way instead of *NO* way, which is a way of not to give anything not even a thank you what to talk of care and support.

"No one who achieves success," said Alfred North Whitehead, "does so without acknowledging the help of others." The people who count their blessings are not luckier than others. They are thankful for their past life because if there was any lack in the past that certainly motivates to try harder in the future. The poor tries to get rich; the ill person tries to get healthier; the fat person tries to get slim and the ignorant tries to learn. All of people feel happy when they achieve what they aspire.

It's easier to be thankful for good times but being thankful for rough times gives a sense of fulfillment in life. Step one is important to reach to step two. When we reach at the top of stairs we can't forget all the lower steps instead we should be thankful to all the lower steps because without those we couldn't reach to the top. It's a truth that you have to start from where you are and with whatever you have. Be thankful for the friends that turned into family and the likes that turned into love. Therefore, we must be thankful to the present in any case.

LIVE IN PRESENT PHILOSOPHY

"Each second brings comfort and joy from above."

P.K. Hallinan, *I'm Thankful Each Day*

You can live the life you dream, provided you live the one you've been given. You can use and develop your own inner resources, just by living in the present moment. Whenever we think back or think ahead we lose the chance to enjoy the present. In fact we are not able to see the present in its total beauty. Often we miss smell of earth on first rain; the smell of roses; the food flavours; the pleasure of touch; listening the music, winds and our child's laugh. I call it sense intelligence. Osho, who was an Indian mystic, guru, and spiritual teacher calls this a state of "No Mind", the salvation. In my view, he was the greatest believer of "Live in Present" Philosophy who garnered an international following.

Bhagwan Nayagar Ji, my spiritual master used to say a quote: "God works in strange ways, and one day we possibly will identify what they are, and where we blend in." I like the long-standing aphorism, "Past is History, Future is a Mystery and Today is Gift and hence it is called the Present." In fact, I love Present because it is a gift. Take pleasure in today, this moment and don't adjourn your enjoyment because you can't act on yesterday, the psychological past and you can't act on tomorrow either the psychological future. I am against daydreaming but in favour of intentional dreaming.

You act where you are right now, and you must do all that you can do where you are in order to reach where you want to be. You must try to make everyday a successful day because successful life is sum total of successful days. Each day counts. Each activity contributes to a successful day. I insist you to do as much acts in a day possible but in an efficient manner without any haste, fear or worry. Go as fast as you can but never hurry. "If you are in rush, you begin to compete whereas real accomplishment lies in creation not in competition."

THE POWER OF RELAXATION

> *"A smile is the light in your window tells others that there is a caring and sharing person inside. The people will contribute in your life and you will also give them your wholehearted love and support. A feeling of gratitude and appreciation towards God and God's Men will reflect on your face and in your actions and that to me is the perfection of a human being."*
>
> Dennis Waitley, an American writer

This LIP or "live in present" philosophy can only be implemented when you are completely relaxed and have total peace of mind. You can't see the reality unless the mirror is clear. Any apprehensiveness, annoyance and aggravation will influence the sense of gratitude. You can't hear the voice unless the echo is clear. You must be thankful in true sense for each mistake because only in failures you can find some lessons. The trinity of fear, uncertainty and doubt (FUD) will prevent you to experience the present. If there is any issue you worry about, the same should be resolved or left permanently. There should not be any excuse, explanation, or regret at the end of the day. This is a condition precedent for proper gratitude.

WHATEVER HAPPENS, HAPPENS FOR OUR BEST

> *"The practice of gratitude bestows many benefits. Anger, arrogance, and jealousy melt in its embrace. Fear and defensiveness dissolve. Gratitude diminishes barriers to love and evokes happiness, keeping alive what has meaning for us."*
>
> Angeles Arrien, *Living In Gratitude*

"THANK YOU." What do we really mean by these two simple words? In answer to this question, I feel affection and deep attraction for proverb "Whatever happens, happens for good." It is a very simple logical statement and gives us the reason to say thank you to each and everyone. This saying shows trust in God. In nearly all of the cases it is true. I have made so many mistakes but I have always learned from my mistake. Every action has a reaction and every reaction is itself an action. I used to say that "Everything happens for good" but now I say that in most of the cases "Whatever happens, it happens for our betterment." My father Sh. Daryao Singh is a paralytic patient and can't move but still he believes there is something right in this condition. He reads a lot, draws conclusions of life philosophy and shares it with people. He affirms: "I am strong believer in God's justice. I am thankful to God in all the circumstances." He establishes further, "Another door opens when one door closes."

I believe everything happens for a reason. We may not always know the reason, but it's out there, good or bad. Even the bad experiences can be learned from. I learned about "health" thing when I underwent serious health issues and problems. Whenever you look at your existing life and then how you have reached this level, you will realize that whatsoever happened in your life was for good only.

This adage should be written this way I propose, "Whatever happens, happens for our best and for a specific reason." This has become my favourite line and I always follow this. I am happy in all situations because I trust whatever happens, happens for our best and for a specific reason.

I believe in good luck only and not in bad luck just because of this strong belief.

I AM HAPPY IN EACH CIRCUMSTANCE

> *"If God is giving you pain, He wants to make you stronger. God never does anything wrong with His people."*
>
> Bhagavan Nayagar (1951–2001)

One of the best examples of observance of the law of thanksgiving is from the life of Borghild Dahl who was born in 1890 at Minnesota. She suffered severely impaired vision from her early years. She attended college against the medical advices. She eventually became the principal of eight schools. "I had only one eye," she explains in her book *I Wanted To See,* "and it was so covered with dense scars that I had to do all my seeing through one small opening in the left of the eye. I could see a book only by holding it up close to my face and by straining my one eye as hard as I could to the left." At the age of 50, she underwent a procedure in 1943 that restored her eyesight to some extent and after that she did enjoy even small things in their entirety like flying of the birds, the sun rising and phases of moon etc. She closed one of her books with these words: "Dear ... Father in heaven, I thank Thee. I thank Thee." She wrote a book *Happy All My Life,* two years before when she died at the age of 92. She authored seventeen books. She had gratitude in her whole life and thus she enjoyed her life.

LOGIC BEHIND THANKSGIVING

> *"Gratitude creates a powerful state of happiness because it returns us to the natural place where we notice what's right and instead of what's wrong."*
>
> M.J. Ryan, *Attitudes of Gratitude*

Gratitude helps us focus on all that we have, rather than our perception of what may be lacking. The logic behind law of thanksgiving is quite simple. When we express our gratitude we feel happy. The heart that gives thanks is a happy one. We don't give thanks because we're happy. We are happy because we give thanks. There is always something to be thankful for. We concentrate on good things with attitude of gratitude. When you allow yourself to experience and express your thanks, you feel happier, younger and healthier. Consequently, we have greater access to our commonsense and understanding. Gratitude is a discipline. We see things in their entireness and we exercise all this out of our increased sense of awareness.

All those who explore, I assure your answers surround you. If you sincerely want to know, the question will be replied. In fact, we can use our senses at the time of gratitude. A scientist has gratitude for his past discoveries and that give him all the confidence to research. I call thanksgiving a form of worship. You must learn to be grateful no matter whatever happens in your life. You'll be amazed by that fact that you feel and see the universe in a different way, when you are grateful for all of your experiences. Gratitude will make you humbled because you know that you are just one small part of a big picture. It will also inspire you because you know that you are born with a purpose.

SUGGESTED STRATEGY

> *"If you give thanks for five gifts every day in two months you may not look at your life in the same way as you might now."*
>
> Sarah Ban Breathnach, *Simple Abundance*

William Arthur Ward (1921–1994) author of *Fountains of Faith* is still one of America's most quoted writers of inspirational maxims. He gives a sound advice in form of a question: "God gave you a gift of 86,400 seconds today. Have you used one to say thank you?" Speak to yourself. The meditation techniques and spiritual studies can be a great help in this regard. I believe that faith is the single shield you can trust to get relaxed. I suggest a remedy when you feel hurry. Stop for a moment and visualize on what you want and begin to give thanks that you are receiving it. This method will strengthen your faith and will renew your purpose. It's high time to start your life-giving journey for the future. You must write two lists of things every day. In the first list, LOPG – List of Present Gratitudes, write what you are thankful for at present in your life. The second list, for which I use the name LOGG – List of Gratitude Goals, contains all the things you wish to be thankful for into your upcoming life. The second list is inspired from Law III of Newton: "To every action there is always an equal and opposite reaction." The concept of prayer to God is there in almost all religions. It is a reflection of thankfulness and makes you feel relaxed in hard times. You should always try to look positive sides of things. Dedicate each single activity in regard to someone whom you love. Hindus pray even before taking food. Musicians, authors and athletes dedicate their performance every time.

ASSIGNMENT

1. Write five blessings daily that you're grateful for in gratitude section of life journal and develop a gratitude list. Simple rule: 5 lines for 5 gifts in "List of Present Gratitudes" and "List of Gratitude Goals."
2. Take a vacation. Enjoy one evening in a week. Plan at least two remote tours in a year – one hill station and another at sea or in jungle, planes and desert etc.
3. Give thanksgiving dinners or lunches every weekend to thank people who help you.
4. Watch *Secret* movie by Rhonda Byrne each month to stay motivated.
5. Listen to the Audio program, *How to Use Gratitude to Attract What You Don't Yet Have* by Marilyn Jenett.

VISUALIZATION

Whenever you feel fear, uncertainty and doubt take deep breaths five times, hold it for a count of ten imagine gathering all the bits and pieces and visualize that with every exhale you release the worries. Breathe out five times. You must visualize a mental thanks to God for all the past successes before each task. "Walk," said Thich Nhat Hanh, "as if you are kissing the Earth with your feet." Your key words must be: "NOT GRIEF BUT GRATITUDE." Remember: Thanks are the highest form of thought.

SELF SUGGESTION

I'm thankful for everything in my life.

Bear in mind: Super achievers always keep their commitments.

[*Promise & Put Your Signature Here With Date*]

24
What Do You Think Of Yourself?

OBJECTIVES

- To learn the "Law of Self-Esteem",
- To employ synergy of willpower and self-discipline to achieve goals, and
- To avoid addictions and contaminated people.

GOLDEN GUIDANCE

"An individual's self-concept is the core of his personality. A strong, positive self-image is the best possible preparation for success in life."

Dr. Joyce Brothers (1927–2013)

CHOOSE YOUR ADVISER CAREFULLY AND USE YOUR OWN JUDGMENT

"You must know that in any moment a decision you make can change the course of your life forever: the very next person stand behind in line or sit next to on an airplane, the very next phone call you make or receive, the very next movie you see or book you read or page you turn could be the one single thing that causes the floodgates to open, and all of the things that you've been waiting for to fall into place."

Anthony Robbins, an American self-help author

Our elders teach us, "Seeking opinion is a good thing." Talking of advices, I am always reminded of a story about a man who once upon a time was selling burgers by the roadside. He was illiterate, so he never read newspapers. He was hard of hearing, so he never listened to the radio. His eyes were weak, so he never watched television. In fact, he wondered what people look in the newspapers, hear on the radio and see on the TV. He sold lots of burgers only just out of enthusiasm. He was intelligent enough to propose some smart schemes to enhance his sales. He had good supporting staff to serve customers. One day his son, who had recently done his M.B.A. from a reputed foreign college, came to home. The son asked, "Father, aren't you aware of the big recession?" The father replied, "No, but let me know about it." The son said, "The global position is very bad so the domestic position is even worse." He further advised, "We should be ready for the approaching bad times." The man removed many high salaried good men and reduced the quality of burger. The sales came down. The profit was also on lower side. He had to close his business one day. The father said to his son, "Son, you were right. Recession is a serious problem."

Moral of the story:

1. The tragedy today is that there are many walking encyclopedias that are living failures.
2. Don't let others decide your value.
3. You can turn a negative situation into a positive situation and this is true the other way around.
4. A positive thought can destroy all the negative thoughts at once.
5. Only one negative thought can destroy the army of positive thoughts.
6. One should choose his adviser carefully.
7. One must also apply his own judgment before acting on any advice.

RELATION BETWEEN SELF-IMAGE AND SELF-ESTEEM

> *"Everything that happens to you is a reflection of what you believe about yourself. We cannot outperform our level of self-esteem. We cannot draw to ourselves more than we think we are worth."*
>
> Iyanla Vanzant, New Thought spiritual teacher

How do you see yourself? What kind of person you think you are? What you believe others think of you? How much do you like yourself? The answers to these questions portray your self-image. Your self-image creates your self-esteem that in result promotes your self-confidence – the appearance to others. You are what you make people believe about you, so you must be careful about what you make people believe. Essentially, you need three things to do any work efficiently. The first is the skill or ability to do a work. Second is the level of inspiration that depends on constant motivation. Thirdly is the attitude that determines your aptitude. Poor or low self-esteem affects every aspect of human conduct especially the competence to grow and change. Even the colour of your dress reflects your attitude. As Miley Cyrus, an American actress said, "Pink isn't just a colour, it's an attitude." All the festivals are also states of mind. Low self-esteem can negatively affect just about every facet of your life. If you acquaint me the level with which an individual looks at his self-esteem, I can inform you, the level with which that individual works in different areas of his life. As John Maxwell says, "people may hear your words, but they feel your attitude." We all have a bad phase(s) in our lives but the key to overcome any bad situation remains the same: "Thoughts and belief have to be positive. Self-talk and elucidations of the circumstance(s) play a significant role in building this positive attitude. We have all earned our sags and wrinkles and rough spots. We should hug them and smile. Stand tall in self-esteem." A person has the pleasing personality because it reflects the approach he has inside. Self-image is the sum total of all the impressions of what you think of yourself and what you believe other people (such as parents, friends etc.) think about you. It is the most important judgment you make about yourself. It is the mental image of that you project in your mind when you think who you are, how you look, what you're brilliant at and what you're not so good at. Self-image can be either positive or negative. You can view yourself intellectual, attractive, ugly, fashionable and stupid and so on. When you begin to appreciate your self-image, then at a snail's pace you develop self-esteem. Nathaniel Branden who is an authority on self-esteem states: "The reputation you have with yourself – *Your Self-Esteem* – is the single most important factor for a fulfilling life." Your self-image has a direct influence over your self-esteem hence when you have a positive self-image you will have a high self-esteem and vice-versa. There is also an "Ideal Self" in everybody where you view yourself with complete idealistic qualities. You will have a better self-esteem when you behave in line with this ideal self. However, if there is a gap between these two ends, your self-esteem will be on lower levels. Therefore, shape of teeth, hair loss, low quality clothes and other appearance disorders can disturb the self-image and hence self-esteem can suffer in the long run. In summary, self-image is what you view of yourself and self-esteem is what you value of yourself.

FDR—AN INSPIRATION

> *"The only disability in life is a bad attitude."*
>
> Scott Hamilton, a celebrated figure skater

We should trust that everything happens for a reason. Often we're not intelligent enough to see it. I have seen many people who have a disability but they don't let it to prevent them from leading complete and well-off lives, in fact some are an inspiration to both disabled and non-disabled people equally. Tolerance, determination and right attitude have an amazing magic. They make difficulties disappear and obstacles vanish. We are told that sky is the limit but look there are footprints on the moon. Winners live, eat and sleep with their passion. They stand tall in their self-esteem. They practice self-discipline and willpower.

One such man was, Franklin Delano Roosevelt, the 32nd President of the United States, a vital figure in world events during the mid-20th century, who led the United States during a time of worldwide economic depression and total war with his popular *Happy Days Are Here Again* as theme song. He contracted Polio in 1921 which left him paralyzed from the waist down. Refusing to accept his paralysis he tried different therapies and methods to try and walk and did master walking short distances using iron braces and a cane. He was careful not to be seen in a wheelchair in public which he used in private. He established a foundation to help others with Polio and directed the March of Dimes program (in his times National Foundation for Infantile Paralysis) which eventually funded an effective vaccine. FDR used a car specially designed for him. He is an inspiration for present youth and generations to follow.

WHAT DIFFERENCE DOES IT MAKE?

All Men Dream But Not Equally

"All men dream but not equally.

Those who dream by night

In the dusty recesses of their minds

Wake in the day to find that it was vanity;

But the dreamers of the day are dangerous men,

For they may act their dream with open eyes

To make it possible."

T.E. Lawrence (1888–1935)

This is a short story about doing the right things even if you are alone. There was a man taking a morning walk at the beach. He saw that along with the morning tide came many fishes and when the tide went back, they were left behind. The tide was fresh and the fishes were alive but they could die of sun rays soon. The man picked one and threw it into the water. He did that repeatedly. Right behind him there was another person who couldn't make out what this man was doing. He asked, "What are you doing? There are many fishes. How many can you save? What difference does it make?" This man picked up another one, threw it into the water, and said, "It makes a difference to this one."

Moral of the story:

1. You should believe and do what you think is right.
2. Big or small, difference does matter.
3. A small difference will end up in a big difference.

LOW, MEDIUM AND HIGH SELF-ESTEEM

> *"If you don't like the way you are, don't worry about it. You can change the way you are."*
>
> Zig Ziglar (1926–2012)

Self-esteem can be low, medium and high. Researchers Block and Thomas (1955) have shown that self-esteem is curvilinear and inverted U Shape but a few others like Chodorkoff (1954), Karmos and Karmos (1979) found a U shaped relationship between self-esteem and emotional adjustment. However, self-esteem is socially and emotionally harmful for a person when it is high and low. Many researchers like Rosenberg, Owen and Guindon have reported the effects of low and high self-esteem. A person with low self-esteem becomes shy and less confident to try new things hence they fear from making mistakes and accuse circumstances and people for who they are. A person with high self-esteem becomes bigheaded, overconfident, self-seeking and egoistic and hence lives in delusion of fake high self-worth. This high self-esteem is responsible for apartheid, caste and other discriminations. The one is famous as inferiority complex and the other

is notorious as superiority complex. However, the truth is that both are unacceptable in the society because society requires an active contribution and not an arrogant attitude.

SUCCESS LIES IN PROPER SELF-ESTEEM

> *"It is not easy to find happiness in ourselves, and it is not possible to find it elsewhere."*
>
> Agnes Repplier (1855–1950)

In today's disorganized and aggressive world self-esteem is indispensable to our personal and professional influence. Success lies in having the proper image. Self-esteem at medium level is at its best and hence socially and emotionally useful for a person. Children have a good level of self-esteem but gradually their family, social and work environment increase or decrease their self-esteem.

So, *here is the golden tip*: "When you achieve targets continuously your self-esteem will get stronger. Most of the people think high of themselves but in adverse circumstances they think negatively because of low self-esteem, low self-worth and low self-respect. These negative feelings result into guilt and this guilt turns into shame eventually. Therefore, low self-esteem leads you to life of passiveness and high self-esteem directs you to activeness and hence high success follows high self-esteem. But, this high self-esteem is at the medium level and not at the ends."

We do not have to follow a family practice. We can pick our own self-worth. Self-esteem is found by connecting to our internal kid. This internal kid is the storehouse of self-worth. You must avoid self-defeating and self-important beliefs and have good positive beliefs about yourself. I love a quotation of Lil Wayne and that can be the guiding law: "Love me or hate me, I swear it won't make or break me."

DON'T IGNORE

> *"Success is easy but so is neglect. For every disciplined effort, there are multiple rewards."*
>
> Jim Rohn (1930–2009)

Everybody knows that early to bed early to rise, makes a man healthy, wealthy and wise. It's as easy as that but it's also easy not to do. We take things for granted. How many of us prefer to go to bed early and dare to get up early? Most of the people are in habits of watching daily soaps on TV and spending time on internet and for these they often neglect their health, the biggest wealth. People prefer to eat what they like and soon they get out of shape, and then they do what is nothing more than a status symbol, dieting and getting membership of famous gym. Success is a matter of sticking to the little disciplines because even a slightest failure will affect your self-esteem and success level eventually. Success is a journey wherein you achieve targets after targets by steady and daily efforts. Your physique will get better and you can get compliments from your friends if you exercise daily at gym.

THE ROSE WITHIN

> *"People who are unable to motivate themselves must be content with mediocrity, no matter how impressive their other talents."*
>
> Andrew Carnegie (1835–1919)

There is a story on unleashing the true potential. A man planted a rose in his home. He used to water it enthusiastically. He was also inspecting it constantly. The bud that was sure to blossom into a good flower. One day he saw thorns upon the stem and thought, "How can any attractive flower come from a plant loaded with so many spiky thorns?" Disappointed by this thought, he ignored to water the rose, and just before it was set to bloom... it died.

Moral of the story:

1. The God-like qualities are in us by birth.
2. Many of us look at ourselves and see only the thorns, the faults.
3. We feel anguish, thinking that nothing good can perhaps come from us.
4. Qualities grow among the thorns of our faults.
5. We neglect to water the good within us, and eventually it dies.
6. We never realize our latent talent, and consequently die in mediocrity.
7. Never make your most important decisions when you are in your worst moods.

MOST PEOPLE THINK NEGATIVELY

> *"Attitude is a mindset. It is the way you look at things mentally. A positive attitude is the outward manifestation of a mind that dwells primarily on positive matters."*
>
> Elwood N. Chapman, *Attitude: Your Most Priceless Possession*

You may be a little apprehensive about "Do 95% people really think negatively?" People are governed by their conventional wisdom that is taught and spoon- fed from day one and generally not based on firsthand experience. They are trained to look for the negatives. Attitude is contagious. One research cited in the book, *What a Great Idea!* by Charles Thompson disclosed that, at home, parents speak 18 negative statements for every positive one, usually to a curious child who wants to know how something works. The average is 432 negative statements per day. Therefore, it is indispensable to "Train The Brain" to think optimistically and that is the only way to facilitate the process of success, wealth and happiness. According to research conducted by psychologists, good health and the ability to overcome stress are also linked to a positive attitude. I may be 95% wrong when I say that the 5% positive people are ruling over 95%

of negative thinking population but 5% ruling men will agree with me on this hypothesis.

I want to share a story on this. There was a hunter who came into the possession of an extraordinary dog. The dog was the only one of its kind, because it can walk on water. One day he invited a friend to go hunting with him so that he could show off his cherished possession. They went to a river with dog. They shot a few water birds and animals like ducks, heron and swan etc. which fell into the river. The man ordered his dog to run and fetch the birds. The dog ran on water to get the birds. The man was expecting praise about the unbelievable dog, but did not get it. Being inquisitive, he asked his friend if the friend had observed anything strange about the dog. The friend replied, "Yes, I did see something strange about your dog. Your dog can't swim." The man laughed and went away with his dog.

Moral of the story:

1. Don't expect compliments from the negative people.
2. Negative people can't understand the value of outstanding things.
3. You shouldn't mind the comments of negative people.

INFLUENCE OF NEGATIVE SOCIETY

> *"There is little difference in people, but that little difference makes a big difference. That little difference is attitude. The big difference is whether it is positive or negative."*
>
> Robert Collier (1885–1950)

Nobody cares about the negative influence produced by this negative society everywhere and every time. Parents, teachers and friends all are part of the negative society because most of them don't encourage children in the field of their chosen activity. Ask them a new approach. They will say, "Are we fools?" "We have done it this way always." "It can't be done." Charles

Thompson attaches a label to these negative responses "killer phrases." And, I have seen, if a child fails in one thing, he is being tortured on that failure and his esteem is challenged in other fields also. People feed the inferiority feeling because they hate any change. As said by Michael Jordan, "If you accept the expectations of others, especially negative ones, then you never will change the outcome." Parents, teachers and friends and in fact the child compares himself with others and often the comparison is unfair and unrealistic because worst features are compared with someone else's best features. Nobody cares about the impact a pornographic movie does to the mind and often the children who watch these dirty stuffs become juvenile delinquents. These things look little but make big impacts.

NO EXCUSE APPROACH

> *"Most people think success comes from good luck or enormous talent, but many successful people achieve their accomplishments in a simpler way: through self-discipline."*
>
> Brian Tracy, *No Excuses*

Brian Tracy is one man whose website briankim.net attracts me a lot. He was born in eastern Canada in 1944 and grew up in California. After dropping out of high school, he travelled and worked his way around the world, eventually visiting eighty countries on six continents. His extensive personal studies in business, sales, management, marketing and economics enabled him to move up to become the head of a $265 million company before he turned his attention to consulting, training and personal development. He is the president of three companies with operations worldwide. He affirms: "A little self-discipline goes a long way." You come to the crossroads in your life. You know what is right? But the same age old disease prevents you from doing the right thing. People should enforce strict disciplines in their lives otherwise somebody else will do. The doctor will enforce dietary and other physical disciplines like exercise etc. if somebody will ignore health, the employers will enforce career discipline if somebody ignores the professional requirements, the courts and banks will enforce monetary disciplines if somebody will ignore money, friends and family members will enforce relationship discipline if somebody will ignore friends and family members, God will enforce spiritual discipline if somebody will ignore meditation and gratitude prayers, society will enforce living discipline if somebody will ignore the contribution in society and the countrymen will enforce citizenship discipline if somebody will ignore the public life. I find that the definition of discipline given by Elbert Hubbard still holds the actuality and admiration. He defined self-discipline as "the ability to do what you should do, when you should do it, whether you feel like it or not." Take my advice: "Convert yourself into a self-disciplinarian." Success is a game of small wins each day, it's not a one shot matter, and even for hitting bull's eye with a single shot the player does daily practice.

SELF-DISCIPLINE LEADS TO SELF-ESTEEM

> *"If there is one character trait whose benefits are endorsed by traditional and progressive educators alike, it may well be self-discipline."*
>
> Alfie Kohn, an American author

Self-discipline gives you the power to stick to your decisions and follow them through, without changing your mind and self- discipline is therefore one of the imperative requirements for accomplishing goals. Instead of devoting a lot of hours one day, and none the other and then a few on another day and so on, harness the power of routine. You are working on tasks in small increments, not all at once. The story of rabbit and tortoise explain the virtue of self-discipline. The people who have poor self-esteem can be identified by the bad habits of Idleness, making excuses and laziness. Another characteristic of these people is to use profanities. Self-control and discipline are the words of foreign language for them. Dedication and discipline will lead to distinction; and distinction will lead to self-respect. You must be ready to accept responsibility for your own life because it is the treasure trove from which the gold of self-respect comes.

You begin with willpower. You complete what you start with self-discipline. Self-discipline is the product and thus higher level of willpower. When you persist with willpower, it becomes self-discipline. Willpower is the initiating power and the self-discipline is the staying power. You need willpower to start a task and self-discipline to continue with it. Self-discipline controls your actions, builds your confidence and allows you to stay focused on your goals. One of the main characteristics of self-discipline is the ability to reject instant gratification and pleasure in favour of some greater gain. It is also called as self-control, perseverance, the ability of not to give up and the ability to resist temptations etc. When you achieve your goals continuously your self-esteem will grow. Jim Rohn was an American entrepreneur, author and motivational speaker who always insisted on self-discipline. He asserts: "The least lack of discipline starts to erode our self-esteem." So we have the paramount law: "Self-discipline leads to better self-esteem."

JUST ONE MORE

> *"Drug addiction is not a choice of lifestyle, it is a disorder of the brain and we need to recognize this. Drug addiction and alcohol are problems."*
>
> Bhagavan Nayagar (1951–2001)

Addiction is a complex disorder characterized by compulsive use. According to Medi-lexicon, Addiction is habitual psychological or physiologic dependence on a substance or practice that is beyond voluntary control. In other words, addiction may refer to a substance dependence (e.g. drug addiction) or behavioural addiction (e.g. gambling addiction).

On a sweet morning of 8th January, 2013, I was reading the morning newspaper *NavBharat Times*. A study attracted my attention. World Cancer Research Fund has found, "Alcohol in any form advances obesity and cancer." I give you the reason: Alcohol contains high calories and often encourages high fat food intake and that promotes obesity. Drugs and alcohol are not the only things that cause addiction but certain pleasurable activities, such as gambling, shopping and sex can also do the same. Addictive drugs provide a shortcut to the brain's reward system by flooding the nucleus accumbens with dopamine and other neurotransmitters. The hippocampus lays down memories of this rapid sense of satisfaction, and the amygdala creates a conditioned response to certain stimuli. Addiction can also damage your emotional stability, finances, career, and your ability to build and sustain satisfying relationships.

Christopher J. Mruk, a Professor of Psychology, opines: "Self-esteem is a critically important influence on psychological adjustment and quality of life. Lack of self-esteem is frequently a precursor to depression, suicidal behaviour, and other personality disorders." Richard Bednar and Scott Peterson found that "Low self-esteem is a common element in different types of disordered behaviour." Most of the people first try alcohol and drugs out of curiosity, to have a good time, because friends are doing it, or in an attempt to advance athletic performance or ease another problem, such as stress, anxiety or depression. After some time, people with low self-esteem look addictive substances or/and behaviours as a shelter to escape the negative feelings. People with low self-esteem use addictive substance or behaviour to feel good about them. Ask yourself every day: "What did I do today that lower or raise my self-esteem?" Please act on twin advices: "1. Associate with high-quality people. 2. Avoid low-quality people." People don't realize when their habit becomes an addiction unless psychological and/or physical effects are visible. You can stop a habit till psychological and/or physical issues get involved because then it becomes an addiction. The concept of "Just One More" becomes a cliché excuse at the time of rehabilitation program. We need to support the victim during his/her rehabilitation period.

SUGGESTED STRATEGY

> *"You can search throughout the entire universe for someone who is more deserving of your love and affection than you are yourself, and that person is not to be found anywhere. You, yourself, as much as anybody in the entire universe, deserve your love and affection."*
>
> Gautama Buddha, the founder of Buddhist religion

You feel less confident when somebody threatens your self-image and that means when somebody appreciate you honestly your self-confidence will rise and your self-worth, your self-respect and your self-esteem will rise eventually. So, the key lies in surrounding yourself with good positive people who think you are a genuine person who wants to improve day by day. Learn the lesson: "You are sum total of all the people you have met." The next advice is: "You should learn to smile everyday when you look in mirror." The facial feedback theory suggests that your mind tends to register certain emotions. When you habituate the smiling look you will learn to be comfortable with yourself. You can repeat past successes and some positive affirmation during the process of looking at yourself in mirror. You can also boost your self-esteem by helping others. Positive affirmations and self-determination are also very good-self-esteem builders.

ASSIGNMENT

1. Make a list of your positive qualities. Ask your good friends to help you in listing these qualities. You can also keep a ready Positive Qualities Reckoner (PQR) in form of a pocket card to keep you in true spirit.

2. On the back of PQR you can also keep a List of Past Successes (LPS) to boost your self-confidence.
3. Use positive language: If someone asks you: How do you do? Instead of saying "Fine" use the empowering words like "Excellent." You can use "involved in work" instead of "office or work tension."
4. Buy Jack Canfield's audio Program *Maximum Confidence: Ten Secrets of Extreme Self-Esteem* to celebrate and capitalize on your strengths and accept your weaknesses without guilt or remorse.

VISUALIZATION

You can visualize your God or Guru behind you, showering blessings when you do good things. Iyanla Vanzant, new thought spiritual teacher, once said: "If you know who walks beside you, you can never be afraid." Remember: Within every soul there is a rose. Your rose will blossom surely if you remain careful of negative people, negative comments and negative habits.

SELF SUGGESTION

I am a creative and powerful being. I have a strong sense of self-identity, self-esteem and self-value. I recognize and honour my talents, abilities and skills.

Bear in mind: Super achievers always keep their commitments.

[*Promise & Put Your Signature Here With Date*]

25

Are You Motivated To Be Successful?

OBJECTIVES

- To learn the "Law of Continuous Motivation",
- To work on intrinsic motivation, and
- To get better at your twin forces.

GOLDEN GUIDANCE

"Nothing will ever be attempted if all possible objections must first be overcome."

Samuel Johnson (1709–1784)

WHAT'S YOUR JOB?

"The law of work seems unfair, but nothing can change it; the more enjoyment you get out of your work, the more money you will make."

Mark Twain (1835–1910)

The word motivation is derived from Latin word *movere* means "to move" therefore I call motivation as a driving force that reinforces a behaviour towards a desired goal. It can be as negative as drive reduction theory like when you are thirsty you crave for water and as positive as goal setting theory (Edwin Locke 1960) which states that specific and challenging goals along with appropriate feedback contribute to better task performance. Most of the persons who are employed anywhere come to their workplace just to do minimum required. I always insist that higher self-efficiency (self-confidence) and goal commitment are necessary to achieve goals and therefore employees should be encouraged to set the goals themselves in conformity with the organizational goals and for that one must choose his inherent profession. How will you find your calling? Find an answer to the question: What will you do with your time if you need not to work to earn a living? You must look into your past habits, skills and education. You can also seek help of a career counsellor. I have already discussed this aspect in detail in previous chapters. You must find a way to serve others through your passion. When you choose your passion as your profession, it becomes your calling, not your job but your career. You are stylish, sharp and you have a job but do you really have the motivation to work and succeed?

I tell you a story that is often quoted by motivational experts. Three persons, John, Robert and Peter were working in a construction project. A spiritual master who was passing by asked them: "What is your job?" John answered: "My job is to work here till evening so that I can get money to feed my family." Robert replied: "My job is to break the stones." Peter said: "My job is to build a temple." Which of these three individuals do you think would be more motivated, most creative and give the added value? John, like most of us was working for the necessities of life, to support himself and his family. John's approach stops you to transform your profession into calling. Robert is pessimistic. Both John and Robert are not motivated. The answer, no doubt is Peter, who knew, his job was far bigger, than just breaking the stones. He realized he was contributing to a reason superior than his own reasons.

Moral of the story:

1. You have a responsibility to conduct yourself in a way that gives an example to others.

2. Every calling is great when greatly pursued.
3. You should transform your attitude towards your job to make it a calling.

STAYING MOTIVATED—THE REAL BATTLE

"A creative man is motivated by the desire to achieve, not by the desire to beat others."

Ayn Rand (1905–1982)

You must set a big goal to stay motivated. "Shoot for the moon. Even if you miss, you'll land among the stars." This quote really inspires me, as something very true, as being motivated would surely get us the stars if not the moon. Success requires passion, enthusiasm and stamina to make it. It often demands a super charged life. Success is a ladder that cannot be climbed with your hands in your pocket. The big question is: How can you motivate yourself? You should have the desire to achieve your big goal. You must seek pleasure in the journey to your success. Memorize Aristotle's Law: Pleasure in the job puts perfection in the work. Every success is a race to the finish. Hence, you have to run at your best speed to be best and not to beat the rest. There will be times when the going gets harsh, when things move slowly and where things don't work out as you'd anticipated. This is a common problem that happens to everyone. We start anything new with excitement but we discontinue after sometime. We all have plans to achieve success in life but we fail to convert plans into actions because of lack of motivation. In the journey of success, staying motivated is the real battle since you lose the momentum every now and then because your desire to work is always attacked by automatic negative thoughts and anxiety about the future and as a result you doubt your ability to perform and eventually there is every chance that you can go under depression.

So, *here is the golden tip*: "Average people discontinue in adverse circumstances but the super successful people keep moving forward. The ability to keep moving forward makes all the difference. In fact, it is the difference in itself. It is the game changer." Everybody fails but big winners pull themselves out of a slump before it gains momentum. Most of the great and successful people failed temporarily without being a permanent failure. All the greatest people were acquainted with the secret of staying motivated. They knew how to cherish motivating thoughts, defuse negative ones, and focus on the mission at hand. They knew the effect of thoughts on emotions and applied it in their life.

DAVID AND GOLIATH

"Our attitude towards life determines life's attitude towards us."

John N. Mitchell (1913–1988)

A man who has a positive mental attitude asks how something can be done rather than finding the reason why it can't be done. I can tell you a fact from the research I have done on the mindsets of winners that: It all begins in mind. We all know the biblical story of David and Goliath. Goliath was a giant of man. He struck fear in everyone's heart. One day, a 17-year old sphere boy came to visit his brothers and asked, "Why don't you stand up and fight the giant?" The brothers were terrified of Goliath and replied, "Don't you see he is too big to hit?" But David said, "No, he is not too big to hit, he is too big to miss." Dressed in his simple tunic, carrying his shepherd's staff, slingshot and a pouch full of stones, David approached Goliath. The giant cursed at him, hurling threats and insults to God of Israel. Goliath made the first move, but his big size made him a little slow on his feet. David, on the other hand, darted towards the giant. He put a stone into his sling and flung it at Goliath's head. Direct hit. The stone put a hole in Goliath's head, and the giant fell to the ground with a thud. David then took the injured giant's sword and cut off Goliath's head. When the rest of the Philistines saw this they ran away and David became a hero to all the people in Israel. "Ability," said Lou Holtz, "is what you're capable of doing. Motivation determines what you do. Attitude determines how well you do it."

The moral of the story:

1. Your attitude determines your win.
2. You rarely succeed unless you have fun in what you are doing.
3. You can control your attitude towards what happens to you.
4. The willpower to win is the greater part of winning.
5. Your attitude becomes optimistic when you have a clear vision of your goal.
6. The optimist sees opportunity in every danger.
7. Act or act not. There is no attempt.

ALWAYS SET NEW COMMITMENTS

> *"Commitment is a big part of what I am and what I believe. How committed are you to winning? How committed are you to being a good friend? To being trustworthy? To being successful? How committed are you to being a good father, a good teammate, a good role model? There's that moment every morning when you look in the mirror: Are you committed, or are you not?"*
>
> Lebron James, an American professional basketball player

The very first thing you can do to motivate yourself is to set your goal clearly because a clear goal leads to clear results. You will lose the momentum to work in the direction of your goal achievement unless you have a clear reason to realize your goal: Why do you want to achieve your goal? What purpose will it serve? Your clarity in explanation of goal-accomplishment will keep you on track and will help you to stay committed. Learn by heart: Commitment is an act, an attitude and not a simple word. You will make choices and decisions in this journey and you must accept 100% responsibility for any success or failure at any stage. You should be absolutely clear: It's only you who makes all the difference. However, I strongly advise to get professional help in whatever activity you are doing because it will increase the chances of success to a great extent. You will need affirmations in this process. Your affirmations have a great effect on your subconscious mind and will turn into your beliefs and soon into faiths. Your self-image will improve during this transformation of belief to faith. And, when you have rock-solid faiths, success will soon become a habit, the only thing that remains to be done regularly is to always set new commitments. Did you get the secret? A commitment to excellence will enable you to attain the success you seek out. The excellence of a person's life is a reflection of his commitment to excellence, in spite of his preferred field of effort. There's no success that is long-lasting, unshakeable and permanent without commitment. Productivity does not come by chance. Any achievement requires commitment to excellence, a good planning and focused endeavour.

EMOTIONAL MASTERY

> *"If you master your emotions, you will more likely be moved by positive emotions to take positive action and create positive results."*
>
> Bruce Elkin, a personal life coach

Emotions are a natural and integral part of humans. People generally choose whatever creates less pain and more pleasure. Emotion is a driving force much like breathing and drives us to do certain things. My observation: You will find yourself often in disastrous situations if you allow your emotions to control you. Sigmund Freud, the grandfather of modern-day psychology explained human conduct with what he called "The Pain/Pleasure Principle." Winners are no exception to this rule but they employ what I call "Emotional Mastery" in which they acquire the ability to associate pleasure with their vital professional goals. In simple words, they feel good when they work towards their goals and objectives and here lies the solution: You stay motivated when you feel good. Emotional mastery does not mean you will ignore all your emotions ... that actually would be a foolish thing and impossible too. This mastery calls to emote right emotion at right time and for that my recommendation is: Be self-aware. In this art you learn to work with emotions in a constructive way instead of becoming destructive. Emotional mastery is an art wherein you recognize your emotions, and after that you use logic to decide the best course of action, and ultimately you portray the most effective emotion for that situation.

Emotional mastery becomes all the more necessary because bad mood will kill your all motivation. There is a big need for emotional integrity and emotional maturity otherwise one can lose his relations, health and money. Often, you and I see divorces which are just an outcome of emotional immaturity. An average person reaches to top because of his emotional integrity. A person who is habitually anxious and worried lacks emotional mastery. Don't be your emotions. Use your emotions, don't let them use you. Drama queens are best examples because they are their emotions. The person who gets angry quickly lacks emotional mastery because he finds faults for his anger in others' activities. Nigel Bloomfield said: "When others, a man begins to blame. He'll soon find himself alone, the same." You have to choose your emotion without being affected by any emotion. This mastery is an ability that consists of controlling the prevailing and choosing the acting emotion.

Winners know that more often *decisions come out of emotions*. It is the language of social success. Positive professionals like teachers, sports stars, great leaders and doctors possess emotional mastery. I love my emotions because without them, I will become a robot but still I want to use my emotions and will not allow any automatic emotion to put me in any unwanted situation. I employ my emotions to further my commitment towards excellence. I use emotions to get motivated. How? I control my thoughts and emotions get controlled automatically. Meditation is one of the best examples of this thought-emotion exercise. I can tell from personal experience of meditation that you can certainly view the things from an unbiased emotional dominance and let me tell you meditation is not an unemotional exercise. Act on recommendation: A high-quality meditator has a good control of his mind as compared to a non-meditator.

THE MOST IMPORTANT RELATIONSHIP

"In youth, it was a way I had,
To do my best to please.
And change, with every passing lad
To suit his theories.
But now I know the things I know
And do the things I do,
And if you do not like me so,
To hell, my love, with you."

Dorothy Parker, *The Complete Poems of Dorothy Parker*

I like to mention Bessie Coleman, an African–American who had to go to a flight school in Paris in order to learn how to fly. But she did, becoming the first woman in America to earn her pilot's license in 1920. The bottom line is: Success is outcome of a prepared mind. There is a quote of Antoine de Saint-Exupery that really hits home with me: "A goal without a plan is just a wish." When you have a goal and you work on a plan to achieve that goal in term of successive objectives, there is nothing that can stop you; the reason is pretty simple, you stay motivated because you continue to achieve objectives after objectives. But when you are not in total alignment with yourself, you challenge the most important relationship of this world, the relationship with yourself, and once this relationship gets in trouble, the tragedy happens, in fact I call it the biggest tragedy because you start to hate yourself when there is any inconsistency in your nature. We cannot do better than our level of self-esteem. "The past is not simply the past," asserts Doris Kearns Goodwin, "but a prism through which the subject filters his own changing self-image." Self-Esteem is about how you feel about yourself. It is not about how others see you. My advice: Give your body a workout. I have come to the conclusion that your level of self-approval goes higher with physical activity. Read or watch something funny. Write your life journal. The smart solution remains: You must fall in love with yourself every day. This approach will keep you motivated. Commit to memory: It's you only who can motivate yourself.

ACT LIKE AN ANTIVIRUS

"Motivation is simple. You eliminate those who are not motivated."

Lou Holtz, an American football coach

Alignment requires that you remove from your life all the stuff that is inconsistent with your passions and goal. You must act like an antivirus sometimes to remove negative thoughts and people. Keep in mind: Some people are good for negative things only, therefore, it's better to stay far from them. John Foster Dulles who served as U.S. Secretary of State under Republican President Dwight D. Eisenhower from 1953 to 1959 once said: "The measure of success is not whether you have a tough problem to deal with, but whether it's the same problem you had last year." Dr. M.S. Verma, an Indian Supreme Court lawyer and one of the proud members of my RPG opines: "You can achieve success if you can just avoid two things: bad thoughts and bad people. I have seen that these two can stop you from getting ahead in your life." Negative thoughts, bad habits and average people are nothing more than obstacles in your road to success. A mistake becomes a blunder when it is committed twice. Moreover, negative thoughts and people obstruct your constructive imagination.

THINKING CREATIVELY

"To raise new questions, new possibilities, to regard old problems from a new angle, require creative imagination."

Albert Einstein (1879–1955)

Imagination is the workshop of the mind and unless you think creatively, you can't connect to infinite intelligence and without the support of infinite intelligence you can't discover your breakthrough ideas. Leo Burnett (1891–1971) an advertising executive was among the most creative men in the advertising business. He said: "Curiosity about life in all of its aspects is still the secret of great creative people." A creative man is motivated by the craving to attain. You need positive frame of mind and in fact harmony of mind to be in touch with that infinite intelligence. Only then, I see, one can see, what others have seen and ultimately the thoughts start to come, the thoughts that no one has ever thought. You will get highest motivation when you connect with infinite intelligence. Nikos Kazantzakis was a Greek writer and philosopher, celebrated for his novel *Zorba the Greek*, which is considered his magnum opus. He became known globally after the 1964 release of the Michael Cacoyannis film *Zorba the Greek*, based on the novel. He gives a nice suggestion for creative visualization: "You have your colours; you have your brushes, paint paradise and walk right in." You will put your mind to think in synthetic way based on previous knowledge, prevalent ideas, and popular practices but that's okay to start with but when you get at peak of your imagination you create your own breakthrough ideas. Don't bother to get it right. Most results are built on the work of others. Vincent van Gogh (1853–1890) was a Dutch post-Impressionist painter whose work, notable for its rough beauty, emotional honesty and bold colour, had a far-reaching influence on 20th-century art. He said: "If you hear a voice within you say, 'You cannot paint,' then by all means paint, and that voice will be silenced." Just get it going. Collect maximum ideas and then throw the bad ones. The indispensable part of creativity is not being anxious to fail.

When an action joins a dream, success ensues. Creating great imaginations and a strong urge about an idea that we cannot live without can be a great motivation technique. You will stimulate the weaker brain (right or left) and when this happens imagination encircles the whole universe. So, just start with your faculty of imagination and it'll take a while to get going and remember: you need to spend time in workshop of your mind to get great ideas. Dr. Seuss asserted: "Think left and think right and think low and think high. Oh, the thinks you can think up if only you try." Please Mark: People will commit you to their memory for your contribution and not for human potential.

FIND MEANING IN YOUR LIFE

> *"In the beginning, God created the earth, and he looked upon it in His cosmic loneliness. And God said, 'Let Us make living creatures out of mud, so the mud can see what We have done.' And God created every living creature that now moveth, and one was man. Mud as man alone could speak. God leaned close to mud as man sat, looked around, and spoke. 'What is the purpose of all this?' he asked politely. 'Everything must have a purpose?' asked God. 'Certainly,' said man. 'Then I leave it to you to think of one for all this,' said God. And He went away."*
>
> Kurt Vonnegut, *Cat's Cradle*

Life is without meaning. You bring the meaning to it. The meaning of life is what you assign it to be. For the meaning of life differs from man to man. For me life is ad infinitum being ambitious, to get newer and richer experiences and to achieve my greatest self. Your motivation level is at seventh sky, when you have a meaning for your life. The meaning of life is not simply to exist, to live, but to progress forward and to be a winner. Yu the Great (2200 BC–2100 BC) was a legendary ruler in ancient China who is famed for his introduction of flood control. Genghis Khan was the founder and

Great Khan (emperor) of the Mongol Empire. He had a dream to make his kingdom the largest contiguous empire in history, and he did. Bruce Lee had a dream to spread martial arts and he did. Mahatma Gandhi had a meaning to his life: to get the Independence for India. Bill Gates has made the computers a whole new world. Quaid-E-Azam Mohammad Ali Jinnah changed the course of history in South Asia and carved out a homeland for the Muslims of India. In his bestselling book *Man's Search for Meaning,* Frankl compared his own "Third Viennese School of Psychotherapy" (after Freud's and Adler's schools) to Adler's analysis: "According to logo therapy, the striving to find a meaning in one's life is the primary motivational force in man. That is why I speak of a will to meaning in contrast to the 'pleasure principle' (or, as we could also term it, the will to pleasure) on which Freudian psychoanalysis is centred, as well as in contrast to the will to power stressed by Adlerian psychology." As you read Frankl's book it really makes you stop and think about the meaning and purpose of your life. This is one of the great books of all times and one of the outstanding contributions to psychological thought also in the last many years. "A man exists for a generation," says Les Brown, "but his name lasts to the end of time. At the end of the day you get satisfaction because you contributed in some way to make things better."

INSPIRATION v. MOTIVATION

> *"If wishes were horses, beggars would ride. Having the will to win is not enough. Everyone has that. What matters is having the will to prepare to win."*
>
> Bob Knight, *The Power of Negative Thinking*

Everybody knows that he must work with persistence to get success. Every now and then, people get motivated when they meet super leaders, watch motivating movies or read some good books but why can't they keep themselves on the route to success and quit so early. You must get inspiration from within to be persistent and constant motivation from outside can be a great influence. I often say to my students: "Great things happen when you act inside out."

Negative thinking can actually produce more positive results, in sports and in daily life. Coach Bob Knight, the second-winningest coach in NCAA history with 902 victories, explains that victory is often attained by the team that makes the fewest mistakes. A critical thinker recognizes the strengths and weaknesses in his team and, instead of pushing people to do what they can't do, pushes them to do what they can to best take advantage of their talents.

All the mentors, friends, books, institutes, courses and movies can motivate you but you will act only on inspiration, and that is totally an internal affair. Your inspiration comes from sound personal philosophy. You act when you feel inspired by your personal philosophy and then life becomes effortless. Therefore, as a business leader you must motivate your fellow men through increments, appreciations and promotions to get inspired to learn and improve in their weak areas. All the super leaders have been a resource of motivation.

FORMS OF MOTIVATION

> *"People would prefer activities where they can pursue three things. Autonomy: People want to have control over their work. Mastery: People want to get better at what they do. Purpose: People want to be part of something that is bigger than they are."*
>
> Daniel H. Pink, *Drive*

Most people believe that the best way to motivate is with rewards like money—the carrot-and-stick approach. That's a mistake. The secret to high performance and satisfaction – at work, at school, and at home – is the deep human need to direct our own lives, to learn and create new things, and to do better for ourselves and our world.

If you value the distinction between intrinsic, extrinsic, positive and negative motivational factors, you have a better probability of motivating yourself and others. The more reasons you find to motivate yourself to take on a specific behaviour, the more likely you will continue with and persist in that behaviour. Let me give you few examples –

Extrinsic Motivation: All my friends are successful.

Intrinsic Motivation: I can contribute in my chosen field of activity.

Positive Motivation: I want to learn new things in my chosen field of activity.

Negative Motivation: If I don't succeed my friends will think I am good for nothing.

You may look at your successful friends for motivation but if you look at the things closely you will find that your friends are successful in the fields of their interests and if you are ready to learn new things and serve in your field, you can also be successful. The fear of failure is a negative motivator and I believe you learn from your successful failures. You must pursue your burning desire. There are successful people in each profession. Trophies, academic recognition, medals, money, bonuses, commission scales, discount cards, coupons, bribery, threats of punishment, grades, entrance to programs or schools, higher commission percentages, new clothes, cheering crowds and losing weight are all examples of extrinsic motivators. Extrinsic motivation gets its support from incentive theory that treats motivation and behaviour as they are influenced by beliefs. According to Reinforcement theory (BF Skinner) positive and negative reinforcement can be used for increasing desirable/required behaviour. I also like Skinner's concept of Radical Behaviourism that means a person's behaviour always has social ramifications. In simple words, people look for social appreciation and approval.

I am not denying the influence of external factors but I recommend inside evolution because it leads to revolution outside. You enjoy an activity, course or skills when you are intrinsically motivated, and when you enjoy you learn and have fun. Success will follow if you are after competency. Natural motivation is driven by an interest and hence it is derived from a self-concept, or personal philosophy opposed to extrinsic motivators. External motivators are typically not stabilizers. The real power is within yourself and unless you are motivated inside you can't excel outside. The motivation has to be intrinsic and positive. You can work hard out of irritation, jealousy and fear but you will excel only out of love, passion and enthusiasm.

UNDERSTAND BOTH ENDS OF THE SPECTRUM

> *"In theory there is no difference between theory and practice. In practice there is."*
>
> Yogi Berra, an American Baseball catcher

Every behaviour has an underlying cause, and understanding the cause of behaviour means you know the motivating factors and that is the key to changing or improving results. There are always blends of reasons why people do, achieve, behave, learn and react; therefore, there are many theories about what motivates people. Theory helps you in applying what you learned solving one problem to different problems. There is a theoretical and a practical side to knowledge and both are valuable. The true masters of any craft or discipline understand both ends of the spectrum. Where theory is learning from the experience of others, practice is learning from your own experience. There are good arguments for both sides, but I think the best way to learn is through a combination of theory and practice. However practice without theory is undirected. So let me take you through few theories of motivation.

Abraham Maslow's Theory (1943) is based on the assumption that there is a hierarchy of five needs within each individual. According to Maslow, individuals are motivated by unsatisfied needs. The physiological needs include air, water, food, clothing and shelter. Safety needs include physical, environmental, emotional safety, job security, financial security, protection from animals, family security and health security. Both physiological and safety needs constitute the lower-order needs. These lower-order needs are mainly satisfied on the outside. The social needs include love, affection, care, belongingness and friendship. Esteem needs are divided into internal and external esteem needs. Internal esteem needs include self-respect, confidence, competence, achievement and freedom. External esteem needs include recognition, power, status, attention and admiration. Self-actualization needs include the urge to become what you are capable of becoming and constitute the higher-order needs.

Clayton Alderfer's ERG theory is a redefined version of Maslow's need hierarchy theory. The premise of this theory is that an employee has various needs that must be satisfied at the same time. Existence needs include physiological, physical safety needs or basic material needs. Relatedness needs include social needs and external esteem factor like maintaining significant interpersonal relationships with family, peers or superiors, getting public fame and recognition. Growth needs include self-actualization needs and intrinsic esteem like self-development, personal growth and advancement.

In 1959, Frederick Herzberg, a behavioural scientist proposed a two-factor theory or the motivator-hygiene theory. According to Herzberg, if hygiene factors like pay, clear company policies and fair administrative policies, fringe benefits, working conditions and job security are non-existent at workplace, then they lead to dissatisfaction. The hygiene factors cannot be regarded as motivators. Motivating factors like praise, recognition, promotion, responsibility and challenging nature of work motivate the employees for a superior performance.

In 1960, Douglas McGregor formulated Theory X (negative) and Theory Y (positive) suggesting two aspects of human behaviour at work. Theory X suggests that an average employee resist change, dislike responsibilities, intrinsically does not like work and tries to escape it whenever possible. Therefore, theory X recommends using close supervision and strict control to induce required behaviour. Theory Y suggests that employees can take responsibilities if the job is satisfactory, rewarding and utilizes the natural talent and potential of employees.

David McClelland's theory of needs states that human behaviour is affected by three needs – Power, Achievement and Affiliation. Victor Vroom in 1964 propounded expectancy theory that suggests that the deserving employees must be rewarded for their exceptional performance. Equity theory demonstrates that the individuals are concerned both with their own rewards and also with what others get in their comparison. The employees who perceive inequity and are under negative tension can make the choices of change in input or quitting the job. The gender, salary, education and the experience level are moderating variables.

BUILD YOUR SELF-CONFIDENCE

> *"People often say that motivation doesn't last. Well, neither does bathing – that's why we recommend it daily."*
>
> Zig Ziglar (1926–2012)

The blunder that an average person makes is that he concentrates completely on what he wants and ignores what he already has. The human mind creates weeds in form of negative thoughts and finds support in the past failures, personal weaknesses and bad times often out of jealousy because when you start comparing with your friends and competitors, the mind produces all the reasons and explanations for why you aren't getting it. This is a total negative thought pattern of mind and unfortunately you can think, feel and visualize about yourself and others only in negative in this state. So, here is my observation for this lesson: It is during over self-critical or self-deprecation state that your motivation levels can drop.

The line of attack to counter or prevent this negative state of mind is to concentrate on what you have already and to express gratitude for possessing the same. By making an endeavour to undergo gratitude, you'll understand how talented and successful you already are. I strongly advise you to make a list of your strengths, good qualities, past successes, and existing advantages and repeat the list as many times as you find convenient. We have a tendency to take our strengths for granted and dwell on our failures. Set aside some time to focus on everything positive in your life. This will restore your self-confidence and get you motivated to make your existing achievement bigger.

Leadership is not only about position, but who we are. Unless we first lead ourselves, we can't imagine leading others. You need to be your own salesmen. You must be your brand ambassador yourself. It is also found that once you tell others the most positive things you wish to achieve the task is half done; giving self positive affirmations and positive talk all the time mentally helps you to stay motivated and on the move always. You must create a want in yourself to get something. You must take good rest and sleep enough. Taking a healthy and balanced diet would certainly help you to feel strong to pursue your goals in life. Laughter and humour could also act as your great motivators because after all the philosophy of this present book is to "live, love and laugh to inspire." Success is all about living a satisfactory and useful life.

WHAT EXACTLY IS IT THAT YOU WANT TO ACCOMPLISH?

> *"Most of us spend too much time on what is urgent and not enough time on what is important."*
>
> Stephen R. Covey (1932–2012)

It's certain that you'll bump into periods of low liveliness, bad times, and even the successful failures. If you don't discipline your mind, these minor speed bumps can turn into mental monsters. You must do two things to propel yourself on route to success. The first one is to count your blessings and second one is to progressively realize your goal. These two go side by side. In fact, I call them twin forces; if one is there it will attract the second. Instead of concentrating on a goal, most of the people think what they don't want. As a student of success philosophy, you must set priorities and a have day-to-day strategy if you want to get success. You must prepare a list of the activities that lead to success and then you must cling to the listed activities. It gives you a lot of motivation. Obviously, you will make the list from smallest and first step to biggest and last step. You keep procrastination away by doing these listed activities and you keep yourself motivated and on the route to success. You move slowly in the direction of a goal. You have to be conscious of the reasons, fears and insecurities for the simple reason because these compel you to put things off. You have to observe your avoidance methods also that you employ to put things off. Understand: You have to keep yourself in the direction and somewhere down the line of realizing your ultimate goal because knowing the life purpose is an evolutionary process. After all, success is progressive realization of a goal. My great thinker friend, Aman Vasishtha is known in our circle as "Osho" because of his thinking abilities. He asserts: "People normally think in terms of fears of poverty, disrespect and loneliness. In place of doing something about their fear, people feed on fear based thinking and that sucks their motivation."

If you're in habit of fear based thinking, the first step is to concentrate your heartiness on a clear-cut goal. By having a clear-cut goal, you plan your actions to achieve a set of objectives and that will automatically lead you to that decided goal, for example if you want to earn money then focus on money and not on poverty, devise a plan to raise your income, join some personality or career development courses, apply for higher paid jobs, or develop a money-spinning website. The key is moving from an intangible desire to tangible and assessable steps towards success. It's better to fix goals for each stretch of work.

By concentrating your mind on a positive goal instead of a confusing fear, you prepare your brain to work to achieve a set objective. It immediately begins devising a plan for success. The best thing is that instead of worrying about the future you start to do something about it. This is the first step in motivating yourself to take actions. When you know what you want, you become motivated to take actions. Yamamoto Tsunetomo Hagakure affirms: "You don't have to be great to get started, but you have to get started to be great."

SUGGESTED STRATEGY

> *"Have a big image with microscopic details as it facilitates in deciding your next move."*
>
> Bhagavan Nayagar (1951–2001)

Look backward, connect the dots in your life, and create a life map of the future. I think this is probably the most useful thing I can get from the life map. By creating a life map, you will see patterns in your life and that will help you to find out where you should go. You will get answers to the questions and you will come to know about your mistakes also. Since you now have the big picture, it becomes easier to see where you should go next. You are looking at the whole path you have passed, so it is easier to guess where the next step should be. It will help you plan your current and coming years better.

ASSIGNMENT

1. Read the stories of successful people who inspire you and learn from them.
2. Make a list of things that really interest you or create a liking for example – exercise, music, reading inspirational quotes and then do them.

3. Find someone that you are comfortable with and share your problems with him/her.
4. Go through the list of your short-term, mid-term and long-term goals at least once every day when you need a little nudge to keep going.
5. No matter what, just start with a small step that you need to do either you like it or not.
6. Develop an index of all the external, internal, positive and negative motivators for the list of goals and think why you want to achieve them.
7. Listen to the Audio program *The 7 Hidden Secrets of Motivation* by Todd Beeler.

VISUALIZATION

Imagine yourself living the life you dream of. Feel the emotions involved; see yourself in the life in colourful detail with sense intelligence. A "VB – Visualization Board" filled with pictures of your new life will really help and you can look at it as often as you like. Remember: People like David and Peter do wonders simply by their attitude and vision.

SELF SUGGESTION

I am enthusiastic to take inspired and right action for each goal and dream I undertake.

Bear in mind: Super achievers always keep their commitments.

[*Promise & Put Your Signature Here With Date*]

26

Can The Imagined Reality Be The Actual Reality?

OBJECTIVES

- To learn the "Law of Sense Intelligence",
- To employ synergy of "Auto-Suggestion & Visualization" before doing anything, and
- To reprogram the subconscious mind for habits of success.

GOLDEN GUIDANCE

"The universe desires you to have everything you want to have. When you make a failure, it is because you have not asked for enough; keep on, and a larger thing then as you were seeking will certainly come to you. We are thinking substance and thinking substance always takes the form of that which it thinks about. Remember this."

Wallace D. Wattles, *The Science of Getting Rich*

DEFINITION OF SUCCESS

"Success is the progressive realization of a worthy ideal."

Earl Nightingale, *The Strangest Secret*

Success is a process of getting achievements after achievements towards the ultimate life goal. In terms of success, this is my standard definition. Our step by step growth in form of habits towards something significant is what makes us successful. A student who wanted to become a teacher is successful person if he is a teacher at present because being a teacher is his lifelong goal. He had to clear the teaching eligibility test after getting all the prescribed qualifications.

That student is successful because he has realized his ideal of being a teacher making progress step by step. He planted the image of teacher in his mind and gradually moved ahead. We develop into what we think about. The most important resolution that you will ever take in your entire life is to set your goal in your mind. Wattles calls humans as thinking substance and thinking substance always takes the form of that which it thinks about.

The successful people have clarity and certainty about what they want (and don't want) for their life. They actually visualize and plan their best reality while others are merely spectators of life. So, *here is the golden tip*: "You should never begin a day unless you have visualized it the night before. You should never begin a task unless you have finished it mentally. Imagination leads the way and makes an ordinary person – an extraordinary leader." Anyone can become a star. "Everyone," said Marilyn Monroe, "is a star and deserves the right to twinkle."

LAW OF ATTRACTION

> *"Whatever you can do, or dream you can do, begin it. Boldness has genius, power and magic in it."*
>
> Goethe (1749–1832)

One of the space laws, I believe, is that whatever we hold in our thought will come exact in our lives because whatsoever is going on in our mind is what we are attracting. This is known as LOA – Law of Attraction. I love the universal law of attraction: What we think about we bring about. You really are what you think about most. When you go back in time through your past miseries it becomes clearer that you are your own prey attracting everything with your doubtful thoughts. I began learning more about creative visualization from the time when I watched "The Secret" movie which introduced me to the Law of Attraction. My life has changed ever since. I have been able to attract a number of positive things to my life. The process involves the simple law of "Like attracts like", based on this logic that as we think and feel, a corresponding frequency is sent out into the universe that attracts back to us events and circumstances on the same frequency. The whole point is: Every thought has a frequency. For example, if you think angry thoughts and feel angry, it is claimed that you will attract back events and circumstances that cause you to feel more anger. On the other hand, if you think and feel positively, you will pull towards yourself positive events, people, money, connections and circumstances. Virender Duhan, one of our RPG friends, went on an adventure camp in June 2011 in 25 people group. The destination was 11,500 feet high but he covered 12,500 and got the best trainee award. In the next tour in June 2012, the target was 13,500 feet high but again he went further and climbed up to 15,500 feet. He beholds in his imagination: the Mount Everest – 18,000 feet. He is undergoing training nowadays at Manali. The secret of law of attraction is: Visualize. Play the picture in your mind and focus on the end result. Be thankful for what you have, you'll end up having more. You will get what you have given. Your performance always equals your input thoughts. What is *IN* will come *OUT*. Abraham Hicks calls this, power of deliberate intent. And it's no wonder. He calls humans as Vibrational Beings who has a receiving mechanism. When you put forward a vibration, in form of a constant thought, the Universal forces function with each other to facilitate your intention. You, if truth be told, are the centre of the Universe. This thesis finds reflection in the computer phrase also, *GIGO – Garbage In Garbage Out* which explains *Positivity In Positivity Out, Negativity In Negativity Out*. You must offer thoughts in support of your desire then you will feel a pure enthusiasm in your day to day life and if you are feeling down it simply means your thought offering is exact opposite of your desire. That's why, one of the best self-help gurus, Napoleon Hill asserts: "Let a person radically alter his thoughts, and he will be astonished at the rapid transformation it will affect in the material conditions of his life." Please Memorize: Law of Attraction does not complain or demand. It simply magnifies the vibration that is within you.

CONSCIOUS AND SUBCONSCIOUS MIND

> *"I have seen miracles happen to men and women in all walks of life all over the world. Lung cancer has been cured and optic nerves made whole again. Your subconscious mind can win you friends, peace of mind, and even help you to attract the ideal mate. Prosperity, happiness and perfect health are yours when you use the power of your subconscious mind."*
>
> Dr. Joseph Murphy, *The Power of Your Subconscious Mind*

You need to plant the thought of success in your subconscious mind through the conscious effort of conscious mind. Of the two brains, the subconscious is more powerful and behaves like a land, it does not discriminate, whatever you will plant; you will get that. If you plant good thoughts you will have good habits or success eventually and if you plant bad thoughts you will have bad habits or failures. Positive and negative are paths. The path you choose determines your future. All the great leaders change the organization they join just because they have programmed their subconscious mind. I often claim: An organization is an outcrop of the leader's subconscious mind. Similarly, if you can maintain positive mental attitude in conscious mind, you will change yourself and your life completely just out of a programmed subconscious mind. Sigmund Freud has compared the conscious mind to a fountain playing in the sun and falling back into the great subterranean pool of subconscious from which it rises. Understand: The subconscious mind can be our friend and enemy. Whenever there is constant failure, that means, we need to reprogram the subconscious mind through the conscious repetitions till it becomes an automatic act or habit. You will become unbeatable once you know this most well-known secret. Rex Todhunter Stout (1886–1975) was an American writer noted for his detective fiction. He is best known as the creator of the fictional detective Nero Wolfe, described by Will Cuppy as "that Falstaff of detectives." He once said: "The only difference between me and most people is that I'm perfectly aware that all my important decisions are made for me by my subconscious. My frontal lobes are just kidding themselves that they decide anything at all. All they do is think up reasons for the decisions that are already made." W. Clement Stone (1902–2002) was born in Chicago. His father died when he was 3. At the age of 6, Stone began hawking newspapers and at 13, he owned his own newsstand. At the age of 16 he went to Detroit to help his mother in the insurance agency from office to office to sell casualty insurance, and he was soon making $100 a week. In his autobiography *The Success System That Never Fails* he tells about the selling of newspapers in restaurants and how he gradually won over managers of restaurants due to his politeness, charisma and persistence. His philosophy was: Whatever the mind can conceive and believe, the mind can achieve with Positive Mental Attitude. He asserted: "You affect your subconscious mind by verbal repetition." He learned the art of selling insurance policies out of the selling of newspapers and ran $100 into millions with a powerful desire to succeed. He built a company providing accident and health insurance coverage in 1919. The name of the company was the Combined Insurance Company of America. He had over a thousand agents selling insurance for him across the United States by 1930. His insurance company exceeded $1 billion in assets by 1979. He was greatly inspired by Napoleon Hill's book *Think and Grow Rich* and joined Hill to propagate his philosophy. Norman Vincent Peale said that Stone and Hill have the rare gift of inspiring and helping people. He often said: "All I want to do is change the world." Learn the law: Subconscious mind expresses what the conscious mind has impressed on it. Your conscious mind is the gatekeeper at the door. The subconscious looks conscious mind for all its impressions. Jeanette Winterson, a British writer, asserts: "In my subconscious, my books were part of a single emotional journey." An English musician, singer and songwriter Florence Welch has always been able to just concoct a melody quite easily. She affirms: "It's just kind of instinct, really. You've got to channel your subconscious."

SENSE INTELLIGENCE

> *"The way it actually works is the reverse. You must first be who you really are, then do what you need to do, in order to have what you want."*
>
> Shakti Gawain, *Creative Imagination*

We should use mental imagery and affirmations to produce positive changes in one's life. One should also be vigilant that creative visualization will not serve greediness or shallow-minded thinking. For example, the author discourages the cycle of trying to have more money and then do what you want in life and ultimately to be happier. You have to go by the law: "First you work on yourself and then on the things you want." People can pull off a perfect way of life just through psychological visualization. All men who have achieved great things have been great dreamers. W. Clement Stone was also a great believer in the synergy of visualization and affirmation. Take my advice: Put an end to thinking about all the reasons you cannot be victorious and as a replacement prepare a list of all the reasons why you can. It's easier for a human being to think negatively than positively. That's why only 5% of people are successful.

Auto-suggestion or self suggestion is a statement made at the conscious mind to provide a stimulus to subconscious mind through the five senses, that I call "Sense Intelligence" because you perceive the reality before it becomes the actuality. Sense intelligence calls for synergy of auto-suggestion and visualization because positive affirmations will not work alone and hence they must be observed with proper and full visualizations through all the senses.

You suggest something to yourself and then you see the mental picture as a reality. For example, if you want to be in a great shape, start the exercise, and at least twice a day, try to visualize and perceive that you are already in great shape. Close your eyes and see that, touch that and listen the good comments till you feel it as a reality with open eyes. See yourself doing all things you will be doing when you have reached your goal.

A person who repeats a statement with visualizations long enough lets it sink into the subconscious mind. I prefer to prolong the behaviour till thirty days to convert it into habit. "I am enough of an artist," said Albert Einstein, "to draw freely upon my imagination. Imagination is more important than knowledge. Knowledge is limited. Imagination encircles the world."

EFFECT OF POSITIVE SUGGESTIONS

> *"If you feel you are falling short of your potential, or you have lost control over your life, Affirmations may be the jump-start you need to put you powerfully back on track."*
>
> Dr. Anne Marie Evers, *Affirmations*

Your reality is nothing more than a reflection of your subconscious thoughts. You can find many affirmations in *Bible* and Hindu *Upanishads*. Dr. Anne Marie Evers calls affirmations as passport to happiness. The effect of doing affirmations is that a few days after, you'll feel strongly confident to make bolder decisions and to live a more rewarding life. In cricket, a batsman gets 0.5 seconds to react to a ball, sometimes even less than that. He can't think of what ABC has said about him. He needs to submit himself to his natural instincts. His subconscious mind knows accurately what to do. It is trained to react. Indian cricket team skipper Mahendra Singh Dhoni's mind wanders in several directions while he is batting but he manages to keep the focus by humming songs even when the bowler is running in from the other end. When the bowler is running in to bowl, he starts to sing but as soon as the bowler gets to his delivery stride, Dhoni focuses on the ball. Singing when the bowler is running in empties his mind of unwanted thoughts. At the moment of the performance, we all have to return to a new level of unconsciousness. I always believe: There is somewhat genuinely known deep down, not consciously, but subconsciously. Another thing, I drew out of various interviews of players published in various magazines and newspapers is that at home, most of players' family doesn't discuss media coverage because this can affect a player's performance negatively also.

Self suggestions should always be in positive sentences. Positive affirmations are generally used in sports and medicine. Negative statements should never be used like I will not eat much sugar; I will not be angry etc. You feel tired also because of the fact that you suggest yourself that you are tired. Negativity is like a drug that induces sadness because you imagine the worst, and at last become weak and sad. Why I am asking you not to use negative statements in self suggestion is for the reason that human mind thinks in pictures not in words. Moreover, the negativity of negative statement will be planted in your mind. For example, if I ask you to close your eyes and ask not to think about your mother. What picture will come to your mind? Of course, of your mother because of this fact, the memory experts advise you to combine your left and right brain in form of charts and instructions while studying something.

USE PRESENT TENSE

"Life isn't about finding yourself. Life's about creating yourself."

George Bernard Shaw (1856–1950)

Mind can't distinguish between an imaginary and actual occurrence. It has been said that if you treat yourself well, the world will treat you even better. Your self-respect will get you respect from others. Albert Einstein appropriately supports LOA. He said: "Your imagination is your preview of life's coming attractions." For example, presume you are a student and you are anxiously waiting for your result and expecting good position in your class. Your good friend informs you on your phone that you have stood first in your class, you will jump up in excitement however later you come to know that he was kidding and you passed in first division only. Ralph Waldo Emerson calls a thought as the ancestor of every action. Your mind believes what you say to it. You've got to win in your brain before you win in your game or life. The sports coaches use this tool like "You are a good player" to back up the performances of players. Taking advantage of this fact, we should use positive affirmations in present tense, like "I am a good player" because it helps our mind to perceive the reality. Once that belief becomes a deep conviction, things commence to happen. Most doctors use this strategy by fixing the schedule of treatment. At the end of treatment good doctors often say to a patient: "You are all right now." I believe that the most crucial conversation is the one you have with yourself. You should select the affirmation from a list and change the words of the affirmation until it matches what you want accurately. You may truly end up with a completely special affirmation and be on the way to creating your own private list of positive affirmations.

THE PLANS WILL APPEAR

> *"Man is master of his earthly status especially his financial status. Man can become master of himself and of his environment because he has the power to influence his own subconscious mind."*
>
> Napoleon Hill (1883–1970)

An American spiritual authority Orison Swett Marden (1850–1924) calls it psychological law. Know the secret: You have to impress the subconscious mind with a conviction that you are a success. You must feel intensely about an idea or goal and then the idea that is buried deep down in your subconscious mind will direct you. Sachin Tendulkar, the greatest batsman also affirms: "At the start of my career, when I used to toss and turn at night, I was fighting that feeling and wanting to go to sleep. Now I know that's normal, so I'll just get up and watch TV or something. I know it's just my subconscious mind getting ready for a game." Your subconscious mind knows no difference reality and imagination. It has no humour. And that's why a visual artist Andrew Wyeth (1917–2009) said: "I dream a lot. I do more painting when I'm not painting. It's in the subconscious." We can gain cooperation from infinite intelligence if we use our sense intelligence correctly. Don't wait for the perfect moment or perfect plan; just imagine yourself in the possession of the thing right now. All the "How will you do it" will appear when you clearly see "What do you want." The thing is when the plans appear you must act on those plans immediately.

SUGGESTED STRATEGY

> *"Our life is the creation of our mind."*
>
> Buddha, the founder of Buddhist religion

Are you a dreamer? Do you have certain aims in your life? Everybody dreams. In fact, many times in our life, we have lived the awaited future in our imagination. Write what you want in full details like I am a guy with 16 inch biceps, 44 inches chest, 34 inches waist or I have one million dollars etc. Then, repeat these written statements at least twice a day. Place as many copies as you like in different places where it is visible. At first, these thoughts will look abstract skeptic thoughts as they are new for your subconscious mind; it is against our belief system but soon these will become beliefs and eventually will get transformed into deepest faith. You can use sense-intelligence in any area with positive changes. Be conscious of the law: "We become what we think about."

ASSIGNMENT

1. Make a list of positive habits, which you want to learn to be successful.
2. Make a list of negative habits which you want to unlearn.
3. Make a list of your self suggestions based on assignment 1 and 2.
4. Plan and do your visualizations accordingly.
5. Listen to the Audio program *The Power of Visualization* by Dr. Lee Pulos.

VISUALIZATION

You must develop a tendency to visualize before doing anything. The master key is to begin with an end in mind. Visualize the whole process and end it perfectly. Remember: Whatever we place in our subconscious mind and feed with verbal repetition and visual emotion will one day become an actuality. We need to condition our reflexes. All the great super achievers knew this well-known but strange secret.

SELF SUGGESTION

I visualize before I do anything.

Bear in mind: Super achievers always keep their commitments.

[Promise & Put Your Signature Here With Date]

27

How Well Do You Take Care Of Yourself?

OBJECTIVES

- To learn the "Law of Good health",
- To find out the best training program for yourself, and
- To develop a healthy diet for yourself.

GOLDEN GUIDANCE

"Illness is the night-side of life, a more onerous citizenship. Everyone who is born holds dual citizenship, in the kingdom of the well and in the kingdom of the sick. Although we all prefer to use only the good passport, sooner or later each of us is obliged, at least for a spell, to identify ourselves as citizens of that other place."

Susan Sontag, *Illness as Metaphor*

DO YOU HAVE A PERFECT HEALTH ROUTINE?

"How do I stay so healthy and boyishly handsome? It's simple. I drink the blood of young runaways."

William Shatner, a Canadian actor

Are you satisfied with shape of your body? Are you having a good physical health? Are you free of all diseases? If your answers to above questions are in negative, then, it is high time to develop a routine for exercise, a daily meal plan and a habit of drinking lots of water. I consider a body that is healthy and in shape is the most excellent style or fashion statement. Your health and well-being are necessary. Herophilus points out what happens when health is absent. He asserts: "When health is absent, wisdom cannot reveal itself, art cannot manifest, strength cannot fight, wealth becomes useless, and intelligence cannot be applied." Keeping your health standards right is surely a private ride. You must follow the basic holistic laws. Lance Armstrong rightly confirms: "I exercise every day. I swim, I bike, I run and I go to the gym." Every champion does so. I follow and advise to follow the best rule and that is: Listen to your body. Your body will tell you if you are not eating well or not exercising regularly. You must manage your stress. You should stay away from taking chemist's advised drugs for common aches and pains. One must avoid no pain, no gain approach also. Your exercises should include more aerobics. In other words, by training aerobically, you can burn body fat and this in turn will lead to a lifetime of health and fitness. You must see your doctor and dietary nutritionist for a perfect health routine. Daily exercise and good eating habits are two habits of successful people. Let me clarify at the outset that the information given in this lesson is for informational purposes only and it is not intended as a substitute for advice from your physician or other health care professional. You should not start or stop any diet, exercise, supplementation program or medication without proper medical advice. In fact, a good professional advice is recommended.

YOU SHOULD NOT TAKE LIFE FOR GRANTED

> *"Health is a state of complete harmony of the body, mind and spirit. When one is free from physical disabilities and mental distractions, the gates of the soul open."*
>
> B.K.S. Iyengar, the founder of Iyengar Yoga

There is somewhat strange in sickness that breaks down the arrogance of a man. Everybody loves life and wants to extend it as long as possible. Everybody wants to be immortal because time is nonrenewable resource. This is more essential than making money and becoming famous. However, people get serious about fitness when their doctors strictly ask them. There's nothing worse than an old, fat and depressed man. Health experts talk about energy in sense of fuel and electricity and the fact remains the more energy we have, the easier it is to concentrate, and the higher the quality of our pursuit is. One of Richard Branson's keys to success was staying in great physical shape. I am your well-wisher so I advise you to make exercise a routine part of your life and believe me, it will definitely increase your chances at success.

You need energy to work so let us talk about your energy level. If you get short of breath with the slightest bit of exertion and often feel like you don't have enough left to be able to concentrate on your goals, then this is the time to get serious about your fitness if you want to enhance your life, both qualitatively and quantitatively and give yourself more time to enjoy the world and life. I have found, during the research for this chapter, that the patients who had a heart attack reported to have fatigue, sleep disturbances, shortness of breath, indigestion and anxiety at least one month before their heart attack. After surgery they realize how precious life is, and most of operated people say: "You've got to take care of your machinery." "You shouldn't take life for granted."

Trivialization is another reason. Little things when accumulated make big difference. High Blood Pressure and Sugar are called as V.I.P. diseases. We ignore health issues despite of believing that "Health is first wealth." We consider "Health Issues" trivial things somewhere in our thinking till we are caught with serious wakeup calls in form of diseases like heart attacks and paralysis.

We need to keep fit so that we can live quality lives. A good medicine doctor friend of my RPG, Dr. Sahid Ali Quereshi, M.D. opines: "Today, transportation, technology and fast food have made us more sedentary. This sedentary lifestyle is responsible for obesity, diabetes, heart disease, cancer and high mortality rates. Consequently, fitness is a multi-billion dollar industry." If you want something done, the adage goes, "Give it to a busy person." You can see in your surroundings. Nowadays people from rich and busiest class are more health conscious as compared to an average accumulator of wealth. The key is to be in parks or gyms at 5 a.m. One of the greatest challenges you will face in your journey of self-development is starting the day early, at 5:00 AM, and it is a habit successful people follow every day. It is also one of the most rewarding habits.

Most of the ultra-successful persons do meditation and exercise in morning and that's why they are consistent because meditation and exercise are a part of their morning routine. Successful people know the significance of "recharging their batteries." They value the need for balance and the fact that so as to operate at a confident level, they must be concerned of themselves at physical, mental and emotional level.

PAY A HEAVY PRICE FOR IGNORING THE HEALTH

> *"Listen to the people who love you. Believe that they are worth living for even when you don't believe it. Seek out the memories depression takes away and project them into the future. Be brave; be strong; take your pills. Exercise because it's good for you even if every step weighs a thousand pounds. Eat when food itself disgusts you. Reason with yourself when you have lost your reason."*
>
> Andrew Solomon, *The Noonday Demon*

When somebody talks about health, I often remember my father, who is a paralytic patient. He can't move on his own. He used to be in a good physical health in his young days. He got retirement from Indian Air Force and joined Haryana Welfare Department at a high administrative post.

The habits of healthy food and exercise went far away from his routine because in military services good health is a compulsion but in civil life it is a discipline. He has tasted the very best foods in the world even at the cost of ignoring the medical advices. He has been fond of sweets. Edward Stanley rightly asserts: "Those who think they have no time for exercise will sooner or later have to find time for illness." He developed the high blood sugar level and high blood pressure during his uncontrolled health regime. One unfortunate morning, the family members noticed his half body had got paralyzed. Doctors confirmed that he got a heart attack also. Thanks to health insurance plan. He got his life saving treatment well in time.

My health also deteriorated during the writing of this book. I left gym and even skipped food for the stupid logic of losing the momentum. I also had another reasons, although foolish ones such as, I have done a lot of exercise. I have eaten good body building material. I will resume after this book. I was obsessed with completion of this book. It happens to 95% of people. We tend to sacrifice or I should say ignore the most important asset of a human being, our health. Just at the age of 35, when I got my annual medical tests report, I was having all kind of troubles. In short, my health was not in good standards. In just 14 months, my health numbers were more of a warning to me. "Thirty-five is when you finally get your head together and your body starts falling apart." This quote of a graphic artist and copywriter Caryn Leschen was a perfect application in my life. I had to make a fresh start and I did. I am now regularly working on my health with my fitness coach. I have included this chapter as a tribute to "OBW – Our Biggest Wealth." I crack a joke often nowadays: Our OBW is costlier than BMW.

Moral of the story:

1. Health consciousness is a costly habit as it comes often from a life threatening ailment.
2. Often the health gets ignored for money and bad food habits.
3. Over-work is a dangerous threat for health at any age.

4. There will be a great change in your success when there is a great change in your health.
5. Your health suffers when you ignore proper medication, regular exercise, good food habits and sound sleep or any of these four health pillars.
6. You should keep your life and health numbers in a standard range.
7. You should get a good health insurance plan also.
8. One must get his complete health check-up at least once in a year.
9. One must avoid no pain, no gain attitude.
10. One must be a carrier of health consciousness.

PHYSICAL STRENGTH COMMANDS RESPECT

> *"About 10,000 years ago, males and females were acting equitably and were treating one another as equals, and then males took over the power, because they have physical power and physical strength."*
>
> Jane Elliot, an anti-racism activist

Zahir-ud-din Muhammad Babur (1483–1530) was a direct descendant of Timur through his father, and a descendant also of Genghis Khan through his mother. Babur is said to have been extremely strong and physically fit. As one of his exercises, Babur would carry two men, one on each of his shoulders, then run around and climb slopes. It is also believed that Babur swam through every major river in India, sometimes even against the current. Akbar, the son of Humayun and the greatest of the Mughal emperors was also famous for his exercises to keep him physically strong. Historians claim that Plato was a nickname, referring to Plato's broad physical build. In fact, Plato is Greek for broad. Together with his mentor, Socrates, and his student, Aristotle, he provided the main opposition to the Materialist view of the world represented by Democritus and Epicurus. He gave himself as a wrestler in the Isthmian Games. In *Republic* he outlined a plan for a perfect society. The first group of children needs to be brought up by state, the second group of children, Mob as he calls it, needs to be taken care of by labourers and farmers and third one by soldiers and fighters. Abraham Lincoln, the 16th President of USA, was one of the tallest and strongest presidents USA has had. According to some sources, Lincoln did have his famous wrestling matches with some local boys. At 6-foot-4-inch and 214 pounds, he was a man of action, who didn't hesitate to wade into a fight. Theodore Roosevelt (1858–1919) was the 26th President of the United States. He is renowned for his exuberant personality, range of interests and achievements, and his leadership of the Progressive Movement, as well as his cowboy persona and robust masculinity. Do you know one thing about him? Roosevelt was 42 years old when sworn in as President of the United States in 1901, making him the youngest president ever; he beat out the youngest elected president, John F. Kennedy, by only one year. He also won the Nobel Peace Prize. He was also fond of gymnastics and weightlifting. He always found time for physical exertions including hiking, riding horses and swimming. No president ever loved sports more than Theodore Roosevelt. Gurdjieff was also a man of immense physical strength who also loved to exercise. In today's modern world, the combination of spirituality and physical strength is a rarity. The whole discussion under this caption looks little bit a historical display of power. My whole point is: History has always been favourable to the men who had great physical strength and in modern world the situation has not changed much. Histories make men wise. I often advise the youngsters to go for weightlifting as it gives you a strength that in turn gives you self-confidence that builds your self-image. Many of the fitness coaches I consulted during the writing of this chapter confirm: Cardio does help with fat loss, but it only breaks down your existing tissue. What you get out of cardio is: soft and skinny fat look. Take my advice: To get toned look, a person must lift heavy weights. Men or women don't get bulky by strength training. You simply need to shed the fat to disclose the gorgeous new muscle beneath. Didn't you feel super-confident when you bench/squat a heavy weight or did an unassisted chin-up for the first time? Understand: You feel unstoppable if you know that you are physically more powerful and stronger than majority of men. Don't you?

IT IS ALL COMMON SENSE

> *"Some people don't do well simply because they don't feel well. Take good care of your body. It's the only place you have to live."*
>
> Jim Rohn (1930–2009)

"It's by and large commonsensical," says a doctor friend of my Resourceful Psyche Group, Dr. Swasti Sharma. "You must be up to date with your LHN (Life & Health Numbers) like blood pressure, body mass index, blood sugar, cholesterol and family history." He further affirms: "You ought to consult your doctor to keep these numbers in a standard range." Take my advice: You must learn to take care of yourself by saying say "No to Stress" and you have to find a routine wherein you put your health on top in your priority list. You have to start taking care of yourself, for your benefit and for the benefit of those who love you.

Another doctor friend of my RPG, Dr. Anil Dahiya states: "It's not easy to combine exercise and a livelihood. I advise a combo of a rich diet and regular exercise. The diet should be rich in fruits and vegetables and low in fat, sugar and salt. The combination of these two can improve heart and health a great deal." I also try to exercise enough and watch what I eat is good enough for my health. I try to cultivate good health habits in my children also. Depression is spreading in our society and, if truth be told, there is no better antidepressant than enthusiastic exercise. The alertness about lifestyle, diet, oil consumption needs more enthusiastic attention.

So, *here is the golden tip*: "Exercise is the source of youth and energy. Super leaders live supercharged life and stay super-fit because for them, it's not an option but a regular part of their daily hygiene, like showering and brushing the teeth."

TYPES OF EXERCISES

"Anything that affects your physical health also affects your mental health."

Napoleon Hill, the author of *Think and Grow Rich*

Exercises and physical activities fall into four basic categories – endurance, strength, balance and flexibility. Doing them all will give you more benefits. Endurance or aerobic or cardiovascular exercises, like playing sports like basketball or tennis, raise your heart rate and condition your lungs and circulation so these are quite useful in preventing diabetes and heart disease. Strength training for example lifting weights and resistance band is good for building muscles. Balance exercises like standing on one leg and toe walk etc. prevent sudden falls which is a common problem in older age. Flexibility exercises like yoga, pilates, dancing and martial arts stretch your muscles and give you more freedom in your movements.

EXERCISE HAS MANY BENEFITS

"Exercise enhances memory, improves reaction times and aids in the generation of unique and spontaneous ideas."

Brian Walsh, *Unleashing Your Brilliance*

Regular exercise gives you better blood-flow to your brain, improved alertness and enhanced concentration. Vigorous physical activity increases metabolism and burn more calories all day because of this raised rate which leads to weight loss. It can also build muscle and strength. Exercise can help in fighting chronic disease by preventing high blood pressure and regulating cholesterol levels. People who don't exercise are more prone to illness and earlier death than those who do. It elevates your mood, makes you feel well toned, strengthen your bones and improve your overall appearance. My fitness coach Nitin Chauhan opines: "Weightlifting makes a difference. It really does. The intense stretching releases endorphins and gives you a sense of well-being. Daily aerobic exercise depletes stress hormones and makes you more functional." I also earn my breakfast by working out for an hour before I leave my home.

WATCH YOUR FOOD HABITS

> *"Human mind makes food-related decisions, more than 200 a day, and many of them without pause for actual thought."*
>
> Brian Wansink, *Mindless Eating*

All the food psychologists transform our awareness. We are really not aware of how much, what, and why we're eating—often without realizing it. All the super-successful celebrities are watchful eaters. I have found that film stars choose to eat from a list few things in their breakfast, lunch or dinner. I also advise you to prepare a list of few things with calorie amount. Why? The logic is simple so that you can predict your daily calorie intake without much hard work. This list can prove to be your opening to carve a new path of physical transformation for yourself. The message of my philosophy is straightforward: Say goodbye once and for all to people, thoughts and activities in your life that bring you little or no worth. Diet is a habit for super leaders and they are often well-established in taste. One and in fact, first important food habit, I have noticed in all the winners is that they treat breakfast as the most important meal of the day and because of this winning edge they have been able to maintain a standard weight and look trim all their lives. Experts agree that eating a healthy breakfast reduces hunger right through the day, and therefore decreases the chance of overeating.

The second habit is that highly successful fit people drink at least 6 to 8 glasses of water daily. Your body is composed of about 60% water. The functions of these bodily fluids include digestion, absorption, circulation, creation of saliva, transportation of nutrients and maintenance of body temperature. Many of them take 2 to 3 glasses of fresh lime juice with salt and sugar to replenish electrolyte and others prefer to take at least 2 glasses of hot water with one teaspoon of honey to reduce weight. Coaches, trainers or nutritionists can help you develop an individualized hydration and electrolyte replacement program.

Third habit, the successful people maintain their cortisol levels and thus they deposit less fat and they do so by eating small foods after every 2 hours. A good breakfast jump starts metabolism and small meals keep it going. You should divide your daily calorie intake into small meals. Eating throughout the day also makes you less tempted by combo and jumbo packs of pizza, chocolates, chips, snacks, cold drinks, sandwiches and burgers. Most of the rich and successful people I know are very choosy in their calorie intake and they eat smart. They eat plenty of high-fiber foods; I call these good carbohydrates like fruits, vegetables, beans and whole grains. They limit their intake of sugary food and animal fat. Most of them if they don't feel satisfied at the end of a meal, they add more leafy green vegetables or rounding off the meal with fresh fruit. I urge you to make small steps, like adding a salad (full of different colour fresh vegetables) to your diet once a day or switching from butter to olive oil when cooking. You can also include few supplements in your daily diet. As your small changes become habit, you can continue to add more healthy choices to your diet. You should decide and balance your daily diet with carbohydrates, proteins and fats with the help of a good nutritionist. Aristotle once said that the only goal of all human activities should be happiness. To be truly happy, it takes thought and planning.

DECIDE YOUR MEDICINE SYSTEM

"Although we experience our bodies as solid, they are in fact more like fires that are constantly being consumed and renewed. We grow new stomach linings every five days, for instance. Our skin is new every

five weeks. Each year, fully 98 percent of the total number of atoms in our bodies is replaced. Ayurveda gives us the tools to intervene at this quantum level, where we are being created anew each day."

Deepak Chopra, *Perfect Health*

You must also decide an appropriate medicine system good for your health like allopathy, homeopathy, ayurveda and alternative systems. In the modern times there has been a growing interest in Traditional, Complementary and Alternative Medicine (TCAM) and its significance in health. Although for proper medical examination and major operations allopathy is still the only option with doctors and if you have a serious physical problem or medical emergency allopathic treatment seems the remedy. Benefits of allopathic treatment come with its side effects also. Allopathy removes the symptoms but ayurveda attacks the roots of disease and slowly removes the outside symptoms. Modern medicine is most important when there is an urgent medical condition. Most medical ailments are a result of improper lifestyle. Natural remedies help much at initial stages. People generally don't prefer natural cure because they are not in habits of a disciplined life and they want hasty relief. Natural remedies demand a restricted life. Indian Ayurveda stresses the use of plant-based medicines and treatments. The Sri Lankan tradition of Ayurveda is very similar to the Indian tradition. Ayurvedic theory and practice dates back in India more than 5,000 years. There are ancient traditions in Buddhist cultures also. Maharishi Mahesh Yogi, the founder of Transcendental Meditation formed a medical council to create authentic herbal formulations according to Ayurvedic texts. I am in favour of ayurvedic practitioners and practices because I believe that only ayurvedic therapy will give us longevity and perfect health especially in chronic diseases. Ayurvedic healing encompasses panchakarma, meditation, primordial sound, pulse diagnosis, marma therapy, bliss technique, aroma therapy and gandharva music therapy. This is my firm conviction that ayurveda is the science of life and a much necessary discipline for our well-being. Integration of Ayurveda, Siddha and Unani, the three Indian systems of medicine (ISM), along with homoeopathic and allopathic systems of medicine can do wonders.

TIME-OUT

> *"Brain dysfunction is the number one reason people fail at school, work, and relationships. The brain is the organ of learning, working, and loving – the supercomputer that runs our lives. It's very simple: when our brains work right, we work right – and when our brains have trouble, we have trouble in our lives."*
>
> Daniel Amen, *Making a Good Brain Great*

Time-out can be your best stress management plan. If truth be told, the simple consciousness that you're controller of your life is the base of stress management. There will never be more hours in the day. Identify the sources of stress in your life: habits, excuses and attitudes. Write in stress journal if there was any stress on any day with proper identification of causes. Whenever there is any stress remember my advice: Focus on the positive. You must also know your limits in your personal and professional life. Learn to say no when it's out of your comfort zone. It's vitally important for your overall well-being to make time to switch off. Let the rest of the world take a back seat for an hour or two and relax. Both your mind and body will thank you for it. I am in favour of a nod in the noon if you can afford in your schedule. Go for a long bathing. Spend time in nature. Work in your garden. Get a massage. Watch a comedy. You often fall into the trap of working long into the night believing that you will get more work done. The irony? You rarely do. You are usually so tired that you don't feel good and the day after is a write-off. Work is good but don't overdo it.

SUGGESTED STRATEGY

> *"I promise you nothing is as chaotic as it seems. Nothing is worth your health. Nothing is worth poisoning yourself into stress, anxiety, and fear."*
>
> Steve Maraboli, *Unapologetically You*

As your small changes become habit, you can continue to add more healthy choices to your diet. When you decide to have good health, you have half of your health. But understand: Healing is a matter of time. You should decide and balance your daily diet with carbohydrates, proteins and fats with the help of a good nutritionist. Similarly, I would advise you to join a fitness program instead of doing exercises at your home for better results. I hope that after reading this chapter you will feel motivated and empowered to make constructive changes in your life and learn to participate in your own physical and emotional healing and development.

ASSIGNMENT

1. Look out for a good nutritionist and decide your daily diet.
2. Join a fitness program.
3. Get a full Ayurvedic body massage this month and continue further if you like it.
4. Listen to Dr. Deepak Chopra's audio program *Magical Mind, Magical Body*.

VISUALIZATION

You should paste poster of your favourite movie star on walls of your room and should compare yourself with him/her while doing any physical activity or exercise. It will boost your self-esteem. Remember: Health is the greatest of human blessings. Don't wait for a serious ailment to have a health consciousness. Your body listens what your mind speaks.

SELF SUGGESTION

I am in great physical shape. I take care of my body's needs because I love and respect my body.

Bear in mind: Super achievers always keep their commitments.

[*Promise & Put Your Signature Here With Date*]

28

Is Your Life In Balance?

OBJECTIVES

- To learn the "Law of Balanced Life",
- To excel in the seven areas of life and
- To make a commitment to increase three assets.

GOLDEN GUIDANCE

> *"I believe that being successful means having a balance of success stories across the many areas of your life. You can't truly be considered successful in your business life if your home life is in shambles."*
>
> Zig Ziglar (1926–2012)

GOLDEN TOUCH

> *"Making money isn't hard in itself... What's hard is to earn it doing something worth devoting one's life to."*
>
> Carlos Ruiz Zafón, *The Shadow of the Wind*

We all know the story of the greedy king named Midas who was fond of having and counting gold. One day while he was counting his gold a stranger came from nowhere and said he would grant him a wish. The king was pleased and said, "I would like everything I touch to turn to gold." So the stranger said, "Starting tomorrow morning with the sun rays you will get the golden touch." But the next day when he woke up, he touched the bed, his clothes, and everything turned to gold. He was getting hungry and he said to himself, "I can't eat and drink gold." Just about that time his daughter came running and he hugged her and she turned into a golden statue. The king bowed his head and started crying. The stranger who gave the wish came again and asked, "What would you rather have, your food and loving daughter or lumps of gold and her golden statue?" The king cried and said, "I will give up all my gold. Please give me my daughter back." The stranger said to the king, "You have become prudent than before," and he reversed the magic charm. The king got his daughter back and learned a lesson that he never forgot for the rest of his life.

Moral of the story:

1. Money can purchase you expensive medicine but it can't purchase you excellent health.
2. Money can purchase you an address but it can't purchase you a happy home.
3. Money can purchase you an engagement for the nighttime but it can't purchase you true love.
4. It's fine to have money and the things that money can buy, but it is fine, as well, to check occasionally and confirm that you haven't ignored or lost the things that money can't purchase.
5. Money can buy the things but not the happiness.

LAW OF BALANCED LIFE

"It's all about quality of life and finding a happy balance between work and friends and family."

Philip Green, a British retail giant

My point is that if you put yourself in place of Midas, you'll find and feel the lesson of balance. I am in favour of finding a balance between what you can acquire and what you can use. Gentleman! Please find a balance between work, love and play. Balance is always well-designed. How many things do you juggle in one day? Do you sometimes think like with all this juggling you have lost yourself in the process? Our lives are a mixture of different roles. The test is to balance what we have to do with what we get pleasure from and crave to do. It does not mean doing everything you can. You must have some targets in different areas of life. I strongly speak that one needs to balance his inner and outer life. Inner life includes psychological development, love, physical shape and outer life includes occupation, society, family and enjoyment. Live a balanced life. Live a life of order, rhythm and harmony because balance is the fruit of a successful life. Balance is beautiful.

An athlete is the best example to display the importance of balance. When an athlete trains for any competition, he requires combination of sleep, exercise and nutrition. He also needs to keep himself motivated by maintaining the right mindset. Any imbalance can lead to an upsetting defeat. Now consider yourself. Are you not an athlete? Yes! You are an athlete who is running in the game of life. You also require all the things—sleep, exercise, nutrition and not to mention the right personal philosophy. In fact, if one can maintain the discipline and dedication of an athlete, he can excel in his personal and professional life at an outstanding level.

So, *here is the golden tip*: "The common idea of balanced living is that you divide your life into seven areas—family, finances, career, friends, social life, health and spirituality. Balance is all about rhythm and harmony. Every human being should try to give the same amounts of consideration to each of these seven areas." In fact, the art of balanced life is a lost art. Our elders were much better in terms of having a perfect balance between all the areas of life. How can we have a balance in our life?

FORMULA OF ONE

"One thing at a time, all things in succession. That which grows fast withers as rapidly; and that which grows slow endures."

J.G. Holland (1819–1881)

You must ask yourself, what is the single best activity in all seven areas you can do in each of the zones that will have the best constructive effect on your life and help you in becoming a man of balance? This is real greatness. I am a seeker and artist of truth. I take inspiration from truths of life. I will suggest the "Formula of One." Take one morning walk for yourself. Take one evening family walk with your wife and children. Make one daily call to a friend and for that I recommend to follow alphabets. Do one daily meditation session for your spiritual growth. Talk to one person per day in your office. Get one big achievement per year for your career. Do one big investment each year. The key is to simplify the things. You can concentrate in a better way on few things. You have to get better every day in every way. Eliminate the unnecessary things and people from your life. Give a personal definition to your life balance. The right balance for you today will possibly be dissimilar for you tomorrow. You'll feel less stress when you are in balance. "Achievement and Enjoyment" are two sides of one coin i.e. life. How will you implement formula of one? Remember these golden words "Everything starts in your mind."

PERFECT HUMAN BEING—MOST IMPORTANT NATIONAL ASSET

> *"Nothing is permanently perfect. But there are perfect moments and the will to choose what will bring about more perfect moments."*
>
> Mary Balogh, *Simply Perfect*

Do you at times consider whether your life is in balance? It is effortless to identify if you live a balanced life, because, if you implement, then you take pleasure in each minute and each second. These days the world all the time tries to throw you out of balance.

This "Perfect Person" who has a perfect life is the ultimate human that is in making when you are reading this book and the moment you will finish the last sentence of this book and start living my laws, you will be a perfect person who has perfect health, perfect relationships, financial independence, wealth and freedom and your life will be full of love, joy and spiritual bliss.

HEALTH IS FIRST WEALTH

"The way you think, the way you behave and the way you eat can influence your life by 30 to 50 years."

Deepak Chopra, an American physician

Health is the biggest wealth and I would call it first wealth because without good health you will not be able to enjoy the life in its full swing. Moreover, you will put more energy in your daily activities with good health. Your mind will also function smoothly as the old saying goes, "Sound mind lives in a sound body." You should maintain a proper record of your blood pressure, ECG reports, Sugar levels and other tests on monthly basis and you must see a good doctor if there is any problem in any test. You will feel relaxed, full of vitality and in an ecstatic state of bliss all day long if you are in perfect health. This aspect has been discussed in detail at appropriate place in this book. (See Chapter 27)

EMOTIONAL INTELLIGENCE QUOTIENT (EQ)

"EQ is unique intersection of both, heart and head."

David Caruso, an American actor

Nearly all the leading experts agree that emotional intelligence is an extremely important skill for personal and professional success. In the speedy business life today, people use more time on computers, mobiles and messengers calls than they do in personal communication. You're supposed to reconstruct broken conversations, cryptic voicemails, and abbreviated text messages to make out how to go on. In this progressively more multifarious web-society, emotional intelligence is more imperative than ever before. It's no top secret that emotional intelligence is at the core of life success.

You must have good connection with your family members. Your relation with your brother, sister, mother and father is equally important as your relation with your wife, son and daughter. Your friends are angels in your life. You must love your family members and friends and more importantly help them timely otherwise they will not be caring, loyal and empowering. The golden rule is reflected in relationships. All the great relationships are built on three things, proximity, intimacy and commitment. You must treat others as you want to be treated. The one thing that is to be remembered is that the commitment is towards values basically. For example, you stand behind your friend because you believe in what he believes in. Your friend was honest and that's why you stood behind him. You can use this affirmation to boost any relationship: "I and (Insert name) have the perfect relationship of love and commitment." Remember: You do not have to be exceptionally superhuman to be successful but you have to be exceptionally genuine to be successful.

The rules are changing. We are being judged by not just how physically attractive we are but also by how well we understand ourselves, our goals and our responses and more importantly how well we understand others and their feelings. In relationships, sympathy and empathy are important tools. You express sympathy in the way how you feel the pain of other but empathy is much more – it is expressing the pain as felt by the victim. Emotional Intelligence Quotient (EQ) is as much relevant to an organization as to a family.

I feel in the approaching five or ten years we will notice more sophisticated and serious research on Emotional Intelligence. Emotional skills and abilities will rule the world. One will need this intelligence to maintain and excel in his family, in school, and at work. In my own view, it is much more important than personality and IQ aspects and for this, I see both teachers and parents need to work on their children, because I endorse psychologists who opine that emotional literacy is effective in earlier years.

PERSONAL ARENA

> *"Man's main task in life is to give birth to himself, to become what he potentially is. The most important product of his effort is his own personality."*
>
> Erich Fromm (1900–1980)

You must be good enough in your personal arena also. Being progressive in personal life gives you a sense of satisfaction. You should pursue your left studies. You should get training or attend workshops for your career advancement. You should write blog or maintain a website to be creative. You can travel to other countries or within your country to have a perfect vacation time. You can also join art classes or cookery classes. You can also learn to play your favourite instrument like guitar etc. You can join yoga classes or take therapy for a past hurt. You can learn meditation in meditation camps. You can start to go to your religious places and offer prayers. You can search for a perfect living guru to advance spiritually.

The idea is to develop yourself up to the full potential. I teach self-leadership i.e. to lead oneself, which means to lead inside out. Discover your greatness by an analysis of your talents and potential, and believe me, if you nurture these, you will become a guaranteed leader.

COMMUNITY LIFE

> *"I alone, cannot change the world, but I can cast a stone across the waters to create many ripples."*
>
> Mother Teresa (1910–1997)

"A man not only needs to know how to fish, he needs to have the freedom to do it and a place to do it." This famous quote of Bill Ayers who is an American elementary education theorist emphasizes the importance of a nice society. I think that's where community comes in. We have to help

each other, and we feel government has a very important role therein. The societies in which you are living also demand active contribution from your side. You should help your locality in looking great and operating perfectly by taking diverse initiatives. You should organize and be a part of community activities. You should be member of your professional organizations and play your part honestly.

You should carry out some charitable work also to help others and try to make a difference by sincere desire to support the under- privileged members of the society. You should also make enough contributions in any national cause and campaigns.

BALANCE RELATES TO GOALS

> *"I have never met a woman, or man, who stated emphatically, 'Yes, I have it all.' Because no matter what any of us has—and how grateful we are for what we have—no one has it all."*
>
> Sheryl Sandberg, *Lean In: Women, Work, and the Will to Lead*

How do you attain balance while working in the direction of your goals? Normally, our lives get out of balance when we have not clearly defined our goals or we are not energetically working in the direction of our goals. Once you set your goals in each of the seven areas, you will and have to definitely realign the time management from time to time, as Work–Life Balance is not a one-shot deal. You must make changes necessary to achieve the goals but at the same time reserve the time for other areas also to keep your life in balance, or else you will have a lot of money to spend on your ill health and divorce case. At the end of the life, if you are not a good husband in the eyes of your wife, a good father in the eyes of your children, a good citizen in the eyes of society and a good friend in the eyes of your friends what is the purpose of your life.

SUGGESTED STRATEGY

"Healthy citizens are the greatest asset any country can have."
Winston Churchill (1874–1965)

There are three assets, as I have found, first is your health, second your relations and third your money. You should be committed in increasing these assets. You should value your health at top most priority. Don't spend your hard earned money on unnecessary things. Invest more and spend less. Plan before you shop. You should make yourself count by helping and supporting your friends and relatives when they need you most. Make every effort to increase these three assets and be cautious when you lose bit of them.

ASSIGNMENT

1. Take an online test of EQ.
2. Define your roles in each capacity, like a great father, great husband, great teacher and great human etc.
3. Listen to audio program *Brilliant Life* by Michael Heppell.

VISUALIZATION

You must visualize succeeding in all the seven areas in full details with sense intelligence. Remember: We'll not get a second chance as King Midas did.

SELF SUGGESTION

I am becoming better every day in every way. I am living a balanced life.

Bear in mind: Super achievers always keep their commitments.

[*Promise & Put Your Signature Here With Date*]

29
How Relevant Are You?

OBJECTIVES

- To learn the "Law of Sharing",
- To understand that significance glows, and
- To serve through your calling.

GOLDEN GUIDANCE

"I cannot believe that the purpose of life is to be happy. I think the purpose of life is to be useful, to be responsible, and to be compassionate. It is, above all to matter, to count, to stand for something, to have made some difference that you lived at all."

Leo Calvin Rosten (1908–1997)

GREEDY PERSONS HAVE AN UNHAPPY END

"Earth provides enough to satisfy every man's needs but not every man's greed."

Mahatma Gandhi (1869–1948)

A farmer named Pahom said to his wife, "If I had plenty of land, I shouldn't fear the Devil himself!" The devil who was listening accepted the challenge and said, "If you will reach your starting point by sunset that day, the entire area of land your route encloses will be yours, but if you do not reach your starting point, you will lose and receive no land." He stayed out as late as possible, marking out land until just before the sun sets. Towards the end, he realized he was far from the starting point and so he ran back as fast as he could. He finally arrived at the starting point just as the sun set, but exhausted from the run, Pahóm dropped dead. His servant buried him in an ordinary grave only six feet long. This story is based on "How Much Land Does a Man Require?" which is an 1886 short story by Leo Tolstoy about a man who, in his lust for land, forfeits everything.

Moral of the story:

1. Greedy persons have an unhappy end.
2. There is a very thin difference between comfort and greed.
3. There is no torrent like greed.
4. Greed is a never-ending tunnel which exhausts the person.
5. Greed is a never-ending exertion to satisfy the ego without ever reaching satisfaction.

HOW RELEVANT ARE YOU?

> *"Experience has shown, and a true philosophy will always show, that a vast, perhaps the larger portion of truth arises from the seemingly irrelevant."*
>
> Edgar Allan Poe, *The Mystery of Marie Rogêt*

Yes, you read it right. It is not "How successful are you?" It is "Who are you?" It is "What do you stand for?" I am talking of your value, your relevancy and not magnitude of your success. Albert Schweitzer (1875–1965) who received Nobel Peace Prize in 1952 for his philosophy of "Relevance for Life" also acknowledged the principle of sharing. He said: "The purpose of human life is to serve, and to show compassion and the will to help others." My spiritual master used to say: "I want to be part of grand tales that are told to inspire and for them the only way, I have, is to be relevant."

So, *here is the golden tip:* "Our favourite words are 'Mine! Mine! Mine!' and we use them all the time. The only thing, we share is our tales and not our belongings. But is it divine to act in this way? Nothing is ever owned by us, things are only entrusted. People will talk about you for generations because of your relevancy and not for your riches." In fact, life itself characterizes a shared energy dispensed into the world generously by the Divine Creator – "the One in Whom we live and move and have our being."

GENERATIVITY OR STAGNATION

> *"It is not enough to be busy... The question is: what are we busy about?"*
>
> Henry David Thoreau (1817–1862)

You have to be creative if you want to leave this world with a feeling of satisfaction. A student of Sigmund Freud, Erik Erikson attributes generativity or stagnation to the age of 25–64 years. Generativity is a sense of productivity or making contributions to the society. The primary developmental task during the middle age is to raise the family and guiding the future generations. The persons with generativity are happy with their life and mission. On the other hand, a person who is self-centred and unable or unwilling to help society move forward develops a feeling of stagnation and remains dissatisfied due to lack of creativity. Do you have a simple wish to get respect from the people? Yes, everybody does. Everybody wants to become but nobody wants do what it takes to become. You have to be someone who matters.

LOVE-IN-ACTION

> *"If we have no peace, it is because we have forgotten that we belong to each other."*
>
> Mother Teresa (1910–1997)

If you want to succeed as bad as you want to breathe, then only you will and can be successful. But can you feel the same breathlessness for others' success? Do you want to act like life catalyst? Do you want to carry your significance? You can reap real rewards when you reflect the fullness of your calling. I give you my law: "Success is in directly proportionate to our significance and money is the byproduct of this process."

You should personally measure success in terms of the contributions you make to the life of your fellow human beings. Sharing is significance. Love in its true sense can only grow if it is available at no cost. People can only grow if they are available at no cost. Dale Carnegie was an American writer, lecturer, and the developer of famous courses in self-improvement, salesmanship, corporate training, public speaking and interpersonal skills. He also supported the law of sharing. He said: "The world is full of people who are grabbing and self-seeking. So the rare individual who unselfishly tries to serve others has an enormous advantage. He has little competition." I will not hesitate to call "sharing" as "Love-in-Action".

ACCLAIMED GUARDIAN OF WORLD'S LARGEST FAMILY

> *"You are forgiven for your happiness and your successes only if you generously consent to share them."*
>
> Albert Camus (1913–1960)

Our hero explains a story in his own words: I have been 9–10 years old. One day my shirt got a tear during playing. It was my beautiful and favourite shirt. I was cribbing. My father saw me crying and asked: "Why are you weeping?" My anger grew due to this question. I told him while weeping: "My shirt has torn." My father called me near him, held the shirt from the torn point and tore the complete shirt to pieces. I recollect: "I was even more hurt." He then made me understood – "See my son! Never get so deeply attached to something materialistic or lifeless things if you want constant peace, comfort, respect and satisfaction. Love fellow human beings, adore human feelings, love the duty towards mankind and work hard."

Our hero of the story is Subrata Roy Sahara, founder and chairman of Sahara Group of Companies. I came across this story when I was reading *Navbaharat Times*, Dated 01 April, 2013. He started his journey with a vision that emotion is the key to success, with a meager savings of Rs. 2000 in the year 1978 with a table, two chairs, one small office, a lambretta scooter, and a staff of one clerk and a runner boy. He states: "My biggest achievement is that I am guardian of world's largest family—Sahara India Pariwar." He mentions, "Always be contented in receiving and be discontented in giving" is the golden law that his father gave to him. This quote of his father is once again a reflection of law of sharing.

Moral of the story:

1. Family traditions play a crucial role in development of a child.
2. Anyone with a vision, commitment and sharing can rise to top.
3. One should not develop too much addiction for lifeless things.
4. One must payback what he has got from the society.
5. Parents must spare some time for their children also.

SHARE EVEN AT THE COST OF YOUR DESIRE

> *"I have three precious things which I hold fast and prize. The first is gentleness; the second frugality; the third is humility, which keeps me from putting myself before others. Be gentle and you can be bold; be frugal and you can be liberal; avoid putting yourself before others and you can become a leader among men."*
>
> Laozi, a Chinese philosopher

This is an old story. A 15 year-old boy entered a hotel and asked, "How much is an ice cream sundae?" "Fifty rupees," replied the waiter. The little boy pulled his hand out of his pocket and counted the money he had. "Well, how much is a plain dish of ice cream?" he enquired. "Thirty-five rupees," the waiter replied. The little boy again counted his money. "I'll have the plain ice cream," he said. The waiter brought the ice cream, put the bill on the table and walked away. The boy finished the ice cream, paid the cashier and left. When the waiter came back, he found that there placed neatly beside the empty dish were fifteen rupees. You see, he could have the sundae but he chose the plain one because he had to leave a tip. In my view, the little boy depicted by his behaviour the principle of sharing. He demonstrated the age-old good manners that a gentleman of a civilized society has to observe. My question to you: "What would have you done if you were in his place?"

Moral of the story:

1. A gentle behaviour pleases everybody.
2. One has to sacrifice even his desires to get a good feeling from others.
3. One who shares outshines the selfish man.

LAW OF SHARING

> *"Whatever we possess becomes of double value when we have the opportunity of sharing it with others."*
>
> Jean-Nicolas Bouilly (1763–1842)

What do we call people who steal other's clothes? We call them a thief. What about the man who can clothe the undressed but does not? The food in your refrigerator belongs to the starving; the old used clothes in your box belong to the needy; the shoes decaying in your store belong to the barefooted; the money which you gather belongs to the deprived. The desirable quality of selfless sharing has long been taught by all the religions of the human race. If Edison did not invent the light bulb, we would have nothing to do but sleep when the sun set. If Graham didn't invent the telephone, we wouldn't have our precious cell phones today. In fact, the people with sharing attitude are the most valuable asset of a nation.

So, Share! Smile! Shine!

GIVE WHAT YOU WANT

The Bridge Builder

"An old man, going a lone highway,
Came, at the evening, cold and gray,
To a chasm, vast, and deep, and wide,
Through which was flowing a sullen tide.
The old man crossed in the twilight dim;
The sullen stream had no fear for him;
But he turned, when safe on the other side,
And built a bridge to span the tide.
"Old man," said a fellow pilgrim, near,
"You are wasting your strength with building here;
Your journey will end with the ending day;
You never again will pass this way;
You've crossed the chasm, deep and wide,
Why build this bridge at the evening tide?"
The builder lifted his old gray head:
"Good friend, in the path I have come," he said,
"There followeth after me today,
A youth, whose feet must pass this way,
This chasm, that has been as naught to me,
To that fair-haired youth may a pitfall be;
He, too, must cross in the twilight dim;
Good friend, I am building this bridge for him."

Will Allen Dromgoole

Everyone gets drilled with certain lessons in life. I was taught many laws – some through recurring demonstrations and some through distinct dominant experience. One of laws that has really got to my skull is "You grow when you share." I have always loved Will Allen Dromgoole's poem *The Bridge Builder* even as a child. I thought that I knew the meaning of the poem but in reality I really didn't know until I wrote the present book. I understood the old man's mission in life. The old man wanted to help the next generation journey down the road of life. The old builder had successfully gone through dangers in life. This act of building a bridge when he didn't have to do so created a controversy with a fellow traveller who raises the meaning of what seemed like a waste of time.

You will get what you want when you will share with other what you have because of the simple logic that others will give what they have. Zig Ziglar was an American author, salesman and motivational speaker. He also endorsed the principle of sharing. He asserted: "If we will help others get what they want we will in turn get what we want." If we want to be successful, we should consider ourselves servants of other people. What can we do to help them and make them better?

I am asking you to share your truthfulness, concern, passion, respect, weaknesses, experience and help. On the whole, what we want to do is to help others. "Increase the number of people you help and I promise you'll see increase in the number of people who help you." But how will we really convert success into significance? I give you a golden mantra to maximize the achievements, not only in business but also in life: "Commend, celebrate and commemorate your smallest success with people. You will see that this ritual will increase the successes. Your success will soon turn into the significance. Your light will start to glow."

HAVE YOU FIND YOUR BEST WAY TO LIVE?

> *"Have you had a kindness shown? Pass it on; 'Twas not given for thee alone, Pass it on; Let it travel down the years, Let it wipe another's tears, 'Til in Heaven the deed appears – Pass it on."*
>
> Henry Burton (1840–1930)

Most people are walking freaks, and they do not find out the best way to live this life, until just before they die. Ask them what do they want? They are always in run for positions, cars, big homes and big bank accounts. They are chasing their tails. There will never ever be a perfect tomorrow. In fact, I give an advice: "If you want to really experience the mental pain, start wishing different things." There will be another hilltop to climb; another objective to accomplish. And, what a man really wants has it already, inside of him. And in fact, nobody actually wants the materialistic things.

HIDDEN MAGICAL PULL

> *"The things you own end up owning you. It's only after you lose everything that you're free to do anything."*
>
> Chuck Palahniuk, *Fight Club*

Always buying the latest, greatest, most expensive stuff doesn't lead to a better life. I want you to imagine yourself in a situation wherein people in the world don't have eyes or no one can see except you, would you still buy the big mansions, luxurious cars and expensive clothes etc. What we really crave for, is the feeling of possessing them like appreciation, internal calm and feeling of being in creamy layer. Visual and print media exposes celebrity lifestyles of mansions, cars, clothes, and conditions us to believe if we have all that too, it will give us the good life. We want respect and attention from our social circle. We want "oohs and ahhs". Leadership experts call it "Magical Pull" of materialism.

WHO AM I BECOMING?

> *"It's never too late to be what you might have been."*
>
> George Eliot (1819–1880)

Everyone seeks the answers to Life's Big Questions in his own ways. One of the common ways is comparison. I have observed that everybody counts our success by the quality of things we have rather than by the quality of person we have become. You are chasing goals that will never make you blissful. People count the money or material things you have instead of the number of people you have won over. Who I am becoming is far more important than what I own. So what am I asking you to do? Gentleman! Make a start of sharing. It can be a small sharing, but make a start. It's never too late to make a brand new start. It is a morning whenever you open the eyes. It is branding yourself, the Big Reputation, you need to sustain and backup. The real personality comes from real genuineness and THAT my friend comes from inside. It can't be purchased.

DON'T LET THINGS DEFINE YOU

> *"They have succeeded in accumulating a greater mass of objects, but the joy in the world has grown less."*
>
> Fyodor Dostoyevsky, *The Brothers Karamazov*

Everybody is fond of having aesthetic and luxurious things around. Everybody wants that his clothes, his accessories and his furniture etc. are of great class, and once in life time, everybody makes a commitment to have a first class life, and it's not a sin. Oscar Wilde put it rightly: "Anyone who lives within their means suffers from a lack of imagination." If you feel rich, you'll become rich. I tell you to carry beauty, luxury and comfort with yourself wherever you go. The person with rich mentality admires extraordinary music. He loves to be in extraordinary fun places. But they do not let things define who they are. I have found after observing the wealthiest people that: "A rich person do not use his possessions to characterize him." Richness is a byproduct of your main products. You are always a brand in the making. Take my case. I want to be known by my teaching, my works, my deeds, my books, my keynote lectures and not through my riches. Richness is a byproduct of your main products.

SUCCESS v. SIGNIFICANCE

> *"Until you make peace with who you are, you will never be contented with what you have."*
>
> Doris Mortman, American writer

What of success? I have found few characteristics of success. It is unpredictable, second it is specific and third it is conditional. As to its lack of reliability, success may be held one moment and taken away the next. Success is relative to a focus. You may be great at business but fail as a husband/wife, father/mother or friend. And not everyone holds success to the same level. In any set of circumstances you may be a huge winner in people's eyes or you may be a loser. Success comes from selfish efforts when you help yourself.

Significance requires success as a stepping stone. You add values to yourself and then to others. This difference is going to change your thinking pattern. Contentment is a matter of giving than having. Yes, I believe success can be a sin in vacuum. Success comes when you get what you want whereas significance comes when you help others in getting what they want.

Your circle of influence will increase with significance as it is like a chain reaction. That's why, I produce leaders, and believe a true leader generates leaders, because a leader influences all those who seek inspirations from him. A great leader becomes a resource for producing good leaders. So seek significance and stop chasing success. Look at the life of all the great people. They sought happiness in significance after they crossed the line of success. They inspired others to leave their cages after they had left their cage. This is true success and makes a successful person—a person of significance. Stephen S. Wise also once said: "An unshared life is not living." I teach significance which is highest level of excellence – 'Relevance' – to be exact – being able to matter. Relevance and not the excellence is the highest manifestation of human life. I believe in living a life worth copying.

SERVE THROUGH YOUR CALLING

> *"I have come to believe that each of us has a personal calling that's as unique as a fingerprint."*
>
> Oprah Winfrey, American talk show host

We confirm our reality by sharing. The amount of sharing tells the humanity of a person. I suggest you to launch a business or do a job – a "Career of Significance" – as a way to share your obsession, your talents, and your understanding with the rest of the humankind. Ask yourself how you can dispense your talents in the best possible way that benefits others. And, then move ahead step by step starting with a little step. Gautam Buddha, the founder of Buddhist Religion, also confirmed the principle of sharing in his life. He said: "Thousands of candles can be lighted from a single candle, and the life of the candle will not be shortened." Happiness never decreases by being shared. He who shares does not lessen, but greatens his life.

In your business or job, never concentrate on what you can get from others (how much money you can make etc.), instead concentrate on what you can give to others (how much you can help give etc.). Sigmund Freud, an Austrian neurologist who came to be known as the founding father of psychoanalysis, called sharing as poetry in the prose of life. In fact, I suggest you to devise various ways to cast a positive impact on the society through your job or business. I believe that everybody has a matchless personal calling as matchless as a fingerprint. The best way to be successful is to find out what you love, and then find a way, to offer it to others in the form of service or product. You must also enjoy the work, and permit the power of the universe to guide you.

In each transaction, recover your actual worth and then add some additional gifts as reflection of your belief in the principle of sharing. Remember, I am asking you to over-deliver on a regular basis in your business and over-perform in your job, deliver more than expected in each transaction. And, if you identify that you are not earning money in spite of the fact that you are making the dreams of people come true, I suggest you to look in your offer. You must get all the answers from the customers' feedback, customers' needs and your true research of the market trends. You should always concentrate on two things: firstly improve the contents of your offer each time and secondly adequately advertize to attract good number of customers.

LET YOUR LIGHT SHINE

> *"Those who bring sunshine into the lives of others cannot keep it from themselves."*
>
> James M. Barrie (1860–1937)

Success ends on the day you die. So apply the principle of living the life after death and achieve significance. Gentleman! Always remember the golden words: "Success is in close proximity if people are not making payment for your work." Never hope for any return (money) and just concentrate on becoming a person of significance (doing your job) and the success will follow. This is another way of thinking, another way of being. Let your light shine. Significance always lasts. It will outlast you. Shine within you so that it can shine on someone else. Let your light shine. We must share (let your light shine) the fruits of success (light) with society. Success is your light that must shine others' life also. Everybody is a dreamer so we must help others in achieving their aims in life without any hope of any return.

Napoleon Hill was another person who believed in law of sharing. He had an amazing gift of helping others by sharing his knowledge. He was born in a one-room cabin near the Appalachian town of Pound, in Southwest Virginia. Hill's mother died when he was nine years old, and his father remarried two years later. At the age of 13, Hill began writing as a reporter for small-town newspapers. He later used his earnings as a reporter to enter law school, but soon he had to withdraw for financial reasons. He became an advisor to President Franklin D. Roosevelt from 1933 to 1936. He authored one of the best books on success philosophy *Think And Grow Rich* (1937) which still remains and tops the bestseller list. He said: "It is literally true that you can succeed in best and quickest way by helping others to succeed." The law of sharing is indispensable to achieve success. This can give you biggest adventures of your life. Can you deduce the formula of success: "Give your best to the world and in return the best will come to you." You can ask any good author or expert for guidance. A true motivational writer learns from his life so he doesn't leave his personal life out of his books, lectures and workshops. Real life gives the best lessons. He is always accessible and personable. I urge you: "If you have knowledge, let your light shine and let others light their candles in it."

INTERDEPENDENCE

> *"Coming together is a beginning; keeping together is progress; working together, togetherness is success."*
>
> Henry Ford (1863–1947)

Each person needs other people to help them in achieving their dreams. Leon Duguit, a respected French jurist propounded the thesis of Interdependence of men and the concept of social solidarity. Stephen R. Covey also talked this concept in his audio programs. U.S. President Bill Clinton read Covey's *Seven Habits of Highly Effective People* and invited him to Camp David to counsel him on how to integrate the book into his presidency. I always cite his one quote: "Organizational behaviour is individual behaviour collectivized." Our society has interdependence, and I tell you that your attitude towards other people will have a mammoth impact on your forthcoming success. I want you to seriously consider a thought of G.B. Shaw who was an Irish playwright and a co-founder of the London School of Economics. He said: "If you have an apple and I have an apple and we exchange apples, then you and I will still each have one apple. But if you have an idea and I have an idea and we exchange these ideas, then each of us will have two ideas." Dependent people need others to have what they crave. The level of help depends on their physical, mental, emotional and intellectual level. Independent people can have what they crave through their own endeavour. Independent people can be high-quality individual producers or performers, but they won't be high-quality leaders or team players. As an interdependent person, you have the opening to share yourself genuinely, significantly, with others, because you have reach to the enormous resources and potential of other people. Interdependent people have the intellectual ripeness to think and act in this way. A man without interdependence is simply an animal. In fact, friendly cooperation is the sweetener in human life.

RESOURCEFUL PSYCHE GROUP

> *"Lofty words cannot construct an alliance or maintain it, only concrete deeds do that."*
>
> John F. Kennedy (1917–1963)

Friendship is the fruit of sharing. Friendship is among life's sacred gifts. I call my friends angels. "Friends are your chosen family." Soon you and your friends get transformed into what I call Resourceful Psyche Group (RPG). The idea behind resourceful psyche group is to gather good psyche people with special resources from diverse fields to help each other as a friend. I love this word "Psyche" because I use it to refer human intelligence in totality – conscious mind, unconscious mind and the soul. You and your friends will get everything and every help from resources within this psyche group.

I consider human being as the biggest resource than all material and other resources. A source can be a person, a thing, or an activity. Whereas, a resource is an available supply that you need and which can be drawn on when needed from that source, for instance a sun is a source of sunshine or solar energy. All the successful persons turn sources into resources. This is not a new concept. Indian emperor, Akbar, a contemporary of Elizabeth I of England, attracted nine best contemporary minds of extraordinary talents, who shone brightly in their respective fields, were known as Akbar's nine gems. They were: Abul Fazl who documented the history meticulously. Faizi was a poet who composed verse in the Persian language. Tansen was a classical singer of an unparalleled fame. Birbal was famous for his wit as well as wisdom. Raja Todar Mal was Akbar's finance minister. Raja Man Singh was lieutenant of Akbar. Abdul Rahim Khan-I-Khan was a poet. Fagir Aziao Din and Mullan Do Piaza were two advisors. There were some other persons also. Daswant, the painter, Abud us-Samad, a brilliant calligrapher and Mir Fathullah Shirazi, who was a financier, philosopher, astrologer, and an astute physician, were also part of his court. You can find an observance of this group formation in the life of Benjamin Franklin also. He and his acquaintances formed a club *Junto* in 1727 with different people from diverse occupations and backgrounds for mutual development. A sense of mutual confidence, mutual allegiance and mutual benevolence develops between people who are well-known with each other for a long period of time. A "RPG" can be the source for the supply of resources you are looking for.

A Resourceful Psyche Group (RPG) consists of two or more minds working energetically and collectively in faultless synchronization towards a common and precise goal. It is about developing and enlarging the area of overlap in form of area of agreement between two or more individuals. It is about finding the solutions and possibilities. The members of group contact regularly, interact frequently, influence mutually and most importantly have a common sentiment of camaraderie. Another observance can be found in the life of C.S. Lewis who had a great faith in his friend J.R.R. Tolkien. They were both members of the informal literary discussion group known as the Inklings. He said: "Friendship is unnecessary, like philosophy, like art ... It has no value; rather it is one of those things that give value to survival." We see reflections in practical life also in form of associations, clubs and societies. True friendship gets reflected in this group.

RPG v. MPG

> *"When someone loves you, the way they say your name is different. You know that your name is safe in their mouth."*
>
> Jess C. Scott, *The Intern*

We want social benefits that come with materialistic things. If you are a "teaching freak" like me, you don't give a damn to Ferrari people; success to you is people like Aristotle, Socrates and Vivekananda. It is the social circle that matters. If you are an environmentalist, and you buy a hummer, you can be excommunicated from a Resourceful Psyche Group (RPG) which believes in environment protection.

Your Psyche Group shares same values and same visions as you do. So going for a Psyche Group who believes in you is the most important step you have to take to create your own identity and value. Once you do that no external stimulus can move you, not even the majority group – MPG–Most Popular Group – that is a group of materialistic people who have nothing to do with Resourceful Psyche Group (RPG).

RIPPLE EFFECT

> *"Whenever I found out anything remarkable, I have thought it my duty to put down my discovery on paper, so that all ingenious people might be informed thereof."*
>
> Antonie van Leeuwenhoek (1632–1723)

If you drop a stone into a pool of water, there will be a ripple effect extending all throughout that pool. I have a small circle of friends, with an outer expansive ring around it that includes acquaintances, akin to the ripple effect on a pool of water. I am asking you to behave like Angels who are ready to help others. Your action is the pebble that must produce ripple effect in your surroundings.

SHINING SHARING—CSR

> *"Money is like manure. It stinks when you pile it; it grows when you spread it."*
>
> Jehangir Ratanji Dadabhoy Tata (1904–1993)

Tata Motors has similar goals of sharing, significance and relevance with respect to providing low-cost transportation in the form of the Nano Car. Today's buzzword, Corporate Social Responsibility or CSR has been part of the Tata Group ever since the days of Jamsetji Tata. Even while he was busy setting up textile ventures, he always thought of his workers' welfare and requirements of the country. From granting scholarships for further studies abroad in 1892 to supporting Gandhiji's campaign for racial equality in South Africa to giving the country its first science centre, hospital and atomic research centre to providing relief and rehabilitation to natural disaster affected places – they have done it all. Tata initiated various labour welfare laws, like the establishment of Welfare Department was introduced in 1917 and enforced by law in

1948 or Maternity Benefit was introduced in 1928 and enforced by law in 1946. Over the years, the Tata philosophy to "Give back what you get" has been followed by all their enterprises across India. Be it relief measures, rural development, health care, education and art and culture, they have been very forthcoming. Tata Group is loved by the people in India, not just by their employees, for the contributions their companies have made to Indian society. Tata Steel bagged the corporate social responsibility award at the seventh edition of "India Business Leader Awards 2012" (IBLA) – Asia's most distinguished awards for excellence in leadership, held in New Delhi at The Lalit, Connaught Place, on January 17, 2012. The Godrej Group has constructed schools, medical clinics, and living facilities for employees. Sahara Group of Companies has adopted 1000 Indian villages. How many companies anywhere could make that claim?

REBUILDING A NEW WORLD—REDISCOVERY OF HUMAN POTENTIAL

> *"Whatever we possess becomes of double value when we have the opportunity of sharing it with others."*
>
> Jean-Nicolas Bouilly (1763–1842)

Habitats are specific to a population. Each population has its own habitat. For example, a population of ants has its own habitat. But several populations may share a habitat. For example, in a small pond several aquatic populations may co-exist in the same water at the same time. An aquarium is a good example of a shared habitat. We can always build a new world. We should start from selfless sharing. We will have to maintain the values of accommodation and cooperation. The world has not seen the beautiful living yet. The best is yet to be.

PASS YOUR LEGACY

"Our greatest responsibility is to pass on a legacy that the coming generations can be proud of."

Shiv Khera, Indian author on motivation

You should know that you are creating today a legacy for tomorrow. Your legacy is the "Best Gift" you can give to coming generations. Socrates passed a legacy to Plato; Plato passed a legacy to Aristotle; Aristotle passed a legacy to Alexander the Great. Knowledge must be passed otherwise it would perish. A quote of Todd R. Tresidder, a financial coach can be the guiding star: "If you die right now while reading this sentence, what would your legacy be? What incomplete work do you have?" We have to finish our lives with best end possible. Nobody wants to leave a burden to loved ones after they die. Successful people want to be remembered lovingly. Successful people believe in leaving an inheritance that people can cherish.

SUGGESTED STRATEGY

"Those who have much are often greedy, those who have little always share."

Oscar Wilde (1854–1900)

Significance should be started from this moment onwards. Start with your child or your poor neighbour. Real love begins to end never. Forget the dollars and care for people. Stop investing in shares and invest in sharing. Don't fall into the trap of "first being rich and then share". When you will be successful you will be more able to shine your light with much more glow and influence. But however dim your light is, still you can shine it on few if not on many, and eventually there will be ripple effect.

ASSIGNMENT

1. Decide your legacy and let it pass on to next generations.
2. Make a contribution in your profession by serving and training the needy persons freely.
3. Donate your old and unused articles, things and goods to a foundation which is working for the underprivileged.
4. Listen to the Audio program *Born To Win* by Zig Ziglar.

VISUALIZATION

Always deal with your fellow men with the *Life-Image After Death* in your mind. "If you want a wise answer," said Goethe, "ask a reasonable question." For example you can ask yourself: How will people remember you after your death? Whose life would you like yours to be like? I mean you must find your revealed destiny, love your profession and relive your own bliss by sharing your heritage with next generations. Remember: Pahóm died out of greed.

SELF SUGGESTION

I am overjoyed to live my revealed divine-destiny and I create value in other peoples' lives through my legacy.

Bear in mind: Super achievers always keep their commitments.

[*Promise & Put Your Signature Here With Date*]

30

Will You Dare To Begin From This End?

OBJECTIVES

- To learn the "Law of Beginning",
- To understand that you create change by action, and
- To start a chain reaction by sharing of the ideas.

GOLDEN GUIDANCE

> *"Don't let life discourage you; everyone who got where he is had to begin where he was."*
>
> Richard L. Evans (1906–1971)

IT'S TIME TO PUT IDEAS INTO ACTION

> *"Every new beginning comes from some other beginning's end."*
>
> Seneca (4 BC–AD 65)

The book's job is just about to finish. This is not an end because every man makes new beginning when some other makes an end. This is a new beginning for you. In parting, I hope that this book will help you in recovery of your true potential. I expect that the laws of this book will maximize your personal and professional achievements. Certainly, you must have done your logical share of thinking on the laws and ideas I championed.

You must have read this book with all your senses. You must have read, saw and felt every word. I mean you must have read, reread, taught, thought deeply about and tried to relate the laws to situations of your life. These laws are so universal, in verity, that they can be regarded as laws like gravity. However, at this time, it is time to act on these principles, for, no principle will work unless you begin to work on the principle.

At last, I am going to share with you an amazing Baton-Law of Beginning from an End. I have full faith in it. It is altogether different from persistence. Sometimes, you have to start fresh, and that's where this law helps a lot. It's about beginning from almost an end, whereas in persistence you continue despite little failures. I believe that no matter how hard the past was, you can always begin again. One best observance of this law of beginning was in the life of George Washington Carver, an American scientist, botanist, and inventor who discovered 325 uses for the peanut. He was recognized for his many achievements and talents and was subject of biographies and articles. In 1941, *Time* magazine dubbed Carver a Black Leonardo. He once said: "99% of failures come from people who have a habit of making excuses." My friend! You have always taken lame excuses but for your new self, please no excuses this time.

ABRAHAM LINCOLN—LIFE IS TOO SHORT FOR BEING WORRIED

Life Is Short

"Life is short, break the rules,

Forgive quickly; kiss slowly, love truly,

Laugh uncontrollably, and

Never regret anything that made you smile.

Twenty years from now,

You will be more disappointed

By the things that you didn't do

Than by the ones you did do.

So throw off the bowlines.

Sail away from the safe harbour.

Catch the trade winds in your sails.

Explore. Dream. Discover."

Mark Twain (1835–1910)

This life is too short to get worried and take rest. The time available is so less as compared to the targets set to be achieved. The life of Abraham Lincoln, the 16th president of the United States is also one of the most well-known examples of observance of law of beginning. He was in office during the American Civil War where he held the people together and is the only reason that the nation did not break into smaller parts. He also ended slavery in the U.S. by signing the Emancipation Proclamation. Here is a brief account of Lincoln's journey:

He was born on February 12, 1809 in a log cabin in Kentucky. His family was forced out of their home in 1816. He had to work to sustain them. His mother died in 1818. He failed in business in 1831. He contested for state legislature in 1832 and got defeated. He lost his job in 1832. He wanted to join law school but couldn't. He borrowed some money in 1833 from a friend to start a business and by the end of the year he was bankrupt. He used up the next 17 years of his life paying off this debt. He contested for state legislature again in 1834 and won. He was engaged in 1835 to be married but his sweetheart died and his heart was broken. He had a total nervous breakdown in 1836 and was in bed for six months. He contested to become speaker of the state legislature in 1838 and got defeated. He contested to become elector in 1840 and got crushed. He contested for Congress in 1843 and got beaten. He contested for Congress again in 1846, won and went to Washington. He contested for re-election to Congress in 1848 and got defeated. He applied in 1849 for the job of land officer in his home state but got rejected.

In 1854, he contested for Senate of the United States but got beaten. He fought for the Vice–Presidential nomination in 1856 at his party's national convention and got less than 100 votes. He contested for U.S. Senate again in 1858 but again got defeated. In 1860, Abraham Lincoln, six-foot-four-inch man, was elected as the sixteenth President of the United States. He served USA between 1861–1865. On April 14, 1865, Lincoln was assassinated at Ford's Theatre in Washington, D.C. while attending a play with his wife. Lincoln was faced with defeat throughout his life. He worked as a labourer on farms and flatboats, and even, for a while, as a store clerk in New Salem. He lost eight elections, twice failed in business and suffered a nervous breakdown. He became one of the greatest presidents in the history of U.S. Lincoln reached to the most powerful building of the world, the White House which is the official residence and principal workplace of the President of the United States, located at 1600 Pennsylvania Avenue Northwest, Washington, D.C. It has been the residence of every U.S. president since John Adams in 1800. In my view, probably the greatest example of law of beginning is Abraham Lincoln. He truly fulfilled the popular ethos in America: "Anyone can make it in America."

INDIA'S PRIME ICON 2012

> *"The world is round and the place which may seem like the end may also be the beginning."*
>
> Ivy Baker Priest (1905–1975)

It reminds me of an accident that changed the course of Indian cinema. It happened on July 26, 1982. Our superhero, a six-foot-two-inch man, sustained a severe injury while he was shooting a fighting scene with Puneet Issar for Manmohan Desai's "Coolie" at Bangalore University Campus. In a television interview, he told that he was supposed to fall on the table and then on to the ground for the scene but he mis-timed the jump and hit his abdomen on the edge of the table, which caused him internal bleeding. He required 17 bottles of blood. The actor was rushed to St. Philomena's Hospital where he underwent an emergency surgery. He was then flown to Mumbai to be treated at the Breach Candy Hospital and went through another surgery. He didn't come out of that one for a very long time and he was clinically dead for a couple of minutes. Then doctor pumped 40 ampules of cortizone injections and then he revived. He survived the accident but people tried to convince him to leave his film career.

This accident received worldwide coverage and made the movie a super hit. He entered into politics in 1984 and defeated Hemvanti Nandan Bahuguna, but soon left it. He fell into a major debt while running his company ABCL in its initial years. On his 61st birthday, he relaunched ABCL as AB Corp. He first gained popularity in the early 1970s as the "angry young man" of Hindi cinema, and has since appeared in over 180 Indian films in a career spanning more than four decades. He was born on October 11, 1942 in Allahabad to a well-known poet Harivansh Rai Bachchan and Teji Bachchan. He went to Sherwood College, a boarding school in the hill-station town of Nainital, and from there to Delhi University where he earned a double MA degree. When he was just trying to get a break in movies he was told to soften his deep voice. Nevertheless, it was soon realized that his deep rich voice was excellent for narration. He has provided narrations for several films. He had to go through 12 flop films before his 1973 super hit film *Zanjeer*. He made his debut in 1969 with film *Saat Hindustani*. The Government of India honoured him with the Padma Shri in 1984 and the Padma Bhusan in 2001 for his contributions towards the arts. Yes, he is none other than Amitabh Bachchan, who received India's Prime Icon award in 2012. He has been attributed with the Star of the Millennium by BBC in a poll. He is the first Asian actor having a wax model of his likeness displayed at Madame Tussaud's in London, U.K. The facial caricature of the Indian comic book character "Supremo" is based upon him. He is one of the best examples of observance of Law of Beginning. He does not use any techniques. He simply enjoys working in films, an observance of law of passionate profession. It's more instinctive rather than anything else. He is still one of the most influential and greatest actors in Indian film industry.

QUIT TALKING AND BEGIN DOING

"It's time to start living the life you have imagined."

Henry James (1843–1916)

One lesson we can learn from all the big personalities is that they talk less and work more. Yes my friend! It's time to quit talking and begin doing. Failure is the chance to begin once again with greater commitment. Your dreamed reality will not be actual reality unless you begin. Begin to be in present what you'll be in future. Live each day as a separate life. Be a leader.

When we have leaders in our family; we will have a revolution. Revolution comes from re+valuation. This revaluation will come from evaluation of yourself. Accordingly, keep revaluing yourself with the tools suggested in this Bible of Believers.

YOUR JOB IS TO BEGIN FROM HERE

"The chief beauty about time
Is that you cannot waste it in advance.
The next year, the next day, the next hour are lying ready for you,
As perfect, as unspoiled,
As if you had never wasted or misapplied
A single moment in all your life.
You can turn over a new leaf every hour
If you choose."

Arnold Bennett, an English writer and novelist

Will you dare to make a start? – Say YES because the top secret to a flourishing life is to have more beginnings than endings. Will you dare to begin from this end? Say YES because all the brilliance in this world comes from dare to begin. The place where you are at present and which seems like an end may be the beginning because the whole world is round.

What I learned from my Spiritual Master was *not* to be like him. The principle that overpowers my own sense is: "Don't go after the footsteps of the masters, but rather seek what they sought." But Nayagar Ji was a saint who was trying to train, teach and make a difference to world. In this pursuit, I *do* aspire to be like him. You must also apply the laws only. You've waited so long to begin. Take action now. This being the case, I think, I shouldn't take more of your time and end here so that you can begin. You need to put your old life behind you! Be proud of the new you! "If you carefully consider what you want to be said of you in the funeral experience," Stephen Covey said, "you will find your definition of success." Your job is about to begin from here. A new beginning towards a new ending!

SUGGESTED STRATEGY

> *"We are told to let our light shine, and if it does, we won't need to tell anybody it does. Lighthouses don't fire cannons to call attention to their shining – they just shine."*
>
> Dwight Lyman Moody, an American evangelist and publisher

Let your light shine. Life is like a light. In this context, Dwight Lyman Moody always comes to my mind, who founded the Moody Church, Northfield School and Mount Hermon School in Massachusetts, the Moody Bible Institute and Moody Publishers. He was a great believer in silent sharing and never demanded any appreciation although he did some of the brilliant deeds. So Share! Smile! Shine! Cheerfulness and kiss are same in one respect. Both requires sharing to get pleasure from them.

It is up to you! You're not going to wake up being the person you want to be. Allan Rufus aptly says: "Life is like a sandwich! Birth as one slice, and Death as the other. What you put in – between 'The slice' is up to you. Is your sandwich tasty or sour?"

You have to take action. You have to take positive steps of personal and professional improvements. It will take time, dedication and a few mistaken choices along the way.

Yes! It is you! You are the one that can produce a ripple effect.

ASSIGNMENT

1. Preach the laws.
2. Live the laws.
3. Be the change.
4. Give back what you get. Be a part of the change.
5. Suggest this book to those who need it most. Sharing shines.
6. Listen to the Audio program *Master Strategies for Higher Achievement* by Brian Tracy.
7. Record your Audio program based on your study of this book.

VISUALIZATION

Celebrate your new awareness! Remember: If Abraham Lincoln can make it to top, you can do the same with more resources and better age than him.

SELF SUGGESTION

I am the one that can start a chain reaction.

Bear in mind: Super achievers always keep their commitments.

[*Promise & Put Your Signature Here With Date*]

Always Remember:

"It is indispensable to 'Train The Brain' to think optimistically and that is the only way to facilitate the process of achieving success, wealth and happiness."

Dr. Anupam Kurlwal (Acharya)

The best is yet to be! –
Be Happy!!
Good Luck!!!

Theme Poem

This poem contains a conversation between a tree and a woodcutter. The tree symbolizes the goodness and the woodcutter stands for a normal human being. The author expresses a special gratitude to the Dead Poet (http://deadpoet.blogspot.com) for composing this poem that summarizes the 30 laws of this book.

THE TREE AND THE WOODCUTTER

Tiny particles of sand, they would rise and fall;
By the passage of wind, summoned to the nature's call.
That turned one to cut the wood, and the other to give his all.
Both unaware at the birth of what they could become,
One lost to the whims of life, the other to life's way had come.
The woodcutter fell the trees; drawing axe and life,
No numbers of wood cut his agony, but grew his strife.
While the tree stood tall on purpose and fruits bade,
Severe to the shades of life, it prospered with its shade.
The tree and the woodcutter, thus of same tiny particles were made.
In belief one roamed and razed, tempted to the bait,
While the tree fixed to its faith, it served to sate.

The woodcutter crossed this wood too often, but this once his hunger rose best in time,

Lured all over by a tree, that blossomed; too in prime.

He took a decision to fell the tree, and the axe was drawn,

Of all decided in life, this at best moment was born;

Destined to make him aware of the plan,

A mellow voice appeared and spoke to the man.

"O man! Thy greedy sins spread the sorrows afar

And incite the devout order, that afraid to war.

So cease the march to untimely doom and peace make,

Before you anger it more, O man! come awake."

The bemused man was shaken and bothered in fear,

He kneeled before the tree, thus fell near.

Of guilts borne throughout the life, he pondered deep,

And on learning of the evils he had done, the woodcutter began to weep.

Conscious of the self and truth, he spoke to the tree,

"O silent bearer of fruitful virtues, thou so blessed be.

O humble tree, the eternal learner of the noble pursuits,

Unaffected to the numbing cold and torrid heat, steadfast to thy roots,

The quiet leader of selfless service, the great sage standing still,

Thou embrace the blows of my greed, unyielding on the sacrificing will.

I tread onto greed, thou stand unmoved to the seed

And timely bloom in health and harmony, happily commanding over thy need

Fecund, with fruits and wisdom, the inspirer whom upon I feed.
I abhor now the glories and greatness, the greed and gain
What beauty be that dies; no worthy and in vain.
It shines true when shared with all, however hard and plain,
I shall begin now, let us all unchain, let us all unchain."

Dead Poet

TRANSLATION OF THE POEM—THE TREE AND THE WOODCUTTER

Lines 1–5

All beings come to life and cease to exist out of it, bound by the norms and laws of nature. Birth, adolescence, youth, adulthood, old age and death are all phases, made to pass through life, in the same manner as particles of sand do rise and fall. Different roles are taken and surrendered in life's mold based on the conscious self.

Responsibilities act as burdens to some, while some embrace them as means of living, in order to accomplish the divine roles or duties they think that are assigned to them. No man is aware of his potential/abilities at the time of birth in full. Thus, some lose hold over the rudder of their lives and get lost in the waves, high and low, of this unending ocean named life. They end up having lived frustrated lives, perceiving it to be their destiny, which on the contrary is their rebuilt destiny.

While some, although handful in number, live up on their vision, firmly taking control of the rudder of their lives and stick to their morals to take it to where its purpose is served.

Lines 6–10

Some take pleasure in indulgences their whole lives, but fail to sate them, as their desires are fuelled by their greed.

While some find life's meaning in service and worth to others around them, being wholly content in fulfilling others' desires. The tree prospers with its shade, finding meaning and worth in its ability to relieve passers-by with its shade and fruits.

As grows a tree, so grows its shade and as grows a tree's shade, so grows its usefulness to travellers in searing heat. Regardless of being born with the similar fleshly bodies, individuals differ drastically, depending on the type of decisions made at appropriate/inappropriate times.

Lines 11–12

There is a subtle difference between beliefs and faith. Beliefs are subject to change all our lives, we adopt one, discard the other and modify one too. But, faith is constant. Once faith is reposed, it either stays fixed for life or is shattered for life. Faith is the focal point from where beliefs disperse into awareness. It is the impulse that drives to the creation, realization and cessation of beliefs.

Lines 13–17

These lines record the incident of the woodcutter being lured by the tree at a particular moment in time, which proves in contrast to be a moment of serendipity in disguise.

Lines 18–22

The discourse in these lines is self-explanatory.

Lines 23–27

A man's wrongdoings pile up one day, the bubble finally bursts and induces fear in him in some form or the other. This ghost of fear tends to grow only bigger and bigger in size. And, when all the realities are taken care of, self is employed into introspection, and awaits realization of one's guilt, consciousness of actions of the self and truth. A discourse/conversation then starts with one's inner being, of what needs to be done and how to be done.

Lines 28–34

Learning never ceases, it continues throughout life. Learning the nobilities/ virtues is the cause to be cared for. This depends on a man's personal philosophy, the cause close to his heart makes him live it and be it.

The leaders lead by example, performing the roles taken by them resolutely and so aptly. That everyone benefits from it.They do not compromise even one bit on their principles, steadfast to their roots, thus, caring for self-esteem.

Being happy internally, checking upon needs, thus, being truly happy with gratitude dwelling in all their senses, despite of the very little and less they take and all and much that they give, to others.

Lines 35–39

Whereas motivation moves upon the outer layers and fails to impregnate the inner layers, they inspire inside out with all their nobilities, thus, moving the heart and inspiring the soul. It is with their creative zeal of life that they are able to provide us with invaluable virtues, scrumptious fruits filled with nectar of wisdom, maintaining a healthy balance in all spectrums of life.

Difference between success and significance – Success that breeds ego and arrogance leads to doom. It is of no worth and use and dies in vain, all alone. The same success becomes significant and truly beautiful when it is wielded to leave an indelible mark in others' lives, no matter how hard it is to wield.

There are no permanent endings that obstruct the new beginnings in life. All it takes is the willingness to learn and collect the lessons dispersing from life and entrench them deep, in memory and heart.

So let us all begin, freeing the chained awareness, we shall begin.

Praises For Dr. Anupam And His Success Philosophy

"I have pleasure in commending Dr. Anupam's successful merging and presenting of so many bits and pieces of lives of greats into understandable and logical lessons in his inspiring book. In short, recommended!"

Vinay Singhal, Managing Director,
SJV Consultants Pvt. Ltd., Advance
Management Program, Harvard Business School

"Dr. Anupam is known as a law teacher who motivates the students not only in their studies but in their life also. He has been a successful writer of law books. This new self-help book is a great resource for anyone who is feeling down or unenthusiastic and need a good boost. I've read many motivational books; this is possibly one of the best."

Mr. Anubhav Arora, Director, Universal Law
Publishing Company Pvt. Ltd., New Delhi, India

"If you have read a lot of self-help books, and didn't take any action, then it's time to get this magnum opus. Dr. Anupam has written a superb book for the individual of this age."

Dr. M.S. Verma, Advocate, Supreme Court of India

"In this positive and pragmatic guide, Dr. Anupam outlines a 30 lesson program for everyone who wants to be successful. He has shared an innovative philosophy that will turn average individuals into super achievers. Great book! Dr. Anupam."

Prof. (Dr.) Naresh Kumar, Professor-in-Law,
Former Head and Dean, M.D. University,
Rohtak, (Haryana), India

"This is an engaging, helpful, and comprehensively enjoyable book. Dr. Anupam offers important laws for structuring one's personal and professional lives. Well done!"

Prof. (Dr.) Gurpal Singh, Former Head & Dean, Faculty of Law,
Punjabi University, Patiala (Punjab), India

"To sum up, I highly recommend the book to those who believe that they can bring change in their personal and professional spheres. Great Read!"

Prof. (Dr.) Raj Kumar, Institute of
Management Studies and Research,
M.D. University, Rohtak, (Haryana), India

"Success in life and business is never easy. If you think so, it's time to listen and read Dr. Anupam who gives dependable advices to get maximum success in your personal and professional life."

Prof. (Dr.) Satish Arya, Professor-in-English and Principal, B.L.J.S.
P.G. College, Tosham, Bhiwani (Haryana), India

"This book is outstanding. It will change the way you think, not only about the world around you, but also about yourself."

Rahul Aggarwal, Deputy General Manager, Human Resource,
Rockland Hospital, Manesar, Haryana, India

"If you are a person who is obsessed with aspiration and aim, then give Dr. Anupam, a patient listening or reading, your life not be same again."

Sanjay Kumar Sharma, Quality Head, Six Sigma Champion, Donaldson India Filters System Pvt. Limited, Manesar, Haryana, India

"This is a profound book, with deep and far-reaching implications. It is engaging, fresh, user friendly, and packed with thoughtful insights."

Dr. Traun Arora, Coordinator, Baba Farid Law College, Faridkot (Punjab), India

"It doesn't matter if your goals are to be the student of the year, become a leading professional, lose weight, become a better parent or child, boost confidence, get your dream home or earn a lot of money; Dr. Anupam Acharya's Success Philosophy actually helps."

Sandeep Aggarwal, Management Teacher and Corporate Consultant, Gurgaon, Haryana, India

"The laws in this book are universal. They are elementary to success whether in any organization, in the family, or perhaps most importantly, for any individual."

Jai Hind, Team Leader, Thales, Hong Kong

"This is probably the most outstanding book that teaches us to lead a balanced life by taking accountability at each and every step. A Must Read!"

Rishiraj, Assistant Bank Manager, Bank of Baroda, Mumbai, Maharashtra, India

"This book is a rare gem that will be treasured by all who will read it. Rarely have I read a work as thoughtful and life-changing as this one. A Remarkable contribution to the field!"

Priyank Tanwar, MBA & LLM, University of Kent, England, Qualified Solicitor in the High Courts of England and Wales

"A Masterpiece! Passionately argued, superbly researched, and filled with indelible stories of real people, it has the potential to permanently change the way you think, behave, and live your life, both personally and professionally."

Harsh Sharma, Engineering Program Manager,
Jupiner Networks, Bengaluru, India

"Dr. Anupam has a matchless and gifted method to make the reader understand how to deal with the world around and how to make personal and professional changes to best match with one's life goals. For instance, understanding the distinction between choice and decision can make a big difference in one's life experiences."

Praveen Kumar, Deputy Manager in Corporate
Quality function, Bosch Ltd., Bengaluru, India

"Dr. Anupam knows the art of teaching and writing. He has, with crystal clarity, crafted the definitive success guiding system. I am sure that the reader will find inspiration and motivation on each page."

Mr. Rajiv Arora, Director, Central Law
Publications, Allahabad, Uttar Pradesh, India

"The book is well written and there are many references to back up the claims made. I definitely suggest this book."

Sunil Anchal, MBA, PMP, CSM, Agile
Project Manager (Scrum Master) AT&T,
Plano (Dallas, USA)

"This is a book, all and sundry, need to read. There's no better gift you could give yourself. Go on! You are worthy of it!"

Dr. Ajit Singh Chahal, Legal Jurist and Social
Thinker, Kurukshetra University, Haryana, India

"This book illustrates the reader how to exactly practice the winning laws that lead to success. Dr. Anupam draws on people, stories and quotes to motivate and inspire the reader to get success. It is simple to read and apply in life!"

Aditya Arya, Senior Engineer,
PMA Consultants, New York, USA

"Dr. Anupam is fascinating to read – clearly a master presenter. His approach is refreshing and based on sound NLP principles."

Saranendu Chaki, founder of Brandbox
Solutions, New Delhi

"What a book! I am an admirer of Dr. Anupam's pursuits! He not only motivates you, but teaches you tools and techniques on how to achieve success."

Rakesh Kumar, Assistant Manager, Supply Chain, Jubilant Life
Sciences, Noida, Uttar Pradesh, India

"Dr. Anupam is a great orator when you require that push to get you going. He not only tells you accurately what you are supposed to do in life but also teaches you how to realize success."

Gopal Sharma, Business Development Manager,
Puremed Surgical, Gurgaon

"Dr. Anupam knows and understands the importance of success at personal and professional level, as he himself has excelled in his life. This book will give to common man the opportunity to analyze and make decisions in Real World Events and live a balanced life."

Dr. Vijay Rathee, Management Teacher and Corporate Trainer,
Gurgaon (Haryana), India